The Development of Judgment
and Decision Making
in Children and Adolescents

The Development of Judgment and Decision Making in Children and Adolescents

Edited by

Janis E. Jacobs
Paul A. Klaczynski
The Pennsylvania State University

LEA LAWRENCE ERLBAUM ASSOCIATES, PUBLISHERS
2005 Mahwah, New Jersey   London

Lawrence Erlbaum Associates, Inc., Publishers
10 Industrial Avenue
Mahwah, New Jersey 07430

Cover design by Kathryn Houghtaling Lacey

Library of Congress Cataloging-in-Publication Data

The development of judgment and decision making in children and adolescents /
edited by Janis E. Jacobs and Paul A. Klaczynski.
p. cm.
Includes bibliographical references and indexes.
ISBN 0-8058-4256-X (hardcover : alk. paper)
1. Judgment in children.   2. Decision making in children.
3. Judgment in adolescence.   4. Decision making in adolescence.
I. Jacobs, Janis E.   II. Klaczynski, Paul A.

BF723.J8D48   2005
155.4'1383—dc22   2004050658
                                                   CIP

Books published by Lawrence Erlbaum Associates are printed on acid-free paper,
and their bindings are chosen for strength and durability.

Printed in the United States of America
10 9 8 7 6 5 4 3 2 1

Dedicated to
Wayne Osgood and Logan Osgood-Jacobs
and to the memory of Nancy Klaczynski

Contents

vii

Preface

In recent years, newspaper articles, television specials, and other media events have focused on the numerous hard decisions faced by today's youth, often pointing to teen pregnancy, drug use, and delinquency as evidence of faulty judgment. Over the past 10 years, many groups—including parents, educators, policymakers, and researchers—have become concerned about the decision making of children and adolescents, asking why they make risky choices, how they can be taught to be better decision makers, and what types of age-related changes occur in decision making. Evidence of this concern comes from the multitude of decision-making programs currently being implemented in schools around the country, some at the explicit request of legislators trying to lower the numbers of teen pregnancies, drunken drivers, and substance abusers. Too often, these programs have been implemented with little regard to basic research on cognitive, emotional, and contextual changes that sometimes support and sometimes inhibit decision making.

Although many universities currently teach courses on decision making within psychology, education, and/or business, and those courses generally include sections on social judgment and decision making, developmental trends in decision making are often given sparse, if any, attention. Indeed, a quick scan of any child-development textbook reveals very few references to decision making. With few exceptions, even in adolescent textbooks, the processes underlying decision making are discussed only briefly, and when the topic is mentioned, the research focuses exclusively on reasoning capabilities and is typically rooted in traditional developmental models that may not work as we try to understand the social and contextual, as well as cognitive, underpinnings of the ontogeny of judgment and decision making. Thus, despite widespread interest from policymakers, the media, educators, parents, and psychologists in how youth make decisions, and despite numerous programs aimed at improving adolescent decision making, little research has focused on the cognitive, emotional, and contextual processes that underlie the development of judgment and decision making.

Why is there such a dearth of developmental research on these issues? Most traditional theories regard cognitive development as a unidirectional progression from either intuitive thinking to logical, scientific reasoning (e.g., Inhelder & Piaget, 1958); from an initially inefficient state to a state of greater efficiency (e.g., information-processing); or from states of limited understanding and complexity to more advanced understanding and computational complexity (e.g., neo-Piagetian "theory-theory"). As we have discussed elsewhere (Jacobs & Klaczynski, 2002), these perspectives do not mesh very well with research on adult judgment and decision making. Specifically, research with adults has shown that, although adults are surprisingly proficient on some decision tasks, they commonly fall prey to judgment biases, ignore important information, or make non-optimal decisions across a wide array of situations. Portraits of adults as irrational decision makers are incongruent with the traditional developmental position that development is marked by progression toward more efficient, logical, and computationally complex judgments. Indeed, data accumulated over the past decade indicate that the traditional theories of cognitive development cannot provide viable explanations for counterintuitive, age-related trends in judgment and decision biases observed by a number of scholars. Although relatively small, this corpus of evidence suggests that new models are needed that can account for both the development of inferential limitations and judgment biases and the improvements in reasoning that are typically associated with development. These new models must also go beyond cognitive perspectives to include a broader array of explanatory variables and contexts if we are to truly understand the development of judgment and decision making.

We hope that this volume will serve as a starting place for those interested in considering new ways of thinking about the development of these issues. Because the area of study is relatively novel, relevant research has been published in disparate places; thus, assembling a coherent picture of development in this area is an exceedingly difficult task. The purpose of this volume is to bring together the voices of several authors who are conducting cutting-edge research and developing new theoretical perspectives related to the development of judgment and decision making. Due to the newness of this area of study, we also wanted to be thinking deeply and critically about this work; therefore, we included commentaries and an afterward by noted researchers in the fields of developmental psychology and decision research.

The volume includes three parts: Part I: Cognitive Developmental Approaches to Judgment and Decision Making (emphasizing different theoretical perspectives on the cognitive aspects of decision making and research supporting each); Part II: Contextual Influences on Decision Making (stressing the social nature of decision making and the importance of context); and Part III: Decision Making in the Real World (highlighting research that uses current theoretical perspectives in applied settings). Each section begins with an overview to highlight critical links and differences between the chapters, and each section is followed by a commentary by developmentalists noted for their work in related fields. Finally, we conclude the volume with an Afterword written by Baruch Fischhoff, one of the leading researchers on the topic of decision making in adults and a long-time advocate of investigating and understanding the developmental roots of adult risk assessment, judgment, and decision making.

Part I, on the Cognitive Developmental Approaches to Judgment and Decision Making, presents three distinctive developmental models that offer different explanations of "what develops" and the relative importance of different cognitive components and experiential components that may be important for developing judgment and decision-making skills. The differences and similarities in the theoretical perspectives lead to different predictions and diverse explanations for patterns of development. The goal of presenting such disparate perspectives is to provide a variety of lenses or frames for the chapters that follow. We hope this will allow readers to consider numerous underlying causes and developmental trajectories as they digest the studies highlighting context and real-world applications.

Part II, related to Contextual Influences on Decision Making, emphasizes the emotional, cultural, and social aspects of decision making, three topics that have been influential in the adult literature on judgment and decision making, but are just beginning to be explored in the developmental area. These chapters again represent diverse perspectives, but present a coherent picture of the many noncognitive aspects of decision making that play a role in development. These are especially important considerations for those interested in adolescent risk taking and risky decisions. As a group, these chapters represent important advances in our understanding of decision making and its development. Although the particular contexts and variables of interest differ in each chapter, these chapters consistently show that decision making is affected by particular cultural, peer, and family contexts; by the emotions that often accompany decision making; and by age-related changes in these contexts and emotional experiences. Collectively, these chapters support the contention that, to fully understand judgment and decision making during childhood and adolescence, we must continue to explore the contexts in which decisions are made.

Finally, Part III, Decision Making in the Real World, provides three examples of research that apply developmental and decision-making models to practical research questions. The applications vary from legal decisions to personal goals to abortion decisions, but they all involve decision making in important settings in which children and adolescents function. This section provides much-needed "grounding" for research in this area, highlighting the need for more interaction among basic and applied researchers, as well as collaborations with policymakers. These chapters were included to begin to draw attention to some of the factors (e.g., media, peers, parents) that might be considered by those interested in understanding child and adolescent decision making within meaningful, real-world situations.

When we began this volume, the overarching goal was to present a coherent picture of the current state of research and theory on the development of judgment and decision making. As we invited authors and solicited chapters, we found that the word "coherent" dropped out of our description of the project. Indeed, the theoretical perspectives, research, and concepts began to appear more chaotic than coherent as we realized that we wanted to include a broad array of conceptual and empirical ideas. These choices were intentional, because this is a new and dynamic area of study—one that will benefit most by presenting a variety of perspectives and topics in order to fuel the next generation of ideas and research. Thus, our ultimate goals are to encourage readers to consider new ideas for why adolescents might be making particular decisions; to apply innovative models to policy and programming questions; and finally, to stimulate novel and wide-ranging research on these topics.

—*Janis E. Jacobs*
—*Paul A. Klaczynski*

REFERENCES

Inhelder, B., & Piaget, J. (1958). *The growth of logical thinking: From childhood to adolescence.* New York: Basic Books.

Jacobs, J. E., & Klaczynski, P. A. (2002). The development of judgment and decision making during childhood and adolescence. *Current Directions in Psychological Science, 11,* 145–149.

I

COGNITIVE DEVELOPMENTAL APPROACHES TO JUDGMENT AND DECISION MAKING

As we noted in the Preface, the developmental study of decision making is in its infancy. Although substantial research documents the cognitive underpinnings of adults' decisions, far fewer attempts have been made with children and adolescents. Fortunately, cognitive developmental research on decision making appears to be on the rise. The chapters in Part I represent three distinct cognitive approaches to the understanding of the development of decision making. Although the authors' perspectives are similar in some respects, they differ in the emphases they place on different forms of processing, the importance of different types of information processing, and, especially, in the role that intuitive processing plays in making adaptive decisions. Each author converges on the belief that the construction, extension, and evaluation of developmental models of decision making is crucial if research is to progress beyond its current, infantile state.

In chapter 1, Byrnes outlines his Self-Regulation Model (SRM) of decision making, the role of self-regulated thinking in development, and the importance of investigating the development of different components of self-regulated thinking when evaluating age differences in decision competence. Byrnes' SRM model focuses on both functional aspects of decision-making competence (i.e., goal-setting abilities, the abilities to generate, evaluate, and implement decision options) and structural aspects of decision

making (e.g., a relevant and accurate knowledge base; working memory capacity) that support and sometimes constrain the utilization of decision-
making competencies. The SRM model thus shares some assumptions with
traditional competence–performance theories of cognitive development and
the "bounded rationality" theories that are currently in vogue among adult
decision theorists. More importantly, Byrnes' theory pinpoints a variety of
sources that may help explain the developmental mechanisms responsible for
age differences in decision making, as well as inter- and intra-individual variability in decision making.

The focus of Klaczynski's chapter (chap. 2) is on the role of dual processing for understanding the development of reasoning and decision making. In
the dual-process theory he presents, development is conceived as occurring
in two separate information-processing systems. The "analytic" system involves conscious deliberation, metacognitive reflection and monitoring of
reasoning, decontextualized task representations, and attempts to arrive at
precise, accurate inferences and decisions. By contrast, the "experiential"
system relies on processing that occurs at or below the "periphery" of consciousness. This system is considered the predominant or default processing
system on most everyday reasoning and decision tasks. Klaczynski augments
his analysis of dual processing by arguing for the importance of metacognitive
functioning in normative reasoning and decision making. Specifically, a case
is made that, although contextual cues typically result in the automatic activation of heuristics and stereotypes, this preconscious activation does not
necessarily lead to preconscious implementation. Children, adolescents, and
adults have at least the opportunity to "metacognitively intercede" before
the products of experiential processing are actually applied, allowing reasoners to reflect on experientially produced responses and to override their implementation with analytically based responses. Klaczynski suggests that this
ability increases with age, particularly around the beginning of the adolescent
period.

In the final chapter of this section, Reyna, Adam, Poirier, LeCroy, and
Brainerd (chap. 3) also propose a dual-process model of decision making and
apply this model to adolescent sexual risk taking. In their "fuzzy-trace" theory, Reyna et al. argue that real-life decision making cannot be adequately
explained by traditional decision analysis. Fuzzy-trace theory thus predicts
that decisions are not based on "rational" integration of risks and rewards.
Rather, decisions are based on "gist" processing. Reyna et al. further argue
that adaptive decisions are typically made on the basis of intuitive semantic
representations (i.e., gist—the "core meaning" of a decision) that are en-
abled by experiences, culture, and development. A key assumption of fuzzy-
trace theory is that decision makers' default processing preference is to operate on the least precise representation available to accomplish particular
tasks. That is, decision makers prefer to operate in gist representations (qual-

itative representations involving holistic distinctions such as "more" vs. "less") and are disinclined to use verbatim representations (i.e., based on precise quantification of task demands). In contrast to most decision-making theories, they argue that this "fuzzy-processing preference" increases with age. An important difference in the conclusions of these researchers is that effective decisions can be achieved from reliance on predominantly intuitive processing; therefore, interventions should focus on priming and enabling intuitions rather than improving the abilities required for precise, analytic computations.

In reviewing these approaches, we note that there are numerous areas of convergence. For example, each position highlights the idea that development involves the acquisition of an increasingly diverse array of decision strategies and heuristics and that decision making involves selection from among an array of strategies that becomes increasingly complex with development. Some divergences among the theories are also evident. For example, Byrnes acknowledges that unconscious processes play a role in decision making, but emphasizes conscious self-regulation, particularly in making important decisions. By contrast, Klaczynski and Reyna et al. emphasize implicit processing. However, Reyna et al. argue that adaptive decisions are more likely produced through implicit, "gist-level" processes; Klaczynski similarly argues that many adaptive decisions arise from predominantly intuitive processing, but (like Byrnes) argues that conscious regulatory mechanisms are more likely to produce normative decisions than purely intuitive processing.

Part of what makes cognitive developmental research on decision making interesting is that different theories sometimes make very different predictions. As Byrnes suggests, the task for the future is to resolve discrepancies both through further theoretical refinements and through additional empirical data that clearly juxtapose predictions from these different theories. With little doubt, the future of cognitive developmental theory and research on decision making promises exciting insights into the processes that underlie decision making and its development.

1

The Development of Self-Regulated Decision Making

James P. Byrnes
University of Maryland

Over the past 50 years or so, a number of theorists have found it useful to ground their perspectives in the construct of *adaptation* (e.g., Anderson, 1991; Bjorklund & Pellegrini, 2000; Jordan & Rumelhart, 1995; Piaget, 1952; Shrager & Siegler, 1998; Stanovich & West, 2000; Todd & Gigerenzer, 2000). Although these perspectives differ in important ways, most seem to converge on the following characterization of adaptive tendencies: (a) People have mental representations that correspond to perceived regularities or relations in the environment (e.g., the belief that smiles evoke friendly responses from other people); (b) these mental representations cause people to behave in certain ways (e.g., smile); (c) experience tends to promote changes in mental representations that serve to increase a person's success in the environment; and (d) humans are unique in their tendency to use various strategies or cognitive shortcuts to overcome limitations on their reasoning abilities (and be more successful than they otherwise would be).

In this chapter, I present a model of decision making (i.e., the Self-Regulation Model [SRM]) that is grounded in similar assumptions. My colleagues and I constructed this model in the mid-1990s and framed it in terms of the construct of adaptation for the following reasons. First, there was a need for a truly developmental model of decision making that could explain the wide range of choices that are normally made by children, adolescents, and adults (Byrnes, 1998; Furby & Beyth-Marom, 1992). Existing models either lacked a developmental mechanism or were designed to explain only certain kinds of decisions (e.g., gambling) or certain phenomena (e.g., framing effects). Second, scholars in the field of decision making were more interested in questions related to the irrationality of adult decision makers (e.g., Why do people ignore base rates?) than in questions such as "Do decision-making skills improve with age?" and "How do highly successful individuals make decisions?" Third, a contrast had been set up in the field between unrealistic normative theories of decision making (that described what people should do, but could never really do, when they make decisions) and descriptive or behavioral theories of decision making (that described the "erroneous" and simplistic things that people typically do). It seemed that this was a false dichotomy that ignored a third possibility: There could be a theory that was realistic, normative, and descriptive all at the same time (e.g., the Self-Regulation Model). Finally, the adaptation perspective affords the possibility of making the leap from basic research to interventions rather straightforward. In particular, theories that are based in the construct of adaptation assume that individuals normally differ in their relative success in securing the benefits of a particular environment and in their longevity (Bjorklund & Pellegrini, 2000). If one assumes that (a) the best choices in a particular situation are those that are most likely (but not certain) to lead to adaptive outcomes (e.g., physical health or financial security); and (b) successful individuals experience adaptive outcomes more often than less successful individuals (by definition), it stands to reason that successful individuals must be skilled decision makers. If so, then studies that contrast the decision-making competencies of successful and less-successful individuals could provide important insight into ways to enhance the decision-making skills of the latter.

The rest of this chapter is organized as follows. In the first section, I provide a primer of the SRM of decision making. In the second section, I describe studies that my colleagues and I conducted to examine elements of the SRM. In the final section, I consider implications of this work and suggest new lines of research that could answer important, yet unresolved questions regarding the development of decision making.

THE SELF-REGULATION MODEL
OF DECISION MAKING

For expository purposes, it is helpful to organize the details of the SRM in terms of its metatheoretical assumptions, its stance regarding the components of decision making, and its stance regarding developmental mechanisms. In what follows, these three aspects of the model are discussed in turn.

Metatheoretical Assumptions of the SRM

Metatheoretical assumptions guide the construction of theoretical models in several different ways (e.g., highlighting the kinds questions one should ask). However, these assumptions tend not to be testable themselves (Byrnes, 1992; Reese, 1994). Instead, they reflect beliefs about "the way things are," and are often definitional in nature, sometimes even axiomatic. An example would be the claim that certain behaviors or tendencies are adaptive (i.e., they improve physical health, emotional health, or promote longevity) whereas others are maladaptive. Other assumptions of the SRM (and many other contemporary theoretical models in psychology) include the following:

Human behavior occurs in contexts. A *context* is a culturally defined situation that (a) occurs in a particular time and place and (b) contains actors who perform culturally defined roles using artifacts and other objects to execute these roles (Cole, 1999). Examples include "dinnertime" at home and "second-period history class" at high school. Although the assumption that behavior occurs in contexts is not testable, the derivative assumption that people form mental representations of recurrent contexts (i.e., "scripts" or event representations) is somewhat more testable. Event representations help people recognize contexts (e.g., I am in a restaurant) and indicate what they should do in these contexts (Nelson, 1996).

Human behavior is goal-directed and intentional. That is, people set goals to change contexts (I am at work and would like to go home now) and also to accomplish things within specific contexts (I intend to finish this work-related task by 5 p.m.). Whereas this assumption appears to be testable, it has been no small matter to prove the existence of goals and intentions to "nonbelievers" (e.g., certain radical behaviorists). Instead, most scholars these days simply accept the proposal that people have goals because it seems self-evident (e.g., Bandura, 1997; Baron, 1994; Wentzel, 1991) or because studies consistently demonstrate an empirical link between measures of intentions and behavior (e.g., Albarracin, Johnson, Fishbein, & Muellerleile, 2001). Note, though, that many goals seem to operate at an unconscious and automatic level (Bargh & Chartland, 1999).

Psychological theories should be able to predict what a person will do in particular contexts. Regardless of whether developmental scientists study children or adolescents in their homes, schools, or in the lab, many hope to be able to describe, predict, and explain the behavior of children and adolescents in these contexts (e.g., what they remember, what errors they make, the prosocial behaviors they exhibit, etc.). For example, researchers might present three options to participants and make predictions regarding which option will be selected at different ages. This claim that theories should explain behaviors within specific contexts would, of course, be rejected by some scholars. Certain intelligence or personality theorists, for example, believe that it is more important to explain consistencies of behavior across contexts.

The rate at which people perform a given behavior is jointly a function of (a) the frequency with which they find themselves in a context that is conducive to performing the behavior and (b) their propensity to perform the behavior when given the opportunity. This proposal has been given labels such as the *opportunity* × *propensity thesis* and the *propensity-event theory* (e.g., Gottfredson & Hirschi, 1990; Osgood, Wilson, O'Malley, Bachman, & Johnson, 1996). One of the virtues of this approach is that it could be used to predict that some people report low levels of a behavior (e.g., underage drinking) mainly because they are never given the opportunity to perform it (e.g., their parents monitor them closely and they live in a "dry" town with strict controls on liquor consumption). However, these same individuals might be very likely to engage in the behavior if given the opportunity. Conversely, there are also people who report low levels of a behavior, not because they have not been given the opportunity, but because they refrain from doing so even when given the opportunity.

Contexts are rife with uncertainty. It is often the case that people are unsure about the following things: (a) the kind of context they find themselves in ("Is this the restaurant I was looking for?"); (b) what they can or should do in that context ("Should I wait to be seated or just go find a table?"); (c) whether an action performed in that context will have its intended effect ("Will this new dish be tasty?"); and (d) how to get themselves into or out of a particular context. Moreover, they may be unsure about whether a given opportunity will arise again in the future ("If I decline this job offer, will better ones come along?").

The Component Processes of Decision Making

So far, I have only considered aspects of the SRM that make it similar to other theories, even those that fall outside the domain of decision making per se (e.g., memory theories). The next step is to provide an answer to the question "What do people do (in their minds and actions) when they make decisions?" To paraphrase Kosslyn and Koenig (1994), psychological theories "carve the mind at its joints." That is, they decompose an intellectual or social–emotional competence into its constituent processes. To determine which processes to include in their models, cognitive theorists often rely on a combination of rational task analysis, computer simulations, self-report, experimentally induced responses, and findings from neuropsychology. Relying on such sources, I have argued (Byrnes, 1998), and others have argued as well (e.g., Baron, 1994; Furby & Beyth-Marom, 1992), that people engage in four core processes when they make decisions in a particular context: (a) They set goals (e.g., find something to eat); (b) they consider one or more ways to accomplish these goals (e.g., look in the refrigerator, go to a fast-food place); (c) they evaluate their options (i.e., a fast-food place is a better idea because the food in the fridge is not very appealing); and (d) they implement the option that seemed like the best way to proceed. In other words, they engage in goal-setting, option generation, option evaluation, and option selection.

In proposing the existence of these four core processes, note that decision theorists (including myself) are not committed to believing any of the following: (a) that people always engage in all four processes when they make a decision (e.g., they only engage in option evaluation and selection because they are presented with two options by someone else); or (b) that they engage in the processes in a rigid, steplike order (goal-setting first, option generation second, etc.); or (c) that they carry out the processes in a conscious, analytical, rational, exhaustive, or optimal way. To illustrate, consider the case of a person who briefly and sleepily scans a closet for something to wear to work (on the basis of unstated goals that he has to go to work every day), notices two shirts that seem reasonable, and chooses the more comfortable of the two (all while mainly thinking about many other things such as work-related tasks and an emotional fight with a spouse the prior day). Hence, the decision was largely semiconscious, unreflective, and unidimensional, but it still involved the consideration of more than one option and the evaluation of at least one dimension (comfort). Note that the only alternative to advocating the four core processes is to believe that people make decisions without comparing options that could fulfill goals. Take away goals (even unconscious ones), and a theorist is left with unintentional, aimless wandering. How would we explain the fact that the person was scanning the closet in the just-mentioned illustration, for example? Moreover, take away the comparison of at least two options, and we are no longer talking about making a decision. If a person repeatedly and reflexively does the same action whenever a goal motivates this behavior, that person did not engage in decision making. It is regrettable that theorists who advocate the existence of the four processes are often assumed to believe that people are rational, logical, metacognitive, and systematic decision makers. This assumption is a non sequitur.

However, comprehensive models in psychology generally extend beyond descriptions of such functional aspects of competence (i.e., the four core processes). They also describe structural aspects that either support, or place constraints on, the operation of the functional aspects (Byrnes, 2001). In the SRM, the structural aspects include a decision maker's (a) declarative, procedural, and conceptual knowledge in long-term memory; (b) values represented in long-term memory; and (c) working-memory capacity. To illustrate the supportive role of these structural aspects, note that highly knowledgeable individuals should be able to generate a larger array of possible courses of action than someone who had less knowledge (Wagner & Sternberg, 1985). However, existing knowledge and values also constrain the magnitude and direction of changes precipitated by the experienced consequences of one's actions. For example, it is possible that a person who is lacking in certain kinds of conceptual knowledge might fail to understand the consequences of his or her actions when they occur. In addition, many different streams of research have revealed limitations on the number and type of dimensions that people can process or interrelate at the same time (Halford, 1999; Siegler, 1998). For example, it is generally not possible for most people to effectively compare options that vary along 8 to 10 "pros" and "cons" that sometimes conflict (e.g., the size of car, its horsepower, its gas mileage, etc.). There simply is not enough computing space to combine all of this information and figure out the best choice even if one wanted to (Gigerenzer & Todd, 1999). Moreover, even if one used strategies to help process the information (e.g., writing lists of pros and cons), the massive array of often-conflicting pieces of information would overwhelm the average person.

But so far, the story remains merely descriptive and applicable to all instances of decision making. Whereas it is useful to know the kinds of things that all decision makers probably do when they make decisions and also the kinds of constraints they all face, from a scientific and public-policy standpoint, it is also useful to characterize the quality of decision making in defensible terms. In other words, what many developmental scientists, parents, and policymakers really want to know is whether decision making improves with age and whether children possess adequate levels of decision-making competence by the time they reach early adulthood (and are "on their own"). Addressing the latter issues requires that we have some way to evaluate the quality of decision making. As will become clear, one further benefit of introducing the quality dimension into a theoretical model is that doing so often makes it more testable.

At a basic level, the issue of quality boils down to four key insights: (a) Not all of the options available to an individual in a particular context are equally "good" (i.e., some are better than others); (b) people differ in their ability or tendency to discriminate between good and not-so-good options; (c) people differ in their ability or tendency to engage in behaviors that maximize their chances that they will discover adequate or better options; and (d) not all decisions require the time and energy needed to carry out effective discovery techniques (Byrnes, 1998; Klaczynski, Byrnes, & Jacobs, 2001; Payne, Bettman, & Johnson, 1993; Simon, 1956; Stanovich & West, 2000; Todd & Gigerenzer, 2000). Note again that good options are those that are more likely to lead to positive outcomes than not-so-good options. Sometimes good options fail to have their intended or usual effects. When this occurs, it is incorrect to assume that a bad decision was made. Relatedly, sometimes options that have a low probability of success lead to positive outcomes. When such an outcome occurs, it is incorrect to assume that a good decision was made. Quality, then, takes a long-term perspective of decision making over time.

From a measurement (i.e., operational definition) standpoint, the aforementioned characteristics of quality decision making need a bit more "unpacking" before studies can be conducted. First, a researcher needs to develop a set of options that could be rank-ordered in terms of their goodness (e.g., the worst option up to the best). This is no easy task because of regular relativist objections raised by, for example, reviewers of one's submitted manuscripts or the readership of a published study (Stanovich & West, 2000). For instance, relativist critics often ask, "Who is a researcher to say what the best choices for another person are?" Here again is where the adaptation perspective comes in handy. It is difficult to argue with the idea (although people often do!) that an important indicator of competent decision making is the ability to choose options that are likely (but not certain) to maintain or improve the decision maker's physical, emotional, or financial well-being (and hopefully improve two or more of these aspects at the same time). This is why choices such as smoking cigarettes, alienating friends and family, and dropping out of school are considered bad choices (because they often, but not always, lead to detriments in physical health, emotional health, or financial well-being, respectively); and why choices such as exercising, repairing important relationships, and doing well in school are considered good choices (because they often, but not always, lead to improvements in physical health, emotional health, and financial well-being, respectively). Within each of these categories (e.g., actions promoting physical health), choices can be further rank-ordered according to their efficacy (e.g., some actions have been shown to produce greater improvement in health than others) and other issues (the possibility of negative side effects, costs, etc.). Of course, this is not to say that the bad decisions just listed have nothing good about them or that the good ones have no costs. For example, some bad choices (e.g., smoking) could increase peer popularity. Moreover, making bad choices and experiencing the consequences (or watching others stumble in such ways) may be the only way for decision making to improve. So in this sense, failure may have adaptive benefits if it is short-lived and does not cause irreparable physical, emotional, or financial harm.

After careful construction of a set of ordered alternatives, a researcher can then present the options to a sample of participants and rate respondents in terms of the frequency with which they choose the best options. This ability to discriminate among poor, acceptable, and very good choices should be an important index of decision-making competence (Byrnes, 1998). But from an intervention standpoint, it is more important to gain further insight into the differences between individuals who can identify the best options and individuals who cannot. The SRM and other perspectives such as Klaczynski (2000; chap. 2, this volume) imply that the next step in the research process is to determine differences in participants' knowledge, beliefs, and values. The premise is that people make flawed choices for four possible reasons: (a) They have faulty knowledge or beliefs (i.e., they think that an action will have a desired effect but it won't, or they think that they are in a certain type of context but they are not); (b) they have maladaptive values (i.e., they do not value their own physical, emotional, or financial well-being); (c) they have accurate knowledge and adaptive values but fail to activate this stored knowledge in a particular situation; or (d) they activate accurate knowledge and values but cannot figure out how to coordinate multiple goals in that situation. To clarify the fourth issue, it is reasonable to argue that an option that is likely to improve several aspects of physical health and emotional health and financial well-being (or at least does not ruin the latter) is to be preferred over options that are likely to only improve one of these aspects (or options that improve one while damaging the other two). Because the world is rather complex (i.e., it contains tangles of intertwined variables) and most people care about lots of things (Rokeach, 1979), focusing on single goals when one has several is bound to lead to losses or problems in one or more areas of one's life. But it often takes a certain amount of talent to figure out solutions that satisfy multiple conflicting goals (e.g., how to stay sober while avoiding ridicule from one's friends at a party). Hence, many people make poor decisions in such situations. Future research may also show that the ability to coordinate multiple dimensions is a key aspect of developmental change in decision-making competence.

From an assessment standpoint, participants in studies need to be presented with multidimensional options (that have two to four dimensions maximum) where the dimensions sometimes conflict (e.g., the taste of foods and their fat content). Higher levels of competence should be assigned to participants who consider more goal-relevant dimensions and figure out ways to combine them (the best possible combination). Note that even in various shortcut models of decision making (e.g., Todd & Gigerenzer's, 2000, ABC model), people still combine or inquire about at least two variables. In addition, however, these models correctly suggest that more credit should be given to individuals who effectively utilize highly diagnostic dimensions (i.e., more is not always better). By *diagnostic*, I mean dimensions that are highly predictive of an outcome such as the size of a city and the number of universities it contains. Note further that the tasks used to test the ABC model (e.g., predicting the number of universities in a city) are not the same as considering whether several options satisfy multiple goals that one has.

The third aspect of quality decision making is required because, in the real world, people are rarely confronted with neatly arranged sets of options in a relatively unambiguous context (as they are in laboratory experiments). Instead, people need to find out what options they might have by reading such things as menus or reference materials, and by going to locations that contain possible choices (e.g., Web sites of universities or guidance offices when considering potential colleges; showrooms of auto dealerships to see what kinds of cars are available; real estate offices to see the kinds of houses available; the employment section of periodicals to see what other jobs are available, etc.). The question for researchers is "What discovery strategies do people use to find options?" These strategies can be rated in terms of the likelihood with which options that meet a person's adaptive, multidimensional goals will be discovered. Relatedly, competent decision makers "look before they leap." That is, they use the strategy of information gathering to clarify the nature of the situation in which they find themselves. For example, an effective public speaker often tries to discover the level of knowledge, attitudes, and interests of his or her audience while deciding what to say. Similarly, most people spend a little time getting to know a conversation partner before stating controversial opinions or telling jokes. Further, good drivers need to carefully determine whether other cars are approaching before making turns onto busy or winding roads. These strategies are not foolproof, of course, and additional information may sometimes increase uncertainty rather than decrease it. In general, however, competent decision makers use a variety of effective strategies to reduce uncertainty about contexts and to compile sets of options that are likely to produce adaptive outcomes they desire.

The final aspect of competent decision making also has its grounding in the construct of adaptation. Not all of the decisions faced by decision makers pose immediate threats to their physical, emotional, or financial well-being. In effect, one could say that it does not really matter what option is selected in these situations. Examples include which book to buy using a gift certificate, which parking spot to select, and which shirt to wear. Given that efficient use of resources is a key aspect of adaptiveness in evolutionary theory (Pinker, 1997), one could argue that effortful or obsessive deliberation over options in these instances is a poor use of resources and that heuristic processes are more adaptive and efficient (Klaczynski, 2000; chap. 2, this volume). Conversely, however, impetuous or unreflective decision making is unwise when one is in the middle of making important decisions (e.g., choosing careers, considering marriage, making major financial investments, or opting for medical treatments). Why? As noted earlier, it often takes some "digging" to discover options that meet several goals. It also takes some intellectual effort to consider multiple, conflicting aspects of a set of options. Of course, a person could "luck out" in such instances even though decisions were arrived at in a hasty or one-dimensional manner, but generally speaking, failure to use available resources for important decisions is a recipe for problems. In sum, then, competent decision makers use effective discovery and evaluative techniques only for important decisions. They can rely on intuitive or highly limited processing for unimportant decisions. Note that in accepting this claim, one eventually has to provide criteria for what counts as an important decision. As implied in the examples and arguments just made, I believe that important decisions involve the potential for losses that are serious and difficult to rectify. Wearing the wrong shirt will generally not have long-term, serious effects on one's physical, emotional, or financial well-being, but marrying the wrong person could.

The arguments so far have laid the groundwork for appreciating the relevance of the construct of self-regulation to the field of decision making. The term *self-regulation* has a number of connotations reflecting its multifaceted role in both domain-general theories of cognitive or social development (e.g., Bandura, 1997; Piaget, 1952; Vygotsky, 1978) and domain-specific perspectives within fields as diverse as memory, reading, emotion, personality, and academic achievement (e.g., Baumeister, Leith, Muraven, & Bratslavsky, 1998; Brown, Bransford, Ferrara, & Campione, 1983; S. G. Paris, Byrnes, & A. H. Paris, 2001; Thomson, 1994; Zimmerman, 2000). Collectively, these approaches suggest that self-regulation is manifested in (a) the tendency to use strategies to overcome the obstacles and distractions imposed by limited resources, lack of knowledge, certain personality traits, and strong emotion; (b) the ability to "know when you know and know when you don't know" (i.e., have calibrated likelihood beliefs); and (c) the tendency to respond appropriately to decision-making successes and failures (i.e., change representations in ways that increase environmental success or increase the use of effective strategies). In addition, self-regulated individuals demonstrate the preceding three attributes even when they are not closely supervised by competent decision makers who have a vested interest in the decision maker's well-being (e.g., parents, teachers, spouses, friends, employers, etc.). In the opportunity × propensity framework, the latter attribute is a key feature of people who refrain from making poor choices when given the opportunity (e.g., declining an offer of a ride home from an intoxicated friend).

When applied to the case of decision making, these self-regulatory tendencies enhance a person's ability to make good choices. For example, the strategy of information gathering often, but not always, helps reduce uncertainty about the nature of a situation (as discussed earlier). In addition, strategies such as writing lists of several important pros and cons may help a decision maker overcome working-memory limitations and coordinate multiple goals. Relatedly, the strategies of advice-seeking and self-talk may help a decision maker overcome obstacles imposed by lack of knowledge of options and impulsivity, respectively. As for correctly assessing one's knowledge, calibrated beliefs are essential to processes related to identifying contexts, evaluating options, and selecting options. By *calibrated*, I mean that a person's intuitive expectations of the likelihood of an outcome match the actual likelihood of these consequences. Misjudging the likelihood of the consequences of one's actions (e.g., the likelihood of skidding on an icy road) could lead to rather poor choices. In this way, both over- and underconfidence can be problems. Overconfident people experience failure more than they should (they take too many risks), whereas underconfident people experience success less often than they should (they take too few risks). In new and unfamiliar situations, errors of calibration and faulty knowledge are to be expected. Over time, however, feedback from the environment should serve to modify beliefs and knowledge structures such that they are more in tune with the "statistical properties of the environment" (Anderson, 1991, p. 471), but it is possible that inappropriate lessons could be learned from experiences as well. For example, failure sometimes follows the right choice (e.g., friendly behavior is sometimes responded to in less-than-friendly terms) and poor choices do not always lead to negative consequences (e.g., drunk driving does not always lead to auto accidents). As I discuss later in this chapter, we know little about the effects of feedback in such instances but will assume, for now, that feedback has the potential to modify knowledge and beliefs in appropriate ways. It can also be assumed (until studies demonstrate otherwise) that feedback is essential in recognizing the need for, or effectiveness of, strategies that can be used to identify contexts, discover options, evaluate options, or regulate one's troublesome traits (e.g., emotionality or impulsivity).

From an assessment standpoint, the foregoing discussion suggests that a researcher would measure self-regulated decision making by presenting decision problems that require a certain amount of intellectual work to discover good options and evaluate them along several dimensions. Moreover, options need to be linked to consequences in probabilistic terms (reflecting the way options are linked to outcomes in real decisions). As the saying goes, there are relatively few sure things in life. Further, there should be multiple trials with feedback to determine the extent to which (a) beliefs, knowledge, and calibration change (i.e., become more accurate); (b) participants increase their use of effective uncertainty reduction, discovery, or evaluative strategies; and (c) participants vary the use of effortful approaches across decision problems (i.e., using effortful approaches only on important problems). The complexity of the study can be further enhanced by (ethically) engendering strong positive or negative emotions in subjects and by assessing personality traits that make it difficult to discover good options (e.g., impulsivity, emotionality). In addition to showing how emotions and personality traits can sidetrack decision makers, one can also determine whether participants use strategies to counteract strong emotions or troublesome personality traits.

The goal in any case is to show the strong linkage between self-regulatory tendencies, competent decision making, and frequent attainment of desired outcomes. Finally, it is important to measure both the opportunity to make certain kinds of decisions (i.e., "How often do participants find themselves in contexts conducive to making these decisions?") and an individual's propensity to choose certain options when in these contexts (e.g., beliefs, values, personality traits, strategies).

In addition to guiding one's methodological decisions in such ways, the SRM has important implications for the patterns of correlations that one would expect in a given study. Note that the contextual assumptions of the SRM imply that one would not necessarily expect high correlations across different decision tasks or even trials within the same task (Byrnes, Miller, & Schafer, 1999; Miller & Byrnes, 1997). As noted earlier, people arrive at decisions on the basis of their knowledge of possible courses of action, their goals, and their use of decision strategies. Moreover, the model assumes that good decision makers learn over time and only engage in effortful processes for important decisions. A person may have knowledge of effective options for one context (e.g., how to solve an interpersonal problem) but may have little idea of how to proceed in another (e.g., how to fix a car that will not start). Hence, people's ability to discover and implement a good option in the first context would not necessarily predict how well they do in the second. Relatedly, contexts need not invoke the same values or concerns and people may feel somewhat more strongly about, say, physical health than, say, financial well-being. Moreover, there is also the distinction between short-term goals, long-term goals, and aspirations that affect decisions (see Klaczynski & Reese, 1991). For these reasons, high correlations in performance across contexts would not obtain. Finally, people may not pursue good options the first few times they find themselves in a context but eventually use good options after repeated failures prompt them to seek advice regarding good ways to proceed. Again, performance on early trials would not necessarily predict performance on later trials. The key, then, to finding correlations is to place people within, or ask them about, contexts that would invoke the accurate knowledge, adaptive values, and effective strategies they have (and keep the importance of decisions essentially the same across problems). Note that I am not attributing performance variations to random error nor do I assume that low correlations should always be the norm (the way some who invoke a competence–performance distinction explain poor performance; see Stanovich & West, 2000, for more on this). I think that one could explain a considerable amount of the variance in performance by measuring a person's knowledge of options and level of understanding in a domain, their confidence and expectations, their values (including those related to the importance of decisions), their working memory capacity, their personality traits, and the extent to which they used strategies during the discovery or evaluative portions of the decision-making process. Relatedly, performance on ability tests such as the SAT or Wechsler Intelligence Scale for Children (WISC) would be expected to correlate with performance on decision tasks to the extent that these tasks tap into working memory capacity (as Stanovich & West, 2000, argued), but correlations might also be found given the possibility that these tasks all require (a) the ability to "know when you don't know"; (b) values common to decision and ability measures (e.g., doing well on tests; giving the experimenter what he or she wants); and (c) strategies needed for both kinds of measures. Performance on the SAT or WISC need not correlate with the tendency to learn from decision outcomes; the latter should be more correlated with a person's existing domain-specific knowledge, values, and strategies (a point I made earlier and return to later).

In support of our claims of the context-specificity of decisions, Byrnes, Miller, and Schafer (1999) showed in a meta-analysis of 150 studies that the size and direction of gender differences in risk taking depended very much on the kind of risk taking at issue and the age of the participants. For some contexts (e.g., driving), males at all ages showed greater risk taking than females. For other contexts, females in certain age groups showed greater risk taking than males (e.g., smoking in 20-year-olds) or no gender differences obtained (e.g., performance on classic "framing" tasks).

Developmental Mechanisms in the SRM

Earlier it was noted that models of decision making that were in existence prior to 1990 generally failed to include factors that might serve to increase decision-making skills over time. This lack of emphasis on developmental mechanisms was probably due to the fact that, at that time, only a handful of developmental scientists were interested in decision making. In addition, the zeitgeist was that adults were rather poor decision makers (Kahneman, Slovic, & Tversky, 1982; Stanovich & West, 2000). As such, researchers may have considered developmental comparisons and explanations to be rather fruitless given this apparent "floor effect."

Notwithstanding this zeitgeist, my colleagues and I considered it important to look for improvements and developmental mechanisms for several reasons. The first reflected our assumptions regarding the nature of decision-making competence. As noted earlier, competent decision makers tend to make good decisions because they (a) have accurate knowledge regarding the likely consequences of various courses of action; (b) value their physical health, emotional health, and financial well-being; (c) have a repertoire of strategies that can be used to reduce uncertainty, discover good options, evaluate options, and overcome obstacles and distractions imposed by limited resources, lack of knowledge, personality traits, and strong emotion; and (d) activate their knowledge, values, and strategies in contexts that call for these aspects of competence. It seemed reasonable to assume that children were not born with the knowledge, values, or strategies they needed to be good decision makers, but numerous studies conducted in other domains (e.g., memory, reading, motivation, etc.) suggested that children could acquire these aspects of decision making over time (Bjorklund, 2000; Byrnes, 2001). Another reason to search for developmental improvements and mechanisms was that we felt it was important to know whether children were acquiring the kinds of skills they needed to be competent decision makers by the time they reached early adulthood. We expected to find individual differences in the level of skills manifested in early adulthood and hoped to link these differences to antecedent factors. In other words, if we could determine why only certain people acquire decision-making skills by early adulthood, we might be able to create interventions to help those who failed to acquire them.

Although our search for developmental mechanisms began late in our program and continues still, the tentative list includes the following: preexisting knowledge and belief networks, preexisting values, personal experience, vicarious learning, schooling, and authoritative parenting. Collectively, these factors provide answers to questions such as (1) How do decision makers acquire knowledge of effective courses of action? (2) Why do they maintain erroneous beliefs about the effectiveness of certain courses of action? (3) Why do they value certain outcomes more (or less) than they used to? and (4) Why are some decision makers incapable of making good decisions when left to their own devices? Answers to the first question include: (a) They personally experience the consequences of their actions, (b) they observe others experiencing the consequences of similar actions, and (c) they are given instruction on effective courses of action in school settings. Generally speaking, however, such experiences tend to produce fairly conservative changes given the powerful effects exerted by preexisting knowledge and belief networks (the answer to the second question). Regarding the third question, we expect that personal experiences in conjunction with cultural influences (e.g., peers, family, the media, etc.) and preexisting values conspire to alter values in a slow and steady manner. As to individual differences in self-regulated decision making, we assume that children will eventually internalize strategic approaches to decision making if they are afforded reasonable autonomy by authoritative parents (who allow them to safely experience outcomes of their decisions and who model, scaffold, and explain competent decision making as well).

EMPIRICAL SUPPORT FOR THE SRM

In the previous two sections of this chapter, I described the nature of competent and self-regulated decision making and also highlighted predictions of the SRM (e.g., patterns of correlations that one would expect). As I describe next, my colleagues and I used these aspects of the model to examine age changes in eight aspects of competent decision making: coordination of multiple goals, having calibrated beliefs, recognition of the best choices in an array, appropriately responding to outcomes, using knowledge to construct effective options, counteracting dysregulating influences, having adaptive values, and use of effective decision-making strategies.

Coordination of Multiple Goals, Calibrated Beliefs, Recognizing Good Options

In several early studies, my colleagues and I presented multidimensional options to adolescents and adults in the context of a game. In one version of the game, subjects were presented with three decks of cards and were asked to select a card from one of the decks on each trial. Each deck contained one, two, or three different types of cards. The cards differed with respect to what was printed or drawn on them (e.g., a red circle vs. a green triangle) and the decks contained different mixtures of cards. For example, on some trials, the three decks might be constituted as follows:

Deck 1 = 3 cards with red circles and 2 cards with green triangles;
Deck 2 = 2 cards with red circles and 4 cards with green triangles;
Deck 3 = 5 cards that had the words "go back to base" on them.

The decks were placed on a game board that had three paths (one for each deck). Each path had three positions: a starting position (called "base"), a middle position, and an end position (called "home"). Each deck was placed next to a middle position on one of the three paths. To earn points, subjects had to choose a path and move in succession from base, to middle, to home. To get past any of the middle positions along a path and move home, subjects had to draw a favorable card from one of the three decks. Hence, each deck acted as a "gatekeeper." On any given trial, the current rule for earning points determined what card was favorable. For example, a card with a red circle on it would be favorable when the rule was: "If you draw a card with a red circle from a deck, you may move home and win a point. However, if you draw a card with a green triangle from a deck, you may not move home. If a card with 'go back to base' is drawn, you must go back to base." Given this rule, subjects should move from the base position to the middle position next to Deck 1 (because Deck 1 happens to have more red circles in it). In contrast, given the three decks mentioned and a rule that makes green triangles favorable, subjects should choose the path that has Deck 2 at its middle position. On each trial, the ratio of cards in each deck was changed so that the best deck (and path) to choose changed from trial to trial. In addition, the rules changed every four trials (e.g., suggesting green triangles are favorable, not red circles).

Hence, subjects earned points on a given trial by correctly matching decks to rules. When the decks contained colored shapes and there were large differences in the proportions of favorable cards in the decks (e.g., Deck 1 = 4 red, 1 green; Deck 2 = 1 red, 4 green), subjects found it easy to identify the best deck to choose. However, when the proportions of favorable cards in each deck were more similar (e.g., 60% favorable vs. 62.5% favorable), subjects had more difficulty. Subjects also had trouble choosing the best deck when we replaced the colored shapes with easy and hard questions (e.g., Deck 1 = 3 easy questions and 4 hard questions instead of 3 red circles and 4 green triangles). When we used cards with easy and hard questions on them, subjects could only move home (i.e., earn points) if they answered a type of question when it was drawn. Hence, unlike the trials with colored shapes that involved simple probabilities (e.g., 3 red out of 6 cards = a 50% chance of points), trials with questions involved compound probabilities. In particular, if a deck contained 60% hard questions and a subject could only answer 50% of these questions, the probability that the person would earn points by answering a hard question was 30% (i.e., $.60 \times .50$).

In addition to asking subjects to choose decks, select cards, and answer questions on each trial, we also asked them to rate their ability to answer questions and estimate the likelihood that they would earn points on a given trial. Note that for trials involving colored shapes, subjects merely had to compute (intuitively or explicitly) the relative proportions of cards to know which deck yielded the highest percentage of favorable cards. For trials involving questions, however, subjects could only maximize points if they were also well-calibrated in their beliefs about their ability to answer the questions. We assessed calibration by linking expectations to actual performance. Whereas we expected calibrated individuals to choose the best deck and optimize their points, we expected that overconfident individuals would attempt to answer questions that were out of their reach (and earn few points), and that underconfident individuals would avoid many questions that were within their reach.

In two experiments, Byrnes and McClenny (1994) found that 13-year-olds and college students performed moderately well on games of this kind. In particular, 13-year-olds in their Experiment 1 chose the best path on 68% of trials and college students did so on 77% of trials (a significant age difference). In Experiment 2, whereas 13-year-olds chose the best path on 60% of trials, college students did so on 64% of trials (a nonsignificant age difference). Subjects in both age groups performed more poorly in Experiment 2 because (a) they had to take into account compound probabilities involving the percentages of cards and their ability beliefs (i.e., Experiment 2 used factual questions whereas Experiment 1 used colored shapes); and (b) more complex decks were used (i.e., three types of cards in each deck instead of two—easy questions, hard questions, and "go back to base"). Analysis of response patterns revealed that many subjects were unidimensional in their thinking (i.e., they focused on just one type of card in the decks instead of considering all types) and tended to be overconfident in their ability to answer hard questions. For example, they gave ratings indicating they were extremely sure they would answer hard questions correctly and earn points on a given trial, even though they regularly failed to draw the card they wanted or earn points on prior trials involving hard questions.

Assuming that the primary factor that promoted mediocre performance in the Byrnes and McClenny (1994) study was the insertion of ability beliefs into the task, Byrnes, Miller, and Reynolds (1999, Experiment 2) created a different game in which participants were asked to assume that they were physicians who were confronted with a series of fictional patients. All of the patients had the same disorder (e.g., high cholesterol) and participants had to decide which of three medicines to prescribe. Each medicine was paired with a booklet that described its success rate in two studies (e.g., 72% of patients had lowered their cholesterol at the end of the studies), its cost (e.g., $3 per pill vs. $1 per pill), and its side effects (e.g., 42% had painful abdominal cramps). Hence, correct responding required the coordination of three dimensions that conflicted (the one with the highest success rate had the highest cost). Careful construction of the alternatives allowed us to create a best choice (the best combination of effectiveness, cost, and incidence of side effects). On each trial, participants chose a medicine, predicted its likely effects on that patient, and observed what happened (e.g., the cholesterol was lowered but the patient experienced painful cramps). Predictions were used to assess a participant's degree of calibration, but did not evoke ability beliefs in the same way the prior version of the game did. Results showed that adults chose the best medicine significantly more often than adolescents (58% of trials vs. 35% of trials) and also demonstrated more calibrated beliefs (e.g., they predicted the outcomes of patients better than adolescents). However, adults were only perfectly calibrated on 10% of trials (i.e., their predictions were either too optimistic or too pessimistic). In addition, when explaining their choices, adults showed more multidimensional thinking than adolescents. That is, whereas adults appealed to two or three aspects of each medicine on 42% of trials (e.g., effectiveness and side effects), adolescents did so on just 22% of trials.

In summary, then, on the first three indices of competent decision making (i.e., coordination of multiple goals, calibrated beliefs, and recognition of the best options in an array), adults demonstrated more competence than adolescents. However, the performance of adults was far from perfect.

Appropriately Responding to Outcomes (i.e., Adaptive Learning)

As noted earlier, another important indicator of self-regulation is the tendency to modify knowledge structures in ways that make them more in tune with the probabilistic, uncertain nature of the environment (Anderson, 1991; Jordan & Rumelhart, 1995; Piaget, 1952). Doing so helps a decision maker increasingly choose courses of action that are likely to lead to favorable, adaptive outcomes. However, the structural aspects of the SRM (see previous text) imply that feedback will tend to promote changes in a relatively conservative and progressive manner. My colleagues and I assume that the conservative quality of change derives from the fact that a person's knowledge and values are represented in the form of networks (Byrnes, Miller, & Reynolds, 1999). Similar to other researchers and theorists, we propose that elements in these networks are linked to other elements through specific relations (e.g., class membership, causal relations, etc.) and that each item of knowledge, belief, or value is assigned a certain strength of conviction that protects it from being quickly discarded (e.g., "I strongly believe that vitamins make me feel better"; "I strongly believe that it is wrong to steal"; etc.).

These assumptions of the SRM regarding networks in conjunction with its assumptions regarding the probabilistic nature of the environment have consequences for the predictions that one would make regarding appropriate responses to feedback. If, in fact, courses of action are linked to their consequences in a probabilistic manner (i.e., things do not always go as planned), it would typically be unwise for an individual to radically revise a current belief or value on the basis of a single negative experience (Edwards & Smith, 1996). For example, friendly, cooperative behavior generally promotes the formation of friendships and positive exchanges. There are times, however, when friendly overtures are rejected (as any middle schooler can attest). These occasional rejections should not be taken to mean that friendly, cooperative behavior is no longer effective. Similarly, the strategy of buying new cars with good repair records usually leads to trouble-free driving, but occasionally even the best manufacturers create a "lemon" or two. This infrequent outcome should not cause a person to abandon the strategy of buying new cars with good repair records. Conversely, though, a single positive experience should not cause someone to alter his or her beliefs about the likelihood that a dangerous behavior could lead to negative consequences. For example, when a teen manages to avoid crashing his car while driving under the influence, he should not then conclude that drunk driving is less risky than he thought. Rather, the adaptive response is to maintain the original belief that drunk driving is dangerous in the face of this counterevidence.

In some cases, though, counterevidence may well accumulate. One could argue that it would be maladaptive to hold onto an erroneous belief or a misguided value for too long. Hence, the adaptive response (in most cases) is to continue to maintain a knowledge structure or value system for a period of time in the face of challenges, but then eventually revise representations if multiple outcomes suggest that beliefs are incorrect. Of course, the literature on scientific misconceptions and other forms of reasoning shows that it is possible to speed up the normal, untutored process of belief revision through presentation of rationales or explanations that make sense (Byrnes, 2001; Stanovich & West, 2000). But here again, the structural aspects of the SRM suggest that decision makers need to have a certain level of conceptual understanding in a domain before outcome feedback or explanations will make sense to them. It is precisely this lack of understanding that might cause a decision maker to quickly or randomly shift rather than demonstrate dogmatism. But note that shifting and random trial-and-error responding can also be considered adaptive in such situations (see Siegler, 1997). The literature also shows that there are individual differences in belief preservation that derive from being particularly biased in one's opinions and having other perspectives on the origin, acquisition, and certainty of knowledge (Klaczynski, 2000).

In several different studies, my colleagues and I examined the ways in which adolescents and adults responded to feedback. In Experiment 2 of Byrnes and McClenny (1994), for example, subjects received feedback each time they chose a card from a deck and tried to answer questions. Results showed that participants in both age groups showed little evidence of learning across trials. Whereas the percentage of best choices increased only slightly over trials for the college students (i.e., 61% to 67%), the percentage of correct choices significantly decreased across trials for the 13-year-olds (71% to 48%). Hence, experiencing these negative outcomes on early trials (i.e., getting answers wrong and losing points) did not have a positive effect on the choices of 13-year-olds in later trials. Failure experiences seemed to prompt them to increasingly choose paths with the highest number (not proportion) of easy questions.

In Experiment 1 of Byrnes, Miller, and Reynolds (1999), we attempted to use training to improve performance on the same version of the decision-making game that was used by Byrnes and McClenny (1994). Training was provided before subjects played the game and focused on the two sources of error that were revealed by Byrnes and McClenny (1994): (a) a tendency to focus on only one type of card and (b) overconfidence. To reduce the tendency to focus on a single type of card (e.g., the number of easy questions in a deck), 13-year-olds and college students were told that

> Other people your age who have played this game do poorly because they do not consider all of the cards in the decks. A particular problem is their tendency to ignore the "go back to base" cards. This tendency is a problem because the "go back to base" cards are often selected during the game. The best deck to choose is the one that has the best proportions of easy, hard, *and* go back to base cards. (Byrnes, Miller, & Reynolds, 1999, p. 1127)

To reduce overconfidence, subjects were given a pretest that contained exactly the same questions that were typed on the cards. Hence, subjects knew going into the game how many of the easy or hard questions they could answer. Across eight trials, all subjects were asked to choose decks, answer questions, rate their ability to answer questions, and estimate the probability that they would earn points on a given trial.

Results showed that verbal training had absolutely no effect on overconfidence or on the ability to choose the best deck. Treatment and control subjects had nearly identical means for correct choices and ability beliefs (i.e., training subjects were as overconfident as control subjects about hard questions even though they saw themselves getting many of these questions wrong on the pretest). The findings for ability beliefs, of course, are consistent with studies of belief persistence (e.g., Edwards & Smith, 1996; Ross & Lepper, 1980). Training only made subjects more pessimistic about the likelihood of earning points (presumably due to pessimism about the type of card drawn, not their abilities). As for learning based on the outcomes of their choices, results showed that whereas college students selected the best path significantly more often on the last four trials (67%) than they did on the first four trials (52%), the 13-year-olds showed no significant improvement (49% on the first four trials to 51% on the last four trials).

The repeated measures design of that study allowed consideration of different kinds of learning patterns as well. We considered whether people (a) made good choices then shifted to less good choices over time, (b) made less good choices and continued to do so in the face of negative feedback, (c) made good choices and continued to do so, or (d) made less good choices then shifted to better choices in response to feedback. Collapsing the first two and last two categories together (creating less adaptive and more adaptive categories, respectively), we found that whereas 27% of the 13-year-olds showed the two more adaptive patterns, 58% of college students and 50% of noncollege adults showed these patterns. Thus, there was developmental improvement in the level of adaptive responses to feedback.

And yet, the results for both age groups were somewhat lower than expected. As noted earlier, we wondered whether ability beliefs were particularly resistant to change. In addition, we wondered whether adolescents simply needed more trials of feedback to demonstrate a higher degree of adaptive learning. Further, the college students were not only older than the 13-year-olds, they also had more education and could have been more intelligent. These considerations led to the use of the medical decision-making task in Experiment 2 of Byrnes, Miller, and Reynolds (1999) and inclusion of an intelligence measure as well. In addition to removing personal attributions from calibration estimates, we also increased the number of trials from 8 to 32 (two blocks of 16 trials each). In addition, in between blocks, we inserted a different kind of verbal training in which they were shown how medicines in the first block could be arrayed, using a graphic display, along the three dimensions of effectiveness, cost, and side effects. Next they were told that no one drug was great on everything (clearly illustrated in the display), so they needed to find a drug that was reasonably good on all three dimensions (the best possible combination). After this explanation, they were asked to prescribe one of three new drugs for the next set of 16 "patients" who had a different disease than the patients in the first trial block.

Results showed that the combination of increased trials of outcome feedback (i.e., observing what happened to patients) and the new verbal feedback substantially increased the age differences in best choices over time. That is, whereas participants at both age levels showed a significant improvement in performance during the second trial block, the effect was much more pronounced in the college students. Cast in the form of learning patterns, adults were much more likely than 13-year-olds to demonstrate adaptive patterns consistent with the feedback they received (i.e., 73% vs. 8%). The younger subjects also showed a strong tendency to shift among drugs rather than rigidly stay with a particular drug. Consistent with the assumptions of the SRM, however, very few of the college students showed radical changes in their choice behavior (e.g., choosing incorrectly for 16 trials and then choosing correctly for the next 16). Instead, the vast majority of changes occurred slowly over trials.

We interpreted such findings as indicating that existing knowledge and beliefs constrained the extent of learning in participants. This interpretation was bolstered by the finding that responsiveness to feedback was uncorrelated with a measure of intelligence (i.e., a timed verbal and spatial analogy measure). When entered in a regression analysis, intelligence scores did not predict a significant amount of variance in good choices during the last 16 trials after good choices during the first 16 trials were entered. When the reverse order was used, good choices during the first block still accounted for nearly all of the variance (overwhelming the effect of intelligence). This finding was supported by an additional analysis of learning patterns. Subdividing the sample into the bottom third, middle third, and top third of scorers on the intelligence measure (standardized within age), we found no significant association between intelligence group and adaptive learning patterns. The percentages of participants who demonstrated the adaptive, feedback-consistent patterns were 35% (bottom third), 60% (middle third), and 28% (top third).

Before moving on, it is important to note that our findings do not necessarily contradict findings of correlations between measures of intellectual ability and other, well-known measures of judgment and decision making (see Stanovich & West, 2000, for a review). One could argue that the coordination of three dimensions (as required on the medical task) is well within the working-memory capacity of the average adolescent or adult (Halford, 1999). Hence, high-ability subjects are afforded no advantage in such an instance. In addition, we considered learning across trials rather than the ability to discern normative responses on a single trial.

In one additional study that has relevance to the notion of adaptive learning (i.e., Miller & Byrnes, 1997, Experiment 1), we examined the role of learning in the context of a risk-taking task. Half of the participants in the third, fifth, and seventh grades were placed in a peers-present condition in which groups of three classmates took turns engaging in four risk-taking tasks (two requiring skill, two involving chance), and a peers-absent condition in which children engaged in the four tasks by themselves. Once again, the repeated measures design allowed for the consideration of learning across trials. The use of the peers-present condition, however, also permitted a consideration of vicarious learning. To assess learning in either condition, we created two categories of choices: (a) choices consistent with prior outcomes (i.e., choosing the riskiest option after seeing that it paid off for oneself or a peer on a prior trial; avoiding the riskiest option after seeing that it led to negative outcomes for oneself or a peer on a prior trial); and (b) choices seemingly indifferent to outcomes (i.e., avoiding risky options after seeing that they paid off; choosing risky options after seeing that they did not pay off). We then categorized children in terms of being risk takers (choosing the riskiest option on at least three of four tasks) or risk avoiders (choosing it less than three times). We found that 69% of the choices made by risk takers were inconsistent with prior outcomes that they themselves experienced. In addition, when peers were present, risk takers generated 87% of the responses that suggested an indifference to the outcomes experienced by peers. Thus, a key difference between risk takers and risk avoiders seemed to be differing degrees of sensitivity to outcomes. Of course, it is not clear whether risk takers in this study (a) failed to pay attention to outcomes, (b) failed to encode these outcomes properly, or (c) failed to remember outcomes that they paid attention to and properly encoded. A result from Byrnes and McClenny (1994) pointed to the possibility of memory problems. When asked to say how many times they earned points on the decision-making game after they finished playing, 13-year-olds were significantly less accurate than adults. More specifically, they remembered doing better than they did.

These findings are consistent with those of Fong, Santioso, and Kunda (1990), who found a similar kind of self-serving bias in adult's memory, which suggests that adults may show a similar level or distortion as time passes. Regardless of the explanation, the findings as a whole suggest that children seem to be more responsive to outcomes as they move through the adolescent period. It is possible that those who seem impervious to outcomes may well experience negative consequences more often than their more responsive peers, and also experience failure more often than their more responsive peers.

Using Knowledge to Construct Effective Options

It was noted earlier that a major assumption of the SRM is that someone cannot make good decisions on a regular basis if that person does not have accurate knowledge of the likely consequences of his or her actions. To extend the aforementioned studies of learning somewhat, my colleagues and I considered the role of experience in the acquisition of knowledge. Although it seems reasonable to expect that experience would manifest itself in the ability to generate a greater variety of effective courses of action, a sizable literature on the role of expertise in decision making has found relatively few differences between novices and experts on decision-making tasks (see Shanteau, 1992, for a review). For example, faculty members and undergraduates rely on the same sorts of criteria when they are deciding who should be admitted into a graduate program. Similarly, experienced therapists rely on the same symptoms as undergraduates when forming diagnoses. These surprising findings prompted us to probe more deeply into the role of experience in several exploratory studies. Because only one of these studies is published, I only provide a sketch of each.

In the first study (which was never published), we considered whether 15 mothers would differ from 15 women who did not have children in their approach to a parenting decision. Subjects in both groups were in their early 30s and were well-educated. All subjects were presented with the following scenario:

> Imagine that you are the parent of a 3-month-old infant who is not sleeping through the night. You put her to bed at 8 p.m., but every night at 2 a.m., she wakes up crying. Because you get up once a night too, you are always tired at work. Now you are trying to decide what to do.

The primary cause of sleeping through the night is brain maturation. We wanted to see the kinds of causes and proposed solutions that subjects in each group would generate. Results showed that whereas parents ($M = 3.0$)

supplied significantly more causes of waking than nonparents ($M = 2.47$), $F(1, 28) = 7.72, p < .01$, the former were not more likely to suggest the "correct" cause of waking and sleeping in infants. Because parents often attributed the waking to the wrong cause (e.g., fear of being alone), they also were more likely to suggest an ineffective strategy as well (e.g., sleeping with the infant). Thus, experience seems to have prompted parents to try many different things (e.g., cereal before bed) and thereby develop a repertoire of strategies, but these strategies were not necessarily effective.

In the second study (which was published, Byrnes & Torney-Purta, 1995), we presented subjects with two problems (global warming, homelessness) and asked them to generate solutions to these problems. There were three groups of subjects: (a) bright 16-year-olds who attended an intensive 2-week workshop on issues that included global warming but not homelessness, (b) bright 16-year-olds who did not attend the workshop, and (c) college students who did not attend the workshop. Results showed that the 16-year-old workshop attendees and college students generated more potential causes of the global warming problem and generated more strategies for solving it than the 16-year-olds who did not attend the workshop. Those in the former two groups did not differ. However, many of the causes and solutions of the college students were not likely to be effective and were based on faulty causal assumptions (in comparison to those suggested by experts on global warming). For example, college students confused the greenhouse effect with the ozone problem. After rescoring responses in terms of correctness, the 16-year-old workshop attendees were found to have significantly higher scores than the college students on the global warming problem. Thus, although the college students were older and presumably more experienced than the workshop attendees, it would seem that the experiences of the college students led to an increase in incorrect knowledge. The workshop experience, in contrast, led to an increase in correct knowledge in the 16-year-olds.

In the third study (unpublished), my colleague Bonita McClenny and I employed the same methodology that was used in the parenting study to examine possible differences between (a) 16 undergraduates who were diagnosed with bulimia and (b) 16 nonbulimic undergraduates. Participants were presented with two scenarios. One described a 23-year-old bulimic and the other described a 23-year-old woman with obsessive-compulsive disorder (OCD). Statistical analysis of the bulimia scenario showed that whereas there were no group differences in the number of causes generated, group differences emerged within categories of causes. Post hoc analyses showed that bulimics were significantly more likely than nonbulimics to attribute the urge to binge to conflicts in the character's family (50% vs. 19%), and to some eliciting event such as a fight with a boyfriend or poor performance on a test (40% vs. 0%). Nonbulimics, in contrast, were significantly more likely to mention the person's body image (13% vs. 50%). The latter is frequently mentioned in undergraduate texts, courses in child development, and other outlets, so the responses of the nonbulimics are to be expected. For the OCD scenario, no group differences emerged for either the number of causes supplied or the type of causes supplied.

With respect to strategies, no quantitative differences emerged between the groups, but there were differences for the types of strategies suggested. For the bulimia scenario, bulimics were more likely than nonbulimics to mention strategies in two categories: (a) engage in distracting behaviors such as watching TV (63% vs. 6%); and (b) engage in reflective, self-calming behaviors such as journal writing (53% vs. 19%). These two types of behaviors were suggested to the bulimics by the same therapist who was treating them all. In contrast, nonbulimics were more likely to suggest the strategy of seeing a therapist (13% vs. 44%). For the OCD scenario, whereas bulimics were more likely to mention the strategies of being reflective and leaving the situation, nonbulimics were once again more likely to mention the strategy of seeing a therapist.

The findings of the bulimia study contrast somewhat with the findings of the parenting study. In the bulimia study, qualitative (i.e., category) differences emerged but quantitative differences did not. In the parenting study, quantitative differences emerged but qualitative ones did not. In addition, whereas parents were not more likely to be accurate than nonparents, many of the strategies and causes mentioned by bulimics were the same as those suggested by experts who study eating disorders (though there is some disagreement about the causes and best treatments for bulimia). The fact that the bulimic women mentioned strategies such as TV watching is not surprising given that this strategy was suggested to them by their therapist. One can speculate that parents were not more accurate than nonparents because parents did not receive the same level of expert advice regarding infant sleep that bulimics received for their eating disorder (probably because they never asked experts for the advice). Moreover, it is possible that bulimics would not have figured out on their own how to solve a problem with binge eating (just as the parents did not figure out on their own how to solve infant sleep problems). Such speculations require further study. In any case, the primary difference between the topics seems to be that whereas infants eventually do sleep through the night (even when parents use ineffective strategies), an eating disorder will not simply go away in the same manner.

To make sense of the results across these studies, it is useful to consider the collective evidence generated by the studies of adaptive learning (the preceding section of this chapter), the studies of experts and novices (reviewed by Shanteau, 1992, and others), and the three studies described in the present section. The first thing to note is that the repeated measures tasks used in the adaptive learning studies gather together and confront subjects with related experiences in a serial, distilled fashion. Hence, it optimizes the chance that participants will draw appropriate lessons across outcomes. In the real world, however, related experiences are interspersed among a variety of other experiences. Hence, it would be harder to link these experiences together and draw general, appropriate lessons from them (Einhorn, 1982). Second, in retrospect, it seems evident that there are major differences between informal learning opportunities with ambiguous outcomes (e.g., childrearing experiences; reviewing applications to graduate school) and formal educational experiences that provide structured, clear, and accurate feedback (e.g., workshops on targeted topics; advice from experienced therapists). Perhaps only the latter appears to be capable of promoting growth in accurate knowledge. Inasmuch as all experiences are not alike, it seems that one would only expect age differences in the knowledge component of decision making if older decision makers have been given structured feedback from experts (e.g., in courses) and the young ones had not. But this claim might only be true for typical or average participants. Scholars who study practical intelligence would argue that success does not derive from the acquisition of formal knowledge that is presented by others, but by tacit knowledge of important tasks that they pick up on their own (e.g., Wagner & Sternberg, 1985). This ability to discern tacit knowledge is independent of the kind of academic intelligence measured by IQ tests. Given these conflicting claims, more research is obviously needed to fully understand the role of experience in decision making.

Having Adaptive Values

As noted earlier, competent decision makers not only have knowledge of the likely consequences of their actions, they also have adaptive values. To see this, consider the example of two decision makers who are alike in their knowledge of eating habits (e.g., both know that fast foods are not terribly healthy), but who differ in their values (e.g., only one considers physical health to be a high priority). It would be predicted that these individuals would make different choices (e.g., one eats fast foods, the other does not). Relatively few studies of decision making have examined age changes in values or considered how such changes affect the choices of individuals at different ages (in conjunction with their knowledge of options). In two studies, Miller and Byrnes (2001a, 2001b) found a developmental decrease in adolescents' valuing of the importance of social–emotional goals (e.g., "How important is it to you to get along with other people?") and the importance of academic achievement goals (e.g., "How important is it to you to do well in school?") between the 9th and 11th grades. This problematic decrease in values is consistent with the findings of Jacobs, Lanza, Osgood, Eccles, and Wigfield (2002) who found a similar drop in students' valuing of academic subjects and sports between the 1st and 12th grades. It remains to be seen whether this negative change in values is followed by a developmental increase between the 12th grade and adulthood (paralleling the other age increases described earlier for other aspects of decision making). Note that the decrease in valuing of achievement found by Miller and Byrnes (2001a, 2001b) and Jacobs et al. (2002) contrasts somewhat with the findings of others who have shown increases in the valuing of achievement in college-bound students (e.g., Klaczynski & Reese, 1991). Neither Miller and Byrnes nor Jacobs et al. differentiated between college-bound and non-college-bound students in their studies.

Counteracting Dysregulating Influences

In the field of decision making, theorists have often appealed to a competence–performance distinction to explain the tendency of participants to make choices that deviate from idealized normative standards (Stanovich & West, 2000). The SRM shares a certain kinship with these theorists in the sense that my colleagues and I think that decision makers have abilities that they often fail to utilize. That is, we believe that people often make poor decisions even when they know better ("What was I thinking?," they might ask themselves). However, we do not limit our explanations of error to random sources such as momentary lapses of attention or misinterpretations. Instead, we typically appeal to more systematic sources of error. Consider, for example, the case of the bulimic women in the aforementioned study who have told us how they should behave when they feel the urge to binge (e.g., distract themselves with TV; call a supportive friend), but nevertheless find it quite difficult to implement these behaviors when in a strong emotional state. In effect, they know what to do and will tell you that they value their health when in a calm state. In real situations, however, their knowledge and values seem to get overridden by an intense whirlwind of emotion. Relatedly, participants in other studies demonstrate different approaches to evaluating their options, depending on how stressed they feel (Keinan, 1987). Moreover, the introduction of new elements into a situation can often lead to a downturn in good choices by distracting the decision maker or by precipitating the need to coordinate more goals than the decision maker can effectively process at the time.

In a regression framework, we have suggested and shown that it is not enough to measure a person's goals, values, knowledge of options, and strategies for discovering or evaluating options. These factors will explain a considerable amount of variance in a person's choices, but the equation will still fall short of predicting behavior in specific contexts unless it takes into account various dysregulating influences (i.e., factors that "knock one off course," making it hard to behave in ways consistent with one's core knowledge and values). My colleagues and I have found that the following personality traits and contextual factors are correlated with suboptimal choices: sensation-seeking, impulsivity, competitiveness, overconfidence, and the presence of peers (Miller & Byrnes, 1997, 2001a, 2001b). Thus, regression studies suggest that the core aspects of competence (i.e., goals, values, knowledge of options, strategies) will predict good decisions if a person also has a favorable personality profile (i.e., lower in sensation-seeking, more reflective, less competitive, more calibrated). However, if a person has a less favorable profile or is distracted by issues that manifest themselves in the presence of peers (e.g., the desire to show off), that person will chose suboptimal options even though he or she seems to have the right goals, values, knowledge of options, and strategies for discovering and evaluating options. The model further predicts, though, that there could also be a third possibility: a person who (a) has the right goals, knowledge of options, and strategies for discovering and evaluating options; and (b) has troublesome personality traits (e.g., emotional, impulsive, highly competitive); but (c) has an additional set of self-regulatory strategies for counteracting the troublesome traits. The methodology needed to investigate this possibility (which we are currently employing) involves measuring the extent to which participants utilize counteracting strategies and then entering the appropriate interaction terms (e.g., personality trait × counteracting strategy) into regressions.

We suspect that inclusion of both dysregulating influences and counteracting strategies into a developmental study could be an important but overlooked variable related to age differences in good choices. In other words, two age groups may look the same "on paper" (i.e., they report similar levels of knowledge and similar values) but nevertheless make different choices in the real world because they differ on dysregulating influences and strategies to counteract them (e.g., the younger group engages in unsafe behaviors whereas the older group does not). This suspicion is supported by studies that show that people who engage in certain behaviors (e.g., cigarette smoking, unprotected sex, etc.) do not differ from those who refrain from engaging in these behaviors in terms of their knowledge of the consequences of these behaviors or their values (DiClemente, Hansen, & Ponton, 1995). So what explains the difference? The opportunity × propensity thesis may provide clues. Engagers could differ from nonengagers in terms of personality traits (e.g., sensation seeking) that predispose them to find opportunities to engage in risky behavior, or in terms of personality traits that predispose them to make poor choices when in these contexts (e.g., impulsivity, competitiveness, and emotionality). But the developmental aspect of the SRM implies that the propensity factor would be augmented over time by the progressive attainment of counteracting strategies. That is, the presence of a trait would no longer be predictive once the person has acquired counteracting strategies. So, for example, one might expect temperamentally emotional adolescents to engage in an unwise behavior when given the opportunity (e.g., express anger at a superior) but expect that temperamentally emotional adults would not (due to the use of self-calming strategies). These predictions remain to be validated in future experiments.

Use of Effective Decision-Making Strategies

As noted earlier, a central claim of the SRM is that, when faced with important decisions, successful individuals use effective strategies to discover and evaluate their options. In effect, these strategies increase their chances of finding options that will help them attain their adaptive goals. Less successful individuals, in contrast, either pursue less adaptive goals or fail to use effective strategies for discovering or evaluating their options. My colleague David Miller and I have found indirect support for these claims in two studies (Miller & Byrnes, 2001a, 2001b). In each study, we asked 9th and 11th graders to (a) rate the importance of either academic goals (Miller & Byrnes, 2001b) or social goals (Miller & Byrnes, 2001a); (b) indicate their tendency to engage in either achievement behaviors (Miller & Byrnes, 2001b) or social behaviors (Miller & Byrnes, 2001a); and (c) indicate their tendency to engage in effective discovery or evaluate strategies when faced with important decisions (e.g., seek advice). Miller and Byrnes (2001b) found that the following three variables explained about 60% of the variance in achievement behaviors (after controlling for other variables): valuing of academic goals, the tendency to use decision-making strategies for important decisions, and a student's grade point average. Similarly, Miller and Byrnes (2001a) found that the following variables explained an average of 60% of the variance (across two studies) in social behaviors: valuing of social goals (Studies 1 and 2), the tendency to use decision-making strategies for important decisions (Studies 1 and 2), and age (Study 2). Note, though, that social behaviors and academic achievement behaviors are merely correlates of social success and academic achievement, respectively. It would be useful for researchers to find direct support for the link between self-regulation and success in future studies.

CONCLUSIONS AND IMPLICATIONS

Earlier I noted that the SRM was created to help us find answers to the three key questions of developmental science (as they pertain to the field of decision making): (1) *the Developmental Trends question*: Do decision-making skills improve with age? (2) *the Developmental Mechanism question*: Why do decision-making skills improve with age? and (3) *the Individual Differences question*: Why are some people more likely to demonstrate decision-making skills in a particular context than others?

Our results suggest that the most reasonable answer to the Developmental Trends question would be, "It depends on the content of the decision, the complexity of the decision, and the particular aspect of decision-making competence that you had in mind." We have found that by placing decision making in the context of a board game with two-dimensional choices, age differences in aspects such as coordination of multiple goals, calibration, and recognition of good options improves significantly but fairly modestly across the adolescent period. We found that the size of the age gap widened when we explained good decision making to participants and asked them to coordinate three dimensions, interpret data to evaluate their options, and draw lessons across a series of discrete outcomes. In line with the competence–performance framework, the latter procedures seem to reveal a higher level of competence in adults than prior studies had suggested. And yet, the overall success rate with these manipulations was still surprisingly modest in adults. Moreover, we found that experience in and of itself is not necessarily likely to improve decisions across the adolescent and early adult period unless it is structured, unambiguous, and accurate. Hence, if one wants to find age differences in decision making, the content and nature of the decision-making task clearly matters. Relatedly, it would be unwise to assume that adults would always make better decisions than adolescents simply because they performed better on a single task in a single study. We believe that the SRM provides a useful framework for delineating the kinds of situations likely to reveal age differences by highlighting the role of knowledge and beliefs, values, processing capacity, and strategies (related to discovery of options, evaluation of options, and counteracting dysregulating factors). If there is reason to think that adults and adolescents would differ along one or more of these aspects (e.g., adults might have more accurate knowledge or beliefs), then one would predict age differences. Our findings that age differences in decision-making skills are more pronounced when complexity increases are consistent with the findings of other scholars in this area (e.g., Klaczynski, 2001).

As to the Developmental Mechanism question, the findings are still tentative but they suggest that education and scaffolded input from knowledgeable mentors may be more likely to improve decision making than personal experience or vicarious learning. Why? We think that it is because the causal structure of the world is relatively opaque and contains lots of confounded variables and coincidences. This fact combined with the fact that ability beliefs are relatively impervious to outcomes suggests that people may not take what they should take from an experience (Byrnes, 1998; Byrnes, Miller, & Reynolds, 1999; Einhorn, 1982; Klaczynski, 2000). This suggestion implies that it would be important to carefully tease apart factors such as experience and education in future studies. In addition, it would be useful to more fully examine the issue of learning in additional real-life situations. For example, it would be interesting to consider the responses of adolescents and adults to questions such as the following: (a) Have you ever been in a car accident? (if more than one, tell me about the most recent one); (b) Why did the accident happen?; (c) Did the accident cause you to change the way you drive? But again, the literature on practical intelligence suggests that successful individuals discern good ways to proceed on their own. Hence, more work is obviously needed in this area to resolve these issues.

Finally, we believe that we have begun to reveal some of the factors responsible for individual differences in decision making within the same age group. We suggest that a good way to explain such differences would be to measure the following variables in a sample of individuals: (a) their beliefs about the effectiveness and likely consequences of a set of options; (b) their values and concerns (i.e., what is important to them); (c) the strategies they may have used to discover and evaluate these options; (d) their working-memory capacity; (e) factors likely to have a dysregulating influence in the context within which decision making occurred (e.g., emotionality, impulsivity, the presence of peers); and (f) strategies used to counteract these influences. Two individuals could make different decisions if they differ for any of these reasons. These variables need to be combined with measures of individual differences in reasoning capacities and tendencies as well (Klaczynski, 2001; Stanovich & West, 2000).

The task remains to fill in the variety of research gaps that are highlighted the SRM. In addition, it remains to be seen how the various alternatives to the SRM (e.g., other models described in this volume) can be coherently combined into still more comprehensive models. The latter task will not be easy because of the different assumptions and intended functions of these different models. But we submit that the continuing integration of ideas is the best way to explain increasing amounts of the variance in decision making. Perhaps more importantly, we will only gain insight into ways to improve decision making if we increase insight into the nature and development of decision making.

REFERENCES

Albarracin, D., Johnson, B. T., Fishbein, M., & Muellerleile, P. A. (2001). Theories of reasoned action and planned behavior as models of condom use: A meta-analysis. *Psychological Bulletin, 127*, 142–161.

Anderson, J. R. (1991). Is human cognition adaptive? *Behavioral & Brain Sciences, 14*, 471–517.

Bandura, A. (1997). *Self-efficacy: The exercise of control.* New York: W. H. Freeman.

Bargh, J. A., & Chartland, T. L. (1999). The unbearable automaticity of being. *American Psychologist, 54*, 462–479.

Baron, J. (1994). *Thinking and deciding* (2nd ed.). Cambridge, England: Cambridge University Press.

Baumeister, R. F., Leith, K. P., Muraven, M., & Bratslavsky, E. (1998). Self-regulation as a key to success in life. In D. Pushkar, W. M. Bukowski, A. E. Schwartzman, D. M. Stack, & D. R. White (Eds.), *Improving competence across the lifespan: Building interventions based on theory and research* (pp. 117–132). New York: Plenum.

Bjorklund, D. F. (2000). *Children's thinking: Developmental function and individual differences* (3rd ed.). Belmont, CA: Wadsworth/Thomson Learning.

Bjorklund, D. F., & Pellegrini, A. D. (2000). Child development and evolutionary psychology. *Child Development, 71,* 1687–1708.

Brown, A. L., Bransford, J. D., Ferrara, R. A., & Campione, J. C. (1983). Learning, remembering and understanding. In J. H. Flavell & E. M. Markman (Eds.), *Handbook of child psychology: Vol. 3. Cognitive development* (pp. 263–340). New York: Wiley.

Byrnes, J. P. (1992). Categorizing and combining theories of cognitive development. *Educational Psychology Review, 4,* 309–343.

Byrnes, J. P. (1998). *The nature and development of decision-making: A self-regulation model.* Mahwah, NJ: Lawrence Erlbaum Associates.

Byrnes, J. P. (2001). *Cognitive development in instructional contexts* (2nd ed.). Needham Heights, MA: Allyn & Bacon.

Byrnes, J. P., & McClenny, B. (1994). Decision-making in young adolescents and adults. *Journal of Experimental Child Psychology, 58,* 359–388.

Byrnes, J. P., Miller, D. C., & Reynolds, M. (1999). Learning to make good decisions: A self-regulation perspective. *Child Development, 70,* 1121–1140.

Byrnes, J. P., Miller, D. C., & Schafer, W. D. (1999). Gender differences in risk-taking: A meta-analysis. *Psychological Bulletin, 125,* 367–383.

Byrnes, J. P., & Torney-Purta, J. V. (1995). Naïve theories and decision-making as part of higher order thinking in social studies. *Theory and Research in Social Education, 23,* 260–277.

Cole, M. (1999). Culture in development. In M. H. Bornstein & M. E. Lamb (Eds.), *Developmental psychology: An advanced textbook* (pp. 73–124). Mahwah, NJ: Lawrence Erlbaum Associates.

DiClemente, R. J., Hansen, W. B., & Ponton, L. E. (1995). *Handbook of adolescent risk behavior.* New York: Plenum.

Edwards, K., & Smith, E. E. (1996). A disconfirmation bias in the evaluation of arguments. *Journal of Personality and Social Psychology, 71,* 5–24.

Einhorn, H. J. (1982). Learning from experience and suboptimal rules in decision-making. In D. Kahneman, P. Slovic, & A. Tversky (Eds.), *Judgment under uncertainty: Heuristics and biases* (pp. 268–286). Cambridge, England: Cambridge University Press.

Fong, G. T., Santioso, R., & Kunda, Z. (1990). Motivated recruitment of autobiographical memories. *Journal of Personality & Social Psychology, 59,* 229–241.

Furby, L., & Beyth-Marom, R. (1992). Risk taking in adolescence: A decision-making perspective. *Developmental Review, 12,* 1–44.

Gigerenzer, G., & Todd, P. M. (1999). *Simple heuristics that make us smart.* London, England: Oxford University Press.

Gottfredson, M. R., & Hirschi, T. (1990). *A general theory of crime.* Stanford, CA: Stanford University Press.

Halford, G. S. (1999). The properties of representations used in higher cognitive processes: Developmental implications. In I. E. Sigel (Ed.), *Development of mental representation: Theories and applications* (pp. 147–168). Mahwah, NJ: Lawrence Erlbaum Associates.

Jacobs, J. E., Lanza, S., Osgood, D. W., Eccles, J. S., & Wigfield, A. (2002). Changes in children's self-competence and values: Gender and domain differences across grades one though twelve. *Child Development, 73,* 509–527.

Jordan, M. I., & Rumelhart, D. E. (1995). Forward models: Supervised learning with a distal teacher. In Y. Chauvin & D. E. Rumelhart (Eds.), *Backpropagation: Theory, architectures, and applications. Developments in connectionist theory* (pp. 189–236). Hillsdale, NJ: Lawrence Erlbaum Associates.

Kahneman, D., Slovic, P., & Tversky, A. (1982). *Judgment under uncertainty: Heuristics and biases.* Cambridge, England: Cambridge University Press.

Keinan, G. (1987). Decision-making under stress: Scanning of alternatives under controllable and uncontrollable threats. *Journal of Personality and Social Psychology, 52,* 639–644.

Klaczynski, P. A. (2000). Motivated scientific reasoning biases, epistemological beliefs, and theory polarization: A two-process approach to adolescent cognition. *Child Development, 71,* 1347–1366.

Klaczynski, P. A. (2001). Analytic and heuristic processing influences on adolescent reasoning and decision-making. *Child Development, 72,* 844–861.

Klaczynski, P. A., Byrnes, J. P., & Jacobs, J. E. (2001). Introduction to the special issue: The development of decision-making. *Journal of Applied Developmental Psychology, 22,* 225–236.

Klaczynski, P. A., & Reese, H. W. (1991). Educational trajectory and "action orientation": Grade and track differences. *Journal of Youth & Adolescence, 20,* 441–462.

Kosslyn, S. M., & Koenig, O. (1994). *Wet mind: The new cognitive neuroscience.* New York: The Free Press.

Miller, D. C., & Byrnes, J. P. (1997). The role of contextual and personal factors in children's risk-taking. *Developmental Psychology, 33,* 814–823.

Miller, D. C., & Byrnes, J. P. (2001a). Adolescents' decision-making in social situations: A self-regulation perspective. *Journal of Applied Developmental Psychology, 22,* 237–256.

Miller, D. C., & Byrnes, J. P. (2001b). To achieve or not to achieve: A self-regulation perspective on adolescents' academic decision-making. *Journal of Educational Psychology, 93,* 677–685.

Nelson, K. (1996). *Language in cognitive development: Emergence of the mediated mind.* New York: Cambridge University Press.

Osgood, D. W., Wilson, J. K., O'Malley, P. M., Bachman, J. G., & Johnson, L. D. (1996). Routine activities and individual deviant behavior. *American Sociological Review, 61,* 635–655.

Paris, S. G., Byrnes, J. P., & Paris, A. H. (2001). Constructing theories, identities, and actions of self-regulated learners. In B. J. Zimmerman & D. H. Schunk (Eds.), *Self-regulated learning and academic achievement: Theoretical perspectives* (2nd ed., pp. 253–287). Mahwah, NJ: Lawrence Erlbaum Associates.

Payne, J. W., Bettman, J. R., & Johnson, E. J. (1993). *The adaptive decision maker.* New York: Cambridge University Press.

Piaget, J. (1952). *The origins of intelligence in children.* New York: International Universities Press.

Pinker, S. (1997). *How the mind works.* New York: Norton.

Reese, H. W. (1994). The data/theory dialectic: The nature of scientific progress. In S. H. Cohen & H. W. Reese (Eds.), *Life-span developmental psychology: Methodological contributions* (pp. 1–27). Hillsdale, NJ: Lawrence Erlbaum Associates.

Rokeach, M. (1979). *Understanding human values.* New York: The Free Press.

Ross, L., & Lepper, M. R. (1980). The perseverance of beliefs: Empirical and normative considerations. In R. A. Shweder (Ed.), *Fallible judgment in behavioral research* (pp. 17–36). San Francisco: Jossey-Bass.

Shanteau, J. (1992). How much information does an expert use? Is it relevant? *Acta Psychologica, 81,* 75–86.

Shrager, J., & Siegler, R. S. (1998). SCADS: A model of children's strategy choices and strategy discoveries. *Psychological Science, 9,* 405–410.

Siegler, R. S. (1997). Concepts and methods for studying cognitive change. In E. Amsel & K. A. Renninger (Eds.), *Change and development: Issues of theory, method, and application* (pp. 77–97). Mahwah, NJ: Lawrence Erlbaum Associates.

Siegler, R. S. (1998). *Children's thinking* (3rd ed.). Englewood Cliffs, NJ: Prentice Hall.

Simon, H. A. (1956). Rational choice and the structure of the environment. *Psychological Review, 63,* 129–138.

Stanovich, K. E., & West, R. F. (2000). Individual differences in reasoning: Implications for the rationality debate? *Behavioral and Brain Science, 23*, 645–726.

Thomson, R. A. (1994). Emotion regulation: A theme in search of a definition. In N. A. Fox (Ed.), The development of emotion regulation: Biological and behavioral considerations. *Monographs of the Society for Research in Child Development, 59*(2–3, Serial No. 240).

Todd, P. M., & Gigerenzer, G. (2000). Precis of simple heuristics that make us smart. *Behavioral & Brain Sciences, 23*, 727–780.

Vygotsky, L. S. (1978). *Mind in society*. Cambridge, MA: Harvard University Press.

Wagner, R. K., & Sternberg, R. J. (1985). Practical intelligence in real world pursuits: The role of tacit knowledge. *Journal of Personality and Social Psychology, 49*, 436–458.

Wentzel, K. R. (1991). Social and academic goals at school: Motivation and achievement in context. In M. Maehr & P. Pintrich (Eds.), *Advances in motivation and achievement* (Vol. 7, pp. 185–212). Greenwich, CT: JAI.

Zimmerman, B. J. (2000). Attaining self-regulation: A social cognitive perspective. In M. Boekaerts & P. R. Pintrich (Eds.), *Handbook of self-regulation* (pp. 13–39). San Diego, CA: Academic.

2

Metacognition and Cognitive Variability: A Dual-Process Model of Decision Making and Its Development

Paul A. Klaczynski
The Pennsylvania State University

Jim, Dave, and Keith are brothers, ages 9, 11, and 14, respectively. On their father's advice, they decided to spend the day playing golf at a small par-3 course. The daily special, "$10 for all the golf you can handle," thrilled them. Although none had played the game previously, the mere idea of smacking a 1.68″ diameter ball around, trying to sink it into each of the course's nine 4.24″ diameter cups, seemed like a great way to spend an otherwise slow summer day. After all, they had worked hard completing their chores and had earned the $15 their father had given each of them.

But what seemed like a good idea at the time took a few bad turns. The day, which began pleasantly enough, was hot and humid by the time the boys reached the fourth hole. Worse, the difficulties—and the concomitant frustrations—of the game were dawning on them. Shot after shot was sliced, hooked, duffed, or otherwise misplayed. No evidence suggested that their games were improving. And so, the initial fire for the game that had burned in the boys' hearts dimmed to a small, barely glowing ember.

It may seem obvious that the boys should quit, end the humiliation, and move on to an activity from which they could derive at least a modicum of enjoyment. The question must nonetheless be asked: How likely is it that any of the boys will actually quit? Given their different ages, is one of the boys more likely than the others to opt out of the game?

The dilemma would be less apparent, and the decision to quit much easier, if not for the $10 investment the boys made to play "all the golf they could handle." Indeed, had they played for free, had they not "sunk" well-earned dollars into the activity, the brothers would likely leave the golf course behind and head for greener pastures. Yet, cognitions that the irretrievable investment, the "sunk cost," would be wasted if they stopped playing will likely compel the boys to stay (on) the course. To answer the first question, the boys—like the millions of golfers who spend hundreds of dollars for equipment and the "privilege" of playing, and like adults in numerous other situations involving unrecoverable investments—are likely to commit the "sunk cost" fallacy. The second question, "Are the boys equally likely to commit the fallacy?" can be answered in the negative. Recent evidence (Klaczynski, 2001b, 2004; Klaczynski & Cottrell, 2004) pointed to the conclusion that, in contrast to the recent speculations of Arkes and Ayton (1999), Keith, the 14-year-old, is more likely than his younger brothers to realize that the money already "flushed down the toilet" on golf should not govern his decision about future activities. But even for Keith, the eldest of the boys, the probability of committing the fallacy is rather high.

Although the tendency to "honor" sunk costs has been the subject of considerable research and speculation, this fallacy is but one of the many foibles that seem to typify the decision making of children and adults (for discussions, see Byrnes, 1998; Kahneman, Slovic, & Tversky, 1982; Klaczynski, Byrnes, & Jacobs, 2001; Reyna, Lloyd, & Brainerd, in press; Stanovich, 1999). Research on this fallacy—like research on other common phenomena, such as the *conjunction fallacy*, base rate neglect, unrealistically optimistic judgments, belief biases, ratio bias, and numerous other errors and biases studied by decision-making theorists—is illustrative of an unfortunate tendency in the decision-making literature. That is, until quite recently (e.g., Stanovich & West, 2000), the concern of most of this research has been on college students' judgments and decisions on specific tasks. Although inferred by many theorists, the generality of these processes across tasks has been studied by few (Klaczynski, 2001a; Stanovich & West, 1998, 2000) and developmental changes in these processes have been almost completely ignored. The focus of this chapter is therefore not on the sunk cost fallacy per se; instead, my concern is with the development of the information-processing mechanisms that underlie decisions across a variety of situations. I argue that these mechanisms can account for nonnormative decisions and judgments involving sunk costs, conditional inferences, precedents, ratios, counterfactual thinking, and the evaluation of scientific evidence and everyday arguments. The bedrock on which this argument rests is an increasingly solid corpus of evidence that cognitive development is supported by two, mutually influential, but independently functioning, information-processing systems: an "experiential" system and an "analytic" system (Klaczynski, 2001a; Jacobs & Klaczynski, 2002).

The *experiential processing system* involves the preconscious activation of procedural memories that can be used to guide judgments and decisions

(Chen & Chaiken, 1999; Epstein, 1994; Epstein & Pacini, 1999). Specifically, development is in part characterized by the acquisition of judgment and decision heuristics. Although some of these heuristics may be learned explicitly, by and large they are acquired through implicit cognitive processes (see Reber, 1992). Once acquired, judgment and decision heuristics are activated automatically by situational cues. For instance, the circumstances of the three brothers brought into conflict the desires to quit playing and to get their money's worth. The latter goal is likely to take precedence over the former because the situation has activated a general heuristic that implores decision makers to guard against waste (i.e., the $10 investment; see Arkes & Ayton, 1999). The application of heuristics is not only "fast and frugal" (Gigerenzer, 1996), but also leads (at least sometimes) to outcomes that are beneficial—or at least not harmful—to the decision maker. Yet, because their activation is effortless and automatic, because people have only a fleeting awareness that they have been activated, and because their activation elicits intuitions or "gut" feelings that they are "right" for the immediate situation, decision heuristics are often used in situations for which their relevance is dubitable—as appears to be the case on the golf course.

Knowing that an increasingly diverse repertoire of heuristics is acquired from early childhood through adolescence and adulthood suffices to explain neither the frequency with which heuristics are applied to judgment and decision situations nor occasions on which heuristics, although activated, are not exercised. Put more succinctly, and discussed in more depth throughout this chapter, because a particular heuristic is stored in procedural memory does not mean that it will be used when it is activated. The experiential processing system, functioning with little or no conscious awareness on the decision maker's part, continuously assimilates information and matches internal and external cues to memory procedures; this matching process, in turn, activates and makes available specific heuristics for utilization in specific situations.

In general, experiential processing is fast, operates automatically and at the "periphery" of consciousness (Epstein, 1994). This system facilitates information mapping onto and assimilation into existing knowledge categories, operates to convert conscious strategies and tactics into automatic procedures and strategies (e.g., we typically do not "know" or are not consciously aware that a strategy is undergoing or has undergone the transformation from a declarative memory to a procedural, automatic memory) and aids and abets the activation of decision-making heuristics and other memories (e.g., beliefs, vivid episodic memories) that bias judgments and interfere with attempts to reason objectively. Because it likely evolved before the analytic processing system and, more importantly, because it requires little cognitive effort and expends few cognitive resources, experiential processing is often considered the overall system's default (Brainerd & Reyna, 2001; Epstein, 1994).

If not for the codevelopment of the more deliberate analytic processing system, judgments and decision making might well be dominated by "off-the-cuff," automatically activated and *employed* heuristics and biases. This second processing system comprises consciously controlled, effortful thinking, and the numerous competencies that have traditionally been considered essential to cognitive development and normative decision making (Evans & Over, 1996; Stanovich, 1999). Of critical importance to the present discussion are age-related progressions in the abilities to reflect on and evaluate decision options, monitor the progress of reasoning and decision making, and inhibit interference from memories activated by logically irrelevant task contents.[1]

Because the instantiation of analytic competencies in performance is often highly effortful, if they are to benefit developing individuals, analytic competence acquisition must be accompanied by increases in the tendency to consciously employ these competencies. As recent discussions of metacognitive development (e.g., Kuhn, 2000; Moshman, 1990, 1999) and "thinking dispositions" (e.g., Stanovich & West, 2000) highlight, for everyday reasoning and decision making to approach normative ideals, development must proceed beyond the abilities to inhibit memory-based interference, reflect on the processes of reasoning and decision making, and evaluate the quality of decision options. Specifically, developments in analytic competence must be coupled with the acquisition of the dispositions (i.e., personal qualities, such as the "need for cognition") that increase an individual's motivation to use these abilities (the tendency to seek and enjoy intellectual challenges; see Cacioppo, Petty, Feinstein, & Javis, 1996).

METACOGNITIVE ABILITIES, METACOGNITIVE DISPOSITIONS, AND METAKNOWLEDGE DEVELOPMENT

The analytic competencies of greatest concern to the present discussion are those involved in evaluating beliefs, justifying beliefs and decisions, assessing beliefs about decision-making procedures, planning decisions (e.g., setting

---

[1]Throughout this chapter, normative responses refer to those historically advocated by logicians, philosophers, and decision theorists. Although arguments have been made that certain nonnormative responses (e.g., the "sunk cost fallacy" discussed earlier) are, in fact, normative, the Stanovich and West (1998a, 1998b) program of research on individual differences in "rational" responses, as well as Stanovich and West's (1999) research on the "understanding/acceptance" principle, supports assertions that the responses labeled as *normative* in this chapter should, in fact, be considered normative. Although this stance remains controversial, I have retained the normative/nonnormative distinction because it is useful, at the very least, for expository purposes. However, the following caveats are worth noting: (a) The distinction between normative and nonnormative is a loose one and is not absolute; (b) responses traditionally termed *normative* are sometimes maladaptive and responses traditionally termed *nonnormative* are sometimes adaptive (see Evans & Over, 1996; Jacobs & Narloch, 2001; Kahneman, Slovic, & Tversky, 1982; Klaczynski, 2001b; Reyna et al., in press).

goals and subgoals, selecting strategies for goal attainment), and monitoring the progress of goal-directed activities. At the most general level, developments in these abilities represent progressions in metacognitive and executive functioning.

Under the rubric of metacognition are *metacognitive abilities* and *metacognitive dispositions*. Three components of metacognitive ability—likely to function in a partially independent manner and possibly developing at different rates—are central to developments in reasoning and decision making. Briefly, these components include metaprocedural, metacognitive monitoring, and metaknowledge abilities.

Metaprocedural skills include the abilities to assess the type of reasoning (e.g., inductive, deductive), memory strategy, problem-solving procedure, or decision-making tactic called for in a particular situation (see Kuhn, 2000, 2001; Kuhn & Pearsall, 1998, 2000). *Metacognitive monitoring* (see also Byrnes, 1998, chap. 1, this volume; Sternberg, 1985) is similar to metaprocedural ability in its relation to executive functioning. Simply, metacognitive monitoring is the ability to consciously track the course of one's reasoning and decision making, discover flaws and inconsistencies in relevant "online" cognitions, and alter one's approach to a problem and plan for goal achievement as a function of these discoveries. Key to effective metaprocedural and metamonitoring are the abilities to inhibit irrelevant memories (e.g., beliefs) from skewing the evaluation process and to inhibit the "thoughtless" application of automatically activated heuristics. Research on metaprocedural understanding, metacognitive monitoring, and their development is still in its infancy, although Kuhn, Garcia-Mila, Zohar, and Andersen's (1995) microgenetic research on scientific reasoning and research on belief-biased reasoning (Klaczynski, 2000; Klaczynski & Robinson, 2000) suggested that these abilities emerge late in development and/or that, if these abilities do fully develop, neither adolescents nor adults are often disposed to using them.

Metaknowledge includes the abilities to assess what one knows (including knowledge of strategies) and understand the nature of knowledge and the process of knowing (i.e., epistemological theories; e.g., beliefs about the certainty or uncertainty of knowledge). Thus, metaknowledge includes the abilities to distinguish among accepted facts, beliefs, assertions, and evidence, and to understand how and when to apply these distinctions to everyday situations (Kuhn, 2001). Metacognitive knowledge thus involves (but is not limited to) an understanding of the epistemic constraints on beliefs and inferences and the importance of constructing and evaluating justifications for beliefs and decisions (Kuhn, 1991). Thus, as noted by Moshman (1998, 1999), Kuhn (2001), Stanovich (1999), and others (e.g., Schommer, 1994), developments in epistemological understanding and in the dispositions to apply this understanding are essential if adolescents are to make reasoned and justifiable decisions.

Although "theory of mind" theorists (e.g., Gopnik & Wellman, 1992; Perner, 1991) argued that the core ingredients of an advanced epistemological understanding are present by the end of the preschool years, this claim has been heavily criticized (e.g., Chandler, Hallett, & Sokol, 2002; Kuhn & Weinstock, 2002) because substantial evidence for qualitative advances in epistemological thought has been found both during later childhood and adolescence (e.g., Boyes & Chandler, 1992; Kuhn & Weinstock, 2002) and during adulthood (Kitchener, King, Wood, & Davison, 1989; Perry, 1970). Further, some theoretical consensus is now emerging that, at least to some degree, epistemological development is domain-specific (see Hofer & Pintrich, 2002). Together with conflicting theoretical claims, often based on research that relies on different methodologies (ranging from simple theory of mind and false belief tasks to in-depth interviews to questionnaires), this realization makes precise statements concerning the developmental course of epistemological development difficult (Chandler et al., 2002). Nonetheless, some broad conclusions about epistemological development can be drawn. Because it is beyond the scope of this chapter to review the literature on epistemological development (see Hofer & Pintrich, 2002), only a brief overview of epistemic development and individual differences in this development is presented here. Among the key conclusions researchers have reached in recent years are the following:

- Across knowledge domains (e.g., physical, social, aesthetic, etc.), epistemic development occurs in a predictable and possibly invariant, sequence (described further subsequently; Kuhn, Cheney, & Weinstock, 2000).
- Epistemic development is, to some extent, domain-specific. That is, (a) progress is evident earlier in some knowledge domains (e.g., aesthetics) than in others (e.g., values); and (b) it is typical of both children and adults to attain different levels of epistemological understanding in different domains (Kuhn et al., 2000).
- Domain-general limitations in basic information processes and developments in these processes place boundaries on the degree to which epistemic developments can be domain-specific. Thus, the rate at which higher order epistemic stances develop is constrained by the rate at which basic information processes and reasoning capabilities develop.
- Domain-general experiences, in conjunction with metacognitive awareness of inconsistencies between domain epistemic beliefs, make it increasingly likely that as children develop, their epistemologies will become more coherent and internally consistent.
- Many adolescents and adults never fully attain the highest levels of epistemological development (Boyes & Chandler, 1992; Kuhn & Weinstock, 2002; Moshman, 1999).

With the aforementioned qualifications in mind, for expository purposes it is nonetheless useful to discuss epistemic progressions as if they occurred in a domain-general fashion. Thus, using Moshman's (1999) terminology, children initially adopt an absolutist/objectivist epistemology. During early adolescence, this stance is succeeded by a diametrically opposed, radically different subjectivist—and necessarily relativist—epistemology. Finally (for some adolescents and adults), a rationalist epistemology evolves.

Absolutist/objectivists believe that knowledge is a direct copy of experience and that "facts" are accounts of reality that can be stated with certainty. Because they represent the truth, these accounts are not open to question. Because absolutists have a "copy" theory of knowledge, two witnesses to the same event should have the same knowledge of that event. If not, then the knowledge (because, perhaps, of poor memory or perception) of at least one witness must be false or incomplete (an understanding children demonstrate on false-belief tasks). In principle, such correspondence epistemologies assume that differences in understandings of "facts" and "truths" can be resolved by way of empirical observation or appeal to authority (e.g., scientists, priests, God). However, having attained their knowledge from experience, respected authorities, and treasured sources of authority (e.g., the Bible), absolutists often fail to recognize the fallibility of knowledge, particularly of those "truths" they personally accept. Although empirical observations are an accepted means of resolving discrepant truth claims, all too often absolutists rely on any number of nonlogical tactics (e.g., nonevidence-based assertions, the belief that only their own personal observations are trustworthy, and heuristics [e.g., "authorities know best"]) to deny the possibility that their "truths" can be repudiated.

Experiences with diverse belief systems, coupled with cognitive developments that enable the construction and appreciation of multiple realities, allow a transformation from absolutism toward subjectivism to occur. In this epistemic stance, knowledge is considered a construction intimately dependent on the observer's perspective. This relativism leads to the belief that even personal "truths" are tenuous and that the known, as well as the knower, are susceptible to moment-to-moment change. No single point of view is considered right or wrong in an absolute sense. The individual considers "perspective"—as coconstructed, for example, with immediate situational factors or, on a broader scale, cultural forces—as the primary influence on the individualization of knowledge. According to Boyes and Chandler (1992), subjectivists:

> embrace openly the know-nothing consequence of unbridled relativism, and assume that because no source of absolute or undoubtable knowledge is to be found, all authority is undermined and all hope for rational consensus is lost. . . . the rallying cry of such adolescent skeptics is that everyone should be allowed to "do their own thing" . . . (p. 285)

This "believe and let believe" position contrasts starkly with that of the absolutist, and implies a tendency to avoid argumentation because one belief system is no better (or worse) than any other. Yet, implicit in and inherent to this epistemology is a sort of dogmatism and a frequently overlooked contradiction: The subjectivist relies on, and cannot in principle defend, the assertion that nothing can be known with certainty. To maintain consistency, subjectivists must allow for the possibility that their stance is inaccurate. However, unlike other beliefs, because it is the bedrock on which their belief system rests, the assertion of relativism is not questioned by most subjectivists.

A minority of adolescents do question this assertion and realize that to resolve conflicts, make commitments, and justify decisions, a set of ground rules for knowledge acceptance must be laid. Like subjectivists, these "rationalists" acknowledge the inherent uncertainty of knowledge and recognize knowing as a constructive process. The subjectivist view that truth claims and beliefs ought not to be evaluated or contrasted is rejected on pragmatic grounds, however: For the sake of effective discourse, cooperative enterprises, and social progress, and to avoid the "epistemic confusion" of which Boyes and Chandler (1992) wrote, the rationalist believes that "ideas and viewpoints can be meaningfully evaluated, criticized, and justified" (cited in Moshman, 1999, p. 28; see also Kuhn, 1991, 2001). Justifiable beliefs and knowledge claims should be adhered to more closely than beliefs for which less evidence exists or for which weaker reasons can be provided (Kuhn & Weinstock, 2002). A truth or belief is maintained as a basis for action until its justifiability is called into question or a more justifiable claim is discovered.

Within knowledge domains, the absolutist → subjectivist → rationalist sequence may be developmentally invariant and depends on both a set of cognitive attainments and social experiences (Kitchener et al., 1989; Moshman, 1999). However, progress from the absolutism that characterizes much of children's thinking to rationalism during adolescence and adulthood is neither necessary nor inevitable. Some, and perhaps most, individuals never become rationalists, some leave absolutism but remain steadfast subjectivists (or as steadfast as is possible for subjectivists), others vacillate between absolutism (for beliefs in some domains, such as religion and the object world) and subjectivism (for beliefs in other domains, such as aesthetics), and still others remain firmly committed to the objectivity promised by absolutism (Boyes & Chandler, 1992; Chandler, Boyes, & Ball, 1990; Kuhn et al., 2000; Perry, 1970; Schommer, 1994).

The development of epistemic understanding is important to understand because differences in epistemological understanding imply (but do not necessitate) individual differences in the extent to which children and adolescents appreciate the need for engaging in metaprocedural and metamonitoring activities. That is, adolescents who understand the importance of evidence and logical justification (i.e., rationalists) are more likely than absolutist or subjectivist adolescents to engage in principled reasoning and decision making (Klaczynski, 2000). Personal epistemologies are prescriptive in the sense that they include not only beliefs about how one comes to know, but also beliefs about how one should come to know and about how knowledge should be treated. In the domain of religion, for instance, an absolutist adolescent is likely to justify his or her belief that abortion is inherently evil by appeal to authority, to assert that such a justification is the best possible justification, and to argue that anyone with a different perspective must have wrongheaded reasons for that perspective. Concerning decision making, a rationalist is more apt than a subjectivist to consciously weigh the pros and cons of different courses of action and to value evaluating evidence for different decisions.

As important as epistemological development and other metaknowledge developments are to reasoning and decision making, the development of dispositions to use these cognitive abilities is equally important. That is, as with other cognitive competencies, the development of a sophisticated epistemological understanding does not guarantee that an adolescent will use that understanding on a consistent basis. Unfortunately, few theorists (e.g., Keating & Sasse, 1996; Kuhn, 2001; Moshman, 1999; Perkins, Jay, & Tishman, 1993; Stanovich, 1999; Stanovich & West, 1998, 2000) have recognized the importance of distinguishing between *metacognitive abilities* and *metacognitive dispositions*. The former comprises a cluster of skills or competencies that are strictly cognitive in nature; the latter is a constellation of values and motivational attributes that may develop independently from cognitive and metacognitive abilities. For instance, an adolescent may develop a rationalist epistemology, and as such possess an advanced understanding of knowledge and knowing, but (e.g., because he or she prizes cognitively economical processing or is not particularly intellectually curious) may rarely put this epistemology "to work."

Little is known of the development of the dispositions that motivate children and adolescents to engage their epistemological stances, monitor their reasoning, assess the processes by which they make decisions, and evaluate the inferences and decisions produced by these processes. Such metacognitive dispositions could develop as a function of socialization or could develop alongside (and indeed, could be both products and producers of) metacognitive abilities. For instance, although research on the development of curiosity is scant and has typically been restricted to early childhood (Alberti & Witryol, 1994; Henderson & Wilson, 1991), individual differences in curiosity during childhood may well be precursors to such motivational dispositions as the "need for cognition" (see Cacioppo et al., 1996). Unfortunately, hypotheses such as this have received little attention.

Despite the paucity of developmental research, numerous arguments have been forwarded that the acquisition of metacognitive dispositions contributes something unique to reasoning and decision making above and beyond metacognitive abilities per se. Perkins et al. (1993), for instance, argued for "a small set of seven 'master' dispositions" (p. 3). Among the dispositions Perkins et al. (see also Nickerson, Perkins, & Smith, 1985) consider key to "good thinking" are: "Toward sustained intellectual curiosity" (similar to NFC), "to clarify and seek understanding," "to seek and evaluate reasons," "to be intellectually careful," and "to be metacognitive" (p. 6). The essential point is that for metaknowledge, metaprocedural, and metamonitoring abilities to have an impact on reasoning and decision making, dispositions that motivate their usage must also be acquired. Some of these dispositions may be acquired early in development (e.g., to be intellectually curious), but others may develop only as children move beyond an absolutist epistemic stance.

THE ANALYTIC–EXPERIENTIAL THEORY OF REASONING, JUDGMENTS, AND DECISION MAKING

Until recently, cognitive developmental research on decision making has concentrated on the emergence of abilities that are frequently associated with intellectual maturity and on the correlations between these abilities and aspects of decision making (e.g., awareness of costs and benefits). The unfortunate outcome of this exclusive focus on higher order competencies (e.g., formal operations) has been a misleading picture of the cognitive foundations on which decision making rests (see also Jacobs & Klaczynski, 2002).

This claim is founded, in part, on findings that have taken to task the long-held assumption that logical, computational processing is essential for rational decision making (Reyna et al., chap. 3, this volume; Reyna & Brainerd, 1995). Advocates of "two-process" theories have instead emphasized the influence of preconscious processes on judgments and decisions (e.g., Bargh & Chartland, 1999; Evans & Over, 1996). Many (but not all) of those in this theoretical camp believe that rational decision making is dependent on both conscious, "analytic" processing and preconscious, "experiential" processing.

In these theories, cognition is believed to develop along two trajectories— one directed toward increases in computational processing, metacognitive abilities, and the capacity to decontextualize reasoning from problem content; the second directed toward highly contextualized processing (Stanovich, 1999) that relies heavily on both vivid, personal memories and implicit, procedural memories. Several basic assumptions of two-process theories pose serious challenges to most theories of cognitive development. These include the assumptions that (a) experiential and analytic processing occur simultaneously, (b) these systems develop independently, (c) experiential processing is the system's default, and (d) experiential processing is predominant over analytic processing in a multitude of everyday situations. If these assumptions are borne out, theoretical construals of development as a unidirectional progression within a single processing system, with progress defined (at least in part) as progress from intuitive processing to logico– mathematical processing (e.g., Inhelder & Piaget, 1958; Piaget & Inhelder, 1951/1975) will no longer be tenable.

Over the past 10 years, two-process theories have become increasing prominent in social (e.g., Chen & Chaiken, 1999), personality (e.g., Epstein, 1994; Epstein & Pacini, 1999), cognitive (e.g., Evans, 1989; Evans & Over, 1996; Sloman, 1996; Stanovich, 1999), and, most recently, developmental psychology (Klaczynski, 2001a, 2001b; Reyna et al., chap. 3, this volume; Reyna & Brainerd, 1995). Although theorists disagree over the terms used to label the two systems (e.g., *analytic* vs. *heuristic processing*, *rational* vs. *experiential processing*, *systematic* vs. *heuristic processing*, *explicit* vs. *tacit*; see Stanovich, 1999, p. 145, for a more complete listing), descriptions of analytic and experiential processing tend to focus on similar properties. The general properties and functions of each system are now listed.

Experiential processing:

- Is holistic and "peripheral" in the sense that it involves a cursory grasp of the entirety of a situation. When experiential processing is predominant, responses have no basis in reasoning in the "usual" sense (i.e., componential analyses are circumvented) and attempts to break problems down into discrete components are absent.
- Is fast, occurs with minimal conscious awareness, and requires little cognitive effort.
- Consequently, enables the automatic recognition and encoding of information that is peripheral to the individual's current focus of attention and frees attentional resources for computationally complex reasoning.
- Simultaneously, this "peripheral" processing enables the detection of unusual information that could cue shifts in attentional focus.
- Generally operates on "contextualized" representations that are heavily dependent on problem content (e.g., familiarity), information gleaned from the proximal context, and semantic memory structures (e.g., stereotypes, beliefs, "theories").

Among other things, the activation of stereotypes, personal theories (e.g., of personalities), vivid or salient memories (Kahneman & Tversky, 1972; Klaczynski, 2000), and procedural memories often leads to experiential predominance. This predominance may (i.e., without intercession on the part of analytic processing) lead to heuristically based judgments and decisions that have the intuitive "feel" of being correct (Epstein, 1994). Hence, when experiential processing is predominant, preconsciously activated heuristics are applied "thoughtlessly" (i.e., without concern for their limitations; see Arkes & Ayton, 1999); that is, individuals often make decisions on the basis of automatically activated heuristics and, in doing so, do not often wonder why a given heuristic should or should not have been used.

According to Sloman (1996): "[Experiential] thought *feels* like it arises from a different cognitive mechanism than does deliberate, analytical reasoning. Sometimes conclusions simply appear at some level of awareness, as if the mind goes off, does some work, and then comes back with a result . . ." (p. 3).

As discussed subsequently, it is important to note that the automatic activation of a heuristic does not necessarily entail the automatic application of that heuristic. That is, the product of the mind going off and doing some work at a preconscious level is often a heuristic that is, at least momentarily, available in working memory. As such, it is possible (although the heuristics and biases literature indicates that, for most people, it is not likely) for the reasoner to critically reflect on the value of the solution. The ability to reflect on and pass judgment on experientially produced solutions is a quality of analytic processing.[2]

Analytic processing is consciously controlled, effortful, and deliberate. Although preadolescents clearly engage in analytic processing under certain task conditions (see, e.g., Harris & Leevers, 2000), on most tasks in the judgment- and decision-making literature, successful analytic processing depends on the acquisition and utilization of abilities that are frequently prescribed as normative for reasoning and decision making (Epstein, 1994; Sloman, 1996). These competencies include the higher order abilities that enable reasoning consistent with the rules of formal logic, decisions based on comparisons between a priori probabilities, accurate calibration of one's abilities, explicit inductive and deductive reasoning, an understanding of the limitations of induction and deduction, and a host of more specific skills and abilities.

In contrast to experiential processing, analytic processing is less personal, less context-dependent, and more reliant on context-independent principles.

---

[2]Although a great deal of information processing takes places at the "truly" unconscious level, experiential processing may involve various degrees of consciousness. Despite vagaries surrounding definitions of unconscious, minimally conscious, and peripherally conscious processing, experiential processing produces responses with little, if any, effort. Obviously, additional theoretical clarity is needed if two-process theories are to progress. For the present, however, I use the term *unconscious* to mean "minimally conscious" or "on the periphery" of consciousness. This usage is consistent with the belief of some two-process theorists (e.g., Epstein, 1994) that experiential processing is "felt" at some level. Attention to these intuitive feelings may bring the products of experiential processing fully into consciousness, where they may be evaluated analytically.

Unlike experiential processing, analytic processing is directed toward breaking down problems into their component elements, carefully examining these elements, and, from this analysis, deriving a problem solution, judgment, decision, or argument. In further contrast to experiential processing, analytic processing operates on "decontextualized" representations. However, the ability to consciously decontextualize task structure and requirements from logically irrelevant contextual forces (e.g., pressure to conform), superficial task contents, and misleading memories activated by contexts and contents depends largely on the metacognitive abilities (e.g., metaprocedural) discussed earlier and on general executive function abilities (e.g., planning, impulse control, ability to inhibit memory-based interference). The process of decontextualization, in turn, is essential if other analytic competencies are to be engaged consistently and effectively (Stanovich, 1999; Stanovich & West, 1997). Decontextualized task representations—wherein the underlying structure (e.g., logical components) of a problem has been decoupled from superficial contents (e.g., counterfactual information)—thus provide working memory a "structure" on which logico-computational processing can operate (Stanovich & West, 1997; see also Donaldson, 1978).

The relationship between processing systems and task representations is more complex than this portrayal suggests, however (see Reyna et al., in press). First, some degree of experiential processing is necessary (e.g., to automatically process text) even when the analytic system is predominant (for additional detail and examples, see Evans & Over, 1996). Second, the motivation to engage in analytic processing and shift away from the default (i.e., experiential) system leads individuals to attempt the construction of decontextualized representations. However, these attempts may be unsuccessful (e.g., such failures appear to be common on counterfactual reasoning tasks and syllogisms containing belief-relevant premises). Third, although the successful derivation of a decontextualized representation increases the probability of additional analytic processing, these representations do not guarantee normatively correct judgments or decisions (see Reyna et al., in press). Even when working on decontextualized representations, individuals may apply inappropriate decision-making principles, misapply appropriate principles, or fall back on experiential processing (e.g., if a problem appears computationally overwhelming). Further, despite analytic predominance and conscious attempts to reason independently from irrelevant task contents, experiential processing sometimes creates interference that biases the outcomes of these conscious efforts.

As this last statement implies, it is important to recognize that decision making results from the confluence of experiential and analytic processing (Epstein, 1994) and that preconsciously extracted (i.e., not effortful) representations often form the basis for consciously made decisions (Evans & Over, 1996). The former claim requires the caveat that task characteristics (e.g., familiarity), context (e.g., social demands for accuracy), and individual differences (e.g., age, epistemic beliefs, intelligence) interact to determine which processing system is predominant on a given task (Stanovich, 1999). The latter claim is critical in that representations are also essential determinants of the processing system accessed in a given situation; at the same time, representations are partially determined by the extent to which individuals are motivated to derive "correct," precise, and justifiable solutions (see Klaczynski & Narasimham, 1998b).

The experiential–analytic processing theory requires an important and fundamental distinction between process and product (see also Moshman, 2000). Yet, this distinction is often blurred by decision and social-cognitive theorists. For example, it is not unusual for theorists to conflate evidence that a heuristic has been used with evidence that the processes underlying that decision were experiential. However, although processing may be predominantly experiential or predominantly analytic, the products of either system may be normative or nonnormative decisions. Thus, for example, automatically activated heuristics may, at least momentarily, be available in working memory for inspection (Klaczynski, 2001a). Individuals may then consciously decide whether to use or reject these heuristics as guides for their decisions. Thus, the probability of normative decisions increases when analytic system processing is predominant and experiential processing is inhibited, but analytic processing by no means guarantees adaptive decisions and experiential processing is not necessarily tied to nonnormative decisions. In short, all good decisions are not necessarily outcomes of analytic processing; all bad decisions are not necessarily products of experiential processing.

Empirical Evidence for Two Cognitive Systems

Considerable evidence accumulated over the past 30 years or so has not only falsified predictions generated from traditional cognitive developmental perspectives (e.g., Piagetian, information processing), but has also shown that satisfactory accounts of intellectual growth must explain the perplexing frequency of errors on simple logical problems, the relationships between reasoning and memory (Reyna & Brainerd, 1995), and the observation that variability, rather than consistency, is the hallmark of everyday cognition and its development (Jacobs & Klaczynski, 2002; Klaczynski, 2000; Kuhn et al., 1995; Reyna & Brainerd, 1995; Siegler, 1996).

In this section, I briefly review some of the developmental research that supports the claims of two-process theorists. In the next section, I focus more specifically on my own research on developments in reasoning, the belief–motivation–cognition interface, and decision making. Although no individual finding suffices to establish the existence of two processing systems, when examined as a whole, these studies—in combination with work on the prevalence of "magical" thinking in both children and adults (e.g., Subbotsky, 2000), implicit and explicit memory (e.g., Lie & Newcombe, 1999; Newcombe & Fox, 1994), and memory–reasoning independence and dependence (see Brainerd & Kingma, 1985; Reyna et al., in press)—render difficult (if not impossible) arguments that development proceeds within a single system.

Several developmental studies indicate that judgment heuristics are used more often by older than by younger children (e.g., Davidson, 1995; Jacobs & Narloch, 2001; Jacobs & Potenza, 1991; Markovits & Dumas, 1999; Reyna & Ellis, 1994). The importance of these findings is not that it establishes developments in experiential processing per se, but instead that it illustrates increases in the availability of (what have traditionally been considered) nonnormative strategies for decision making. The acquisition of these heuristics, in combination with developments in computational abilities, affords increases in the flexibility of children's and adolescents' decision making, increases the likelihood of "cognitive variability" (problem-to-problem shifts in reasoning or decision quality)—which, in turn, increases the extent and type of feedback on which analytic processing (via metamonitoring of outcomes) can operate—and provides an increasingly diverse arsenal on which experiential and analytic processing can rely.

Findings of age-related increases in certain nonnormative responses are difficult to explain without reference to two cognitive systems. Jacobs and Potenza (1991), for instance, found that reliance on statistical evidence on asocial decision tasks (e.g., about bicycles) increased with age (presumably because of increased analytic competence). On logically isomorphic social problems, however, the opposite trend was observed: With increasing age, children relied more on the "representativeness heuristic" (i.e., the extent to which individual cases conform to existing schemata) and less on statistical evidence (presumably because of increased reliance on experiential processing). Under some conditions, older children commit the "conjunction fallacy" (i.e., judge $p[AB]$ as more likely than $p[A]$ or $p[B]$) more than younger children, a finding that has also been attributed to increased reliance on representativeness (Davidson, 1995).

Similar evidence can be found across disparate methodological paradigms and dimensions of cognitive development. Despite knowledge of normative computational strategies, age (under certain conditions) is positively associated with (a) making probability judgments based on simple, cognitively economical, strategies (e.g., ignoring denominators in ratio problems; Brainerd, 1981); (b) changing decisions as a function of the "framing" of logically identical problems (Reyna & Ellis, 1994); (c) making nonlogical "transitive" inferences regarding social relationships (e.g., "A is a friend of B. B is a friend of C. Therefore, A and C are friends"; Markovits & Dumas, 1999; a "friends of friends are friends" heuristic); (d) committing deductive reasoning fallacies (Klaczynski & Narasimham, 1998a; Wildman & Fletcher, 1977); (e) imputing false beliefs to others (Mitchell, Robinson, Isaacs, & Nye, 1996); (f) misinterpreting the premises of syllogistic reasoning problems (Noveck, 2001), and rejecting evidence on the basis of nonlogical heuristics (Klaczynski, 2000). Although some of these findings could be due to the overextension of logical rules of inference, such overextension is unlikely to be governed primarily by conscious processes. Therefore, because these developmental trends are systematic and yet violate formal rules of inference, they likely arise from a cognitive system that does not rely on logico-mathematical processing.

RESEARCH ON ADOLESCENT REASONING, JUDGMENTS, AND DECISIONS

Despite numerous reports of counterintuitive developmental trends, considerable care must be taken before assuming that experiential processing increases in predominance with age or that the use of decision heuristics increases monolithically with age. Specifically, not all research on heuristics and biases has demonstrated developmental increases in nonnormative responding. In the present section, research on motivated reasoning biases and decision heuristics is described. Embedded in these descriptions is the argument that developmental advances in metacognitive skills can at least partially explain why heuristics are sometimes used more by children than adolescents.

Adolescent Development and the Belief–Motivation–Reasoning Interface

In several investigations, my colleagues and I (e.g., Klaczynski & Aneja, 2002; Klaczynski & Gordon, 1996a; Klaczynski & Narasimham, 1998b) studied how children and adolescents process everyday arguments and "scientific" evidence. The basic tactic in these studies has been to present logically flawed arguments or methodologically flawed scientific investigations, the contents of which are relevant to strongly held beliefs. The conclusions drawn by the "arguers" or "scientists" in these scenarios are either consistent, inconsistent, or neutral with respect to these beliefs. In each scenario, information participants had provided concerning their beliefs and/or groups to which they belonged (e.g., concerning their religious affiliations) was inserted to make the scenarios as personally meaningful as possible. Consider the scenario presented now (adapted from Klaczynski & Narasimham, 1998b), designed for an adolescent who believed that being a Baptist makes a person morally superior to members of other religious affiliations:

> Dr. Robison is a psychologist interested in finding out whether sexual harassment is more likely to occur in some religious groups than in others. To conduct his research, he conducted a study of Baptists, Catholics, Methodists, Hindus, Muslims, and Lutherans. In each religious group, he asked 40 people to be in the study. To measure sexual harassment, Dr. Robison observed people in each group at church meetings and picnics and counted the number of times each person told jokes with sexual content. At the end of his study, Dr. Robison found that the average Baptist told 6.5 sexual jokes per month. Members of the other religions . . . told an average of only 2.0 sexual jokes per month. . . . Based on this, Dr. Robison concluded that Baptists are involved in more sexual harassment than . . . members of other religions.

This conclusion contrasts rather clearly with the adolescent's previously expressed belief. Like most adults, adolescents process such belief-threatening information with considerably more care than information that is either belief-neutral or belief-supportive. Specifically, the evidence is processed analytically and scrutinized closely for flaws; problem representations are based on decontextualizations of the logical structure of the evidence and/or arguments. On the basis of this processing, the evidence is rejected, often by invoking normative principles of logic, argumentation, and scientific reasoning. In dealing with this scenario, the adolescent is likely to display rather sophisticated reasoning by arguing that the operationalization of sexual harassment lacks construct validity. For example, one respondent claimed, "The amount of jokes about sex a person tells hasn't got anything to do with sexual harassment. Plus, you don't know who they're telling the jokes to." Other problems—involving sample size, selection, and experimental confounds—are also much more likely to be detected when evidence (if it appears plausible) threatens beliefs than when evidence is supportive or neutral.

When evidence supports beliefs, experiential processing is usually predominant. Specifically, the evidence is processed at a relatively cursory level, and representations appear to be highly contextualized (i.e., based on superficial contents that support relevant beliefs). Justifications for evidence acceptance derive from personal experiences, category exemplars, positive stereotypes of in-groups, negative stereotypes of comparison out-groups, and simple assertions as to the validity of the evidence.

In the within-subjects designs used in these investigations, participants are presented randomly determined sequences of belief-threatening, supportive, and neutral evidence. This approach provides the opportunity to examine problem-to-problem variability in processing. Of particular importance is the surprising finding that children, adolescents, and adults are very similar in the extent to which they vacillate between experiential processing on supportive and neutral problems and analytic processing on belief-threatening problems. This within-individual variability in processing suggests several hypotheses concerning the relationship between reasoning biases and metacognition (specifically, metamonitoring). First, adolescents in this work may not have used their metamonitoring skills to track the course of reasoning for consistency (e.g., because they were not aware that these skills were relevant). Second, adolescents may have tried to use their metamonitoring skills, but these skills may not have been sufficiently developed to be useful. Third, adolescents may have successfully monitored their reasoning and realized that it was inconsistent between problems, but may not have believed that maintaining consistency is important or valuable (a belief more likely among absolutists and subjectivists than among rationalists; see Kuhn, 2001).

The variability adolescents demonstrate in studies of belief-biased reasoning is a pattern of reasoning like that shown in Fig. 2.1. As the figure illustrates, fluctuations in reasoning and strategy use are not random; rather, they are largely a function of evidence type. The line depicting adolescents' "reasoning" is intended to illustrate their general tendency to invoke their (relative to children) superior analytic competencies. The generally parallel nature of adolescent and child reasoning shows that, despite differences in basic analytic competencies (e.g., argumentation skills, scientific reasoning abilities), the amount of variability—and, by implication, the amount of experiential processing interference—differs little, if at all, with age. What is not shown in the figure is the additional finding (Klaczynski, 2000; Klaczynski & Aneja, 2002; Klaczynski & Fauth, 1997) that the heuristics and other nonlogical strategies used to justify the acceptance of belief-supportive evidence do sometimes differ with age. Because the amount of experiential interference is similar (on these tasks), this last finding illustrates that the use of different heuristics by children and adolescents does not necessarily reflect age differences in reliance on experiential processing. This description also implies that information processing is dualistic: Regardless of evidence

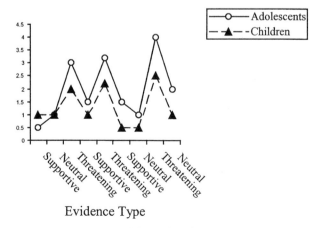

FIG. 2.1.   Variability in belief-biased reasoning.

type and age, elements of both analytic and experiential processing are often apparent in individuals' evidence assessments. It is the predominance of processing systems—rather than the complete "switching off" of one system or the other—that changes with evidence type.

Two sets of evidence illustrate the importance of metacognition in belief-biased reasoning. The first set of evidence is from two studies in which we examined the effects of extrinsic "accuracy" motivation on belief-based reasoning biases. In these studies (Klaczynski & Gordon, 1996b; Klaczynski & Narasimham, 1998b), adolescents were instructed that if they gave confusing, thoughtless, or inaccurate responses, they would be contacted during the next week and required to meet individually with the experimenters to justify their responses. The effect of these instructions was considerable in the sense that reasoning across problem types (i.e., belief-threatening, neutral, and supportive) was much more complex than in the control conditions. However, what did *not* change was the degree of bias in participants' reasoning. That is, although reasoning overall improved, the magnitude of the differences between reasoning on belief-threatening and belief-supportive problems was as large in the "accuracy motivation" conditions as in the control conditions. These findings suggest that participants could not consciously control the biases they introduced into their reasoning; from the improvements in reasoning complexity observed in the "accuracy" motivation conditions, it is apparent that participants made efforts to reason "objectively" and more effectively than control participants. Yet, despite these efforts, biases—evidenced by between-problem type differences in reasoning complexity—did not diminish. This was as true for adolescents who scored poorly on measures of intellectual ability as it was for adolescents whose ability scores were high.

The second set of evidence illustrating the role of metacognition in belief-bias reasoning comes from examination of the data from each of the aforementioned studies. In each study, some participants were not biased in their reasoning, despite holding beliefs as strong as those of their more biased peers (see also Stanovich & West, 1997; for detailed discussions of individual differences in rational thought, see Baron, 1985; Stanovich, 1999; Stanovich & West, 1998, 2000). Perhaps the most obvious individual difference variable that could explain differences in reasoning biases is general intelligence. However, in several investigations, intellectual ability has explained virtually no variance in biases (e.g., Kardash & Scholes, 1996; Klaczynski, 1997, 2000; Klaczynski & Gordon, 1996a, 1996b; see, however, Stanovich & West, 1997). In light of these data, Klaczynski (2000) and Klaczynski and Fauth (1997; see also Klaczynski, Gordon, & Fauth, 1997, Experiments 3 and 4; Stanovich & West, 1997) explored whether individual differences in epistemological beliefs (e.g., "People should always take into consideration evidence that goes against their beliefs"; from Stanovich & West, 1998, p.

167) and metacognitive dispositions (e.g., "It is more important for me than to most people to behave in a logical way"; from Epstein, Pacini, Denes-Raj, & Heier, 1995; see Epstein & Pacini, 1999, p. 996) could explain between-subject variability in biases. Although these investigations relied heavily on self-report questionnaires, they nonetheless accounted for significant and unique variance in each study.

To an extent, relationships between metacognitive dispositions and reasoning biases argue for roles of metaknowledge, metaprocedural understanding, and metamonitoring capabilities. Specifically, each of these aspects of metacognitive ability is necessary for individuals to act effectively on the types of dispositions just listed. Thus, the results implicate metaknowledge (e.g., understanding that personal beliefs should be as open to scrutiny as others' beliefs), metaprocedural competence (e.g., understanding which computational abilities to use under which conditions), and metamonitoring ability (e.g., possibly indexed by items tapping intellectual curiosity and carefulness) as playing important roles in reducing the experiential processing interference with analytic processing and in attempts to reason independently from beliefs (Stanovich, 1999).

Decision Heuristics and Analytic Competence

In three recent investigations (Klaczynski, 2001a, 2001b, 2004; Klaczynski & Cottrell, 2004), I explored the relationships among age, heuristic and analytic processing, and task conditions. In one study (Klaczynski, 2001a), I presented adolescents with a series of problems derived from the "heuristics and biases literature." Among other tasks, participants were presented indicative and deontic versions of Wason's (1966) selection task, several "conjunction fallacy" problems, as well as problems involving covariation detection, statistical decision making, the gambler's fallacy, outcome bias, and hindsight bias. Several findings are noteworthy. First, normative reasoning, judgments, and decisions were, with few exceptions, more common among middle adolescents than among early adolescents. Second, the associations between normative responding and a measure of general intellectual ability were not uniformly positive or significant. For example, although statistical decision making and covariation judgments were related positively to ability, neither the tendency for outcomes to bias judgments nor hindsight biases were linked to ability. Third, principal components analyses revealed two readily interpretable factors. The analytic factor comprised normative statistical reasoning, deontic reasoning, covariation judgments, and the metacognitive abilities involved in assessing the accuracy of one's judgments. The heuristic factor comprised a host of nonnormative fallacies and biases (e.g., outcome bias, hindsight bias, the conjunction fallacy). Whereas the analytic factor was positively related to age and ability, the heuristic factor was related nega-tively to age and was scarcely related to ability at all ($r = .03$).

Two problems from this study are displayed in Table 2.1. These two prob-lems, each of which requires but a modest degree of statistical reasoning competence, are useful in illustrating one of the more important findings. So-lutions to the "law of large numbers" (LLN) problem had high loadings on the analytic processing factor and were related to both verbal ability and age. Outcome bias solutions, although also positively related to age, loaded highly on the heuristic (i.e., experiential) factor and were not related to ability. Questions these findings raise include: Why, despite similar relations to age, would such problems as these load on different factors? Why would they bear

TABLE 2.1
Examples of Judgment Tasks From Klaczynski (2001a)

Outcome Bias

A priori failure probability high, outcome nonetheless favorable

A businessman owned a company that was not making very much money. The man was, of course, very upset; if he did not make more money, he would be forced to shut the com-pany down in the next 4 years. He just learned that he might be able to save his company if he became partners with another company. By joining together, he could make enough money to keep the company going at least 8 more years. However, there was a 10% chance that both companies would go bankrupt and lose all their money if he became partners with the other company.

The person decided to go ahead and become partners. The partnership worked; now the company will last at least 8 more years. Was the man's decision to become partners with the other company a good decision? (Judgments made on 7-point scale)

A priori failure probability low, outcome nonetheless unfavorable

A man has been running a small market for 10 years, but the market has never made very much money. He has learned that, because of a new shopping mall, he will be forced to close his market within 3 years. But he could move his store into the mall. If he moves into the mall, he could keep his market open for at least 9 more years. However, there was a 4% chance that his store would completely fail if he moved it into the mall.

The man decided to go ahead and open a new store in the mall. It failed and he had to close his store. Was the man's decision to move his store into the mall a good decision?

Statistical Decisions

Ken and Toni are teachers who are arguing over whether students enjoy the new computer-based teaching method that is used in some math classes.

Ken's argument is, "Each of the 3 years that we've had the computer-based learning class, about 60 students have taken it. At the end of each year, they have written essays on why they liked or didn't like the class. Over 85% of the students say that they have liked it. That's more than 130 out of 150 students who liked the computer class!"

Toni's argument is, "I don't think you're right. Stephanie and John—the two best stu-dents in the school, both are high honors students—have come to me and complained about how much they hate the computer-based learning class and how much more they like regular math classes. They say that a computer just can't replace a good teacher, who is a real person."

different relations to general intellectual ability? Why was age related to responses to both types of problem?

Each question requires in-depth task analyses that are beyond the scope of this chapter. Nevertheless, required on each task is decontextualization of the formal requirements of the problems from misleading contents. In the case of the statistical reasoning problems, the relatively vivid personal arguments create an "experiential attraction"—"pulling" for predominantly experiential processing and the activation and utilization of such heuristics as, "they saw it with their own two eyes." Reasoners must inhibit the attraction of such heuristics and recognize that one can have more confidence in decisions based on large evidential samples than in decisions based on small samples. Ability is linked to decontextualization skills (Stanovich, 1999; Stanovich & West, 2000) and, to an extent, other metaprocedural skills (e.g., recognition that the problems require application of the law of large numbers).

The outcome bias problem also requires separation of formal requirements from misleading contents. Unlike the LLN problems (and other ability-related problems, such as the contingency detection problems), the two components of the outcome bias problems (e.g., low probability of success versus [relatively] high probability of success) were separated by a number of other problems. In making a judgment, the two logical components (success probabilities in the two problems) that were pitted against one another were not obvious—explicit comparison required both memory for one's judgment on the initial problem and metamonitoring to know that a similar problem had been presented previously. Perhaps more importantly, the low probabilities of success, in combination with explicit knowledge of actual success and failure, may activate "success = good," "failure = bad" heuristics, as well as tendencies to engage in post hoc theorizing and commit the "if only" fallacy (e.g., "If only the man hadn't moved his store into the mall . . ."). Because outcomes are easier to process than probabilities, and because reliance on either usually leads to the same evaluation, the analytic–experiential conflict thought to occur for higher ability adolescents on the more "transparent" LLN problems is considerably less likely on outcome bias and similar problems.

On the surface, neither the LLN nor the outcome bias problems are particularly complex. Given that a rudimentary understanding of the role of probabilities and sample size in making judgments develops prior to adolescence (Jacobs & Narloch, 2001; Jacobs & Potenza, 1991; Klaczynski & Aneja, 2002; S. Kreitler & H. Kreitler, 1986), neither the differences among same-age adolescents nor between differently aged adolescents can be easily explained by reference to differences in intellectual ability (as traditionally measured). Indeed, consistent with the arguments others have voiced (e.g., Ceci, 1990; Berg & Sternberg, 1985; Sternberg, 1985), the metacognitive skills—decontextualizing, inhibiting interference, monitoring reasoning, determining appropriate procedures—important to solving such problems normatively are not well-captured by standard ability tests. As results from tasks that strongly "draw" adolescents toward experiential processing (e.g., outcome bias, hindsight bias, "gambler's fallacy," etc.) illustrate, it would seem that age is not merely an index of raw intellectual talent. Rather, what age may capture that standard measures of ability do not are the higher order decontextualization abilities and metacognitive dispositions that motivate the utilization of those abilities.

Two other studies illustrate the importance of highlighting developmental progressions in metacognition in theories of decision making. In the first investigation (Klaczynski, 2001b), early adolescents, middle adolescents, and young adults made judgments and decisions on sunk cost, ratio bias, and counterfactual reasoning problems. Participants were instructed to solve each problem as they usually would and from the perspective of a perfectly logical person (see Denes-Raj & Epstein, 1994; Epstein & Pacini, 1999; Kirkpatrick & Epstein, 1993). The intent of the usual "frame" was to elicit participants' default manner of processing (presumably experiential). The "logic" frame was intended to elicit a shift to analytic processing. An example of a "usual" ratio problem is:

> You are playing a lottery in which you can win $1,000. There are two jars from which you can select a winning ticket. In the first jar, there are only 10 tickets, and 1 of these is the winning ticket. In the second jar, there are 100 tickets and 10 winning tickets. Think about this situation as you normally would. Which jar, if either, would you select from to have a better chance of winning the lottery?
>
> A. The jar with 1 winning ticket
> B. The jar with 10 winning tickets
> C. It would not matter which jar I selected from.

An example of a "usual" sunk cost problem is:

> A. You are staying in a hotel room on vacation. You paid $10.95 to see a movie on pay TV. After 5 minutes, you are bored and the movie seems pretty bad. How much longer would you continue to watch the movie?
> B. You are staying in a hotel room on vacation. You turn on the TV and there is a movie on. After 5 minutes, you are bored and the movie seems pretty bad. How much longer would you continue to watch the movie?

(For A and B, participants selected from the following options: stop watching entirely, watch for 10 more minutes, watch for 20 more minutes, watch for 30 more minutes, watch until the end; the sunk-cost fallacy occurred when participants indicated that they would spend more time in A than in B; adapted from Frisch, 1993.)

The third type of problem involved a type of counterfactual thinking referred to as the "if only" fallacy. The "if only" fallacy occurs when behaviors are judged more negatively when it appears that a negative consequence could have been easily anticipated, and therefore avoided, in one of two logically identical and equally unpredictable situations. Consider the example below (adapted from Epstein & Pacini, 1999):

> Tom parked his new car in a parking lot that was half empty. His wife asked him to park in a spot closer to where she wanted to shop, but he parked, instead, in a spot closer to where he wanted to shop. As luck would have it, when he backed out after shopping, the car behind him backed out at the same time, and both cars sustained about $1,000 worth of damage.
>
> Robert parked his car in the same parking lot when there was only one parking place left, so he took it. As luck would have it, when he backed out after shopping, the car behind him backed out at the same time, and both cars sustained about $1,000 worth of damage.

Participants indicated which, if either, of the two involved parties acted "more foolishly." Note that in both cases, the accidents were not actually under the control of the involved parties. Yet representations based on cursory task analyses (e.g., Tom had control, Robert had no control) may activate heuristics that link control to fault (i.e., similar to the *fundamental attribution error*—the tendency for observers to overestimate the role of dispositional factors when assessing another person's actions). Tom, whose accident appeared avoidable (if only he had heeded his wife), is believed by most young adults to have made a worse decision than Robert (Denes-Raj & Epstein, 1994; Epstein & Pacini, 1999)—whose parking decision was "forced" on him by uncontrollable circumstances.

Findings from this study were revealing in several ways. First, in both the "usual" and the "logic" frames, the normative judgments were infrequent. For instance, in the usual frame, only the young adult college students' responses were normative on what appear to be the simplest, most straightforward problems (the ratio problems). Second, in both frames, normative responding increased with age on all three tasks. Third, and perhaps most importantly, normative responses were much more frequent in the logic than in the usual frame, regardless of age and task. Even in the logic frame, however, responding was far from perfect and in some cases remained close to or only slightly above chance. The findings, collapsed over the three types of decision tasks, are presented in Fig. 2.2.

The fact that normative responding was better in the logic frame suggests experiential predominance in the usual frame. However, what occurred in the logic frame? It appears that an effortful shift from experiential to analytic processing took place. To achieve such a shift, adolescents must inhibit the "prepotent" response to a problem, evaluate the quality and/or appropriateness of that response, and consider alternative solutions. The main effect of the logic frame indicates that early adolescents may be as able to control

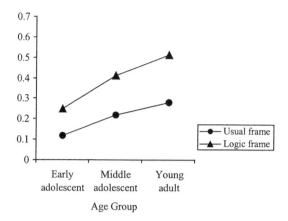

FIG. 2.2. Results from Klaczynski (2001b), collapsed across sunk cost, counterfactual, and ratio bias problems.

such experiential-to-analytic shifts as older adolescents and adults—although at none of these ages did a simple cue to switch processing modes have an overwhelmingly positive impact. At least in the case of the ratio problem, poor performance in the logic frame is probably not attributable to lack of the computational and/or analytic competencies this task calls for, as even preadolescents are capable of solving ratio problems and comparing ratios against one another (S. Kreitler & H. Kreitler, 1986). Rather, there are several possible explanations for participants' poor performance. For instance, participants may have had trouble defining and decontextualizing the logical task. Alternatively, the logic instructions may have been insufficient to induce an experiential-to-analytic shift, (in the case of the counterfactual and sunk-cost tasks) participants may have lacked knowledge of the relevant logical principles, or the heuristics activated by the tasks may have been too compelling for participants to dismiss easily. Indeed, at least in the case of the sunk-cost problems, subsequent research lends some credence to this last possibility.

In other investigations (Klaczynski, 2004; Klaczynski & Cottrell, 2004), a first goal was to determine how often adolescents use heuristics to respond to different decision tasks. A second goal was to examine the effects of arguments for either the normative decision or the heuristic decision on adolescents' decisions. This latter goal was particularly important because of its relevance to the analytic–experiential theory outlined earlier and to questions of adolescent decision-making competence. Specifically, the results of the two previously discussed investigations of adolescent decision making illustrated that under conditions with no instructions to engage in analytic processing (Klaczynski, 2001a) or rather minimal instructions to think analytically (Klaczynski, 2001b), adolescents' decisions are often nonnormative and appear to rely heavily on heuristics. However, it is possible that, if adolescents were instructed to closely inspect arguments for heuristically based responses, they would reject these arguments. In subsequent decisions, adolescents might then rely more heavily on responses produced through analytic processing and thus show evidence of more decision-making competence than the two previous studies suggested.

In this research (Klaczynski, 2004; Klaczynski & Cottrell, 2004), decision tasks involving sunk costs and precedent setting were presented to 8-, 11-, and 14-year-olds (Study 1) and 9-, 12-, and 15-year-olds (Study 2). In the precedent setting problems, each scenario contained information about a publicly established rule (e.g., for classroom behavior, household chores), a rule infraction committed by a particular child, and the circumstances surrounding the rule infraction. The task was to decide whether to enforce the punishment associated with the rule or to make an exception. In Study 1, the circumstances surrounding infractions either appeared extenuating or more clearly fell under the purview of the rule. An example of a "no-mitigating circumstance" problem (adapted from Baron, Granato, Spranca, & Teubal, 1993) is:

> Mr. Miller, the coach of the basketball team, says that every person on the team has to go to all of the team's practices if they want to play in the games. If a person misses a practice, then he will not be allowed to play in the next game. Bill is the best player on the team. He missed three practices in a row, just because he wanted to watch TV instead. Bill is *so* good that the team will probably win if he gets to play, but the team will probably lose if Bill doesn't get to play. Now, it's the day before the game. What should Mr. Miller do?

The normative principle in cases such as this appears straightforward: Unless there are mitigating conditions, failure to enforce the rule establishes a negative precedent for future violations. Thus, if Mr. Miller does not enforce the rule, the rule is likely to lose its moral force and open the door for Bill (and his teammates) to question the rule in the future (see Moshman, 1998). When positive precedents are established by enforcing rules, they should serve to deter future violations; negative precedents, however, provide those expected to heed the rule grounds for arguing for the permissibility of violations.

However, under some conditions a clearly stated rule can be violated without establishing a negative precedent. Specifically, if the conditions surrounding a violation were not anticipated when the rule was created (or, if they were anticipated, they were not communicated to potential violators), then the question of whether the violation establishes a negative precedent is much more ambiguous. For example, in the "mitigating circumstance" version of the just-cited problem, the midsentences of the problem read: "Bill is the best player on the team. He missed three practices in a row because he had promised to do charity work at a hospital instead. Bill is *so* good that the team will probably win if he gets to play, but the team will probably lose the game if Bill doesn't get to play."

The results, depicted in Fig. 2.3, indicated that 9-year-olds responded at chance on both the mitigating and the no-mitigating circumstance problems. By contrast, on the no-mitigating circumstance problems, the 11- and 14-year-olds generally opted for rule enforcement (the normative decision). The opposite was found for the mitigating circumstance problems. Thus, most of the 11- and 14-year-olds elected to "make exceptions" (arguably, the normative decision). These results shed light on an aspect of adolescent decision making that hitherto had been investigated only by Baron et al. (1993). In contrast to children, both early and early middle adolescents evinced flexibility in their decision making, as only the adolescents systematically considered the role of context in their decisions. Children seemed to vacillate between rule enforcement and making exceptions—regardless of the contextual variations that had a pronounced effect on adolescents' decisions.

Adolescents' ability to coordinate social contextual considerations with apparently context-independent rules argues for a developmental progression in the same types of skills involved in coordinating beliefs and evidence that Kuhn and her colleagues have studied extensively (e.g., Kuhn, Amsel, & O'Loughlin, 1988; Kuhn et al., 1995). The findings also suggest application of at least a partially developed rationalist epistemology: Absolutists would likely have focused on rule enforcement on both mitigating and no-mitigating circumstances problems. Subjectivists, on both the mitigating and the no-mitigating circumstance problems, would likely have been predisposed toward making exceptions (i.e., "live and let live"; rules are relative to the individual and to the situation). Rationalists, however, in seeking the most justifiable rea-

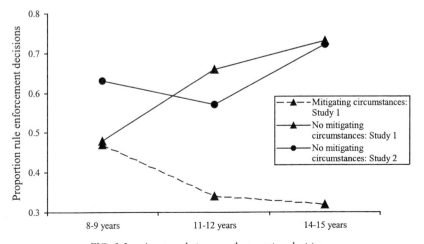

FIG. 2.3. Age trends in precedent-setting decisions.

sons for their decisions, would likely have considered the rule and the implications of its enforcement under the different conditions posed by the problems. Thus, rather than blindly applying rules about rules (e.g., enforce—regardless of context; make exceptions—regardless of context) adolescents (perhaps on the path toward becoming rationalists) were more likely than children to spontaneously apply their metacognitive knowledge.

Despite the attainment of a certain degree of metacognitive competence, adolescents' decision making remained characterized by substantial variability. To illustrate this variability, and again highlight the importance of metacognition in decision making, consider developmental trends in sunk cost decisions. For example:

> On parent's day at Julie's school, there will be a contest where all the students' paintings will be shown. Julie has spent the last 14 days working really hard on a drawing. She wants to win a prize pretty badly and thinks her drawing has a chance to win. Now, at long last, the drawing is almost finished.
>
> Then, just 4 days before the contest, Julie had an idea for a totally different drawing. She was positive that she could draw the new picture in 4 days, just in time for the contest. Not only that, but Julie thinks that the new drawing would be a lot better than the one she's been working on. The problem is that Julie has only one drawing board. That means that if she wants to draw the new picture, she will have to completely erase the picture she's been working on.

In both Study 1 and Study 2, children and adolescents demonstrated clear use of a nonnormative rule. As illustrated in Fig. 2.4, the majority honored sunk costs, presumably because of overreliance on a "waste not" heuristic (see Arkes & Ayton, 1999).

Although the age trends parallel those found on the precedent setting problems, these data illustrate two additional qualities of decision making and its development. First, on some decision tasks, children, like adults and adolescents, do not reply randomly; rather, they systematically use nonnor-

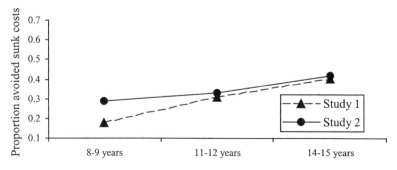

FIG. 2.4.   Age trends in sunk-cost decisions.

mative heuristics (see also Davidson, 1995; Jacobs & Potenza, 1991). Second, despite age-related improvements, nonnormative rule use typified decisions at all three ages. In contrast to precedent setting, these data, as well as those from Klaczynski (2001b), suggested that most adolescents do not spontaneously demonstrate competence at making decisions involving sunk costs. However, the failure to spontaneously make normative decisions does not mean that adolescents do not have the competence to understand and make the normative decision. Instead, it could be that adolescents possess an understanding of the importance of avoiding sunk costs but do not engage this competence because the heuristic against waste is extremely appealing. That is, once activated, the "waste not" heuristic is momentarily available in working memory and can, during this time, be examined for its relevance to a given situation. The heuristic may seem so commonsensical, however, that neither children nor adolescents give any thought to analyzing it.

One way of determining whether the competence to understand sunk costs—and other decision making principles—has been acquired is to have participants evaluate arguments that illustrate the normative principle and arguments that favor the nonnormative heuristic. More so than simple instructions to respond logically, this task is likely to elicit analytic processing predominance because the task itself (i.e., make a judgment about a normative principle, a nonnormative heuristic, or both) requires that the participants' role is effortful and conscious. Thus, presentation of arguments for nonnormative heuristics functions to bring heuristics that are activated automatically into working memory. Once in working memory, analytic processing can be engaged to determine the value of the heuristics and contrast this value with that of the normative principle. If participants embrace the normative rule more often than the nonnormative rule and if they apply the normative rule more often than the nonnormative rule to subsequent decisions, then the case can be made that the requisite competence has, in fact, developed (Stanovich & West, 1999, describe this methodology and its usefulness in helping sort out arguments over adult rationality in greater detail).

Using a variant of the design developed by Stanovich and West (1999) in their work on adult decision making, in Study 2 (Klaczynski, 2004), participants made decisions on a set of "baseline" problems that involved either sunk costs or precedents (results for the baseline problems are shown in Fig. 2.3 and Fig. 2.4). After decisions had been made on the baseline problems (as already described), fairly detailed arguments were presented. Thus, for each baseline problem, an argument for the normative decision, an argument for the nonnormative decision, or arguments for both the normative decision and the nonnormative decision were presented. Examples of these arguments are presented in Table 2.2.

Subsequent to argument presentation, the original problems were re-presented and a set a transfer problems was administered. If nonnormative

TABLE 2.2
Examples of Normative and Nonnormative
Arguments From Klaczynski (2004)

Normative Arguments	Nonnormative Arguments
Sunk costs	*Sunk costs*
Amy thinks that Julie should erase the old picture and draw the new one because "All the time that Julie put into the old picture doesn't make any difference. She wants to win, so she should use the new picture. She shouldn't worry about what she's already done. The work she put into the old one is in the past—she can't let that affect her now. Because she really wants to win, she's got to go with the best picture, even if she has to throw out a picture she worked hard on."	Tara thinks that Julie should keep working on the picture that she's spent 3 weeks on because "Julie's worked on this picture for 3 weeks. Even if the new picture would be better, all of her imagination and effort were in the old picture. She should show a picture that really means something to her. She worked really hard on that picture. If she doesn't use the one she worked so hard on, all of that time and effort will be wasted. If she doesn't use the old picture, she'll just be throwing away 3 weeks of work."
Precedent setting	
Mr. Ward thinks that Bill should *not* be allowed to play because "If Mr. Miller lets Bill play, other players might start breaking rules. He can't make an exception just because Bill is the best player. If Mr. Miller lets Bill break rules, the rest of the team could lose respect for him and might not listen to him if Bill gets away with skipping practice. It'd be better to lose a game than to make an exception."	*Precedent setting*
	Mr. Jones thinks that Bill *should* be allowed to play because "Bill has got to play or the team will lose. It's true that Mr. Miller set a rule, but in this case he has to make an exception. The rest of the team will understand—they probably want Mr. Miller to let Bill play. Nobody wants to lose, so for the good of the team, Mr. Miller should let Bill play."

responses were given on the baseline problems, and if at least some initial level of competence for understanding a particular decision principle had developed, then exposure to normative arguments should have resulted in more normative responding on problem re-presentation and on the transfer problems. Further, if responses on the baseline problems were normative and if the relevant competence was (to some extent) developed, then exposure to nonnormative, intuitively appealing arguments should not have had a negative impact (for a detailed discussion of the "understanding/acceptance" principle, its relevance to decision making, and its role in helping distinguish between responses purported to be normative and responses thought to be nonnormative, see Stanovich & West, 1999).

Importantly, the effects of both types of arguments were qualified by age and type of decision task. Specifically, regardless of age on the precedent-setting problems, normative arguments—both when these were presented by themselves and when presented with nonnormative arguments—led to more normative precedent setting decisions when the original problems were re-presented; this effect carried over to the transfer problems only for the adolescent groups, however. By contrast, when presented by themselves (i.e., without the normative arguments), nonnormative arguments (involving appealing to a "make an exception" heuristic) led to declines in normative decisions at problem re-presentation for all three age groups and, on the transfer problems, for the 9-year-olds. Thus, when adolescents had the opportunity to evaluate the "make an exception" heuristic in working memory, it appears that the metaprocedural competence to recognize the heuristics' shortcomings had not fully developed, even by 15 years of age. However, unlike children, adolescents' reliance on heuristics was short-lived in the sense that they applied the "make an exception" heuristic only to the problems discussed in the arguments.

A very different picture emerged for sunk-cost decisions. First, following exposure to normative arguments, normative decisions by the 12- and 15-year-olds, but not the 9-year-olds, increased for the re-presented problems and the transfer problems. When normative arguments were presented alongside nonnormative arguments, however, only the 15-year-olds accepted and understood the superiority of the former type of argument over the latter. Second, the 15-year-olds were unaffected by exposure to nonnormative arguments (when presented without the normative arguments). By contrast, when the problems were re-presented, both the 9- and the 12-year-olds made more decisions in the nonnormative direction (although this effect did not carry over to the transfer problems). In contrast to the precedent-setting problems, this finding implies that the metaprocedural competence necessary to effectively evaluate the "waste not" heuristic and to evaluate the normative decision principle had developed by middle adolescence.

Findings such as these speak to the complexity involved in both making and disentangling arguments about age-related attainments in cognitive and decision-making competencies. In this case, it would appear (despite recent arguments to the contrary; e.g., Arkes & Ayton, 1999) that an understanding of sunk costs and of the reason for avoiding them does not develop prior to adolescence. Even so, at 12 years, this understanding seems somewhat fragile (given 12-year-olds' susceptibility to nonnormative arguments) and may not emerge "in full" until later in adolescence. But even at 15 years and beyond, people rely primarily on a "waste not, want not" heuristic. By contrast, children's responses to normative precedent-setting arguments appear to suggest some competence at 9 years and a greater degree (as indicated by positive transfer) by adolescence; yet, across ages, nonnormative arguments lowered the frequency of normative decisions. This latter finding illustrates that, once a competence has developed, its utilization is often overridden by situational factors that activate intuitively appealing heuristics. More broadly, decision-making competencies do not develop in an all-or-none fashion and are not displayed under all apparently relevant conditions.

A theme underlying much of this chapter has been that, although all decisions are products of interactions between experiential and analytical processing, the system predominant at the moment of the decision is the more potent determinant of actual decisions. The aforementioned findings illustrate this interplay in that baseline decisions may well have been a function of automatically activated heuristics (e.g., "waste not," "make exceptions"), the "thoughtless" application of which was not (particularly for younger children and for sunk-cost decisions) prevented by metacognitive intercession. Both normative and nonnormative arguments cued analytic processing predominance and, in order to evaluate and apply the arguments, activated metaknowledge and metaprocedural understanding. Whether shifts were from the normative decision to the nonnormative decision (as usually occurred following normative arguments) or vice versa (which sometimes occurred following nonnormative arguments), postargument decisions involved the evaluation and acceptance of a decision rule different from that used at baseline. Further, this rule had to have been extracted from the arguments at some level of abstraction for transfer (whether positive or negative) to occur. Because the baseline, re-presentation, and transfer problems were separated by other problems (e.g., the baseline sunk-cost problems were separated from the re-presentation problems by both the arguments and precedent setting problems [as well as other problems not discussed here]), metamonitoring of decisions had to have been involved for participants to recognize the applicability of the decision rule to the novel problems. Finally, the findings illustrate that metaknowledge understanding and metamonitoring abilities are not always in perfect alignment with one another. For example, following nonnormative arguments, the negative transfer to novel precedent-setting problems can be taken as evidence for successful metamonitoring and, simultaneously, as evidence for miscomprehension at the metaknowledge level.

SUMMARY AND CONCLUSIONS

The principal aims of this chapter were fourfold. A first goal was to outline a two-process theory of reasoning and decision making that, until recently, has not been at the fore of discussions of cognitive development. A second goal was to illustrate the two forms of variability that characterize everyday reasoning, decision making, and development. One form involves moment-to-moment fluctuations in the sophistication of reasoning, analytic strategies, and heuristics that can be considered, to some extent at least, as evidence for rapidly shifting predominance between analytic processing and experiential processing. The second form involves developmental variability in the emergence of the competencies required to understand and apply normative decision rules. As the findings from Klaczynski (2004; Klaczynski & Cottrell, 2004) demonstrated, both in spontaneous decision making and in decision making following cues to process information analytically, there is no single age at which decision making competence is attained. A third goal was to highlight the role of three components of metacognition (metaknowledge, metaprocedural understanding, and metamonitoring) in analytic processing and in reducing moment-to-moment variability in reasoning and decision making. Finally, a fourth goal was to provide empirical evidence for a link between metacognitive development and decision making (see also Byrnes, 1998).

The evidence presented here supports the two-process assumption that, because it is the default system (i.e., that which is typically predominant), experiential processing, more often than not, is not overridden by analytic processing. Consequently, decisions are made and arguments are evaluated on the basis of cursory analyses of the circumstances and stereotypes, beliefs, and heuristics activated by these circumstances. Although this point was not emphasized here, often the outcomes of this processing are in line with those that would have been produced had analytic processing been predominant (see also Denes-Raj & Epstein, 1994; Stanovich & West, 1998, 2000). In other cases, although the decisions produced by the two systems may differ, they may be equally useful in achieving a goal (i.e., via different routes). In many cases, although experiential processing may lead to nonnormative decisions, the outcome of following the actions dictated by those decisions is not particularly harmful to the decision maker (e.g., the decision to continue playing golf by Jim, Dave, and Keith). In sum, reliance on the default-processing system sometimes has adaptive value (e.g., when it produces the same decisions as analytic processing, it does so more quickly, saving time and cognitive effort). A challenge for future research is to determine more precisely the conditions under which experiential processing predominance is more adaptive than analytic processing predominance.

Nonetheless, as research on belief-motivated reasoning illustrates, experiential processing often interferes with analytic processing to produce biases that not only preserve existing beliefs, but also perpetuate stereotypes and inhibit development. In the case of motivated reasoning, novel, but belief-threatening, information that may provide an adolescent new insights into the self and/or others is often rejected, but similar evidence that supports existing views of the self and others is accepted. Experientially biased decisions can have deleterious consequences, both in the short term and in the long term. Variable reinforcement (e.g., occasional winning) may be implicitly processed to create a "schema" for committing the "gambler's fallacy" and may contribute to addictive betting and gambling. Experiential processing of ratios, in combination with unrealistic optimism, may contribute to the widespread tendency of adults to play lotteries. Clearly, there are numerous circumstances that call for analytic processing to override experiential processing. Indeed, as societies become increasingly complex, the need for analytic processing to override experiential processing may increase (Stanovich & West, 2000).

Equally clear is that there is variability—between decision and reasoning situations, between ages, and among individuals at particular ages—in the extent to which individuals can achieve analytic predominance (Stanovich, 1999). Studies of ratio bias and counterfactual decisions indicate that even simple cues to process information analytically can increase normative decisions from early adolescence through early adulthood. Likewise, studies of precedent setting and sunk-cost decisions show that arguments for normative decisions can produce shifts from nonnormative to normative decisions—shifts that require analytic predominance and that are easier to achieve by adolescents than by children. By contrast, as studies of the effects of accuracy motivations on belief-biased reasoning indicate, even adolescents and adults have difficulty inhibiting experiential interference when evaluating evidence bearing on strongly held beliefs.

These investigations indicate that the metacognitive abilities required to inhibit the implementation of automatically activated beliefs and heuristics are not always fully developed or, if they have in fact developed, the individuals possessing these abilities do not often expend the effort required to use them. Although there appear to be developmental improvements in metacognitive abilities, even by adulthood, they may not be fully developed (Kuhn, 2000; Moshman, 1999). It remains to be determined, however, whether poor decisions and biased reasoning are more a matter of acquiring dispositions to be "metacognitively oriented" than of possessing metacognitive abilities per se. Critical to further investigation of these issues will be improvements in the methodologies used to index both abilities and dispositions.

REFERENCES

Alberti, E. T., & Witryol, S. L. (1994). The relationship between curiosity and cognitive ability in third- and fifth-grade children. *Journal of Genetic Psychology, 155*, 129–134.

Arkes, H. R., & Ayton, P. (1999). The sunk cost and concorde effects: Are humans less rational than animals? *Psychological Review, 125*, 591–600.

Bargh, J. A., & Chartland, T. L. (1999). The unbearable automaticity of being. *American Psychologist, 54*, 462–479.

Baron, J. (1985). *Rationality and intelligence.* Cambridge, MA: Cambridge University Press.

Baron, J., Granato, L., Spranca, M., & Teubal, E. (1993). Decision-making biases in children and early adolescence: Exploratory studies. *Merrill-Palmer Quarterly, 39*, 22–46.

Berg, C. A., & Sternberg, R. J. (1985). A triarchic theory of intellectual developing during adulthood. *Developmental Review, 5*, 334–370.

Boyes, M. C., & Chandler, M. (1992). Cognitive development, epistemic doubt, and identity formation during adolescence. *Journal of Youth and Adolescence, 21,* 277–304.

Brainerd, C. J. (1981). Working memory and the developmental analysis of probability judgment. *Psychological Review, 88,* 463–502.

Brainerd, C. J., & Kingma, J. (1985). On the independence of short-term memory and working memory in cognitive development. *Cognitive Psychology, 17,* 210–247.

Brainerd, C. J., & Reyna, V. A. (2001). Fuzzy-trace theory: Dual processes in memory, reasoning, and cognitive neuroscience. In H. W. Reese & R. Kail (Eds.), *Advances in children development and behavior* (Vol. 28, pp. 41–100). San Diego: Academic.

Byrnes, J. P. (1998). *The nature and development of decision making: A self-regulation model.* Mahwah, NJ: Lawrence Erlbaum Associates.

Cacioppo, R., Petty, J., Feinstein, J., & Javis, W. (1996). Dispositional differences in cognitive motivation: The life and times of individuals varying in need for cognition. *Psychological Bulletin, 119,* 197–253.

Ceci, S. J. (1990). *On intelligence . . . more or less.* Englewood Cliffs, NJ: Prentice-Hall.

Chandler, M. J., Boyes, M. C., & Ball, L. (1990). Relativism and stations of epistemic doubt. *Journal of Experimental Child Psychology, 50,* 370–395.

Chandler, M. J., Hallett, D., & Sokol, B. W. (2002). Competing claims about competing knowledge claims. In B. K. Hofer & P. R. Pintrich (Eds.), *Personal epistemology: The psychology of beliefs about knowledge and knowing* (pp. 145–168). Mahwah, NJ: Lawrence Erlbaum Associates.

Chen, S., & Chaiken, S. (1999). The heuristic-systematic model in its broader context. In S. Chaiken & Y. Trope (Eds.), *Dual-process theories in social psychology* (pp. 73–96). New York: Guilford.

Davidson, D. (1995). The representativeness heuristic and the conjunction fallacy in children's decision making. *Merrill-Palmer Quarterly, 41,* 328–346.

Denes-Raj, V., & Epstein, S. (1994). Conflict between intuitive and rational processing: When people behave against their better judgment. *Journal of Personality and Social Psychology, 66,* 819–829.

Donaldson, M. (1978). *Children's minds.* London: Fontana.

Epstein, S. (1994). Integration of the cognitive and psychodynamic unconscious. *American Psychologist, 49,* 709–724.

Epstein, S., & Pacini, R. (1999). Some basic issues regarding dual-process theories from the perspective of cognitive–experiential self-theory. In S. Chaiken & Y. Trope (Eds.), *Dual-process theories in social psychology* (pp. 462–482). New York: Guilford.

Epstein, S., Pacini, R., Denes-Raj, V., & Heier, H. (1995). *Individual differences in heuristic processing.* Unpublished manuscript, University of Massachusetts.

Evans, J. B. St. T. (1989). *Bias in human reasoning: Causes and consequences.* London: Routledge.

Evans, J. B. St. T., & Over, D. E. (1996). *Reasoning and rationality.* Hove, England: Psychology Press.

Frisch, D. (1993). Reasons for framing effects. *Organization Behavior and Human Decision Processes, 54,* 399–429.

Gigerenzer, G. (1996). On narrow norms and vague heuristics: A reply to Kahneman and Tversky. *Psychological Review, 103,* 592–596.

Gopnik, A., & Wellman, H. M. (1992). Why the child's theory of mind is really a theory. *Mind and Language, 7,* 145–171.

Harris, P. L., & Leevers, H. J. (2000). Reasoning from false premises. In K. J. Riggs & P. Mitchell (Eds.), *Children's reasoning and the mind* (pp. 67–86). Hove, England: Psychology Press/Taylor & Francis.

Henderson, B., & Wilson, S. E. (1991). Intelligence and curiosity and preschool children. *Journal of School Psychology, 29,* 167–175.

Hofer, B. K., & Pintrich, P. R. (2002). *Personal epistemology: The psychology of beliefs about knowledge and knowing.* Mahwah, NJ: Lawrence Erlbaum Associates.

Inhelder, B., & Piaget, J. (1958). *The growth of logical thinking from childhood to adolescence.* New York: Basic.

Jacobs, J. E., & Klaczynski, P. A. (2002). The development of decision making during childhood and adolescence. *Current Directions in Psychological Science, 4,* 145–149.

Jacobs, J. E., & Narloch, R. H. (2001). Children's use of sample size and variability to make social inferences. *Journal of Applied Developmental Psychology, 22,* 1–21.

Jacobs, J. E., & Potenza, M. T. (1991). The use of judgment heuristics to make social and object decisions: A developmental perspective. *Child Development, 62,* 166–178.

Kahneman, D., Slovic, P., & Tversky, A. (Eds.). (1982). *Judgment under uncertainty: Heuristics and biases.* Cambridge, MA: Cambridge University Press.

Kahneman, D., & Tversky, A. (1972). Subjective probability: A judgment of representativeness. *Cognitive Psychology, 3,* 430–454.

Kardash, C. M., & Scholes, R. J. (1996). Effects of pre-existing beliefs, epistemological beliefs, and need for cognition on interpretation of controversial issues. *Journal of Educational Psychology, 88,* 260–271.

Keating, D. P., & Sasse, D. K. (1996). Cognitive socialization in adolescence: Critical period for a critical habit of mind. In G. R. Adams, R. Montemayor, & T. P. Gullotta (Eds.), *Psychosocial development during adolescence: Progress in developmental contextualism* (pp. 232–258). Thousand Oaks, CA: Sage.

Kirkpatrick, L. A., & Epstein, S. (1993). Cognitive-experiential self-theory and subjective probability: Further evidence for two conceptual systems. *Journal of Personality and Social Psychology, 63,* 534–544.

Kitchener, K. S., King, P. M., Wood, P. K., & Davison, M. L. (1989). Sequentiality and consistency in the development of reflective judgment: A six-year longitudinal study. *Journal of Applied Developmental Psychology, 10,* 73–95.

Klaczynski, P. A. (1997). Bias in adolescents' everyday reasoning and its relationship with intellectual ability, personal theories, and self-serving motivation. *Developmental Psychology, 33,* 273–283.

Klaczynski, P. A. (2000). Motivated scientific reasoning biases, epistemological beliefs, and theory polarization: A two-process approach to adolescent cognition. *Child Development, 71,* 1347–1366.

Klaczynski, P. A. (2001a). Analytic and heuristic processing influences on adolescent reasoning and decision making. *Child Development, 72,* 844–861.

Klaczynski, P. A. (2001b). Framing effects on adolescent task representations, analytic and heuristic processing, and decision making: Implications for the normative-descriptive gap. *Journal of Applied Developmental Psychology, 22,* 289–309.

Klaczynski, P. A. (2004). *Understanding developmental progressions (and digressions) in decision making: Effects of normative and non-normative arguments on decision about negative precedents.* Unpublished manuscript, The Pennsylvania State University.

Klaczynski, P. A., & Aneja, A. (2002). The development of quantitative reasoning and gender biases. *Developmental Psychology, 38,* 208–221.

Klaczynski, P. A., Byrnes, J. B., & Jacobs, J. E. (2001). Introduction: Special issue on decision making. *Journal of Applied Developmental Psychology, 22,* 225–236.

Klaczynski, P. A., & Cottrell, J. E. (2004). A dual-process approach to cognitive development: The case of children's understanding of sunk cost decisions. *Thinking & Reasoning, 10,* 147–174.

Klaczynski, P. A., & Fauth, J. (1997). Developmental differences in memory-based intrusions and self-serving statistical reasoning biases. *Merrill-Palmer Quarterly, 43,* 539–566.

Klaczynski, P. A., & Gordon, D. H. (1996a). Goal-directed everyday problem solving: Motivational and general ability influences on adolescent statistical reasoning. *Child Development, 67,* 2873–2891.

Klaczynski, P. A., & Gordon, D. H. (1996b). Self-serving influences on adolescents' evaluations of belief-relevant evidence. *Journal of Experimental Child Psychology, 62,* 317–339.

Klaczynski, P. A., Gordon, D. H., & Fauth, J. (1997). Goal-oriented critical thinking biases and individual differences in reasoning biases. *Journal of Educational Psychology, 89,* 470–485.

Klaczynski, P. A., & Narasimham, G. (1998a). The development of self-serving reasoning biases: Ego-protective versus cognitive explanations. *Developmental Psychology, 34,* 175–187.

Klaczynski, P. A., & Narasimham, G. (1998b). Problem representations as mediators of adolescent deductive reasoning. *Developmental Psychology, 34,* 865–881.

Klaczynski, P. A., & Robinson, B. (2000). Personal theories, intellectual ability, and epistemological beliefs: Adult age differences in everyday reasoning biases. *Psychology and Aging, 15,* 400–416.

Kreitler, S., & Kreitler, H. (1986). Development of probability thinking in children 5 to 12 years old. *Cognitive Development, 1,* 365–390.

Kuhn, D. (1991). *The skills of argument.* New York: Cambridge University Press.

Kuhn, D. (2000). Metacognitive development. *Current Directions in Psychological Science, 9,* 178–181.

Kuhn, D. (2001). How do people know? *Psychological Science, 12,* 1–8.

Kuhn, D., Amsel, E., & O'Loughlin, M. (1988). *The development of scientific thinking skills.* Orlando, FL: Academic.

Kuhn, D., Cheney, R., & Weinstock, M. (2000). The development of epistemological understanding. *Cognitive Development, 15,* 309–328.

Kuhn, D., Garcia-Mila, M., Zohar, A., & Andersen, C. (1995). Strategies of knowledge acquisition. *Monographs of the Society for Research in Child Development, 60*(4, Serial No. 245).

Kuhn, D., & Pearsall, S. (1998). Relations between metastrategic knowledge and strategic performance. *Cognitive Development, 13,* 227–247.

Kuhn, D., & Pearsall, S. (2000). Developmental origins of scientific thinking. *Journal of Cognition and Development, 1,* 113–129.

Kuhn, D., & Weinstock, M. (2002). What is epistemological thinking and why does it matter? In B. K. Hofer & P. R. Pintrich (Eds.), *Personal epistemology: The psychology of beliefs about knowledge and knowing* (pp. 121–144). Mahwah, NJ: Lawrence Erlbaum Associates.

Lie, E., & Newcombe, N. S. (1999). Elementary school children's explicit and implicit memory for faces of preschool classmates. *Developmental Psychology, 35,* 102–112.

Markovits, H., & Dumas, C. (1999). Developmental patterns of understanding social and physical transitivity. *Journal of Experimental Child Psychology, 73,* 95–114.

Mitchell, P., Robinson, E. J., Isaacs, R. M., & Nye, R. M. (1996). Contamination in reasoning about false belief: An instance of realist bias in adults but not children. *Cognition, 59,* 1–21.

Moshman, D. (1990). The development of metalogical understanding. In W. F. Overton (Ed.), *Reasoning, necessity, and logic: Developmental perspectives* (pp. 205–225). Hillsdale, NJ: Lawrence Erlbaum Associates.

Moshman, D. (1998). Cognitive development beyond childhood. In D. Kuhn & R. Siegler (Eds.), *Handbook of child psychology: Cognition, perception, and language* (5th ed., pp. 947–978). New York: Wiley.

Moshman, D. (1999). *Adolescent psychological development.* Mahwah, NJ: Lawrence Erlbaum Associates.

Moshman, D. (2000). Diversity in reasoning and rationality: Metacognitive and developmental considerations. *Brain and Behavioral Sciences, 23,* 689–670.

Newcombe, N., & Fox, N. A. (1994). Infantile amnesia: Through a glass darkly. *Child Development, 65,* 31–40.

Nickerson, R., Perkins, D. N., & Smith, E. (1985). *The teaching of thinking.* Hillsdale, NJ: Lawrence Erlbaum Associates.

Noveck, I. A. (2001). When children are more logical than adults: Experimental investigations of scalar implicature. *Cognition, 78,* 165–188.

Perkins, D. N., Jay, E., & Tishman, S. (1993). Beyond abilities: A dispositional theory of thinking. *Merrill-Palmer Quarterly, 39,* 1–21.

Perner, J. (1991). *Understanding the representational mind.* Cambridge, MA: MIT Press.

Perry, W. G. (1970). *Forms of intellectual and ethical development during the college years: A scheme.* New York: Holt, Rinehart & Winston.

Piaget, J., & Inhelder, B. (1975). *The origin of the idea of chance in children.* New York: Norton. (Original work published 1951)

Reyna, V. F., & Brainerd, C. J. (1995). Fuzzy-trace theory: An interim synthesis. *Learning and Individual Differences, 7,* 1–75.

Reyna, V. F., & Ellis, S. C. (1994). Fuzzy-trace theory and framing effects in children's risky decision making. *Psychological Science, 5,* 275–279.

Reyna, V. F., Lloyd, F. J., & Brainerd, C. J. (in press). Memory, development, and rationality: An integrative theory of judgment and decision-making. In S. Schneider & J. Shanteau (Eds.), *Emerging perspectives on decision research.* Cambridge, MA: Cambridge University Press.

Schommer, M. (1994). Synthesizing epistemological belief research: Tentative understandings and provocative conclusions. *Educational Psychology Review, 6,* 293–319.

Siegler, R. S. (1996). *Emerging minds: The process of change in children's thinking.* New York: Oxford University Press,

Sloman, S. A. (1996). The empirical case for two systems of reasoning. *Psychological Bulletin, 119,* 3–22.

Stanovich, K. E. (1999). *Who is rational? Studies of individual differences in reasoning.* Mahwah, NJ: Lawrence Erlbaum Associates.

Stanovich, K. E., & West, R. F. (1997). Reasoning independently of prior belief and individual differences in actively open-minded thinking. *Journal of Educational Psychology, 89,* 342–357.

Stanovich, K. E., & West, R. F. (1998a). Individual differences in rational thought. *Journal of Experimental Psychology: General, 127,* 161–188.

Stanovich, K. E., & West, R. F. (1998b). Who uses base rates and P(D/-H)? An analysis of individual differences. *Memory & Cognition, 26,* 161–179.

Stanovich, K. E., & West, R. F. (1999). Discrepancies between normative and descriptive models of decision making and the understanding/acceptance principle. *Cognitive Psychology, 38,* 349–385.

Stanovich, K. E., & West, R. F. (2000). Individual differences in reasoning: Implications for the rationality debate? *Behavioral and Brain Sciences, 23,* 645–665.

Sternberg, R. J. (1985). *Beyond IQ: A triarchic theory of human intelligence.* New York: Cambridge University Press.

Subbotsky, E. (2000). Phenomenalistic perception and rational understanding in the mind of an individual: A fight for dominance. In K. S. Rosengren, C. N. Johnson, & P. L. Harris (Eds.), *Imagining the impossible: Magical, scientific, and religious thinking in children* (pp. 35–74). New York: Cambridge University Press.

Wason, P. C. (1966). Reasoning. In B. Foss (Ed.), *New horizons in psychology* (pp. 135–151). Harmondworth, England: Penguin Books.

Wildman, T. M., & Fletcher, H. J. (1977). Developmental increases and decreases in solutions to conditional syllogism problems. *Developmental Psychology, 13,* 630–636.

3

Risky Decision Making in Childhood and Adolescence: A Fuzzy-Trace Theory Approach

Valerie F. Reyna
Mary B. Adam
Kristin M. Poirier
Craig W. LeCroy
Charles J. Brainerd
University of Arizona

In this chapter, we discuss the psychological origins of judgment and decision making from childhood through adolescence, with an emphasis on developmental differences in risk taking. First, we outline a developmental theory—*fuzzy-trace theory*—that makes counterintuitive predictions about risk taking. The main prediction, in marked contrast to traditional theories, is that development progresses from compensatory trading off of risks and rewards to intuitive gist-based processing (e.g., Reyna, 1996; Reyna & Brainerd, 1991a, 1993, 1994, 1995a; Reyna & Ellis, 1994; Reyna, Lloyd, & Brainerd, 2003). A central tenet of fuzzy-trace theory is that judgment and decision making tend to be based on simple, gistlike mental representations of options ("fuzzy" memory traces), rather than detailed, quantitative representations of information (verbatim memory traces). *Gist* is defined as the individual's semantic representation of information—its meaning—which reflects his or her knowledge, worldview, culture, and developmental level (e.g., Reyna, 1996; Reyna & Brainerd, 1995b; Romo, 1995). As we discuss, fuzzy-trace theory encompasses social, affective, and neurological development, as well as cognitive development (e.g., Klaczynski & Fauth, 1997; Reyna, 1992; Reyna & Brainerd, 1998; Schacter, Curran, Galluccio, Milberg, & Bates, 1996).

Next, we relate these background principles provided by fuzzy-trace theory to situations of sexual risk taking in adolescence. We then review studies that show evidence of effectiveness in reducing sexual risk taking among adolescents. In that connection, we discuss how programs to reduce risk taking cohere with a range of explanatory theories, specifically for programs addressing AIDS prevention. One lesson to emerge from this review is that even effective interventions become less so over time, and mechanisms for sustaining effectiveness are needed. Furthermore, most risk-reduction programs are predicated on decision analysis (i.e., rational integration of risks and rewards), a prescriptive approach, which clashes with descriptive data about how decisions are actually made and fails to incorporate developmental changes in risky decision making. Finally, we compare alternative theories of decision making with respect to the tension between prescription and description, and discuss what is considered healthy behavior from these highly divergent theoretical perspectives. Throughout this chapter, we are guided by the principle that knowing what works in reducing risk is essential, but, in the long run, practical progress is greatest, and most effectively generalized, when we also know why and how it works.

BACKGROUND: EXPLANATORY PRINCIPLES

Semantics of Risk and Reward

As we noted, the gist of a decision is its core meaning, what it boils down to, and that meaning is influenced by culture, context, and development (e.g., Reyna & Brainerd, 1995a, 1995b). Consider an adolescent's choice between "hanging out" at the mall on a Saturday evening versus going to an unsupervised party where drinking and sexual risk taking might take place. According to fuzzy-trace theory, although objective analysis might uncover hundreds of potential risks and benefits in this situation, the gist of the decision for many adolescents is that they can have some fun at the mall versus take a risk and possibly have more fun at the party (see Table 3.1; Reyna et al., 2003).

This interpretation of the choices is not a given, but instead is shaped by social influences. Going to the mall, and associated socializing, is a cultural phenomenon that is peculiar to certain ethnic groups, social classes, and time periods in history. Social influences, including media, suggest that hanging out at the mall, unsupervised parties, and other activities are fun (Table 3.1). Although adolescents in diverse cultures prefer having more fun to having less, what is considered fun varies. In addition, what is fun changes with development, for example, changing from playing with toys to drinking at parties. Thus, according to fuzzy-trace theory, the gist of the options themselves, and their meaning, reflects social learning through direct and indirect experiences (e.g., Bandura, 1982, 1986, 1994).

Similarly, the interpretation of risk changes with culture, development, and experience. For example, driving without a seat belt or biking without a hel-

TABLE 3.1
Anatomy of a Risky Decision

1. Choices: Go to the mall or to an unsupervised party.
2. Categorical gist representation (lower risk): Can have some fun [at the mall] and not take a risk versus have some fun [at the party] and take a risk.
3. Ordinal gist representation (higher risk): Can have some fun [at the mall] versus take a risk and possibly have more fun [at the party].
4. Verbatim representation (higher risk): Can have twice as much fun [at the party compared to the mall], but the risk is only about 1 in 10 of something really bad happening [at the party].
5. Values retrieved (lower risk): No risk is better than taking a risk.
6. Values retrieved (higher risk): Less risk is better than more risk.
7. Values retrieved (lower risk): Having some fun is better than having no fun.
8. Values retrieved (higher risk): Having more fun is better than having less fun.

met would be considered risky today, but were mundane a generation ago. Cognitive interventions, as illustrated by the effect of educational levels or public health messages on smoking, can be effective in communicating risk. Although it is true that children learn more about risks with development, the common assumption that adolescents are oblivious to the risks involved in such activities as drinking, drug taking, and unprotected sex appears to be false (e.g., Quadrel, Fischhoff, & Davis, 1993). The myth of immortality, which adolescents are assumed to believe, seems to be a myth itself. Carefully conducted studies indicate that adolescents realize that they are at greater risk than adults, and those engaged in higher risk behaviors rate themselves as more vulnerable than those not engaged in these risky behaviors.

Research does support the conventional wisdom that adolescents are deficient in planning or future orientation, less likely to be aware of consequences, and are more prone to risk taking, compared to adults (e.g., Baron & Brown, 1991; Furby & Beyth-Marom, 1992; Reyna, 1996). According to fuzzy-trace theory, what is interpreted as risky reflects the sum total of experience, including education. Objective risk, therefore, is only one factor in risk perception, which is ultimately subjective (acceptable risk) and qualitative (i.e., the nonnumerical meaning of risk to an individual; e.g., Hampson, Severson, Burns, Slovic, & Fisher, 2001; Reyna & Brainerd, 1995a; Slovic, Fischhoff, & Lichtenstein, 1982).

Although we might speculate that experience with consequences increases awareness and future orientation, the developmental trend of decreasing risk taking is more mysterious. Risk taking decreases with age through adolescence even when outcomes and probabilities are explicit, which only serves to deepen the mystery. That is, decreased risk taking cannot be attributed in these situations to lack of awareness of risks and outcomes (although lack of awareness may be operative in some real-life contexts).

Standard decision analysis points to two factors as possible sources of developmental differences in risk taking: valuation of outcomes and attitude toward risks. In this view, developmental differences are a matter of degree; with age, the valuation of outcomes may decline and the perception of risk may increase. For instance, evidence suggests that some adolescents value the outcome of pregnancy more positively than their parents do, and they discount the value of future outcomes relative to immediate ones more sharply than adults do (e.g., Loewenstein & Furstenberg, 1991). Once these developmentally different values are assumed, unprotected intercourse and early pregnancy can be rationalized as broadly consistent with maximizing expected utility (Loewenstein & Furstenberg, 1991; but see Reyna, Lloyd, & Brainerd, 2003). As we discuss in the next section, this explanation of changes in degree of valuation or risk perception is not entirely satisfactory, however, because developmental changes are qualitative, as opposed to merely quantitative. In risky decision making, patterns of behavior emerge with age, such as framing effects, which were not present earlier in development (Reyna & Ellis, 1994).

Fuzzy-Processing Preference in Thinking

Many programs to reduce risk taking assume that teaching adolescents to think analytically about the risks and consequences will reduce unhealthy behaviors (e.g., Baron & Brown, 1991; Beyth-Marom, Fischhoff, Quadrel, & Furby, 1991; Furby & Beyth-Marom, 1992). Thus, interventions are typically focused on how to convey probabilities more clearly, make consequences more explicit, and connect protective behaviors to values (e.g., teach refusal skills to support the value of sexual abstinence in adolescence). It is assumed that, once the decision is properly specified, decisions then hinge on the degree to which risk and reward trade off.

According to fuzzy-trace theory, although such precise and analytic thinking is a cognitive option, the natural habit of mind is to think imprecisely and intuitively about decisions, choosing the option that dominates based on gist representations and retrieved values or principles. This fuzzy processing preference is increased by experience making related decisions, including experience with outcomes. Development, therefore, drives decision making away from trading off toward simple, categorical reasoning, from more precise quantitative distinctions toward qualitative distinctions. For instance, a mature representation of the mall versus party decision is that there is fun to be had at both locations, but no risk is better than taking a risk (see Table 3.1). To be sure, a sophisticated expected utility model would weigh degrees of risks and rewards, as would many an adolescent (i.e., considerations such as how much more fun the party would be or how likely it is that something bad would happen at the party). To the mature decision maker, however, it is not the expected value of the gamble that matters but only the non-negligible possibility of a single categorical catastrophe.

The fuzzy representations that underlie such categorical decision making have been found to be available early in development, along with more precise levels of representation. Carefully controlled experiments that teased out the contributions of representation, retrieval, and processing have shown that multiple representations of the same decision that vary along a verbatim to gist continuum are encoded (e.g., Reyna, 1992; Reyna & Brainerd, 1991a). For example, the mall–party decision can also be framed as a choice between having less fun and lower risk versus more fun and higher risk (Table 3.1). Note that the latter representation is at a finer grain of precision, but consistent with the categorical gist discussed earlier (i.e., that there is fun to be had at both locations, but no risk is better than taking a risk). Ordinal distinctions (less and more; lower and higher) along the outcomes and risk dimensions have replaced categories of *fun* or *no fun, risk* or *no risk*. Still finer distinctions might be imagined, such as those that decision analysts attempt to extract from decision makers in order to determine preferences for complex trade-offs (e.g., von Winterfeldt & Edwards, 1986). These representations at varying levels of precision form a hierarchy of gist roughly analogous to scales of measurement (Reyna & Brainerd, 1995b). The fine-grained quantitative distinctions represented in verbatim memories are analogous to ratio-level information and the categorical distinctions of lower level gist are like crude nominal information.

According to fuzzy-trace theory, decision makers seek the lowest level of precision in this hierarchy of gist that can be used to accomplish the task (see Reyna & Brainerd, 1995a). For example, given a choice between a sure option ($100 for sure) and a gamble with at least one null outcome (50% chance of $200, 50% chance of nothing), the categorical contrast between some money and no money can be used to accomplish the task of choosing between options. According to Reyna (1995), tasks can be distinguished as to whether precise information is required or optional simply to generate a cooperative response. For example, if asked how many dollars one would pay in rent for two similar apartments except that one of them is closer to work (assuming ample information has been given and one is familiar with the market), it is not cooperative to respond that more dollars would be spent on the closer apartment; the question concerns the exact number of dollars that one is willing to pay (e.g., see also Reyna & Brainerd, 1993, 1995a).

When precise information is required, such as memory for details or judgment of exact quantities, verbatim memory representations must be tapped in order to accomplish the task (Reyna & Brainerd, 1995a). Otherwise, gist representations are relied on as the default mode of processing. What develops with age and experience, according to research, is the dissociation between gist and verbatim representations depending on the task (called *task calibration*; Reyna & Kiernan, 1994, 1995). Young children sometimes attempt to answer reasoning questions with rote responses that are retrieved from verbatim memory, eventually learning in the early school years to approach these questions as matters of gist (Brainerd & Reyna, 1993). Conversely, false memories are often gist responses—such as reporting semantic inferences—to verbatim questions (Reyna, 2000; Reyna & Brainerd, 1998; Reyna & Lloyd, 1997). Insightfully and rapidly applying the right representation to the right task (indeed realizing what the task is) increases with development (Reyna et al., 2003).

Some observers have neglected the concept of a *hierarchy of gist* in fuzzy-trace theory, and have assumed that the theory predicts that all decision making is governed by categorical contrasts (Kuhberger, 1995); this is not the case. Given a choice between two gambles, both of which involve null outcomes, a something–nothing categorical contrast does not discriminate between options (i.e., the decision maker cannot accomplish the task), and so decision makers must ascend the hierarchy of gist. For instance, given a choice between two unsupervised parties that both involve risk, the ordinal gist—which party has the potential for more fun and less risk—can be used to discriminate between options.

Within the decision-analytic framework, in contrast, preferences depend on precise distinctions along the dimensions of risk and reward (including social cognitive theory, the theory of reasoned action, and its extensions to "planned behavior," and decision theory; e.g., Ajzen & Fishbein, 1980; Bandura, 1982, 1986, 1994; Beyth-Marom & Fischhoff, 1997; Beyth-Marom et al., 1991; Fishbein & Ajzen, 1975; Furby & Beyth-Marom, 1992; Loewenstein & Furstenberg, 1991). Rationally, it is argued, the mall-versus-party decision depends on the *amount* of fun and risk to be had at the party compared to the mall (or, at least, the perception of the amount of dollars or fun; e.g., Fischhoff & Quadrel, 1991; Kuther, 2002; see also Table 3.1). Most parents would disagree. An unsupervised party is not subject to negotiation as to degrees of risk. The amount of fun cannot compensate for the risk, contrary to a strictly rational cost–benefit analysis. It could be further argued that parents are irrational, especially when it comes to their offspring. (See Reyna et al., 2003, and Reyna & Brainerd, 1995a, for detailed discussions of fair criteria for rationality.) However, fuzzy-trace theorists have maintained that such global categorical policies exist on a higher plane of rationality, cutting across details of amounts of risk and reward in distinct choices. Although situations that tempt adolescents vary in detail, their common gist is that the potential for catastrophe trumps all other considerations.

Consider the amount of money that would be required to play Russian roulette; what dollar amount would make the decision to play rational? We could imagine desperate straits in which a person needed money to avoid death, and a decision to play could be rational in that case. However, in the usual status quo situation (alive without threat of imminent death), what amount would make sense? As we discuss in the final section, rationality in our view does not pivot on the number of dollars because there is no number of dollars that would make such a choice rational. According to fuzzy-trace theory, a point in development is reached for most people at which the categorical gist of the decision—dead versus not dead—overwhelms differences in dollars or probabilities. Not so with younger children for whom differences in dollars and probabilities matter a great deal (Davidson, 1991; Reyna, 1996; Reyna & Ellis, 1994).

Quantitative Decision Making in Childhood

In order to understand adolescent decision making, it is essential to understand its precursors in childhood. Classic decision tasks pit a sure option against a gamble of equal expected value (such as the choice between winning $100 for sure vs. a 50% change of winning $200). Variations on this basic task include reflection problems, in which all outcomes are the same in magnitude but they are reversed in valence; winning money becomes losing money. Framing problems, in turn, involve objectively identical outcomes presented or "framed" as gains versus losses. For example, imagine that you are given $200 to keep but you must make a choice between Options A and B; Option A involves losing $100 for sure and Option B involves a 50% chance of losing $200. (The actual outcomes, subtracted from the initial $200, are identical to the problem phrased in terms of winning.) If decision makers responded only to objective outcomes, they would make the same decisions for gain and "loss" framing problems (whose outcomes are actually the same), but might respond differently to gain-and-loss reflection problems (whose outcomes actually differ from one another). This is the pattern shown by young children (preschoolers and younger elementary schoolers).

In a series of studies using framing and reflection problems, Reyna and colleagues have shown that young children are responsive to the quantitative "bottom line" of decisions (e.g., Reyna, 1996; Reyna & Ellis, 1994). Given a choice between sure wins and gambles of equal expected value, children are more risk seeking than adults, but they respond sensibly to magnitude of risks and outcomes; as risk increases, choice of the gamble declines systematically. As magnitude of outcomes increases (number of prizes), choice of the gamble increases presumably to secure the larger outcomes. Sensitive techniques such as functional measurement have revealed that young children reliably discriminate subtle quantitative differences in probabilities and outcomes (e.g., Acredolo, O'Connor, Banks, & Horobin, 1989; Hommers, 1980), and their preferences follow suit.

Loss aversion (greater risk seeking for losses than gains) has been identified in children as young as 4 and 5 years old, but unlike adults, applies only to real losses not to ersatz losses that are the result of framing (see Reyna, 1996). (This loss aversion result has since been replicated in 6-year-olds using a somewhat different task.) Apparently, from an early age, the pain of a sure loss motivates taking risks to avoid it. Across several studies involving large sample sizes, many decisions, and a range of outcomes and probabilities, the picture that emerges of decision making in early childhood is one of objective trade-offs of risks and rewards. Thus, children begin adolescence with a rich repertoire of decision-analytic skills.

Because these results violate expectations of most developmental theories, it is worth taking a closer look at the methodological details. Reyna and Ellis (1994), for example, presented preschoolers, second graders, and fifth graders with a series of framing problems pitting sure options against gambles of equal expected value (e.g., win two toys for sure vs. spin and either win four toys or nothing with equal probability). Each child received a total of 18 problems (a block of 9 gains and a block of 9 losses) in counterbalanced order. The 9 problems in each gain- or loss-block involved a factorial combination of three levels of risk ($p = .5, .67, .75$) and three configurations of outcomes (the number of prizes that could be won or lost by choosing the gamble option ranged from 2 to 120).

Probabilities were conveyed by how much area of a spinner was covered by the winning color, with the losing area representing the complementary probability. Thus, young children could gauge their chances of winning by perceptual estimation of the relative magnitudes of colored areas, which they are quite adept at doing (e.g., Hoemann & Ross, 1982; Reyna & Brainerd, 1994; Schlottman, 2000). In contrast to adults, who typically choose the sure option as opposed to a gamble of equal or even superior expected value, children were generally risk seeking, preferring the gamble. This tendency diminished steadily with age, demonstrating under controlled conditions that the conventional wisdom about developmental differences in risk seeking appears to be correct.

Subsequent experiments used two spinners, to control for the attractiveness of spinners (the sure option had a single-colored spinner), and elicited similar risk seeking with developmental decline (see Reyna, 1996). Interestingly, risk seeking was obtained under laboratory conditions, suggesting that the kinds of social and contextual factors that we ordinarily consider contributory to eliciting risk seeking are not essential. For example, decisions were not made in a social setting with peers, and did not involve sex or substances that have biological correlates. The tendency to seek risks in youth seems to be a basic feature of cognitive and motivational development that might be exacerbated by other kinds of factors but does not require them.

Given that these decisions were designed so that options were equal in expected value, it was always the case that the non-zero outcome of the gamble involved more prizes than the sure option (four prizes compared to two in our aforementioned example). Thus, risk seeking for these decisions implies that the lure of more prizes overrode the presence of risk in getting those prizes. This reasoning is bolstered by the finding that risk seeking tracked the number of prizes (increasing with the amount of reward). Children also processed level of risk and would respond differently to different levels of risk, so the lure of more prizes occurred in spite of awareness of risk.

Other experiments, in which expected value was allowed to vary across options (e.g., so that the sure option had a greater expected value than the gamble), have shown that children at all three age levels were sensitive to differences across levels of risk and reward; although generally preferring risky options, they decreased risk taking as level of risk increased (e.g., see Reyna, 1996). Results also replicated across types of outcomes, for example, using stickers with a range of age-appropriate content so that "four stickers" was a suitable reward for younger and older children. (Children were instructed that they could pick their stickers from the set for one decision selected at random and played for real at the end of the experiment.)

These data support the inference that younger children's decisions were at a finer grain of analysis than older children's and adults', who were refractory to wide bands of differences in outcomes and risks, preferring sure options for gains (and risky options for losses; see discussion to come). Specifically, preschoolers showed greatest sensitivity to quantitative differences along both dimensions, second graders were less sensitive but lured by outcome quantities, and fifth graders were least sensitive (especially for problems where quantitative differences were small), exhibiting the kinds of qualitative reasoning favored by adults (e.g., Reyna & Brainerd, 1991b, 1995a; Reyna & Ellis, 1994). Ironically, adolescents and adults were more likely than young children to treat objectively identical decisions differently, violating axioms of rationality that require consistency.

Qualitative Decision Making in Adolescence

Research suggests that reasoners encode multiple representations at varied levels of precision; the tendency to rely on more precise representations in decision making, however, declines in adolescence. A conclusion that has emerged from studies of fuzzy-trace theory is that decision making becomes more gist-based with development, as adolescents gain experience in a domain. Adolescents progress from a focus on quantitative differences in outcomes (i.e., an option gives me more fun, money or some other desirable outcome, along with more risk, compared to another option involving less fun with less risk) to an all-or-none focus on qualitative differences (i.e., an option gives me something good for sure as opposed to taking a risk). Thus, children as young as age 4 and age 5 were sensitive to differences in risks and rewards, and favored rewards, whereas adolescents (and adults) were similarly aware of such differences, but apparently made decisions on the basis of categorical gist; having something for sure is better than maybe having nothing.

The conclusion that decision making becomes less sensitive to quantitative nuances with age is not confined to this line of experimentation. Davidson, for instance, has shown that seeking information on multiple countervailing dimensions declines with age, resulting in less trading off across dimensions of a decision. Similarly, Jacobs and Potenza (1991; see also Davidson, 1995) showed that qualitative heuristics supplant previously acquired quantitative strategies as children learn and apply social stereotypes.

The issue is not that children, adolescents, or adults for that matter are incapable of rationally integrating risks and rewards. There is ample evidence that the capability for both fuzzy and precise thinking is present at an early age, and this capability endures. Rather, the issue is the level of representation that is applied in a given situation in which many possible representations support decision making (see discussions of task variability in Reyna & Brainerd, 1994, 1995a; Reyna et al., 2003).

Although a menu of representations and processing styles is available at all ages, adolescents are at a cognitive crossroads. They can exhibit both the quantitative processing of earlier childhood or the categorical thinking of adulthood on the same task. Adolescents encode multiple, independent representations of the same information along a fuzzy-to-verbatim continuum, which ranges from verbatim surface details to vague gist that preserves the core meaning of experience (Reyna & Brainerd, 1995b). They operate at multiple levels in between crude categories and precise quantities, including using ordinal-level distinctions in choosing between two options that are "more versus less" risky, if the options cannot be distinguished categorically (cf. Kuhberger, 1995; Reyna & Brainerd, 1995a). For example, two options that many adolescents would perceive as more versus less risky are confessing to skipping school and risking parental punishment versus keeping quiet and risking being found out. Given the same information, adolescents can engage in qualitatively different kinds of processing, from fuzzy-gist to verbatim-level processing. In other words, they can perceive the same decision situation in multiple ways. From a developmental perspective, they are ripe for interventions that foster health-promoting, gist-based representations. Whether such gist seeking is rational is a question taken up in the last section, but it is clear that semantically derived qualitative representations of decisions are likely to engender violations of traditional axioms of rational decision making. (Intuitionism, as reflected in fuzzy-trace theory, provides a different view.) Nevertheless, we argue that gist-based decision making is generally healthy because it reduces the attractiveness of risky options.

As we alluded, the conventional understanding of why risk aversion increases is that, at least in part, adolescents are unaware of risks, or are unaware of their true magnitude—the myth of invulnerability. The implication of this view is that interventions to reduce risk taking must provide precise information about vulnerability to risks. Alternatively, it may be possible to uncover adolescents' perceptions of risks and rewards to discover the hidden incentives in seemingly self-destructive behaviors. However, a well-designed study showed that adolescents who were engaging in risky behaviors correctly saw themselves as more vulnerable than those not engaging in those risky behaviors. Although these risk perceptions can only be evaluated relative to one another because exact risk estimates were not available for these behaviors, it seems that youth had a realistic appraisal of their risk, neither as invulnerable nor as inevitably doomed. When objective risk information has been available to gauge perceptions, respondents have generally overestimated the risks associated with AIDS-related behaviors. In many cases, providing objective information would lower risk estimates.

Thus, encouraging more precise representations of risks is likely to backfire. Adolescents, who perceive that they are at some risk, may discover that the objective risk is less than they imagined. Trading off risks and rewards could then increase risky behaviors, which are objectively perceived as not quite as dangerous as once thought. As in Russian roulette, in fact, the objective odds for a single encounter favor the adolescent, cold comfort to their parents and society. In contrast, encouraging adolescents to operate on the lowest (or least precise) level of gist has advantages, such as that gist representations are more stable over time and easier to think about compared to verbatim representations (e.g., Reyna & Brainerd, 1991a, 1992). Thus, encouraging adolescents to recognize the gist of common risky situations has the potential for longer lasting effects on behavior (compared to standard fact-based interventions) because memory for gist endures over time, whereas verbatim memory for facts is forgotten.

Values and Principles

Research has also suggested that values or principles are vaguely represented in long-term memory, as simple operations on qualitative gists as opposed to precisely articulated blueprints for actions (e.g., Larrick, Morgan, & Nisbett, 1990; Reyna & Brainerd, 1991a, 1991b). For example, in framing problems for which subjects must choose between saving some lives for sure versus taking a chance and possibly saving none, we argued that decision makers respond on the basis of a general principle such as "Saving some people is better than saving none" (see, e.g., Reyna & Brainerd, 1991b, 1995a, for details).

Other findings, such as framing effects diminish if subjects are told that their choices will be executed repeatedly, rather than once, are also consistent with fuzzy-trace theory's predictions (Gigerenzer, 1994; Keren, 1991; Wedell & Bockenholt, 1990, 1994). That is, one-time gambles result in categorical outcomes: Money was won or not; pregnancy occurred or not; HIV-infection occurred or not. Repeatedly engaging in risky behavior, however, virtually eliminates categorical contrasts between occurrence versus nonoccurrence, and decision makers shift their preferences if they are told that a gamble will be executed repeatedly rather than once. This contrast between one time and repeated (cumulative) risk, then, can be used to encourage retrieval of appropriate risk-reduction heuristics (e.g., Slovic, Fischhoff, & Lichtenstein, 1982).

Misovich, J. D. Fisher, and W. A. Fisher (1996, 1997) have recently demonstrated that such simple qualitative "decision heuristics" are associated with HIV risk behaviors (see also Holtgrave, Tinsley, & Kay, 1994). For example, endorsement of such decision rules as "monogamous relationships are safe" or "known partners are safe" predicts unsafe sexual practices among heterosexual college students and adults. Although Misovich et al. (1996, 1997) focused on negative heuristics that increased risk taking, we assume that there are complementary positive heuristics that reduce risky behaviors. Generally speaking, as knowledge and experience in a domain increase, these adaptive decision heuristics are more likely to be retrieved and implemented (e.g., Reyna, 1991, 1995, 1996).

Thus, fuzzy-trace theory does not imply that preferences are entirely constructed anew in different situations (as some have claimed; cf. Payne, Bettman, & Johnson, 1992), but are, instead, based on preexisting values and principles that are not fully articulated in long-term memory (e.g., Rokeach, 1970). However, adolescents, and adults for that matter, may not recognize the applicability of their abstract values in concrete situations. In addition, multiple values and principles often apply to the same decisions; applying certain representations and principles blocks the retrieval of competing representations and principles. For example, young women may seek affiliation in relationships, but simultaneously value independence. They may fail to recognize that choosing to have sex, and risk pregnancy, addresses needs for affiliation but limits their independence.

Qualitative "gist" memory representations address compatibility between concrete situations and values or principles. By representing decision information at a gist level (simple, meaningful, qualitative representations), adolescents can learn to map decisions onto comparably vague gist-level values and decision heuristics. For example, adolescents can come to realize that having sexual relations with multiple partners, despite practicing serial monogamy, violates principles about "avoiding high risk." According to fuzzy-trace theory, the ability to recognize the relevance of general principles in specific and superficially disparate contexts is an important feature of advanced reasoning.

The ability to recognize general principles across contexts seems to be similar to the idea of decontextualization used by other theorists (e.g., Klaczynski, 2001; Stanovich & West, 2000). However, although the effect is similar, the underlying explanation is quite different. Most theorists assume that analytical, quantitative, or computational thinking is abstract and decontextualized, whereas intuitive thinking is highly concrete and context-bound. We claim the opposite—namely, that intuitive, fuzzy, gist-based thinking facilitates bridging across contexts that differ in verbatim detail (Reyna, 2004). Further, it is the concrete cues in superficially disparate contexts that reasoners must learn to link with relevant knowledge and decision principles. Making that process automatic requires a great deal of practice with concrete cues in multiple, differing contexts. Thus, gist representations of decision contexts capture meaningful content, rather than being abstract structural representations.

In summary, fuzzy-trace theory makes strong predictions about the form in which values, preferences, and emotion-laden attitudes are represented in long-term memory, namely, as fuzzy gists. The valence of these dimensions determines behavior in judgment and decision tasks. Simply put, adolescents encode dimensions of decisions as "good" or "bad," and prefer more good and less bad (e.g., Brainerd & Reyna, 1990; Reyna & Brainerd, 1991a, 1991b, 1992, 1995a). Moral values and preferences constitute decision principles, and these vaguely represented principles interact with task requirements, problem representations, retrieval of principles in context, and competing principles (e.g., Reyna & Brainerd, 1991a, 1992).

Dual Processing: Emotion and the Brain

An exciting development in recent research is the integration of concepts of *values* and *emotion* with those of *cognitive representation* and *processing* (e.g., Byrnes, 1998; Davidson, 1995; Isen, 1993; Klaczynski & Narasimham, 1998; Levin, Schneider, & Gaeth, 1998). For example, Klaczynski and Fauth (1997) argued that emotion and cognition interact in self-serving bias. When evidence contradicts cherished beliefs about the self, subjects engage in nonpreferred, verbatim-level quantitative reasoning. When evidence supports their beliefs, however, the same adolescents rely on qualitative gist. These findings suggest that challenging adolescents' assumptions about themselves could be used as part of risk-reduction interventions to jar processing into an analytical, quantitative mode. Challenging adolescents' assumptions about themselves may encourage analytical thinking for a time, but intuitive gist-based thinking is likely to reassert itself as the dominant mode of decision processing.

Another recent development in research is the growing work on developmental cognitive neuroscience. Data from experiments using functional magnetic resonance imaging (fMRI) and other techniques that dynamically capture information processing cohere with many of the concepts that we have discussed. The gist–verbatim distinction of fuzzy-trace theory has been extensively studied in a variety of populations, ranging from amnesics to the aged (Israel & Schacter, 1997; Koutstaal & Schacter, 1997; Koutstaal, Schacter, Galluccio, & Stofer, 1999; Schacter et al., 1996; Schacter, Israel, & Racine, 1999; Schacter, Kagan, & Leichtman, 1995; Schacter, Verfaellie, & Anes, 1997; Schacter, Verfaellie, & Pradere, 1996; Tun, Wingfield, Rosen, & Blanchard, 1998). Developmental data also implicate the increasing ability in childhood to resist interference in cognitive tasks (e.g., Dempster, 1992). Interference from competing representations and decision principles are a well-documented source of errors in judgment and decision-making tasks, and these effects have been found to decline with age and experience (see Table 3.2 for a summary of error types).

TABLE 3.2
Degrees of Rationality[a] in Judgment and Decision Making

1. Knowledge: HPV (human papilloma virus, which causes genital warts and cervical cancer) prevalence is high among sexually active young people.
2. Accurate representation of information: Most cases of cervical cancer are linked to strains of HPV. (This does not mean that most women with these strains of HPV infection get cervical cancer.)
3. Recognizing the gist of risky situations: A clean-cut, but highly sexually active, college student is a high-risk partner. Being alone with a boy and drinking means being at risk.
4. Reliance on appropriate gist representations that promote health: Choice boils down to having a relationship without risking AIDS or having a relationship and risking AIDS.
5. Retrieval of relevant values/principles in the situation: Having sex to be loved violates self-respect.
6. Resisting social pressures that interfere with acting on principles: Movies that depict adolescents having sex are not about *me*.
7. Implementing principles reliably: Avoiding risk on a date, among peers at an unsupervised party, and other settings.

[a]"Degrees of rationality" in fuzzy-trace theory refers to the idea that rationality is not an all-or-none attribute that people have or lack, but that a behavior can be more or less rational depending on the underlying processing that produced it (Reyna & Brainerd, 1995a; see Reyna et al., 2003, for a detailed description of different processing errors and what they indicate about rationality). This idea stands in contrast to traditional claims that variability in reasoning across tasks indicates that there is something wrong with people and to newer claims that variability across tasks indicates that there is something wrong with tasks (at least the ones that make people look bad). Instead, fuzzy-trace theory explains how reasoning competence actually shifts from context to context, depending on people's knowledge and how that knowledge is represented, retrieved, and implemented given shifting contextual cues (Reyna & Adam, 2003).

Preliminary evidence supports the dual-processing assumptions of fuzzy-trace theory, in particular, that multiple modes of processing exist within the same individual and can be brought to bear on the same task. For example, Bowden and Beeman (1998) found hemispheric differences in coarse, gist processing versus narrow, verbatim processing. Subjects are asked to solve remote association problems in which solution words are sought that complete a phrase or compound noun for three stimulus words (e.g., NEWS-WALL-FLY; the solution word is PAPER). Problems are presented to the left or right visual field to assess processing in the contralateral hemisphere.

When problems are solved, priming (reduced naming and recognition time for words that are problem solutions) occurs in both hemispheres, but when the problem remains unsolved, priming nevertheless occurs for solution words in the right hemisphere. In a sense, the brain knows the solution, but the mind does not; the correct solution is activated in the right hemisphere, but it remains unconscious and unavailable to the reasoner. Such right-hemisphere processing corresponds to the unconscious intuitive processing that has been linked to false recognition of semantically related words in memory experiments (see Brainerd, Stein, & Reyna, 1998; Reyna, 2000; Reyna, Holliday, & Marche, 2002). That is, false recognition of broadly related semantic associates is unconscious and relies on gist memories, whereas immediate memory for presented words is verbatim and conscious.

Similar results have been found for probability judgment with split-brain patients, namely, that the right hemisphere solves such problems using optimal strategies, whereas the left hemisphere relies on suboptimal strategies (i.e., frequency matching; see Wolford, Miller, & Gazzaniga, 2000). In fact, these probability judgment strategies have been related to survival in animals (e.g., identifying foraging strategies that are optimal, and so promote survival), and form the core competence that adolescents can draw on to make judgments about risk and uncertainty. An analogous example that has survival value for adolescents is the following: Assume that there is a 65% probability that young men will abandon their pregnant girlfriends. The optimal strategy based solely on probabilities is to predict, for any given young man, that he will abandon his girlfriend. Frequency matching, attempting to predict the 35% who are reliable, is a suboptimal strategy, and will always produce more prediction errors than the optimal strategy (assuming that diagnosticity is anything less than perfect).

The upshot of these examples about dual processing in the brain is not that they identify hemispheric asymmetries, which would not be apparent in everyday behavior in any case because the corpus callosum ordinarily connects the hemispheres. The implication is also not that the hemispheres are necessarily specialized for gist versus verbatim processing; subsequent evidence may show that both types of processing occur in both hemispheres. The relevance of these findings to our concerns about judgment and decision making is that they point up the availability of multiple modes of processing within the same individual, some of which are more adaptive than others. The locus of effective interventions, then, is not necessarily teaching new knowledge and skills, but rather, accessing and implementing health-promoting intuitions that lie dormant.

SEXUAL RISK TAKING IN ADOLESCENCE

Although the literature on risk-reduction interventions generally does not draw on research in cognitive development or judgment and decision making, effective interventions have been identified. Most interventions reflect features common to several prominent social-science theories (e.g., health-belief models, theory of reasoned action) that are supported by a number of lines of research looking at health-related behaviors, including adolescent sexual behaviors (Fishbein & Ajzen, 1975; Fishbein et al., 1991). We now review that literature with respect to sexual risk taking in adolescence in order to identify profitable points of contact. In particular, we identify several shortcomings of the best interventions that could be addressed using recent research that we have reviewed. In the last section, we discuss the clash between the prescriptive decision-analytic framework of most risk-reduction interventions and descriptive data suggesting that actual decision making is intuitive rather than analytic. The surprising implication of this juxtaposition is that advanced reasoning can be achieved using intuitive processes.

Sexually transmitted diseases (STDs) are a significant public health problem, infecting over 3 million adolescents annually (Institute of Medicine, 1997). In spite of increased reports of condom use, rates of infection among adolescents continue to rise (Kann et al., 1998). As a result, AIDS has become the seventh leading cause of death among youth between the ages of 15 and 24 (Hoyert, Kochanek, & Murphy, 1999). About one out of four AIDS cases are reported among adults age 20 to 29 years, who were probably infected as teenagers. Risky sexual behaviors remain the primary mechanism for contracting HIV/AIDS, as well as non-HIV infection (e.g., May & Anderson, 1987; Reiss & Leik, 1989).

Although some research has addressed the effectiveness of abstinence education, reducing risk through such measures as condom use has been the primary prevention methodology. Interventions have been directed at increasing knowledge of AIDS and other STDs, skills training (including refusal skills and resistance to social pressure), and inculcation of beliefs and attitudes that promote healthy behavior (e.g., self-efficacy). Multicomponent approaches that incorporate many of these techniques simultaneously have produced the largest positive effects (e.g., Byrnes, 1998).

Several interventions to reduce risky sexual behavior in adolescents have been identified as effective with respect to at least some behavioral outcome measures (e.g., Eisen, Zellman, & McAlister, 1990; J. B. Jemmott & Fong, 1998; J. B. Jemmott, L. S. Jemmott, & Fong, 1992; Kirby, Barth, Leland, & Fetro, 1991; Howard & McCabe, 1990; Hubbard, Giese, & Rainey, 1998; Main et al., 1994; Rotheram-Borus, Koopman, Haignere, & Davies, 1991; St. Lawrence et al., 1995; Stanton, Li, Galbraith, Feigelman, & Kaljee, 1996; Stanton, Li, Ricardo, Galbraith, Feigelman, & Kaljee, 1996; Walter & Vaughan, 1993). For example, Jemmott et al. (1992) randomly assigned 157 African American male adolescents to either an AIDS risk-reduction intervention aimed at increasing AIDS knowledge and reducing risky sexual behaviors or to a control intervention on career opportunities. The career-opportunities condition was designed to control for Hawthorne effects, that is, to reduce the likelihood that differences favoring the AIDS intervention could be attributed to nonspecific features such as group interaction and special attention. Follow-up data gathered at 3 months indicated that adolescents in the AIDS-intervention condition engaged in intercourse less frequently and with fewer partners, and were more likely to use condoms.

Stanton, Li, Ricardo, Galbraith, et al. (1996) investigated whether short-term increases in self-reported intentions and behaviors regarding condom use, such as those obtained by Jemmott et al. (1992) were sustained over longer intervals. They also implemented a theory-based, randomized control trial involving African American adolescents ($N = 383$). Self-reported condom use intentions and behaviors were significantly higher among intervention than control youths at 6 months. However, by 12 months, condom use rates and intentions were no longer significantly higher among intervention youths. These authors concluded that strong short-term improvements in behaviors and intentions followed by relapse over longer periods "argue for a strengthened program and research focus on sustainability" (p. 363).

Several interventions have emphasized behavior skills training, arguing that to achieve substantial and sustainable changes in risky behavior, programs need to incorporate informational needs, motivational influences, and behavior (W. A. Fisher & J. D. Fisher, 1992). Main et al. (1994), for example, used a quasi-experimental design, assigning 17 schools to either a skills-based HIV risk-reduction program or to comparison conditions ("their usual HIV programs," p. 411) involving minimal HIV education, yielding 979 students with baseline and 6-month follow-up data. Among students who were sexually active at follow-up, intervention students reported fewer sexual partners, greater frequency of using condoms, and greater perceived vulnerability to HIV infection. However, at 6 months, intervention and comparison students did not differ in terms of the onset or the frequency of intercourse.

Similarly, St. Lawrence et al. (1995) compared education plus behavior skills training to an education-only control condition. Participants in both groups completed self-reported assessments of knowledge, attitudes, and behaviors and engaged in simulated role-playing exercises involving risky interactions. Of 246 African American adolescents assigned to an intervention, 225 completed baseline, 2-, 6-, and 12-month assessments. Relevant to sustainability, risk reduction was maintained at the 12-month follow-up for skills-trained adolescents relative to their education-only peers. Among initially abstinent youth, fewer had initiated intercourse in the skills group at the 12-month follow-up (11.5% compared to 31% in the education-only group) and fewer had engaged in unprotected vaginal intercourse. Condom use increased but then gradually decreased among males in the skills-training group, whereas intervention-related decreases were sustained in female adolescents after 12 months.

Kirby et al. (1991) also demonstrated an impact on the initiation of sexual activity over a sustained period. Using a quasi-experimental design, classes at 13 California high schools were assigned to either a treatment or control group, and assessed at baseline (preexposure to the curriculum), immediately after exposure, and at 6 months and 18 months. The treatment group received "Reducing the Risk: Building the Skills to Prevent Pregnancy, STD, and HIV," a sexuality curriculum (based on social learning, social inoculation, and cognitive–behavioral theory) aimed at increasing information, motivation, and skills to reduce pregnancy, STDs, and HIV risk behaviors (Barth, 1996). The control group received sexuality education as part of their standard health curriculum. Many effects of the curriculum extended to both non-Hispanic Whites and Hispanics. Among all 758 students, participation in the treatment group was associated with greater knowledge and parent–child communication. As in the St. Lawrence et al. (1995) study, among initially abstinent youth, the curriculum was associated with a reduction in the rates of initiation of sexual intercourse 18 months later. Also, females and lower risk youth in the treatment group were less likely to have unprotected sexual intercourse at 18 months than were their counterparts in the control group.

Finally, Hubbard et al. (1998) investigated whether the effects of "Reducing the Risk" could be duplicated in a southern rural state quite different from California. They found that, among students who were initially abstinent, the curriculum reduced the chance of initiating intercourse after 18 months. Among students who became sexually active during the study, condom use and the use of effective contraceptives increased for treatment students relative to controls. Parent–child communication was also enhanced for two out of four topics. These results generally corroborated those of Kirby et al. (1991) in a different population, reinforcing the conclusion that a theory-based curriculum that provides information and skill building is more effective at reducing risky sexual behaviors among adolescents than standard health education or abstinence-only curricula.

Because the "Reducing the Risk" curriculum has demonstrated effectiveness for White and Hispanic adolescents, we discuss its theoretical underpinnings in greater detail (Hubbard et al., 1998; Kirby et al., 1991). Many of the other successful HIV prevention curricula for adolescents have been aimed at African Americans, although major components of these curricula are also present in "Reducing the Risk." "Reducing the Risk" is based on three interrelated theoretical approaches: social learning theory, social inoculation theory, and cognitive behavior theory. As applied to STD prevention, social-learning theory posits that the likelihood of an action such as condom use is determined by (a) an understanding of what must be done to avoid risk, (b) a youth's belief that he or she is able to perform the action, (c) a belief that the action will prevent STDs, and (d) the anticipated benefit of performing the action. These ideas are learned through observation (role playing) and experience (practicing the skills required for the behavior). *Social inoculation* refers to the ability to recognize social pressure, and becoming motivated and capable of resisting it. Frequent practice in developing strategies to resist social pressure to engage in risky behaviors is offered in the "Reducing the Risk" program. This program explicitly emphasizes avoidance of unprotected intercourse, either by not having sex or by using condoms (to reduce STD risk) or other contraception (to reduce pregnancy risk). The curriculum also requires parent–child discussion about such issues as abstinence and birth control. Topics are covered with respect to both heterosexual and gay/lesbian sexuality and behavior. Last, cognitive-behavior theory has many similarities to social influence theory (and to the other two theories). It requires personalizing information about sexuality and risk, training in decision-making and communication skills, and practice applying these skills.

Many studies examine ethnic differences by simple categorization of participants based on a single question about ethnic identification. By conceptualizing and using ethnicity as a discrete categorical variable, one is employing what Bronfenbrenner (1986) labeled the *social address* of the subject. Like street addresses, social addresses provide specific information, that is, they tell us that differences exist between groups of people and direct our attention to these differences. Research has clearly shown that Hispanics are at increased risk for STDs and adolescent pregnancy. Nationally, during the 1990s, AIDS cases shifted toward a growing proportion of Hispanics, as well as African Americans and women (Centers for Disease Control and Prevention, 1999). In Arizona, for example, Hispanics are estimated to be 4.5 times more likely to have chlamydia infection than non-Hispanic Whites, and Hispanic adolescents are 2.7 times as likely to become pregnant (Mrela & Jimenez, 1997). Individuals within ethnic groups are not homogeneous in their beliefs, values, experiences, or behaviors (P. J. Pelto & G. H. Pelto, 1978; Phinney, 1996; Whiting, 1976), and it is these cultural variables that are likely to have explanatory power. By examining the relationship between ethnicity and cognitive representations of risk, and with the values, beliefs, and attitudes that adolescents have about sexual behavior, we can begin to "unpack" these ethnic differences and to target interventions more appropriately (LaVeist, 1994; Walsh, Smith, Morales, & Sechrest, 2000).

In summary, programs found to be effective in reducing self-reported HIV risk behaviors tend to be based on theories with established effectiveness in other health domains, to be multicomponent approaches addressing both risk avoidance (by delaying initiation of intercourse) and risk reduction, and to have been subject to rigorous evaluation. Although HIV risk-prevention programs for adolescents have demonstrated effectiveness using behavioral outcomes, the sustainability of those effects is uncertain. A few studies have documented long-term outcomes (12 to 18 months), but the effects of interventions were not sustained for all outcome measures and for all subgroups at the longer intervals. Replication of interventions across geographical and cultural subgroups is rare, but at least one curriculum, "Reducing the Risk," has been successfully implemented in two populations.

Relatively few studies of HIV risk prevention have focused on Hispanics, and still fewer have documented effective interventions among Hispanics (e.g., Kirby et al., 1991; Schinke, Gordon, & Weston, 1990), a group at heightened risk for HIV infection. Literature reviews in this area cite the need for studies that build on successful and theoretically motivated interventions, and that involve random assignment, large sample sizes, long-term follow-up, and behavioral measures. Thus, as concluded in a recent review of the literature, HIV-prevention programs "have not come close to eliminating unprotected sex and have often lacked a long-term impact" (Kirby, 1999, p. 2; see also Kirby, 1997). Therefore, it is crucial to identify ways to increase the effectiveness and durability of HIV-prevention programs in adolescents for whom risk-related behaviors lead to an array of harmful outcomes.

RATIONALITY AND PRESCRIPTION

Building on prior research on effective programs, it is apparent that new knowledge is needed in at least three areas: (a) psychological processes underlying risky decision making in adolescents; (b) differences among subgroups of adolescents (e.g., Hispanics and non-Hispanics; low- and high-risk adolescents) in decision making; and (c) comparisons of results to those of alternative abstinence-only programs. The latter contrast incorporates the distinction between risk reduction and elimination. Notably, some programs achieved greater success in reduction of initiation of intercourse, as opposed to reduction of risky behaviors. Among adults, eliminating risk is ordinarily strongly preferred to merely reducing risk; categorical insurance that eliminates risk for certain diseases is preferred to so-called probabilistic insurance that provides uncertain protection for a greater range of diseases. Similar cognitive processes may underlie the differential effectiveness of some programs in delaying initiation of intercourse, but such conclusions await evidence from detailed process analyses of adolescent decision making.

With respect to the first area of knowledge, recent advances in cognitive developmental research might be used to enhance HIV risk-reduction programs for adolescents. The thrust of such an enhanced intervention would be to instill new ways of "framing" risky sexual decisions for adolescents, which research indicates will increase the durability and effectiveness of interventions (e.g., Reyna, 1996; Reyna & Brainerd, 1995a; Reyna & Ellis, 1994). The second area of knowledge about psychological differences among subgroups of adolescents, especially Hispanics versus non-Hispanics and those who do and do not engage in risky sexual behaviors, requires testing hypotheses about ethnic differences in perception of risks, desirability of outcomes, decision heuristics, and in the meaning of sexual activity, as well as in behavioral responses to risk-reduction interventions (Holtgrave et al., 1994; Misovich et al., 1997; Schulenberg, Maggs, & Hurrelmann, 1997). Regarding the third area, abstinence-only programs should be compared to multi-component interventions using such outcomes as initiation of intercourse, use of condoms, number of partners, and treatment for STDs (again, controlling for baseline characteristics).

Specifically, our analysis based on fuzzy-trace theory suggests that processing analyses should include categorization according to theoretically specified patterns, for example, whether decisions are represented as quantitative tradeoffs or qualitative gist and whether key decision heuristics are endorsed (e.g., appeal to the "known partners are safe" heuristic to explain risky choices). According to fuzzy-trace theory, gist representations of the same sexual scenarios are expected to differ across gender, ethnicity, and developmental level because the gist is the meaning or interpretation of events. A quantitative tradeoff would involve representing a decision situation as a choice between having a little fun with very low risk or a lot more fun with more risk (see Table 3.1). (Comparing the amount of fun and amount of risk across the options in order to make a decision would reflect a quantitative representation of the scenario.) A qualitative gist representation would involve representing this situation as a choice between having some fun without taking a risk versus taking a risk (an all-or-none contrast with respect to risk). Based on prior research, we hypothesize that low-risk adolescents will be more likely to have qualitative gist representations of sexual scenarios, compared to high-risk adolescents. Also, Hispanic and non-Hispanic youth are expected to exhibit systematic differences in perceived options, social norms, and (culturally derived) values, including differences in perception of abstinence, pregnancy, and in importance of other family members' values.

Fuzzy-trace theory predicts specific distortions in risk perception, which should be reflected in interpretations of public health messages, such as Centers for Disease Control and Prevention (CDC) and Federal Drug Administration (FDA) statements about condoms' effectiveness in reducing sexually transmitted disease. Because mental representations of risk are qualitative (gist-based), basing risk estimates on the gist of categories (e.g., the category "STDs") is predicted to produce risk underestimation associated with atypical category members (e.g., human papillomavirus [HPV]; Holmes et al., 1999; Orr, Brizendine, Fortenberry, & Katz, 1999). Therefore, STD risk should be underestimated, but condoms' effectiveness (relative to published estimates) should be overestimated, for psychologically atypical but prevalent diseases (such as HPV). Although CDC and FDA statements concerning risk reduction apply primarily to fluid-borne illness, risk estimates are predicted to reflect inappropriate generalization to skin-to-skin transmission, as in HPV. Although knowledge deficits contribute to such risk-estimation biases, biases are also caused by other factors that we have discussed, such as failures to apply known decision heuristics and psychological processing errors. Hence, instructional interventions that are designed to improve risk perception among teenagers must incorporate more than knowledge dissemination. They should also provide support for effective retrieval of relevant values and principles and accurate processing of risk information in realistic situations.

Fuzzy-trace theory also predicts specific cognitive illusions in adolescents' judgments of HIV risk behaviors that involve cumulative or combined probabilities (e.g., Byrnes, 1998; Reyna, 1991; Reyna & Brainerd, 1995a; Reyna & Ellis, 1994). These illusions include (a) systematic underestimation of cumulative risk across repeated behaviors (as opposed to single instances of risk taking, such as unprotected intercourse); (b) underestimation of risk of sex with someone who has had multiple partners (as opposed to having multiple partners oneself); and (c) underestimation of risk due to a failure to "unpack" multiple sources of risk (i.e., risk estimation of STDs as a generic category as opposed to estimation of risks for each STD separately followed by combining of estimates). Reversing these cognitive illusions by changing the elicitation procedure (e.g., manipulating phrasing of risk-estimation questions) in ways that are known to produce higher estimates of risk would be another objective of an enhanced intervention.

One way to effect this enhanced intervention would be to stress simple narratives (i.e., parables) that illustrate major risks and consequences, nonquantitative representations of cumulative risk, and a "framing" of decision options that mimics the representations of lower risk (but culturally similar) adolescents (including lower perceived cohort norms for sexual activity). Thus, adolescents would be taught to recognize common scripts that signal risk despite superficial differences in how situations appear. Rather than construing sexual decisions as gambles involving tradeoffs between risks and rewards, the curriculum would emphasize clear, categorical information about large, highly undesirable risks, such as the high cumulative probability of contracting a STD given certain risk-related behaviors. By applying recent advances in cognitive developmental research to the design of intervention programs that promote risk reduction, it should be possible to develop new ways of "framing" risky sexual decisions for adolescents.

Traditional theories of cognitive development predict that decision makers progress from intuitive (gist-based) to computational (verbatim) thinking, whereas fuzzy-trace theory makes the opposite prediction. That is, decision making becomes less compensatory and more intuitive and categorical as development proceeds. These predictions have been confirmed in a series of experiments with children, adolescents, and adults (e.g., Davidson, 1991; Reyna, 1996; Reyna & Ellis, 1994). However, inconsistencies and biases in decision making, such as framing effects, also emerge with development, and become greater with age. Thus, in a narrow sense, mature thinking is irrational because it does not necessarily reflect quantitative, compensatory trade-offs between risks and rewards. Note that fuzzy-trace theory differs from developmental theories that argue that quantitative trading off is the key to adaptive decision making (e.g., Byrnes, chap. 1, this volume; although self-regulation remains a powerful explanatory concept). Not only are qualitative, gist representations of decisions used more by more advanced decision makers (compared to detailed quantitative representations), but for important decisions, often the key to adaptive decision making is rejecting the notion of trading off (Reyna, 2004). Mature adults reject calculations about the number of bullets in Russian roulette (or the number of instances of intravenous drug use, unprotected sex, and so on) that would make such activities safe enough. We have argued that it is the latter sort of mature thinking that should be emphasized to enhance educational interventions with adolescents.

Most adults are risk-averse, and they prefer a sure gain to a gamble of equal expected value. So long as risk aversion is consistent, this behavior is ordinarily not considered irrational. Even if the amount to win is increased, making the gamble superior in expected value, adults often reject the wager. Similarly, most decision makers would not play Russian roulette regardless of the amount of the potential winnings (and despite favorable odds, five out of six, of survival). In contrast, school-age children prefer to gamble with gains or losses, although they are sensitive to the magnitudes of risks and outcomes. Risk aversion—despite objectively favorable odds—steadily increases through adolescence (Reyna, 1996; Reyna & Ellis, 1994).

Reyna et al. (2003) discuss how such developmental trends can be used as one source of evidence as to which behaviors are globally adaptive. However, they argue that ascribing rationality to specific behaviors requires a process analysis. Such an analysis suggests that the gist-based processing that produces framing and other effects is globally adaptive. Moreover, gist-based processing is essential to achieve the most fundamental criterion of rationality—consistency across superficially disparate but ultimately similar decisions. Nevertheless, framing effects, the conjunction fallacy, and similar biases violate coherence. Unlike recent ecological and naturalistic reasoning approaches, we do not argue that what is natural is necessarily good or rational. The conjunction fallacy, for example, is not "smart." Perfect rationality satisfies criteria of both internal coherence (e.g., with relevant rules of logic and probability) and external correspondence with reality. The denouement of this analysis is a categorization of different loci of processing errors, all of which fall short of perfect rationality, but some of which are more advanced than others (see Table 3.2). Therefore, the goal of risk-reduction interventions should be to avoid predictable processing errors, so that judgment and decision making are as nearly coherent and consistent with objective reality as possible (e.g., consistent with the objective risk for various STDs, or with the effectiveness of various forms of birth control). Our review of the literature in sexual risk taking indicates that research should focus on encouraging memory for risks in a form that will endure and be more likely to be applied in actual decision making. This enhanced intervention should produce effects that are significant for a broader range of outcome measures and that are more long-lasting.

OVERVIEW

Research has demonstrated that reasoning tends to operate on the lowest (or least precise) level of gist that can be used to accomplish a task, such as making a choice (Reyna & Brainerd, 1995a; Reyna et al., 2003). This fuzzy-processing preference has advantages for reasoning, such as that gist representations are more stable over time and easier to think about compared to verbatim representations (e.g., Reyna & Brainerd, 1991a, 1992). Indeed, after several months, because adolescents ultimately recall the gist of educational interventions (which is filtered through their understanding), the residue of interventions may be dramatically different from what was initially communicated (Brainerd, Reyna, & Mojardin, 1999; Brainerd et al., 1998; Reyna & Brainerd, 1995a; Reyna & Titcomb, 1997). Thus, encouraging adolescents to recognize the gist of common risky situations has the potential for longer lasting effects on behavior (compared to standard, fact-based interventions) because memory for gist endures over time, but verbatim memory for facts is forgotten.

Whereas Piaget characterized *reasoning* as the application of logical rules, and information-processing theorists characterized it as computation, we have identified reasoning with the fuzzy processes of intuition. Thus, although fuzzy-trace theory shares important features with other developmental theories, it differs in assuming that advanced reasoning is intuitive and parallel (cf. Sloman, 1996). The alternative to computational models is not necessarily affective models, as some have argued (e.g., Loewenstein, Weber, Hsee, & Welch, 2001). Although we do not deny that better theories of affect are needed, there are cognitive models such as fuzzy-trace theory that are not computational. Much of the evidence and arguments adduced against computational models supports the claim that reasoning is naturally intuitive and gist-based. In general, gist representations allow adolescents to treat superficially different problems similarly, supporting the consistency criterion of rationality (Tversky & Kahneman, 1986). Thus, adolescents can learn to recognize common scripts that signal risk despite superficial differences in how situations appear.

According to fuzzy-trace theory, processing more information more precisely, even if it were possible, is not the key to rationality. In practice, adolescents process verbatim details in parallel with gist, and ultimately rely on imprecise gist in making judgments or decisions. Our conception of rationality is the degree to which reasoning fits an ideal whose components are (a) knowledge, (b) accurate representation of information, (c) recognizing the gist of risky situations, (d) reliance on appropriate gist representations that promote health, (e) retrieval of relevant values/principles in the situation, (f) resisting social pressures that interfere with acting on principles, and (g) implementing those principles reliably. Paradoxically, developmental evidence suggests that quantitatively trading off risks and rewards, as in expected-utility and other decision-analytic approaches, is not globally adaptive. Instead, the most powerful enhancement of risk-reduction interventions is not necessarily teaching new knowledge and skills, but rather, accessing and implementing health-promoting intuitions.

REFERENCES

Acredolo, C., O'Connor, J., Banks, L., & Horobin, K. (1989). Children's ability to make probability estimates: Skills revealed through application of Anderson's functional measurement methodology. *Child Development, 60,* 933–945.

Ajzen, I., & Fishbein, M. (1980). *Understanding attitudes and predicting social behavior.* Englewood Cliffs, NJ: Prentice-Hall.

Bandura, A. (1982). Self-efficacy mechanism in human agency. *American Psychologist, 37,* 122–147.

Bandura, A. (1986). *Social foundations of thought and action: A social cognitive theory.* Englewood Cliffs, NJ: Prentice-Hall.

Bandura, A. (1994). Social cognitive theory and exercise of control over HIV infection. In R. DiClemente & J. Peterson (Eds.), *Preventing AIDS: Theories and methods of behavioral interventions* (pp. 25–60). New York: Plenum.

Baron, J., & Brown, R. V. (1991). *Teaching decision making to adolescents.* Hillsdale, NJ: Lawrence Erlbaum Associates.

Barth, R. P. (1996). *Reducing the risk: Building skills to prevent pregnancy, STDs, and HIV.* Santa Cruz, CA: ETR Associates.

Beyth-Marom, R., & Fischhoff, B. (1997). Adolescents' decisions about risks: A cognitive perspective. In J. Schulenberg, J. L. Maggs, & K. Hurrelmann (Eds.), *Health risks and developmental transitions during adolescence* (pp. 110–135). New York: Cambridge University Press.

Beyth-Marom, R., Fischhoff, B., Quadrel, M. J., & Furby, L. (1991). Teaching decision making to adolescents: A critical review. In J. Baron & R. V. Brown (Eds.), *Teaching decision making to adolescents* (pp. 19–59). Hillsdale, NJ: Lawrence Erlbaum Associates.

Bowden, E. M., & Beeman, M. J. (1998). Getting the right idea: Semantic activation in the right hemisphere may help solve insight problems. *Psychological Science, 9*, 435–440.

Brainerd, C. J., & Reyna, V. F. (1990). Gist is the grist: Fuzzy-trace theory and the new intuitionism. *Developmental Review, 10*, 3–47.

Brainerd, C. J., & Reyna, V. F. (1993). Memory independence and memory interference in cognitive development. *Psychological Review, 100*(1), 42–67.

Brainerd, C. J., Reyna, V. F., & Mojardin, A. H. (1999). Conjoint recognition. *Psychological Review, 106*(1), 160–179.

Brainerd, C. J., Stein, L. M., & Reyna, V. F. (1998). On the development of conscious and unconscious memory. *Developmental Psychology, 34*(2), 342–357.

Bronfenbrenner, U. (1986). Ecology of the family as a context for human development: Research perspectives. *Developmental Psychology, 22*, 723–742.

Byrnes, J. P. (1998). *The nature and development of decision making.* Mahwah, NJ: Lawrence Erlbaum Associates.

Centers for Disease Control and Prevention. (1999). *HIV/AIDS surveillance report,* 11(No. 2), 1–44.

Davidson, D. (1991). Developmental differences in children's search of pre-decisional information. *Journal of Experimental Child Psychology, 52*, 239–255.

Davidson, D. (1995). The representativeness heuristic and the conjunction fallacy effect in children's decision making. *Merrill-Palmer Quarterly, 41*, 328–346.

Dempster, F. (1992). The rise and fall of the inhibitory mechanism: Toward a unified theory of cognitive development and aging. *Developmental Review, 12*, 45–75.

Eisen, M., Zellman, G. L., & McAlister, A. L. (1990). Evaluating the impact of a theory-based sexuality and contraceptive education program. *Family Planning Perspectives, 22*, 261–271.

Fischhoff, B., & Quadrel, M. (1991). Adolescent alcohol decisions. *Alcohol Health & Research World, 15*, 43–51.

Fishbein, M., & Ajzen, I. (1975). *Belief, attitude, intention and behavior.* Boston, MA: Addison-Wesley.

Fishbein, M., Bandura, A., Triandis, H. C., Kanfer, F. H., Becker, M. H., & Middlestadt, S. E. (1991). *Factors influencing behavior and behavior change.* Final report to the Theorist's Workshop, National Institutes of Health, Washington, DC.

Fisher, W. A., & Fisher, J. D. (1992). Changing AIDS risk behavior. *Psychological Bulletin, 111*, 455–474.

Furby, L., & Beyth-Marom, R. (1992). Risk taking in adolescence: A decision-making perspective. *Developmental Review, 12*(1), 1–44.

Gigerenzer, G. (1994). Why the distinction between single-event probabilities and frequencies is important for psychology (and vice versa). In G. Wright & P. Ayton (Eds.), *Subjective probability* (pp. 129–161). New York: Wiley.

Hampson, S. E., Severson, H. H., Burns, W. J., Slovic, P., & Fisher, J. K. (2001). Risk perception, personality factors, and alcohol use among adolescents. *Personality and Individual Differences, 30*, 167–181.

Hoemann, H. W., & Ross, B. M. (1982). Children's understanding of probability concepts. *Child Development, 42*, 221–236.

Holmes, K., Sparling, P. F., Mardh, P. A., Lemon, S., Stamm, W., Piot, P., & Wasserheit, J. (1999). *Sexually transmitted diseases* (3rd ed.). New York: McGraw-Hill.

Holtgrave, D. R., Tinsley, B. J., & Kay, L. S. (1994). Heuristics, biases and environmental health risk analysis. In L. Heath, R. S. Tindale, & J. Edwards (Eds.), *Applications of heuristics and biases to social issues* (pp. 259–285). New York: Plenum.

Hommers, W. (1980). Information processing in children's choices among bets. In F. Wilkening, J. Becker, & T. Trabasso (Eds.), *Information integration by children* (pp. 99–112). Hillsdale, NJ: Lawrence Erlbaum Associates.

Howard, M., & McCabe, J. B. (1990). Helping teenagers postpone sexual involvement. *Family Planning Perspectives, 22*(1), 21–26.

Hoyert, D. L., Kochanek, K. D., & Murphy, S. L. (1999). Deaths: Final data for 1997. *National Center for Vital Statistics Reports, 47*(19), 1–104.

Hubbard, B. M., Giese, M. L., & Rainey, J. (1998). A replication study of Reducing the Risk, a theory-based sexuality curriculum for adolescents. *Journal of School Health, 68*(6), 243–247.

Institute of Medicine. (1997). *The hidden epidemic: Confronting sexually transmitted diseases.* Washington, DC: National Academy Press.

Isen, A. M. (1993). Positive affect and decision making. In M. Lewis & J. Haviland (Eds.), *Handbook of emotion* (pp. 261–277). New York: Guilford.

Israel, L., & Schacter, D. L. (1997). Pictorial encoding reduces false recognition of semantic associates. *Psychonomic Bulletin and Review, 4*, 577–581.

Jacobs, J. E., & Potenza, M. (1991). The use of judgment heuristics to make social and object decisions: A developmental perspective. *Child Development, 62*, 166–178.

Jemmott, J. B., & Fong, G. T. (1998). Abstinence and safer sex HIV risk-reduction interventions for African-American adolescents. *Journal of the American Medical Association, 279*(19), 1529–1536.

Jemmott, J. B., Jemmott, L. S., & Fong, G. T. (1992). Reductions in HIV risk-associated sexual behaviors among Black male adolescents: Effects of an AIDS prevention intervention. *American Journal of Public Health, 82*(3), 372–377.

Kann, L., Kinchen, S. A., Williams, B. I., Ross, J. G., Lowry, R., Hill, C. V., Grunbaum, J. A., Blumson, P. S., Collins, J. L., & Kolbe, L. J. (1998). Youth risk behavior surveillance— United States, 1997. *MMWR CDC Surveillance Summaries, 47*(3), 1–89.

Keren, G. (1991). Additional tests of utility theory under unique and repeated conditions. *Journal of Behavioral Decision Making, 4*, 297–304.

Kirby, D. (1997). *No easy answers: Research findings on programs to reduce teen pregnancy.* Washington, DC: The National Campaign to Prevent Teen Pregnancy.

Kirby, D. (1999). *Looking for reasons why.* Washington, DC: The National Campaign to Prevent Teen Pregnancy.

Kirby, D., Barth, R. P., Leland, N., & Fetro, J. V. (1991). Reducing the risk: Impact of a new curriculum on sexual risk-taking. *Family Planning Perspectives, 23*(6), 253–263.

Klaczynski, P. (2001). Analytic and heuristic processing influences on adolescent reasoning and decision-making. *Child Development, 72*, 844–861.

Klaczynski, P. A., & Fauth, J. (1997). Developmental differences in memory-based intrusions and self-serving statistical reasoning biases. *Merrill-Palmer Quarterly, 43*, 539–566.

Klaczynski, P. A., & Narasimham, G. (1998). Representations as mediators of adolescent deductive reasoning. *Developmental Psychology, 34*, 865–881.

Koutstaal, W., & Schacter, D. L. (1997). Gist-based false recognition of pictures in older and younger adults. *Journal of Memory and Language, 37*, 555–583.

Koutstaal, W., Schacter, D. L., Galluccio, L., & Stofer, K. A. (1999). Reducing gist-based false recognition in older adults: Encoding and retrieval manipulations. *Psychology and Aging, 14*, 220–237.

Kuhberger, A. (1995). The framing of decisions: A new look at old problems. *Organizational Behavior and Human Decision Processes, 62*, 230–240.

Kuther, T. L. (2002). Rational decision perspectives on alcohol consumption by youth: Revising the theory of planned behavior. *Addictive Behaviors, 27*, 35–47.

Larrick, R. P., Morgan, J. N., & Nisbett, R. E. (1990). Teaching the use of cost–benefit reasoning in everyday life. *Psychological Science, 1,* 362–370.

LaVeist, T. A. (1994). Beyond dummy variables and sample selection: What health services researchers ought to know about race as a variable. *Health Services Research, 29,* 1–16.

Levin, I. P., Schneider, S. L., & Gaeth, G. J. (1998). All frames are not created equal: A typology and critical analysis of framing effects. *Organizational Behavior and Human Decision Processes, 76,* 149–188.

Loewenstein, G., & Furstenberg, F. F. (1991). Is teenage sexual behavior rational? *Journal of Applied Social Psychology, 21*(12), 957–986.

Loewenstein, G., Weber, E. U., Hsee, C. K., & Welch, N. (2001). Risk as feelings. *Psychological Bulletin, 127,* 267–286.

Main, D. S., Iverson, D. C., McGloin, J., Banspach, S. W., Collin, J. L., Rugg, D. L., & Kolbe, L. J. (1994). Preventing HIV infection among adolescents: Evaluation of a school-based education program. *Preventive Medicine, 23*(4), 409–417.

May, R. M., & Anderson, R. M. (1987). Transmission dynamics of HIV infection. *Nature, 326,* 137–142.

Misovich, S. J., Fisher, J. D., & Fisher, W. A. (1996). The perceived AIDS-preventive utility of knowing one's partner well: A public health dictum and individuals' risky sexual behavior. *The Canadian Journal of Human Sexuality, 5*(2), 83–90.

Misovich, S. J., Fisher, J. D., & Fisher, W. A. (1997). Close relationships and elevated HIV risk behavior: Evidence and possible underlying psychological processes. *Review of General Psychology, 1,* 72–107.

Mrela, C. K., & Jimenez, J. (1997, May). *Differences in the health status among ethnic groups, Arizona, 1997.* Phoenix: Arizona Department of Health Services.

Orr, D. P., Brizendine, E. J., Fortenberry, J. D., & Katz, B. P. (1999, July). *Subsequent sexually transmitted infections among high-risk adolescents: Is it time to reexamine screening guidelines?* Paper presented at the 13th meeting of the International Society for Sexually Transmitted Diseases Research, Denver, CO.

Payne, J. W., Bettman, J., & Johnson, E. J. (1992). Behavioral decision research: A constructive processing perspective. *Annual Review of Psychology, 43,* 87–131.

Pelto, P. J., & Pelto, G. H. (1978). Medicine, anthropology, community: An overview. *Health and the human condition* (pp. 401–406). North Scituate, MA: Duxbury Press.

Phinney, J. S. (1996). When we talk about American ethnic groups, what do we mean? *American Psychologist, 51,* 918–927.

Quadrel, M. J., Fischhoff, B., & Davis, W. (1993). Adolescent (in)vulnerability. *American Psychologist, 48,* 102–116.

Reiss, I. L., & Leik, R. K. (1989). Evaluating strategies to avoid AIDS: Number of partners vs. use of condoms. *Journal of Sex Research, 26*(4), 411–433.

Reyna, V. F. (1991). Class inclusion, the conjunction fallacy, and other cognitive illusions. *Developmental Review, 11,* 317–336.

Reyna, V. F. (1992). Reasoning, remembering, and their relationship: Social, cognitive, and developmental issues. In M. L. Howe, C. J. Brainerd, & V. F. Reyna (Eds.), *Development of long-term retention* (pp. 103–127). New York: Springer-Verlag.

Reyna, V. F. (1995). Interference effects in memory and reasoning: A fuzzy trace theory analysis. In F. N. Dempster & C. J. Brainerd (Eds.), *Interference and inhibition in cognition* (pp. 29–59). San Diego, CA: Academic.

Reyna, V. F. (1996). Conceptions of memory development with implications for reasoning and decision making. *Annals of Child Development, 12,* 87–118.

Reyna, V. F. (2000). Fuzzy-trace theory and source monitoring: An evaluation of theory and false memory data. *Learning and Individual Differences, 12,* 163–175.

Reyna, V. F. (2004). How people make decisions that involve risk: A dual-processes approach. *Current Directions in Psychological Science, 13,* 60–66.

Reyna, V. F., & Adam, M. B. (2003). Fuzzy-trace theory, risk communication, and product labeling in sexually transmitted diseases. *Risk Analysis, 23,* 325–342.

Reyna, V. F., & Brainerd, C. J. (1991a). Fuzzy-trace theory and children's acquisition of mathematical and scientific concepts. *Learning & Individual Differences, 3*(1), 27–59.

Reyna, V. F., & Brainerd, C. J. (1991b). Fuzzy-trace theory and framing effects in choice. Gist extraction, truncation, and conversion. *Journal of Behavioral Decision Making, 4,* 249–262.

Reyna, V. F., & Brainerd, C. J. (1992). A fuzzy-trace theory of reasoning and remembering: Paradoxes, patterns, and parallelism. In N. Hearst, S. Kosslyn, & R. Shiffrin (Eds.), *From learning processes to cognitive processes: Essays in honor of William K. Estes* (pp. 235–259). Hillsdale, NJ: Lawrence Erlbaum Associates.

Reyna, V. F., & Brainerd, C. J. (1993). Fuzzy memory and mathematics in the classroom. In G. M. Davies & R. H. Logie (Eds.), *Memory in everyday life* (pp. 91–119). Amsterdam: North Holland Press.

Reyna, V. F., & Brainerd, C. J. (1994). The origins of probability judgement: A review of data and theories. In G. Wright & P. Ayton (Eds.), *Subjective probability* (pp. 239–272). New York: Wiley.

Reyna, V. F., & Brainerd, C. J. (1995a). Fuzzy-trace theory: An interim synthesis. *Learning & Individual Differences, 7*(1), 1–75.

Reyna, V. F., & Brainerd, C. J. (1995b). Fuzzy-trace theory: Some foundational issues. *Learning & Individual Differences, 7*(2), 145–162.

Reyna, V. F., & Brainerd, C. J. (1998). Fuzzy trace theory and false memory: New frontiers. *Journal of Experimental Child Psychology, 71,* 194–209.

Reyna, V. F., & Ellis, S. C. (1994). Fuzzy-trace theory and framing effects in children's risky decision making. *Psychological Science, 5*(5), 275–279.

Reyna, V. F., Holliday, R., & Marche, T. (2002). Explaining the development of false memories. *Developmental Review, 22,* 436–489.

Reyna, V. F., & Kiernan, B. (1994). The development of gist versus verbatim memory in sentence recognition: Effects of lexical familiarity, semantic content, encoding instructions, and retention interval. *Developmental Psychology, 30,* 178–191.

Reyna, V. F., & Kiernan, B. (1995). Children's memory and interpretation of psychological metaphors. *Metaphor and Symbolic Activity, 10,* 309–331.

Reyna, V. F., & Lloyd, F. (1997). Theories of false memory in children and adults. *Learning and Individual Differences, 9,* 95–123.

Reyna, V. F., Lloyd, F. J., & Brainerd, C. J. (2003). Memory, development, and rationality: An integrative theory of judgment and decision making. In S. Schneider & J. Shanteau (Eds.), *Emerging perspectives in judgment and decision making* (pp. 201–245). Mahwah, NJ: Lawrence Erlbaum Associates.

Reyna, V. F., & Titcomb, A. L. (1997). Constraints on the suggestibility of eyewitness testimony: A fuzzy-trace theory analysis. In D. G. Payne & F. G. Conrad (Eds.), *A synthesis of basic and applied approaches to human memory* (pp. 157–174). Mahwah, NJ: Lawrence Erlbaum Associates.

Rokeach, M. (1970). Long-range experimental modification of values, attitudes and behavior. *American Psychologist, 26,* 453–459.

Romo, M. S. (1995). *Cultural differences in memory and logical reasoning.* Unpublished master's thesis, University of Arizona.

Rotheram-Borus, M. J., Koopman, C., Haignere, C., & Davies, M. (1991). Reducing HIV sexual risk behaviors among runaway adolescents. *Journal of the American Medical Association, 266*(9), 1237–1241.

St. Lawrence, J. S., Brasfield, T. L., Jefferson, K. W., Alleyne, E., O'Bannon, R. E., & Shirley, A. (1995). Cognitive-behavioral intervention to reduce African American adolescents' risk for HIV infection. *Journal of Consulting & Clinical Psychology, 63*(2), 221–237.

Schacter, D. L., Curran, T., Galluccio, L., Milberg, W. B., & Bates, J. F. (1996). False recognition and the right frontal lobe: A case study. *Neuropsychologica, 34,* 793–808.

Schacter, D. L., Israel, L., & Racine, C. (1999). Suppressing false recognition in younger and older adults: The distinctiveness heuristic. *Journal of Memory and Language, 40,* 1–24.

Schacter, D. L., Kagan, J., & Leichtman, M. D. (1995). True and false memories in children and adults: A cognitive neuroscience perspective. *Psychology, Public Policy, and Law, 1,* 411–428.

Schacter, D. L., Verfaellie, M., & Anes, M. D. (1997). Illusory memories in amnesiac patients: Conceptual and perceptual false recognition. *Neuropsychology, 11,* 331–342.

Schacter, D. L., Verfaellie, M., & Pradere, D. (1996). The neuropsychology of memory illusions: False recall and recognition in amnesic patients. *Journal of Memory and Language, 35,* 319–334.

Schinke, S. P., Gordon, A. N., & Weston, R. E. (1990). Self-instruction to prevent HIV infection among African-American and Hispanic-American adolescents. *Journal of Consulting & Clinical Psychology, 58*(4), 432–436.

Schlottman, A. (2000). Children's judgments of gambles: A disordinal violation of utility. *Journal of Behavioral Decision Making, 13,* 77–89.

Schulenberg, J., Maggs, J. L., & Hurrelmann, K. (1997). *Health risks and developmental transitions during adolescence.* Cambridge, England: Cambridge University Press.

Sloman, S. (1996). The empirical case for two systems of reasoning. *Psychological Bulletin, 119,* 3–22.

Slovic, P., Fischhoff, B., & Lichtenstein, S. (1982). Facts versus fears: Understanding perceived risks. In D. Kahneman, P. Slovic, & A. Tversky (Eds.), *Judgment under uncertainty: Heuristics and biases* (pp. 463–492). New York: Cambridge University Press.

Stanovich, K. E., & West, R. F. (2000). Individual differences in reasoning: Implications for the rationality debate? *Behavioral and Brain Sciences, 23,* 645–726.

Stanton, B. F., Li, X., Galbraith, J., Feigelman, S., & Kaljee, L. (1996). Sexually transmitted diseases, human immunodeficiency virus, and pregnancy prevention. Combined contraceptive practices among urban African-American early adolescents. *Archives of Pediatrics & Adolescent Medicine, 150*(1), 17–24.

Stanton, B. F., Li, X., Ricardo, I., Galbraith, J., Feigelman, S., & Kaljee, L. (1996). A randomized, controlled effectiveness trial of an AIDS prevention program for low-income African-American youths. *Archives of Pediatrics & Adolescent Medicine, 150*(4), 363–372.

Tun, P. A., Wingfield, A., Rosen, M. J., & Blanchard, L. (1998). Response latencies for false memories: Gist-based processes in normal aging. *Psychology and Aging, 13,* 230–241.

Tversky, A., & Kahneman, D. (1986). Rational choice and the framing of decisions. *Journal of Business, 59,* 252–278.

von Winterfeldt, D., & Edwards, W. (1986). *Decision analysis and behavioral research.* New York: Cambridge University Press.

Walsh, M., Smith, R., Morales, A., & Sechrest, L. (2000). *Ecocultural research: A mental health researcher's guide to the study of race, ethnicity and culture.* Cambridge, MA: Human Services Research Institute.

Walter, H. J., & Vaughan, R. D. (1993). AIDS risk reduction among a multiethnic sample of urban high school students. *Journal of the American Medical Association, 270*(6), 725–730.

Wedell, D. H., & Bockenholt, U. (1990). Moderation of preference reversals in the long run. *Journal of Experimental Psychology: Human Perception and Performance, 16,* 429–438.

Wedell, D. H., & Bockenholt, U. (1994). Contemplating single versus multiple encounters of a risky prospect. *American Journal of Psychology, 107,* 499–518.

Whiting, B. (1976). Unpackaging variables. In K. F. Riegel & J. A. Meacham (Eds.), *The changing individual in a changing world* (pp. 303–309). Chicago: Aldine.

Wolford, G., Miller, M. B., & Gazzaniga, M. (2000). The left hemisphere's roles in hypothesis formation. *Journal of Neuroscience, 20,* RC64.

Commentary:
Development and Decisions

Keith E. Stanovich
University of Toronto

In Part I, we have some of the best state-of-the-art work in the area of the development of judgment and decision making. This area is not overinvestigated, so we must welcome the systematic program of research that each chapter reports. An equally important contribution of these chapters is represented by the theoretical perspective presented. In very different ways, the chapters advance our theoretical understanding. Byrnes' model of self-regulated decision making (chap. 1) juxtaposes a large number of factors that have been implicated in decision research, and it synthesizes them in some very creative ways. In chapter 2, Klaczynski takes a matrix of theoretical insights that have been well worked out in the adult literature—two-process theories of cognition—and applies them to the development of decision-making abilities, where they have been relatively undeveloped. This is a wise and useful strategy. Finally, in chapter 3, Reyna, Adam, Poirier, LeCroy, and Brainerd set their research program within the context of fuzzy-trace theory, which has some similarities with two-process theories but also contains some unique and counterintuitive features that are of immense interest.

Because the work in these chapters is some of the best in the field and because I share so many of the metatheoretical assumptions of these authors, there is very little in these chapters I would wish to directly contradict. Rather than artificially trying to pick fights where none exist, I shall do something that is both more fun for me and perhaps more useful for the field. These chapters provide many insights and jumping-off points that illuminate both the field and my own research program, and I structure my comments around some reactions to the chapters that I hope will be additive for the field (in that they add contextual and theoretical richness).

Both Byrnes (chap. 1) and Klaczynski (chap. 2) rightly point to the importance of issues surrounding knowledge calibration for good decision making. Issues of knowledge and metaknowledge (e.g., overconfidence effects) have been underinvestigated in the children's literature on judgment and decision making. I would like to draw attention to another type of knowledge calibration issue that I discussed in a recent book (Stanovich, 2004) because it has not been identified in the literature of decision theory (although it is alluded to in philosophical discussions). It is what I call the *pragmatic calibration of knowledge acquisition*—the calibration of knowledge acquisition according to practical goals.

Over a person's lifetime, it is critical to acquire knowledge in domains that are most relevant to fulfilling one's most important goals. Knowledge acquisition is effortful, and the cognitive resources available for it are limited. There is also a limited amount of time available to spend in epistemic activities. It is important that our effort be calibrated so that it is directed at knowledge domains that are connected to goals we deem important. If we say that something is of paramount importance to us (e.g., our children's safety), then it is incumbent on us to know something about these things we deem to be so important. An emphasis on the pragmatic calibration of knowledge acquisition prevents the tendency to absolve individuals of charges of poor decision making because they can prove that they were not in possession of some critical piece of knowledge. For example, the parents of children unbelted in automobiles are not absolved of irrationality even if they could actually prove that they did not *know* that unbelted children were at unusually great risk. Applying my concept, although a particular act of failing to belt the children cannot be deemed irrational, the parents are irrational in a different sense—they have instead poorly calibrated their knowledge acquisition over a long time period of their lives. Philosophers (e.g., Code, 1987) talk of this under the rubric of so-called epistemic responsibility.

The authors of all three of these chapters are Meliorists in my taxonomy (Stanovich, 1999). They feel that human decision making is not as good as it could be and that it could be improved by instruction, experience, and appropriate modeling. This is most apparent in chapter 3 by Reyna et al., where innovative suggestions for improving AIDS prevention programs are put forth. Their Meliorist prescription follows from several experimental results that are set within the context of fuzzy-trace theory. Perhaps surprisingly, I am in considerable sympathy with their research program even though my research strategy has been different. I have tried to induce theoretical change by making adjustments in traditional decision-theoretic concepts and in canonical two-process models (of the type discussed in chap. 2 by Klaczynski). Reyna et al. (chap. 3) have chosen the more radical theoretical path of altering more drastically the processing assumptions in traditional theory.

Nonetheless, many of the reforms we are urging (with our somewhat different strategies) are moving in the same direction. First of all, it should be noted that my version of dual-process theory shares with fuzzy-trace theory a rejection of what Brainerd and Reyna (2001) called the "illusion of replacement" (p. 52)—the idea that analytic thought replaces heuristic thought. The dual-process notion I have championed (a synthesis of many earlier views; see Stanovich, 1999, 2004; Stanovich & West, 2000; and chap. 2 by Klaczynski) shares with fuzzy-trace theory the assumption that both heuristic and analytic processing modes are available at all points in development, at least after infancy.

As another example, consider the ingenious discussion by Reyna et al. (chap. 3) of why adults may sometimes violate consistency assumptions of normative models that children do not. I have recently discussed similar paradoxes (Stanovich, 2004), but have attempted to explain them by staying closer to classical models than do Reyna et al. Nonetheless, our conclusions have some affinity. For example, I pointed out that all of the classical principles of rational choice (transitivity, reduction of compound lotteries, independence, regularity, sure-thing principle, etc.) have as implications, in one way or another, that irrelevant context should not affect judgment—that choices should be appropriately decontextualized. But in my most recent book, I discuss how a human adult recognizes subtle contextual factors in decision problems that complicate their choices and perhaps contribute to their instability. Because decision theorists debate the rationality of reacting to these contextual factors, it is not difficult to imagine such a debate going on (either explicitly or without awareness) in the mind of the decision maker. Regardless of the outcome of the internal debate, it is nearly certain that such an internal struggle would introduce instability in responses. Such variability would no doubt raise the probability of producing a sequence of choices that violated one of the coherence constraints that define utility maximization under the axiomatic approach of Savage (1954) and von Neumann and Morgenstern (1944). I note that an agent with a less subtle psychology (a child or a nonhuman primate) might be less prone to be drawn into complex cogitation about conflicting psychological states. For example, an agent impervious to regret might be more likely to adhere to the independence axiom in the Allais problem and thus be judged as instrumentally rational.

One common feature of the classical axioms—that they all require the decision maker to abstract away aspects in the contextual environment of the options—explains why the finding that children and lower animals can sometimes fulfill the strictures of instrumental rationality better than adults is not only not paradoxical at all but is actually to be expected in some cases.

Humans are the great social contextualizers (one of what I have termed the *fundamental computational biases* of human cognition; see Stanovich, 1999, 2004). We respond to subtle environmental cues in the contextual surround and are sensitive to social flux and nuance. All of this means that the contextual features humans code into options may lack stability both for good reasons (the social world is not stable) and bad reasons (the cues are too many and varying to be coded consistently each time). In having more capacity for differential coding of contextual cues from occasion to occasion, adults create more opportunities for violation of any number of choice axioms, all of which require a consistent contextualization of the options from choice to choice. The more such contextual cues are coded, the more difficult it will be to consistently contextualize from decision to decision. The very complexity of the information that adults seek to bring to bear on a decision is precisely the thing that renders difficult an adherence to the consistency requirements of the choice axioms.

The recommendation in Reyna et al. (chap. 3) that we foster health-promoting intuitions rather than knowledge or consequentialist decision analyses calls to mind Nozick's (1993) discussion of the importance of principles in decision making, as well as some philosophical debates between consequentialist and deontological approaches. Adhering to a principle may, in the long run, be more advantageous than engaging in a utilitarian calculus in each instance. Thus, paradoxically, global consequentialist criteria may sometimes dictate abandoning consequentialism at the microlevel of decision making. Furthermore, adhering to a principle sends a signal to the self: "I am the type of person who adheres to a principle such as this" (see Nozick, 1993; Stanovich, 2004). Such a signal can serve to shape the future self in ways that engaging in a utilitarian calculus does not. Thus again, through the shaping of the decisions of the future person you will be (Parfit, 1984), adhering to a deontological principle may be more optimal in the long run, even on a consequentialist analysis.

Finally, I have wondered whether some of the important features of fuzzy-trace theory could not be accommodated within some types of two-process views (or vice versa; my point is not to argue about the direction of subsumption but to emphasize commonalities). They both share the assumption that the natural habit of mind is to think imprecisely. Fuzzy-trace theory postulates that both verbatim processing of precise memory information and the intuitive processing of gist both improve with age (see Brainerd & Reyna, 2001). This is not seriously at odds with two-process theory (see Klaczynski, chap. 2). That the fuzzy-processing preference increases with age and experience could perhaps be framed within mechanisms of two-process theories, which emphasize (going as far back as Shiffrin & Schneider, 1977) that repeated execution of computationally expensive, analytic system production rules leads to their compilation in the heuristic system as quick-acting quasi-modules. This processing sequence—analytic responses becoming instantiated in the heuristic system with practice—explains the well-known developmental trend for controlled processes to become automatized with practice.

The Meliorism that fuels Byrnes' analysis is on display in many parts of chapter 1. As an overall rationale for a model of self-regulated decision making, he states that "if we could determine why only certain people acquire decision-making skills by early adulthood, we might be able to create interventions to help those who failed to." Byrnes emphasizes a key aspect of Meliorism when he contrasts the costs involved in making a bad clothes choice versus marrying the wrong person. This is a point that evolutionary psychologists and proponents of fast and frugal heuristics seem to miss. Evolutionary modules may deliver the correct decision 99% of the time, but for the 1% of errors, it may still be critically important to have the correct procedures and strategies for the analytic system to implement—because the 1% of cases may be in domains of unusual importance (financial decisions, personal decisions, employment decisions; see Stanovich, 2004, for a detailed development of this argument). The modern world tends to create situations where some of the default values of evolutionarily adapted heuristic systems are not optimal. As Klaczynski notes in chapter 2, many heuristic systems biases serve to contextualize problem-solving situations. In contrast, modern technological societies continually spawn situations where humans must decontextualize information—where they must deal abstractly and in a depersonalized manner with information. Such situations require the active suppression of the social, narrative, and contextualizing styles that characterize the operation of the heuristic system (Evans, 2002a, 2002b; Oatley, 1996; Stanovich, 1999, 2004). For example, many aspects of the contemporary legal system put a premium on detaching prior belief and world knowledge from the process of evidence evaluation. These situations may not be numerous, but they tend to be in particularly important domains of modern life.

Finally, Byrnes gives us an important Meliorist warning when he notes that within-subjects designs maximize the chances that participants will draw the appropriate lessons across outcomes. He notes that "in the real world, however, related experiences are interspersed among a variety of other experiences." This is a point that some of the founders of the heuristics and biases tradition in decision making (Kahneman & Tversky, 1996; Kahneman & Frederick, 2002) warned us about: Life is a between-subjects design. Many of us studying individual differences use within-subjects designs so as to get an index of normative or nonnormative thinking for an individual (usually in order to correlate it with some other variable). However, in doing so for this methodological purpose, we must really realize that our studies may be minimizing the biases observed (see LeBoeuf & Shafir, 2003).

Many of these points about Meliorism could equally be made by referring to chapter 2 by Klaczynski. Additionally, his manner of interpreting two-process theories in a developmental context is very congruent with my own view. The notion that most decisions involve an interaction between the two systems is critical, as well as the point mentioned that, in common with fuzzy-trace theory (Brainerd & Reyna, 2001), the dual-process theories reject the idea that analytic thought replaces heuristic thought. Klaczynski's chapter is helpfully clarifying on all these points. One final clarifying point that I would add to all discussions of two-process theories is that the term *heuristic system* (or System 1; see Stanovich, 1999) is a misnomer in a sense, because it implies a single cognitive system. In fact, the term refers to a (probably large) set of systems in the brain that operate autonomously in response to their own triggering stimuli, and not under the control of a central processing structure. This is why I have begun to use a substitute terminology: the autonomous set of systems (TASS; see Stanovich, 2004). TASS is referred to as autonomous because: (a) their execution is rapid, (b) their execution is mandatory when the triggering stimuli are encountered, (c) they are not under conscious control, and (d) they are not dependent on input from the analytic system. Included in TASS are processes of implicit learning, overlearned associations, processes of behavioral regulation by the emotions, and the encapsulated modules for solving specific adaptive problems that have been posited by the evolutionary psychologists. Nothing theoretical is changed by this terminology, but it will perhaps be clearer to newcomers to two-process theory.

As I mentioned at the outset, most of the aforementioned comments should be viewed as additive rather than adversarial. The reader, in these three chapters, has been given as good a sampling of theories of the development of decision-making skills as they are likely to get anywhere.

ACKNOWLEDGMENTS

Preparation of this commentary was supported by a grant from the Social Sciences and Humanities Research Council of Canada and the Canada Research Chairs program.

REFERENCES

Brainerd, C. J., & Reyna, V. F. (2001). Fuzzy-trace theory: Dual processes in memory, reasoning, and cognitive neuroscience. In H. W. Reese & R. Kail (Eds.), *Advances in child development and behavior* (Vol. 28, pp. 41–100). San Diego: Academic.
Code, L. (1987). *Epistemic responsibility.* Hanover, NH: University Press of New England.
Evans, J. St. B. T. (2002a). Logic and human reasoning: An assessment of the deduction paradigm. *Psychological Bulletin, 128,* 978–996.

Evans, J. St. B. T. (2002b). The influence of prior belief on scientific thinking. In P. Carruthers, S. Stich, & M. Siegal (Eds.), *The cognitive basis of science* (pp. 193–210). Cambridge: Cambridge University Press.

Kahneman, D., & Frederick, S. (2002). Representativeness revisited: Attribute substitution in intuitive judgment. In T. Gilovich, D. Griffin, & D. Kahneman (Eds.), *Heuristics and biases: The psychology of intuitive judgment* (pp. 49–81). New York: Cambridge University Press.

Kahneman, D., & Tversky, A. (1996). On the reality of cognitive illusions. *Psychological Review, 103*, 582–591.

LeBoeuf, R. A., & Shafir, E. (2003). Deep thoughts and shallow frames: On the susceptibility to framing effects. *Journal of Behavioral Decision Making, 16*, 77–92.

Nozick, R. (1993). *The nature of rationality.* Princeton, NJ: Princeton University Press.

Oatley, K. (1996). Inference in narrative and science. In D. R. Olson & N. Torrance (Eds.), *Modes of thought: Explorations in culture and cognition* (pp. 123–140). New York: Cambridge University Press.

Parfit, D. (1984). *Reasons and persons.* Oxford: Oxford University Press.

Savage, L. J. (1954). *The foundations of statistics.* New York: Wiley.

Shiffrin, R. M., & Schneider, W. (1977). Controlled and automatic human information processing: II. Perceptual learning, automatic attending, and a general theory. *Psychological Review, 84*, 127–190.

Stanovich, K. E. (1999). *Who is rational? Studies of individual differences in reasoning.* Mahwah, NJ: Lawrence Erlbaum Associates.

Stanovich, K. E. (2004). *The robot's rebellion: Finding meaning in the age of Darwin.* Chicago: University of Chicago Press.

Stanovich, K. E., & West, R. F. (2000). Individual differences in reasoning: Implications for the rationality debate? *Behavioural and Brain Sciences, 23*, 645–726.

Von Neumann, J., & Morgenstern, O. (1944). *The theory of games and economic behavior.* Princeton, NJ: Princeton University Press.

II

CONTEXTUAL INFLUENCES
ON DECISION MAKING

The four chapters in Part II comprise various approaches to decision making that address emotional, social, and cultural influences on developmental trends in decision making and related processes. The goal in selecting these authors and topics for inclusion was to highlight a variety of contexts in which children and adolescents must make judgments and decisions. In addition, we wanted to include a range of descriptive and explanatory variables that have been considered in attempting to understand contextual influences on decision making. Thus, the chapters in this section include peer, parental, and cultural contexts, and the potential explanatory variables include emotions, social–cognitive representations, expectancies, collaborative interactions, and cognitive biases and abilities.

In chapter 4, Amsel, Bowden, Cottrell, and Sullivan present theory and evidence that the anticipation of regret affects the decisions of preadolescents and adults. At the core of the Amsel et al. chapter is the notion that cognitive developmentalists have neglected the role of higher order emotions and, specifically, regret, in decision making. Thus, by anticipating outcomes that they would likely regret, both children and adults can avoid nonoptimal decisions. However, the process of regret anticipation involves such skills as (a) systematically generating positive and negative possible outcomes for decision options, (b) making affect-based judgments of these possible outcomes, (c) freeing the self of biases in order to identify the worst possible outcome, and (d) making decisions likely to prevent this outcome. The effective utilization of these abilities involves coordinating anticipated regret with relatively unbiased reasoning to arrive at optimal decisions.

Amsel et al. (chap. 4) take issue with decision theorists who have argued that adolescents are as capable of making good decisions as adults. Specifically, because the models on which many adolescent decision theorists rely pay little attention to affective influences on decision making, theorists tend to overestimate adolescents' abilities. In their research, Amsel et al. found that only when cued to make decisions that anticipated and avoided regret were preadolescents as competent as adults. This finding suggests that preadolescents may be as competent as adults in regret-based decision making. However, in lieu of contextual support, preadolescents chose decision options that they had associated with the worst possible outcome and generated fewer potential negative outcomes than adults. Amsel et al. thus conclude that, in "real-world" risky decision making, the quality of preadolescents' decisions may well be a function of the presence or absence of supportive and informed collaborators.

The issue of bias in adolescents' judgments and decisions arises again in chapter 5, in which Jacobs and Johnston report relations between adolescents' perceptions of the base rates at which their peers engage in deviant behavior and their own actual participation in deviant activities. These authors begin by noting that adults often fail to take into consideration the base rates at which events occur. By contrast, prior work indicates that, in situations that do not involve social content, even young children can effectively use base-rate information. Nonetheless, systematic biases in the use of base rates have been found in both children and adults. The core question addressed in this chapter is the relation between adolescents' estimates for the base rates of deviant activities and their own deviant behavior.

Jacobs and Johnston (chap. 5) note two developments at the outset of adolescence: increases in understanding of base-rate information and increases in deviant behavior. How, these authors ask, might these trends be related? The authors suggest that, if adolescents use their peers to estimate base rates of deviant behaviors, then those who engage in such behaviors may systematically overestimate actual base rates because they may be spending time with others who engage in similar behaviors. By comparing adolescents' base-rate estimates to actual base rates in their schools, the authors found that boys highly involved in deviant activities and adolescents who had been targets of peer victimization were susceptible to more extreme overestimations of base rates of deviant activity and victimization, respectively, than other adolescents. Jacobs and Johnston conclude by suggesting that adolescents' overestimation of base rates may be due to either biased processing or to biased data as a result of the peer context in which they make such judgments.

In chapter 6, Helwig reviews research conducted in Western cultural contexts on the development of conceptions of decision making and how children use these conceptions to evaluate decision-making procedures (e.g., authority-oriented). He then goes on to use cross-cultural evidence to demonstrate similarities between Western and Chinese children's and adolescents' judgments about rights, autonomy, and democratic decision making. Helwig points out that many theorists have assumed that Chinese culture and psychology are "collectivistic" and oriented toward respect for authority and social hierarchy. Although arguments have been forwarded that concepts of *rights* and *democracy* are uniquely Western, in recent years, dissatisfaction with characterizations of cultures as individualistic and collectivistic has been expressed by numerous scholars.

In general, Helwig's data in chapter 6 support the contention that collectivist accounts of Chinese culture cannot adequately explain the responses of the vast majority of Chinese adolescents. Specifically, although there were some modest variations by region (e.g., traditional villages, modernized cities), adolescents frequently rejected adult jurisdiction over decisions in the family and curriculum decisions in schools—although, like their Western counterparts, Chinese adolescents occasionally believed that the authority for some decisions rested with adults. These findings indicate a number of similarities in developmental and contextual patterns in judgments about decision procedures across cultures with different social hierarchies and ideologies.

In chapter 7, Gauvain and Perez discuss research on the relationship between parental expectations and children's participation in planning leisure activities, focusing on specific social interactions and children's daily planning. As these authors note, adult regulation over children's after-school activities has increased in recent years; and an important consequence of this trend is that children's time spent planning by themselves and in collaboration with peers has declined. It therefore becomes critical to explore how children plan their leisure activities and how adults collaborate with or assume regulation over activities that were once left to children. For example, parents' engagement in planning activities with their children is likely to be critical to the development of autonomous planning because they model the importance of self-regulation for children. With increasing age, parents (and other adults) come to expect more autonomous planning and goal setting from children and, consequently, adjust their parenting strategies and patterns of "coregulation." More precisely, based on their sociocultural approach to cognitive development, Gauvain and Perez propose that parents' contributions to the development of children's planning skills reflect both cultural prescriptions and parents' expectations about children's development in general, and self-regulation in particular.

Gauvain and Perez (chap. 7) present findings from two sets of longitudinal data. The first investigation asked whether children's participation in planning-related interactions in the family change from childhood to adolescence. The second study focused on whether children have opportunities to decide on their out-of-school activities and whether parents are involved in this process. Data from the first study indicated, among other things, that children are involved in planning family activities at an early age, mothers are more involved than fathers in these activities, and parenting styles are linked to the extent to which planning is governed by adults and to developments in the initiation of planning discussions. In the second study, most mothers of European American and Latino American backgrounds reported that they and their children jointly made decisions about organized after-school activities, whereas children alone made most decisions about informal activities. In addition, parental expectations about the ages at which children should participate in planning activities differed by the child's age, gender, and ethnic background. Critically, the sheer amount of participation in out-of-school activities was a less important determinant of children's satisfaction with out-of-school activities than their participation in the decision making process.

As a group, these chapters represent important advances in our understanding of decision making and its development. Historically, decision making has been treated as an almost exclusively individual process, bereft of emotion (or, at least, affective influences on decision making have been given short shrift), unaffected by peers and perceptions of peers and independent of culture. Context and affect do affect decision making; collaboration and cultural belief systems are critical to children's conceptions of their autonomy, self-regulatory capacities, and decisions across a diverse array of domains. The theories and evidence presented in these chapters indicate that views of decision making as purely individualistic and affect-free cannot be sustained if our goal is to fully understand decision making in a variety of contexts.

4

Anticipating and Avoiding Regret as a Model of Adolescent Decision Making

Eric Amsel
Troy Bowden
Jennifer Cottrell
James Sullivan
Weber State University

Adolescence is certainly a time of contrast, conflict, and contradiction. This also applies to theoretical characterizations of adolescent cognition. On one hand, adolescence has been described as a time when cognitive abilities underlying rationality are acquired. The cognitive abilities acquired during adolescence are the elements of hypothetic deduction (Inhelder & Piaget, 1958), the foundation of scientific thought itself (Braithwaite, 1957). Such cognitive abilities include logical reasoning (Moshman & Franks, 1986; Mueller, Overton, & Reene, 2001), hypothetical reasoning (Amsel & Smalley, 2000; Fay & Klahr, 1996), and empirical reasoning (Amsel & Brock, 1996; Kuhn, Amsel, & O'Loughlin, 1988; Kuhn, Garcia-Mila, Zohar, & Andersen, 1995). On the other hand, adolescence is also described as a time of engaging in risky behavior, with none other than G. Stanley Hall himself (cited by Arnett, 1999) characterizing it as "normal" for adolescent boys to engage in a period of semicriminality. Adolescents engage in many forms of risky behaviors more frequently than children or adults (Arnett, 1992; Byrnes, Miller, & Schafer, 1999; Irwin, 1993). These ill-considered actions run the gamut from thrill seeking and recklessness to rebelliousness and antisocial behaviors (Gullone, Moore, Moss, & Boyd, 2000).

Like a bad case of cognitive dissonance, the contrasting characterizations of adolescents as thoughtful and impulsive, deliberative and impetuous, or reflective and foolhardy are difficult to hold simultaneously. It comes then as no surprise that these conflicting characterizations are not often presented together. There are book-length treatises that focus exclusively on adolescents' remarkable cognitive achievements (Inhelder & Piaget, 1958; Moshman, 1999) or risky behaviors (N. Bell & R. Bell, 1993) without fully acknowledging the other characterization. Authors sometimes place these characterizations in different chapters of textbook treatments of adolescence. For example, in one of the most popular adolescent textbooks, adolescents are characterized as irrationally making risky and dangerous decisions in the Biology and Health chapter but as hypothetical and logical scientific thinkers in the Cognitive chapter (Santrock, 2003).

These contrasting characterizations of adolescent cognition have played out in interesting ways in the domain of decision making (Jacobs & Ganzel, 1993; Klaczynski, Byrnes, & Jacobs, 2001). On the one hand, the growth of cognitive competencies would suggest that decision-making skills increase from childhood to adolescence (Lewis, 1981). As an acknowledgment of adolescents' cognitive sophistication, it has been argued that adolescents are no less capable than adults of making adequate decisions (Quadrel, Fischhoff, & Davis, 1993); at the very least, little evidence exists for the presumed substantial differences between adolescents and adults (Furby & Beyth-Marom, 1992). On the other hand, adolescents' risky behaviors can be traced back to their cognitions (Gerrard, Gibbons, Benthin, & Hessling, 1996) with a number of researchers suggesting that adolescents lack adults' decision-making competence (Baron, 1990) or self-regulatory skills (Byrnes, 1998), which leads them to make ill-considered decisions (Arnett, 1999; Miller & Byrnes, 1997). Whatever their underlying competence, adolescents' decision-making performance may be affected by their limited amount of practice and experience (Santrock, 2003), alternative perceptions and/or preferences (Gardner, 1993; Moore & Gullone, 1996) and a host of other mediating and/or moderating factors (Byrnes, 1998) including social–contextual (Arnett & Balle-Jensen, 1993; Lightfoot, 1997), psychosocial (Steinberg & Cauffman, 1996), and affective and/or motivational (Caffrey & Schneider, 2000) variables. Thus, there is a conflicting picture of adolescents as fundamentally competent decision makers, incompetent decision makers, or as decision makers whose performance is affected by a range of moderating and mediating factors.

In a majority of cases (but certainly not all), the conflicting accounts of adolescent decision making share one thing in common: Normative claims regarding adolescent decision-making sophistication and vulnerabilities are based on the standard economic decision-making model, typically described under the rubric of Expected Utility (EU) theory (Hastie & Dawes, 2001; Landman, 1993). EU models (including many extensions and variants) propose that good decisions involve comparing options in terms of the likelihood and value or utility of outcomes associated with each option. Competent decision-making processes, as defined from this perspective (Beyth-Marom, Austin, Fischhoff, Palmgren, & Jacobs-Quadrel, 1993; Beyth-Marom, Fischhoff, Quadrel, & Furby, 1991; Furby & Beyth-Marom, 1992), include (a) listing relevant options; (b) envisioning possible outcomes or consequences associated with each option; (c) assessing the likelihood of each outcome or consequence; (d) establishing the relative value or utility of each outcome or consequence; and (e) using rules to integrate or combine the likelihood and value information to specify the best option, which is the one that maximizes expected value.

EU theory and the cognitive processes it implies are often invoked explicitly or implicitly when defining such concepts as *decision-making competence, decision-making incompetence*, and even *moderating* or *mediating decision-making variables*. The tendency to competently engage in the processes just described when making decisions constitutes decision-making competence and failure to competently engage in such processes constitutes decision-making incompetence. Finally, mediating and moderating variables are those such as cognitive biases, personality traits, or emotions that influence, interfere, sidetrack or undermine the processes of decision making already described.

In this chapter, we challenge some characteristics of the EU theory of decision making in general and its implications for adolescent decision making in particular. We do not deny that there are normative standards that apply to decision-making practices (cf. Stanovich, 1999); rather, we question whether the EU model in the form typically applied to adolescent decision making is complete. We outline an extension of EU models that treats decision makers' anticipation of their postdecisional regret regarding option outcomes as normatively justified in the decision-making process itself (cf. Landman, 1993; Zeelenberg, 1999b). We argue that "regret-based" decision making is a normatively justified and descriptively adequate model of decision making. On the basis of this analysis, we present some preliminary research in which we describe the development of adolescents' spontaneous and induced use of anticipated postdecisional regret in decision making. Ultimately, we paint a different picture of adolescent decision-making strengths and vulnerabilities than those derived from the standard EU model.

These arguments and data are presented in two sections. In the first section, we review and analyze regret-based decision-making models, arguing in favor of the central tenet, that it is often rational for decision makers to actively anticipate and seek to avoid options that are associated with outcomes they would regret if those outcomes were to occur (Landman, 1993). Part of our normative argument in this section is the review of evidence demonstrating that adults' decisions in a variety of decision-making contexts are influenced by their anticipation and avoidance of regret. In the second section, we extend the analysis of regret-based decision-making models to adolescents. We outline and present preliminary tests of the claim that adolescents may still be learning to coordinate the component skills required to spontaneously make rational decisions that anticipate and avoid regret. It is argued that their lack of coordination of component skills for anticipating and avoiding regret results in adolescents being particularly vulnerable to make decisions that, in specific contexts, appear to be quite irrational, impulsive, ill-considered, or risky.

REGRET-BASED DECISION MAKING

Imagine that students in a class are each given a free lottery ticket and asked to write their names on it. They are all told that only the students in the class will be given lottery tickets and the lucky holder of the winning ticket will receive $17. Upon writing their names on the ticket and answering some questions about their chances of winning, they are asked to exchange their tickets for other tickets. To (literally) sweeten the offer, each student is additionally offered an expensive-looking chocolate as an incentive to exchange. Do the students agree to the exchange?

This seems like a fairly simple decision from the perspective of standard EU models of decision making. The probability of winning the lottery is the same no matter which ticket the students are holding. That is, their chances of winning the lottery are unaffected by whether they are holding the original ticket (because they rejected the offer to exchange), or a new ticket (because they accepted the offer to exchange). As the decision graph in Table 4.1 makes clear, the outcomes associated with exchanging tickets (Option A) are each more valued than the corresponding outcomes associated with not exchanging tickets (Option B). The value of holding a winning ticket is greater if they exchanged the ticket than if they held onto their original ticket because of the added value of the incentive. Similarly, the incentive increases the value of holding a losing ticket if they exchanged the ticket than if they kept the original one. In popular parlance, the choice is a "no brainer."

TABLE 4.1
Decision Graph for the Lottery Exchange Decision Problem
(See Text for Details)

Initial State	Decision Option	Potential Outcome (p)	Value
Original Lottery Ticket	A: Exchange Ticket	Win the Lottery (.016)[a]	$17 + incentive
		Lose the Lottery (.984)	$0 + incentive
	B: Keep Original Ticket	Win the Lottery (.016)	$17
		Lose the Lottery (.984)	$0

[a]Bar-Hillel and Neter (1996, Study 1) has 61 students in the class who participated in the lottery, making the probability of having the winning lottery ticket 1 in 61.

Regret Avoidance in Lottery-Ticket Exchanges

Despite the obvious superiority of the option to exchange tickets, only a minority of Israeli college students accepted the offer to exchange, with a total of 59% of the students resisting it (Bar-Hillel & Neter, 1996, Study 1). In a series of follow-up analyses and studies, Bar-Hillel and Neter (1996) replicated the finding, ruling out a variety of explanations for the behavior of the lottery-ticket exchange "resisters." For example, most lottery-ticket "exchangers" and "resisters" said that their original lottery ticket was no more or less likely to win the lottery compared to other tickets, suggesting that participants did not misunderstand or miscalculate the probability of an individual ticket winning the lottery. Although many students resisted exchanging lottery tickets when offered an incentive, there was no such resistance for exchanging pencils or the color of the paper on which the lottery ticket was printed (but only if the number on the ticket remained the same), suggesting that there was no general hesitation about agreeing to exchanges with or without incentives. Furthermore, the students resisted exchanging their lottery ticket irrespective of whether or not they wrote their names on their original ticket, suggesting that no simple endowment effect was operating. Although the size of the incentive influenced exchange rates (more exchangers when the incentive was more valued), the framing of the problem did not. Exchange rates remained stable whether the gamble was framed as a choice between two equal gambling options with an incentive for exchanging, or as a choice between unequal gambles (lottery prize or lottery prize plus bonus) with a free option to exchange.

Although Bar-Hillel and Neter (1996) suggested that resisters may be "irrational"[1] they do acknowledge that resistance has a function: It protects one from postdecisional regret. *Regret* is the negative feeling resulting from counterfactual thoughts regarding how a negative outcome, which actually occurred, could have been avoided had an alternative action or choice been made (Roese, 1994; Zeelenberg, 1999b). It is usually characterized by punishing oneself for inappropriate actions or poor decisions (i.e., kicking oneself), feeling that one should have known better, wanting to undo the negative outcome, and wishing for a second chance. Regret is a cognitive emotion in the sense that it involves a comparison of reality to mentally created possible alternatives. Although the counterfactual process that gives rise to regret is spontaneously engaged (Sanna & Turley, 1996), it can be suppressed or blocked (Goldinger, Kleider, Azuma, & Beike, 2003). It is a frequently expressed emotion in interpersonal contexts (Shimanoff, 1984) and a unique emotion, distinguishable from but related to disappointment (Zeelenberg,

---

[1]Bar-Hillel and Neter (1996) described the choice of resisting the exchange as "irrational from the perspective of normative choice theory, because it amounts to the rejection of the dominant option (exchange one lottery ticket for an equivalent lottery ticket plus a bonus)" (p. 19).

Van Dijk, Manstead, & Van Der Plight, 1998), guilt (Boydston, Goodliffe, Hoag, Money, & Amsel, 2002), shame (Amsel, McVaugh, Biggs, & Ferguson, 2003), and other negative emotions (Roseman, Weist, & Swartz, 1994). As an emotion, regret functions adaptively to prepare a person to learn from a poor decision, and to avoid making the same decision again in the same situation (Roese, 1994), although it also has maladaptive consequences in rumination and depression (Stewart & Vanderwater, 1999).

Bar-Hillel and Neter (1996) suggested that to protect themselves from postdecisional regret, the resisters anticipated potential sources of regret and made lottery-exchange decisions that avoid such sources. In the context of decision making, postdecisional feelings of regret can be anticipated regarding various decision options by imagining how, in the postdecision world, a given outcome could have been better had an alternative choice been made. With regard to lottery-ticket exchanges, a compelling source of anticipated regret is the emotionally painful experience of discovering that you held the winning ticket but gave it away to someone else in exchange for the small incentive. One would certainly feel regret about giving away a winning ticket because regret is more strongly associated with narrowly missed positive outcomes (such as missing an airplane flight by only a few minutes) than with greatly missed ones (such as missing the flight by 30 minutes; Kahneman & Tversky, 1982). Although resisting the lottery-ticket exchange insures protection from feeling foolish for giving away a winning ticket, what about the regret of keeping the losing ticket and rejecting a potential winning one? The regret is less intense in the case of inaction (or omission) leading to a negative outcome than in the case of actions (or commission) leading to such outcomes (Landman, 1987, 1993), at least in the short term (see Gilovich & Medvec, 1995). So resisting a lottery-ticket exchange may not protect one from all forms of postdecision regret, just the potentially most intense forms.

Bar-Hillel and Neter (1996) noted that resisters gave indications that they made decisions seeking to avoid regret. Some explicitly justified their resistance by a desire to avoid outcomes about which they would have postdecisional regret. The finding that individuals' gambles are influenced by the potential for experiencing regret in the postdecisional world has been demonstrated in a series of studies by Ritov (1996). She found that when information about the foregone (i.e., unchosen alternative) gamble was unavailable, because only the results of the chosen gamble were revealed, there was a strong tendency for participants to be risk-averse by choosing a low-risk gamble with a higher probability of winning but a lower payoff. The alternative was a high-risk gamble, which has a lower probability of winning but a higher payoff. The preference for low-risk gambles was reversed, however, when information was made available about both gambles. This choice was a way for participants to avoid the regret of later discovering that they would have won a big payoff.

The results support the notion that anticipating postdecisional regrets in a gambling context influences the kind of gamble that will be made. To extend this notion to more real-world decision-making contexts, Richard, Van Der Plight, and De Vries (1996) examined the role of anticipated regret in sexual risk-taking behavior. In the study, participants were told to focus on their feelings about having unsafe sex, or their feelings after having unsafe sex. Then participants were presented with a list of positive and negative affect terms and asked to choose 10 to describe their state of mind. The participants in the "feelings after" condition scored significantly higher on negative affect scales than those in the "feelings about" condition and were more likely to choose regret (58% compared to 33%) as a description of their feelings. Most importantly though, the authors found in a second study that respondents who were induced to think about their feelings after unsafe sex were more likely to have modified their behavior (e.g., condom use) toward safer sex in the 5 months that followed than the respondents told to merely focus on their feelings about unsafe sex (Richard et al., 1996).

The Richard et al. (1996) finding of regret-based decision making inducing less risky behavior is consistent with Caffrey and Schneider's (2000; also see Richard, De Vries, & Van Der Plight, 1998) study of affective motivation of risky behavior in adolescence. Caffrey and Schneider (2000) found that the avoidance of regret was more strongly cited as a primary affective motivator for not engaging in a wide range of risky behavior by a group of teens who never or infrequently engaged in risky behavior compared to a group who frequently or regularly engaged in it. Adolescents who do not engage in risky behavior saying they are motivated to avoid regret is weak evidence of a regret-avoidance decision-making process. Nonetheless, coupled with the previous research presented in this section, the Caffrey and Schneider (2000) study suggests that regret-based decision making can function in some decision-making contexts to decrease the tendency to engage in risky behavior.

Regret Aversion Versus Risk Aversion in Decision-Making Contexts

Regret-based decision making, it seems, is powerful enough to modify the future behavior of people who are induced to consider their postdecisional feelings. Paradoxically, Richard et al. (1996) found that regret-based decision making functions to decrease the tendency to engage in risky behavior, and Ritov (1996) found that regret-based decision making functions to increase the tendency to engage in risky gambles. Although the riskiness of the activities may differ, the decision to do each was motivated to avoid regret. The notion here is that assessing a gamble or behavior in terms of its risk is not the same as its potential for regret.

Zeelenberg, Beattie, Van Der Plight, and De Vries (1996) tested for the difference between focusing on risk or regret as a decision strategy by allowing participants to choose either risky or safe gambles when the outcome of one or the other of those gambles could be known. EU theory supposes that gambles could be predicted simply on the basis of maximizing benefits or utility, although some people may prefer riskier gambles (a low-probability but high-payoff gamble) and others prefer safer ones (a high-probability but low-payoff gamble). However, it was proposed that gambling preferences could be altered by the availability of feedback that provided information regarding the outcome of gambles. In the task, participants could choose either a safe or risky gamble and then discover the outcome of their decision. Prior to their gamble, they were additionally told that no matter what gamble they chose, they would additionally discover the consequences of one gamble or the other. For example, in one condition, participants were told that they were going to receive information about the results of the safe gamble. A tendency to select the risky gamble in such a condition sets up the possibility of discovering in the postdecisional world that choosing the risky gamble was a mistake because only the safe gamble paid off. The only way to avoid any potential regret is to choose the gamble whose outcome will be revealed anyway.

For the most part, the information condition predicted the gamble participants made. Participants chose risky gambles when feedback about risky gambles was going to be received anyway, presumably in order to avoid the regret in discovering that the safe gamble that they did not choose would have won. Similarly, participants chose safe gambles when they were going to receive feedback about them in order to avoid the regret in discovering that the risky gamble that they did not choose would have won. In this study then, decisions that avoided regret were made irrespective of their riskiness.

The finding of individuals strategically attending to and making decisions on the basis of postdecisional regret as opposed to assessing and making decisions on the basis of risk has been confirmed a variety of other studies. Zeelenberg and Beattie (1997) found similar results with regard to regret and risk assessment in a task involving investment decisions rather than gambling paradigms, giving the results more applicability.

Are There Two Types of Regret to Avoid?

A regret-avoidance decision-making strategy would seem to involve a context in which the decision maker knows that foregone (unchosen) options can be resolved and will be known. Indeed, a number of studies just cited demonstrate the power of regret-based decision-making strategies by varying participants' knowledge that the foregone option outcome will be available postdecisionally (Ritov, 1996; Zeelenberg et al., 1996; for a complete review, see Zeelenberg, 1999a).

Bar-Hillel and Neter (1996) also varied the availability of the foregone option in their study of lottery-ticket exchanges. In some conditions, students were told that their exchanged ticket would be recycled and offered to someone else in the room. This procedure adds a particularly strong source of regret as participants must wrestle with the possibility that they will discover someone else has won with their exchanged ticket. However, in other conditions, students were told that they could exchange their lottery tickets and their original ticket would be destroyed. This procedure removes the possibility of regret associated with discovering that someone else won with their original lottery ticket. Surprisingly, the ticket exchange rates were unaffected by varying whether or not potentially regretful information was available. The participants' general reluctance to exchange tickets remained high even in the face of a monetary incentive to exchange, irrespective of whether the original ticket was to be recirculated (and potentially become a winning ticket for someone else) or thrown out (and not potentially become a winning ticket). In addition, the authors found that regret was self-reported at the same rate in the resolution and no resolution conditions, suggesting that the availability of resolution information may have played no role in the decision to resist exchanging lottery tickets.

The notion that one may anticipate regret even when it is impossible to resolve the status of the unchosen or foregone alternative is important because it widens the types of decisions in which regret-based decision-making strategies can be applied. For example, it is impossible to resolve outcomes associated with foregone alternative jobs, marriage partners, or risky behavior because they never get "played out." We label as *anticipated concrete regret* decision-making contexts ones that involve anticipating the actual postdecisional discovery of a more valued outcome of a foregone alternative. Anticipating the regret about actually discovering that someone else won a lottery with your original ticket is an example of a concrete regret that one can avoid by making the decision to resist exchanging lottery tickets. However, decision makers may still anticipate and avoid regret in a decision-making context in which it is impossible to ever know the resolution of the foregone alternative. In such contexts, a decision maker can imagine a scenario of being tormented by thoughts in the postdecisional world in which the actual outcome would have been better if only the foregone alternative had been chosen. We label this *anticipated hypothetical regret* because it involves anticipating postdecisional rumination about a potentially more valued outcome of a foregone alternative that can never be verified. Such regret could be avoided by simply deciding to choose what was envisioned as the foregone alternative.

In two studies (Sullivan & Amsel, 2001), we replicated and extended Bar-Hillel and Neter's finding of participants' use of regret-based decision-making strategies in the hypothetical (Study 1) and concrete (Study 2) anticipated-regret condition. In both studies we added a baseline measure of exchange when no incentive was offered and ran the study individually rather than in a classroom. In Study 1, 26 students from an Introductory Psychology class were interviewed individually and told that they, like everyone else in the class, were to draw a lottery ticket from a jar for the chance of winning a $5.00 gift certificate. After writing their name on the ticket (as contact information in case they won), they were asked to select another ticket from the same container. Participants were then told that they could enter the lottery with their original ticket or exchange it for the new ticket and enter the lottery with it. Students were additionally randomly assigned to a condition in which they were offered no incentive, a small incentive ($.05) or a large incentive ($.25) for exchanging their original ticket. They were told that the ticket they rejected would be destroyed, which should have minimized concrete source of anticipated regret in justifying resistance to the exchange. Nonetheless, the procedure in Study 1 was designed to promote resistance to ticket exchange by having participants form elaborate representations of the original ticket winning (writing contact information on the ticket), which would be activated in predecision simulations of postdecision regrets.

After they made their exchange decision, participants were asked to place their ticket in another "lottery" container and asked whether the ticket they placed in that container was less likely, more likely, or equally likely to win as other tickets in the container. Only 4 students (equally distributed among resisters and exchangers) incorrectly judged their chosen ticket as more likely to win than other tickets, with everyone else acknowledging that all tickets were equally likely to win. When given no incentive, all participants (9 out of 9, 100%) resisted exchanging tickets. However, when given an incentive only a slight a majority of students (9 out of 17, 53%) resist exchanging tickets (Fischer exact probability, $p < .05$), with no difference found between a small and large incentive. The tendency for a slight majority of students to resist exchanging lottery tickets when offered an incentive to do so in a context minimizing concrete sources of anticipated regret replicates the finding of Bar-Hillel and Neter (1996), who also found a slight majority of students (59%) to resist exchanging. The finding further confirms the possibility of a hypothetical source of anticipated regret in lottery-ticket exchanges. Bar-Hillel and Neter (1996) characterized such a strategy in the following way, "Our participants seemed willing to entertain the tenuous counterfactual: 'If only I had not exchanged my ticket, maybe it would have won' and even that vague possibility affected their decision" (p. 20).

The claim that participants anticipate hypothetical regret was further tested in Study 2, which was designed to lower participants' resistance to exchange lottery tickets. Our speculation was that resisters in Study 1 anticipated postdecisional hypothetical regret of their original ticket winning because of having the opportunity to form elaborate representations of the original ticket, maybe even imagining that it might win. Because representations of their original ticket winning were readily available to resisters, they may have concluded that it would better not to exchange tickets. Thus, to lessen participants' resistance to lottery-ticket exchanges when offered an incentive, we minimized their sense of ownership over the original ticket by limiting their time and engagement with it. We hypothesized that this would minimize the tendency of participants to frame the decision as one of relinquishing their ticket for another one. The frame we tried to create instead was one of choosing between two otherwise identical tickets, one of which they just happened to draw first but that had no more association for the participant with being a winning ticket than the ticket drawn later.

Thirty-seven college students from an Introductory Psychology class were interviewed individually and asked to draw two lottery tickets, one at a time, from a container. Rather than writing their names on the original ticket (as was done in Study 1), participants were merely asked to choose between their first and second drawn ticket to enter into the lottery. Students were offered either no incentive or a $.25 incentive to choose the second drawn ticket and told that the ticket not chosen would be returned to the set of active tickets, thereby reinstating the concrete source of regret in the present decision-making context. Thus, unlike Study 1, participants in Study 2 were led to believe that their tickets would be recycled, maximizing concrete hypothetical regret. However, despite this, Study 2 was designed to promote ticket exchange by blocking participants from forming elaborate representations of the original ticket being rejected, recycled back into the pool of lottery tickets, and winning.

The experimenter recorded the ticket chosen by each participant who placed it in the lottery container and then posed the same probability question as was asked in Study 1 (was their ticket less likely, more likely, or equally likely to win as other tickets in the container). Finally, the students rated on a 10-point scale (labeled from $1 = $ not at all to $10 = $ a lot) how much they thought about the exchange before deciding to do what they did and how sad they would feel if the rejected ticket won. Again, few students ($n = 2$) judged their chosen ticket not equal to other tickets in its likelihood to win. As in Study 1, most students (13 out of 18, 72%) resisted the ticket exchange in the no-incentive condition, but now only a minority of students (6 out of 19, 32%) resisted in the $.25 incentive condition (Fisher exact probability, $p < .01$, see Table 4.2). There were more exchangers in Study 2 than in Study 1 when combining the no incentive and $.25 incentive conditions, Fisher exact probability, $p < .05$ (Table 4.2). Finally, exchangers tended to think less about the exchange than did resisters, one-tail $t(35) = 1.95$, $p < .05$, but to feel no sadder if the rejected ticket were to win, $t(35) = .60$, ns (Table 4.2).

TABLE 4.2
Distributions and Judgments of Resisters and Exchangers

Comparison	Condition	Resisters	Exchangers
Incentive (Study 2)**			
	No	13	5
	$.25	6	13
Cross-Study Comparison* (Only Participants in the No or $.25 incentive condition)			
	Study 1	14	3
	Study 2	19	18
Ratings (Only Participants in Study 2)			
	Think*	4.21 (1.99)	3.11 (1.36)
	(n)	19	18
	Feel	4.74 (2.13)	4.22 (3.02)
	(n)	19	18

*p .05. **p .01.

Study 2 showed that the tendency to resist lottery-ticket exchanges even in the face of an incentive, as demonstrated in Study 1, could be overcome. We propose that the procedure in Study 2 lessened participants' sense of ownership regarding the original ticket in Study 2 compared to Study 1, minimizing the tendency to form elaborate representations of the original ticket winning. This speculation is supported by the finding that exchangers (who presumably did not form representations of the original ticket winning) reported taking less time to think though the exchange request than did resisters (predicted to form such representations).

Is decision making affected by two sources of anticipated regret? It seems so. Anticipated concrete regret involves anticipating the actual postdecisional discovery of a more valued outcome of a foregone alternative than the chosen alternative. Evidence of the power of such a form of regret on decision making is well documented in the aforementioned review and in Zeelenberg (1999a). Alternatively, anticipated regret can arise from more hypothetical sources than from discovering the resolution of foregone options in the postdecisional world. Anticipated hypothetical regret involves anticipating postdecisional rumination about an unverifiable but potentially more-valued outcome of a foregone alternative. Such regret is sensitive to the decision maker's encoding of the foregone alternative and its later anticipated availability in memory. As previously noted, making decisions that avoid anticipated hypothetical regret may well play a role in many real-world decisions where foregone alternatives cannot be resolved by virtue of choices that were made, like deciding whether or not to engage in risky behavior. Although one cannot resolve the foregone alternative in such cases as deciding to have unprotected sex, one can anticipate a postdecisional world in which one frequently and intensely wishes one had not made that decision.

Rationality of Regret Aversion

Although making decisions anticipating and avoiding concrete or hypothetical regret may be something we do, the question remains whether or not it is a rational thing to do. In an account of its history, Landman (1993) traced the development of Regret theory, highlighting how tenets of EU theory were extended to account for regret as a normative and integral part of the decision-making process. As described by Landman (1993), the expected utility of an option (x) is still germane to modern Regret models of decision making, but there is the additional component of adding or subtracting a value representing the individual's anticipated regret for not having chosen an alternate option (not y). The value of regret is subtracted from a calculation of the expected utility of a decision-option outcome, if the best possible outcome of the alternative-decision option has a higher expected utility. The value is added to the calculation, if the best possible alternative-option outcome has a lower value. Landman gives the example of a decision between having an operation to improve one's life that comes at some risk and not having an operation that involves living a less than functional life and potentially dying in a few months anyway. The positive outcome of having the operation is being cured (value = 1.0, probability = .6, subjective expected utility [SEU] = .6) and the negative outcome is dying on the operating table (value = .00, probability = .4, SEU = .00). The positive outcome of avoiding surgery is a pretty good life (value = .6, probability = .8, SEU = .48) but could negatively result in death in 6 months (value = .1, probability = .2, SEU = .02). Given that the best possible outcome of having the surgery has a SEU (being cured = .6) that is higher than the SEU values of the no-surgery option outcomes, then that value is subtracted from the SEU of each of the no-surgery option outcomes (SEU pretty good life = .48 − R(.6) = −.12; SEU death in 6 months = .02 − R(.6) = −.58). This reflects the anticipated potential postdecisional regret of deciding to forgo surgery. Moreover, because the best possible outcome of having no surgery also has a SEU (pretty good life = .48) that is higher than the SEU of death by surgery, then the former value is subtracted from the latter (SEU death by surgery = .00 − R(.48) = −.48) to again reflect anticipated postdecisional regret. However, the SEU of a surgical cure is higher than the SEU of the best possible outcome of the no-cure option (pretty good life = .48), so it is added to the latter SEU (SEU surgical cure = .6 + R(.48) = 1.08), reflecting the potential postdecisional elation of having made the best decision! From this analysis, the decision to have the operation (1.08 + −.48 = .60) than forgoing it (−.12 + −.58 = −.70) is normatively justified. According to Landman (1993), this formulation may be too accommodating to the basic decision model, and not exhaust the possibilities of Regret theory. But the formation does reveal how anticipated thoughts about postdecisional feelings can be made relevant in a normative decision model.

Although Regret theory can be normatively justified, that does not end the discussion of whether or not anticipating and avoiding regret is a decision-making practice that is rational. The assessment of rationality additionally requires coordinating the psychological models of actual judgments and decision making and logical or statistical models of normative judgments and decision making (see Amsel, 1985, and Stanovich, 1999, for a discussion of the relevance of this for psychology). The coordination of normative and the descriptive aspects of regret-based decision making is far from fully adequate. Zeelenberg (1999a) acknowledged that there is less-than-perfect support in the decision-making literature for specific tenets of Regret theory. However, it is argued that there is abundant evidence for the central tenet of Regret theory, that decision makers treat anticipated postdecisional regret as important in the process of deliberation (Landman, 1993; Mellers, 2000; Zeelenberg, 1999b). According to Zeelenberg (1999b), the normative basis for accepting the tenet is that anticipating and avoiding regret may be used to maximize both decision utility (i.e., it helps to insure that the decision option chosen is the one most valued) and experience utility (i.e., feeling good about the decision outcome). With regard to experience utility, Regret theory acknowledges the relevance to decision making of postdecision emotions that go beyond the value of the outcome. For example, two people may win the same gift but not feel the same way about it if one discovers she could have had a better gift (which results in regret), and the other discovers that he could have had a worse one (which results in elation; Amsel & Smalley, 2000). With regard to decision utility, Regret theory supposes that decision makers adopt a reference point in their analysis of the utility of a target option as the counterfactual states associated with foregone alternatives.

The normative adequacy of the central tent of Regret theory is important because it acknowledges a pivotal role of human emotions in the process of rational decision making (Landman, 1993; Mellers, 2000; Zeelenberg, 1999b). However, there remain problems standing in the way of the successful coordination between normative and descriptive aspects of regret-based decision making. Among those problems is one particularly relevant in the adolescent decision-making literature: the role of the decision-making context. This source of irrationality in anticipating and avoiding regret concerns the extent to which decision making is influenced by properties of the context, not of the decision options themselves. For example, whether or not hypothetical regret (i.e., anticipating postdecisional rumination about an unverifiable but potentially more-valued outcome of a foregone alternative) is anticipated and avoided depends on the extent to which the alternative is well enough encoded to be available postdecisionally. This was suggested by the Sullivan and Amsel (2001) work reported earlier. They found that when ownership of the first drawn lottery ticket was minimized, there was less anticipated regret (as evidenced by more ticket exchangers) than when such ownership was magnified. Zeelenberg (1999a) claimed that another condition that may heighten the experience of postdecisional regret is the presence of others in the decision maker's social or professional world for whom the decision is significant and may even expect the decision maker to choose a particular option. Besides highlighting possible postdecision regrets, the presence or even just the thoughts of others may force a delay in the decision-making process in order to ensure that it is done right. Additionally, Zeelenberg (1999b) noted that the decision makers' regret-based strategies may be contextually sensitive to whether the regret anticipated is their own or others'. The anticipation of others' regret may be strong in contexts where one's decisions have consequences for others. However, decisions made on the basis anticipating the concrete or hypothetical regret of others may insure neither that the most valued option will be selected (*decision utility*) nor that there will be satisfaction with the option selected (*experienced utility*). All this is further complicated by consideration of who compromises the decision-making context—a friend, an expert, or an authority. Moreover, in these contexts, the veridicality of the regret anticipated may come into question.

There is little doubt that decision makers' sensitivity to the context when anticipating and avoiding regret can be functional and at times serve to maximize experienced utility. But, what is less clear is whether contextual influence on the decision-making process maximizes decision utility. The anticipated regret avoided by making decisions that do not disappoint others may make one feel better about the decision but do not guarantee that a rational decision was made. Such contextual sources for anticipating and avoiding regret seem unrelated, or at least not systematically related to the values of the decision options. Put differently, the extent to which decision makers' anticipation and avoidance of regret are dependent on properties of the context and not on the decision options, the more difficult it is to defend the decision as rational.

In summary, there is good reason to treat the general decision-making strategy of anticipating and avoiding regret as rational, although there remains some lack of coordination between descriptive practices and normative models of regret-based decision making. However, not all uses of the strategy are rational. It may not be rational to make decisions anticipating future regrets if the regrets anticipated are based on a contextual source, which may maximize experienced utility but not decision utility.

ANTICIPATED REGRET AND ADOLESCENT DECISION MAKING

What about the relevance of a regret-based model of decision making for adolescents? As already suggested, regret-based decision making, whether induced or spontaneous, can function in some decision-making contexts to decrease adolescents' tendency to engage in risky behavior (Caffrey & Schneider, 2000; Richard et al., 1996, 1998). In the present section, we examine preadolescents' and college students' abilities to make regret-based decisions spontaneously and their sources of difficulty in doing so.

The Development of Spontaneously Regret-Based Decision Making

To study the spontaneous use of regret-based decision-making strategies, Bowden and Amsel (2002) developed a pencil-and-paper version of the lottery-ticket exchange problem and an equivalent nongambling version of the story. The stories involved a protagonist who had to decide whether or not to trade a lottery ticket (Lottery Story) or an unknown tennis partner (Tennis Story) for another ticket or partner and a cash incentive ($1.00). The stories are listed in Appendix A. In each case, participants were to make a judgment on a 7-point scale and to explain their judgment.

Prior to providing their judgments and justifications, participants were invited to imagine being the protagonist facing the decision. The protagonists (and, by extension, participants) were described as motivated to make a decision they would be satisfied with no matter how the decision turned out. This was meant to motivate participants to respond thoughtfully to the problem (Klaczynski, 2001) and consider strategies that might promote postdecisional satisfaction (experience utility). Experience utility can be accomplished by either of two strategies that promote decision utility. Decision satisfaction can be realized by adopting an EU-based strategy in which decisions are made by computing expected utilities associated with each option, comparing the options' expected utilities, and choosing the option that maximizes expected utility. Postdecisional satisfaction flows from knowing that the best decision was made at the time. Alternatively, a regret-based strategy could be used in which, factored into the comparison of option values, are those associated with anticipating and avoiding postdecisional regret. Postdecisional satisfaction flows from knowing that whatever outcome actually occurs, at least another outcome, which would have been very strongly regretted, did not. Armed with both these strategies, a decision maker can evaluate the decision to be made from multiple perspectives, appreciating both the utility to be gained and the regrets to be avoided.

Appendix A presents the Control condition of the study, but there were two additional conditions. In the Promoting Exchange condition, the following sentence was added at the end of each story, before participants were asked to make and justify their judgment: "While making the decision, you think about trading tickets (partners) and what you would do with the $1.00." This condition was designed to draw participants' attention to the value or utility of exchanging tickets, information that was already contained in the control story. By merely describing the fleeting thoughts of protagonists, the sentence does not add or subtract information from the decision-making context and so does not alter it in objective ways. This was not the case in Sullivan and Amsel (2001), who altered objective properties of the decision-making context. Of interest here was whether the fleeting thoughts of the protagonist that make salient the dominance of exchanging, alter not only participants' decision judgments but also their decision strategies as measured by their justifications for their judgments.

In the Promoting Resistance condition, the following sentence was added about the fleeting thoughts of the protagonists: "While making the decision, you think about how you would feel if you were to trade tickets/partners and discover that Sam/Molly won the lottery/tournament with the ticket/partner you gave her." In this case, the fleeting thoughts of the protagonists make salient the possibility of an outcome that would be regretted. Again, although this possibility can be inferred in the control condition, of interest was whether making it salient alters participants' decision judgments and strategies.

A group of 49 fourth- and fifth-grade students (23 male and 26 female, mean age 11.13 years) and 53 college students (30 female and 24 male, mean age 21.78 years) were randomly assigned to one of three different conditions: Control, Promoting Exchange, or Promoting Resistance. Each group filled out the tasks during class, with the preteens filling out the task as an initial activity in a class discussion and lecture on decision making. The preteens and adults were encouraged to circle their judgment on the 1 (*very likely not to exchange*) to 7 (*very likely to exchange*) scale and to fully justify their judgments, even if it meant writing down that they did not know why they responded the way that they did (no responses were treated as missing data).

An analysis of the judgments ranging from 1 to 7 revealed no significant main effects or interaction effects of the stories (Lottery vs. Tennis), conditions (Control, Exchange Promoting, or Resistance Promoting), or age group (Preteens vs. Adults). The overall mean for the Lottery story was 4.47, for the Tennis story it was 4.42, and each was significantly higher than the value of 4, labeled as *decision neutrality* (Lottery story, $t(102) = 1.99, p < .05$; Tennis story, $t(100) = 1.99, p < .05$). The finding suggests that there was an overall tendency of both groups to favor resisting the exchange but no systematic effects of subject (age group) or contextual (story, conditions) factors on judgments.

One factor that was related to judgments was how they were justified (see Table 4.3). Justifications were coded as either *regret-based* (i.e., justifications based on anticipating and avoiding potentially negative situations, which if realized would be a source of negative feelings), *comparison-based* (i.e., justifications based on determining the option associated with the best outcome as assessed on the basis of comparing the value or benefit and probability of the

TABLE 4.3
Mean Judgments by Decision-Making Strategy and Story

Story	Strategy	n	Mean	SD
Lottery				
	Regret-based	18	5.28	2.08
	Comparison-based	42	3.50	2.40
	Other	40	4.98	2.15
Tennis				
	Regret-based	12	5.33	1.30
	Comparison-based	28	3.18	2.34
	Other	59	4.83	1.90

Note. A rating below 4 reflects an acceptance of the exchange and a rating above 4 reflects resistance to the exchange.

possible outcomes), and *other* (i.e., no justifications or ones based on idiosyncratic, invalid and irrelevant information that goes beyond the story and is unrelated to value, probabilities, or anticipated feelings associated with possible outcomes). The interrater reliability was 87%, based on 60 judgments. In both participants' stories, regret-based justifications were associated with mean judgments of resisting the offer to exchange, and comparison-based justifications were associated with mean judgments of accepting the offer. In separate one-way analyses of variance (ANOVAs; with post-hoc follow-up analyses), run on each story, the mean judgment of participants who expressed comparison-based justifications were significantly lower (i.e., more likely to exchange) than the mean judgment of those offering regret-based ones, with the latter means no different than the mean judgments of those making other justifications (Lottery story, $F(2, 96) = 5.71$, $p < .01$; Tennis story, $F(2, 96) = 8.03$, $p < .001$).

By virtue of differentially predicting judgments, we think that participants' justifications described general characteristics of their decision-making strategies. For example, comparison-based justifications focused on the greater values of potential outcomes associated with certain choices. These justifications were frequently associated with the tendency to accept the exchanges.[2] Such a comparison argument was made clearly by a male college student who explained, "It seems like a win/win situation, either way you come out $1.00 ahead." The same argument was summarized succinctly by a male 10-year-old, "No matter what happens, at least I will have the dollar afterward."

---

[2]The 7-point judgment scale was recoded as reflecting a preference to accept the exchange (1–3), to resist the exchange (5–7), or as no preference (4). Over both stories, 56% of comparison-based judgments showed a preference for making the exchange, $\chi^2(2) = 18.37, p < .001$.

Regret-based justifications often meant resisting the offer to exchange in order to avoid anticipated regret.[3] For example, one male fifth grader expressed his motivation to make a decision to avoid an unwanted potential outcome, "because if he'd trade [the ticket], Sam might win with it." This parallels a college student's explanation for her ticket exchange resistance, "I would probably wonder later if the ticket I traded was better than the one I traded for." A female freshman expressed a related concern about unwanted potential regret when justifying her resistance to trade both tickets and partners: "I always have bad feelings about trading with friends. Whenever I do, it turns bad. . . . I'd prefer to remain friends than harbor resentment for a decision I'd made."

On some occasions, Other justifications could be treated as descriptions of actual decision-making practice as when they referred to information not in the story or to information best described as idiosyncratically, not rationally, relevant. An example of the former decision is a 5th-grade male who decided to trade tickets "because he could buy another ticket." An example of the latter decision is a 5th-grade female who resisted exchanging partners because "she had that name first so she didn't want to trade names." On these occasions, justifications point to the informational (albeit invalid) basis for judgments. However, in other cases, *other* justifications could not be treated as descriptions of actual decision-making practices because they were merely expressions of an inability to decide or to justify a decision. These cases may be best seen as an intuitive or heuristic decision-making process, which has been described (Klaczynski, 2001) as a process in which "the judgment or decision that 'comes to mind' (i.e., into working memory) is not the result of conscious efforts to reason through a situation or to retrieve a decision-making strategy. Consequently, the cognitive basis for such judgments is difficult to access and articulate" (p. 292). Although *other* justifications could not be treated as decision strategies, this does not mean that decision makers' justifications were not strategic, only that they could not verbalize them.

Justifications were fairly consistent over Stories, with 62% of participants responding with the same justification (binomial, $p < .001$, based on $p = .33$ for agreement) and there were no age, gender, or condition effects in consistent responding. As a result, the justification tokens were summed over stories and subject to a 3 (*Justifications*) by 3 (*Conditions*) by 2 (*Age Group*) mixed-model ANOVA, with repeated measures on the *Justifications* variable. There was a marginally significant *Justification* by *Condition* by *Age Group* interaction effect, $F(2, 97) = 2.85$, $p = .063$. Adults consistently used each strategy roughly one third (approximately .67 out of 2) of the time across conditions, whereas the preteens offered *other* justifications ($M = 1.27$) more

[3]Over stories, 70% of regret-based judgments showed a preference for resisting exchange, $^{2}(2) = 22.20$, $p < .001$.

often than comparison-based ones (M = .59) and both of those more than regret-based (M = .02) justification, which varied over condition. This relative relation in the frequency of preteens' justifications varied in the promoting exchange condition, in which comparison-based justifications (M = .94) were offered as frequently as *other* ones (M = .81) and both were made more frequently than *regret-based*, which were made by no preteen in this condition.

The adults in the present study adopted regret-based decision-making strategy as often as they adopted any other one, with 39% of the adults offering the justification at least once. Moreover, they deployed such a decision-making strategy consistently over stories and across conditions. The finding of a sizable percentage of resisters and exchangers in incentive conditions in the present study and the previous ones suggests the possibility of an individual difference factor. One such source may be a tendency to engage in *counterfactual reasoning* (Harris, 2000; Kasimatis & Wells, 1995), which is the cognitive process underlying the anticipation of regret. Although none of the present research was designed to detect the existence of such a factor, its identification would be of central importance in future research.

In contrast to the college students, the preteens did not spontaneously adopt regret-based decision-making strategies, despite the presence of conditions that were designed to promote their use. Indeed, the regret-based decision-making strategy seems to be of limited availability to preteens as there was only one incidence of it. In contrast to the growth of regret-based justifications, comparison-based ones were offered as frequently by preteens (M = .59) as by adults (M = .76), $t(101) = 1.10$, ns. The strategy is based on the EU model of calculating and maximizing expected utility, suggesting that according to this standard, preteens were as rational as adults.

There was a developmental decrease in the frequency of other-based justifications (preteen M = 1.27, adult M = .70, $t(101) = 3.33$, $p < .001$). Moreover, there were negative partial (controlling for age, gender, and condition) correlations between the tendency to make regret-based and other justifications, $r = -.40$ (98), $p < .001$, and between comparison-based and other justifications, $r = -.67$ (98), $p < .001$. The data suggest that the acquisition of rational decision-making strategies (EU or regret-based) is associated with a decrease in idiosyncratic judgments. Such a suggestion finds support in Klaczynski (2001) who, in a very different study, nonetheless demonstrated a similar decrease of idiosyncratic or atypical decision-making judgment errors (but not of typical errors) and an increase in rational judgments in the examined-age period.

The data regarding decision-making judgments and justifications presented here is consistent with many of the claims presented earlier regarding decision making in adolescence. Consistent with those who claim that adolescents are irrational (Baron, 1990) or dysregulated (Byrnes, 1998) decision makers, there was a notable lack of regret-based justifications and heavy use of other justifications. On the other hand, the fact that both age groups offered comparison-based justifications equally frequently gives additional credence to those who claim that adolescents are as rational as adults viewed from the norms of the EU decision-making model (Beyth-Marom et al., 1993; Furby & Beyth-Marom, 1992).

One curious finding in the present study is the limited impact of such contextual factors as story content and salience manipulations on decision making. In other work on adolescent decision making, task content has been found to be a powerful moderator of adolescent decision making (Byrnes, 1998; Finken & Jacobs, 1996; Miller & Byrnes, 1997). However, story type did not influence on decision judgments or justifications, even though the content domains of gambling (lottery) and athletics (tennis), used in the present study, have been shown to affect decision making in other studies (Byrnes, 1998). Perhaps the similar structure of the stories in their focus on interpersonal transactions (trading or not trading a commodity with a friend) overwhelmed any effect of content domains.

Adult decision makers' sensitivity to contextual manipulations that alter the salience of information have been well-documented (Tversky & Kahneman, 1981) and there is evidence of developmental increases in such sensitivity (Reyna & Ellis, 1994). In contrast to this, only preteens but not adults in the present study were influenced by contextual variation that made salient various aspects of the decision problem. However, the present findings are consistent with Berg (1989), who found that adolescents with less knowledge of strategy effectiveness (as rated by experts) responded more strongly and inappropriately to contextual changes in everyday problem-solving tasks compared to adolescents with more strategic effectiveness knowledge. She argued that individuals with little knowledge of strategy effectiveness have a limited basis to determine whether and how to adjust to their problem-solving strategies when faced with contextual changes in a problem. We do not want to overstate the relation between the studies, as the present study has few of the design features of Berg's. But paralleling her results, the preteens in the present study had limited knowledge of decision-making strategy effectiveness as measured by their tendency not to use strategies that experts in decision making have identified as more effective in the sense of being valid and functional (regret-based justifications) and their tendency to use strategies identified as ineffective (other justifications). That is, although preteens used comparison-based justifications at adult levels, their broader knowledge of decision-making strategy effectiveness was less sophisticated, making them particularly vulnerable to such decision-making context effects as highlighting the fleeting thoughts of decision makers.

The present study documents that many adults spontaneously approach decisions seeking to anticipate and avoid regret, whereas preteens do not.

Additionally the growth in regret-based decision making was associated with a decrease in idiosyncratic and unjustified judgments and a tendency to be uninfluenced by contextual factors. Only future research will confirm these connections, but in each case there are other studies that support the claim of a link. The linkage between the growth of regret-based decision making and a decrease in poor decision making and contextual oversensitivity is proposed to be the acquisition of knowledge of strategic effectiveness, that is, the appreciation of decision-making strategies as valid and functional. Acquiring strategic understanding is consistent with Byrnes' (1998) characterization of a self-regulated decision maker, who has good appreciation of the effectiveness of their decision-making strategies, ways to deal with moderating variables, and high standards for successful decision making. The availability of more effective and valid (i.e., rational) grounds for decision making may be the basis for adolescents learning to avoid both overreacting to contextual variation and making idiosyncratic or unjustified decisions.

The Acquisition and Consolidation of Component Skills for Anticipating and Avoiding Regret

The central point of the chapter has been that regret-based decision making is a normatively rational basis on which to make many decisions and one that is often adopted by people actually making them. However, preadolescents do not spontaneously approach decisions by anticipating and seeking to avoid regret. One remaining question is whether 10- and 11-year-old preteens lack the cognitive prerequisite skills for making decisions that anticipate and avoid regret or merely fail to appreciate the strategic value of doing so. Answering that question may clarify the nature of the developmental process underlying the acquisition of regret-based decision making in adolescence.

Cottrell and Amsel (2001) attempted to test for availability of component skills underlying regret-based decision making among 19 college-bound preteens (10-year-old fourth graders who were in a gifted program in which college attendance was highly likely) and 97 college students (psychology students with an average age of 22 years). We decomposed regret-based decision making into four component cognitive skills. The four skills identified as necessary for regret-based decision making include the abilities to (a) methodically generate both positive and negative possible outcomes associated with each decision option, (b) systematically anticipate one's own feelings associated with each possibility being realized, (c) consistently rank-order those outcomes in light of anticipated feelings, and (d) decide to avoid the worst possible outcome. Of course, this does not exhaust the skills involved in regret-based decision making. However, our goal was to identify the decision-making skills that are not only necessary but also unique in the process of anticipating and avoiding regret. For example, we did not assess the ability to compute utilities (Schlottman & Anderson, 1994) even though it is a component skill necessary to reason according to the Regret theory of decision making. However, it is not a component cognitive ability that is unique to regret-based decision making as it is also a characteristic of decision making according to EU theory (Beyth-Marom et al., 1991).

The four component skills uniquely necessary for regret-based decision making are assumed to have two properties that are important to note. First, they are temporally organized in the sense that Skill a (generating positive and negative outcomes) would generally come before Skill b (anticipating one's feelings about the potential outcomes). This does not preclude the possibility of complete or partial iterative processes that involves repeatedly cycling through all or some of the steps. However, given that one step is taken in a given iteration, the later but not the earlier step in the sequence may also be required. The second property is that the skills are hierarchically related in that completing one step is necessary for completing the next step. Unless one has generated possible positive and negative outcomes, potential emotional reactions to them cannot be anticipated, and if those reactions are not anticipated, they cannot be ranked.

The temporal and hierarchical nature of the cognitive skills under investigation required separate tests of each skill. Each test was embedded in a questionnaire containing four different stories, one story testing each of four skills. In each story, a protagonist is described as struggling with a decision about a relationship between friends within a school context (i.e., working together or alone on a school project; giving critical or complimentary academic feedback to a friend) or a home context (i.e., buying a gift for oneself or a friend, going to a movie with friends or studying). The stories were constructed to be familiar to preteens and college students. In each story, decision options were presented as mutually exclusive and participants were asked to advise the protagonist making a decision, by using one of the component decision-making skills (generate possible outcomes, anticipate feelings regarding possible outcomes, rank outcomes, and choose to avoid the most undesired outcome). Appendix B presents an example of one of the stories and each of the tasks. Interviews with and questionnaires distributed to other participants of comparable ages to participants in the present study allowed us to identify decision options that were considered more culturally appropriate or socially desirable.[4] We labeled the culturally appropriate or socially desirable option as *desired* and the alternative option as *undesired* and

_____

[4]There was broad (but not unanimous) agreement among a majority of students in each age group that it was more appropriate and desirable to (a) work together rather than alone with a friend on a school project, (b) give complimentary than critical academic feedback to a friend, (c) buy a gift for a friend than for oneself, and (d) study for an exam than go to a movie.

assumed that a majority of participants in each age group would think—at least initially—that the desired option was best.

Questionnaires were distributed and completed in class. In each questionnaire, the order of presenting decision-making tasks was invariant, reflecting what we believe to be their real-time sequence in actual regret-based decision making. Story 1 tested participants' generation of possible outcomes of decision options. Story 2 involved participants anticipating the feelings about already-generated possible outcomes being realized. Story 3 tested participants' ranking from *best* to *worst* of already generated and evaluated possible outcomes. Story 4 measured participants' decisions to avoid the worst possible outcome given information about already-rank-ordered possible outcomes. The skill tested by a given story was counterbalanced in four different questionnaires resulting in approximately one quarter of the participants being tested for each component with a given story. We review the nature of the skills tested and the results from each assessment in separate sections now.

Generating Possible Outcomes of Decision Alternatives. Participants were asked to generate four possible outcomes associated with the options facing a protagonist (see Appendix B). We asked specifically for four outcomes because we were interested in the types, not the number, of possible outcomes generated. Methodically generating a range of possible positive and negative outcomes for each option is necessary for a complete assessment of potential regrets. However, because one option had been identified as more culturally appropriate and socially desired, we assumed that positive outcomes associated with the desired option (and perhaps negative options associated with the undesired option) would be more available and more frequently generated. That is, the positive consequences of "doing the right thing" and maybe the negative consequences of not doing so are culturally available and may bias participants' generation of outcome possibilities.

Generated outcomes were coded[5] as positive (*good*) or negative (*bad*) for the desired and undesired decision option, tallied, and subjected to a 2 (age group) by 2 (outcome) by 2 (decision option) mixed-model ANOVA. Outcomes were not equally generated by option (*desired* or *undesired*) or outcome (*positive* or *negative*). There was an overall tendency for participants to generate many more positive than negative possible outcomes regarding the desired (positive $M = .93$; negative $M = .37$) than undesired option (positive $M = .58$; negative $M = .58$), $F(1, 110) = 16.07$, $p < .001$. This bias to unevenly generate possibilities over options and outcomes was stronger among the preteens who generated more positive than negative possible outcomes about the desired outcome than did adults. Both groups generated positive

---

[5]The interrater reliability for the five codes (*positive desired, negative desired, positive undesired, negative undesired,* and *nonanticipatory judgment*) for 20% of the participants was 85%.

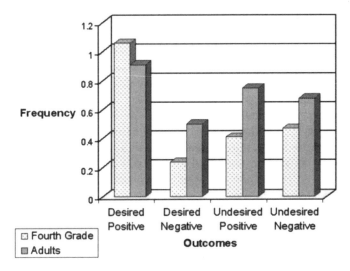

FIG. 4.1.   Frequency of possible outcomes generated by age group and option desirability.

and negative possible outcomes equally frequently regarding the undesired option (see Fig. 4.1). One-way ANOVA follow-up analyses revealed that preteens generated fewer negative desired outcomes and positive undesired ones. The former result is particularly important as fewer negative outcomes generated, means fewer sources of anticipated regret for the desired option.

Anticipating Feelings About Outcome Possibilities.   The second task in the questionnaire required participants to rate their anticipated feelings regarding four given possible outcomes: a positive and a negative outcome associated with a desired and an undesired option (see Appendix B).[6] Systematically anticipating one's feelings about potential positive and negative outcomes would be important in the appropriate use of regret-based decision making (see the previous discussion of experience and decision utility and the role of context in decision making). That is, judgments of anticipated emotion must be made independently of any initial judgments of the desirability of the options. If anticipatory judgments are not made independently of the desirability of the outcome, then the exercise of anticipating regret is a meaningless activity performed merely to find support for a predetermined decision. Just as the confirmation bias serves to merely support a preordained position in a hypothesis-testing context, the influence of the desirability of

---

[6]The options given to participants to rate were developed by the experimenters and identified by a group of nonparticipants in each age group as *positive* and *negative*. However, no attempt was made to try to equalize the options in terms of their affective intensity.

options on anticipated feelings about potential outcomes merely preordains a specific decision in a decision-making context. Thus, to make an appropriate regret-based decision, it would be necessary to anticipate feeling generally happy about positive potential outcomes and sad about negative potential outcomes, irrespective of the apparent desirability of the options with which they are associated.

Participants' anticipated affective ratings were subjected to a separate 2 (Age Group) by 2 (Outcome) by 2 (Decision Option) mixed-model ANOVA. As predicted, anticipated affective ratings were more positive for desired (M = 5.03) than undesired (M = 3.62) options, suggesting that the desirability of an option affected participants' emotional reactions to the potential outcomes. Again this effect was stronger for children, who, compared to adults, anticipated feeling much happier about desired than undesired options, $F(1, 111) = 6.20, p < .01$, and feeling much less happy about positive than negative options, $F(1, 111) = 4.09, p < .05$ (see Fig. 4.2). The results suggest that, not only do preteens generate fewer negative potential outcomes for desired options than do adults (as demonstrated in "Generating Possible Outcomes of Decision Alternatives"), but they also anticipate such potential outcomes to be emotionally less negative than do adults.

Rank-Ordering Anticipated Feelings About Outcome Possibilities. The third task in the questionnaire involved rank-ordering four given outcomes, from the anticipated emotionally best (*most positive*) to worst (*most negative*)

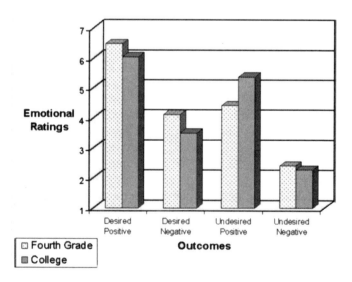

FIG. 4.2. Mean emotion ratings of outcomes (very happy = 7 to very sad = 1) by age group and option desirability.

(see Appendix B). As with the anticipatory affective ratings, anticipatory affective rankings about potential positive and negative outcomes would have to
be systematic for the rational use of regret-based decision making. Participants'
anticipated affective rankings were subjected to the same 2 by 2 by 2 mixed-
model ANOVA that has been used previously. Again, as with the ratings,
affective rankings were higher (*more positive*) for desired (M = 2.05) than undesired (M = 2.83) options, suggesting bias in being influenced by option desirability. Also as before, the preteens' ratings were more unsystematic than
the adults. Preteens' anticipatory affective rankings were much more positive
regarding desired options (M Preteens = 1.82; M Adult = 2.26) than undesired ones (M Preteens = 3.00; M Adult = 2.66), $F(1, 111) = 5.73, p < .05$
(see Fig. 4.3). There was also a 3-way interaction, $F(1, 111) = 5.73, p < .05$,
due to preteens emotionally ranking undesired positive (M = 2.77) and negative (M = 3.24) outcomes no differently from each other, which was the only
pair of outcomes for desired or undesired options that was not differentiated by
this group. Both rankings were higher than neutrality (2.5), suggesting that
both anticipated outcomes of undesired options are ranked by preteens as
emotionally poor. Thus, irrespective of their bias in generating potential outcomes or their feelings about them, preteens are also unsystematic in their
emotional ranking of anticipated outcomes (they judge as emotionally dis-
agreeable even positive outcomes associated with undesired options).

Deciding to Avoid the Emotionally Worst Possible Outcome. Finally,
participants decided which of the protagonists' options they thought would
be best, defined as one the protagonist would *not* regret depending on how it

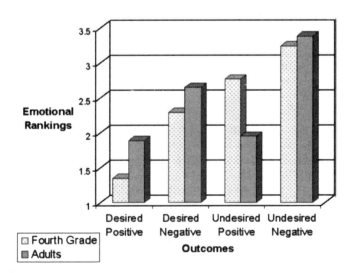

FIG. 4.3.   Mean emotional rankings of outcomes (best = 1 to worst = 4) by
age group and option desirability.

turned out (see Appendix B). Additionally, participants were told that the likelihood of the occurrence of each outcome of a decision option was the same and were given the protagonists' emotional rankings of positive and negative outcomes for desired and undesired options. In three of the stories, the positive outcome envisioned for the desired option was emotionally ranked by the protagonist as the best possible one, and the negative outcome for the same option as the worst. By setting up the ranking in this manner, participants making decisions to avoid the emotionally worst possible outcome would choose the undesired option. It was assumed that the undesired option would not be chosen very frequently, except by participants seeking to avoid regret. To confirm this assumption, the fourth story (given randomly to one fourth of the sample) was designed differently than the other three stories. In the fourth story, the positive and negative outcomes envisioned for the undesired option were emotionally ranked by the protagonist as respectively the best and worst possible ones. It was predicted that under these conditions, adults and preteens alike would choose the desired option as the best decision. This prediction was largely confirmed, with 72% (22 out of 32) of the participants choosing the desired option in this control story. The picture was different in the other three experimental stories, where the undesired option (the option that would avoid anticipated regret) was selected only 40% of the time, $\chi^2(1) = 10.01, p$ .001. Most importantly, there was no difference in the frequency with which preteens (41%) and adults (53%) chose the options that would avoid regret. Thus, given sufficient information about protagonists' emotional rankings, an equally sizable percentage of preteens and adults made decisions that anticipated and avoided regret.

The patterns of results from the present study suggest that preteens are as competent as adults to make decisions that anticipate and avoid regret when sufficiently scaffolded to make such decisions. A sizable percentage of preteens and adults ignored an option's undesirability and chose it as the best decision to make when the desired option was associated with the emotionally worst (and best) possible outcome. However, without the support and left to their own devices, preteens preordained the desirable options; negative potential outcomes anticipated for desired options were generated less often and anticipated to be less affectively negative by preteens than adults. Moreover, preteens ranked outcomes regarding undesired options as emotionally poor, presumably the type of outcome they would try to avoid when making decisions. It should be noted that many of the biases demonstrated by preteens were also seen in adults, suggesting that the preteens were less sophisticated but not fundamentally different than adults in their abilities to anticipate and avoid regret. However, caution should be exercised in interpreting the results. The within-subject design may have produced different carryover effects from task to task for preteens than for college students, whose judgments on most tasks were markedly different. Second, the preteen sample was small ($N = 19$) and atypical (from a gifted and talented program), which are characteristics of selecting preteens who, we were confident, were college bound. Third, despite pretesting and equating the groups for the outcome desirability of each story, the stories were not equated in other ways, including all the perceived consequences of choosing the undesired option.

With these caveats in mind, the findings suggest that preadolescents may have the component skills to make adultlike decisions to anticipate and avoid regret. However, they lack adults' systematicity in coordinating the skills in the service of making regret-based decisions. That is, they have the hypothetical, logical, and theoretical skills to think through a decision at least as competently as adults to avoid postdecisional regret, given sufficient scaffolding, but perhaps lack the metacognitive skills (Moshman, 1999) to do so spontaneously. The proviso in this developmental analysis concerns the consistent finding of only a subset of adults (and in this case preteens) who show a tendency to make regret-avoiding judgments. As noted earlier, an individual difference factor in counterfactual reasoning may be at work in affecting participants' tendency to anticipate regret. But such a factor may not be sufficient to account for all of the anticipatory judgment biases children and the adults demonstrate (Klaczynski & Fauth, 1996). Understanding the individual difference factors within a developmental framework appears to be a very important task in order to construct a complete account of regret-based decision making.

Reconceptualizing Adolescent Decision Making

We introduced this chapter by suggesting that an alternative normative decision-making model may help clarify some of the confusing claims being made about adolescents' abilities to make rational decisions. It was argued that the regret-based decision-making model is best seen as an extension rather than a replacement of EU theory. As an extension of EU, Regret theory has many of the same properties, including the computing of probabilities and utilities of outcomes and combining those values. But beyond allowing decision makers to envision potential outcomes of options, Regret theory permits them to anticipate their feelings about those envisioned outcomes and use such information to inform the decision-making process itself. There remain issues regarding the normative adequacy of regret theory, but work continues (Zeelenberg, 1999b). As for its descriptive adequacy, it appears that a regret-based decision-making strategy is often used by adults in contexts where the decision maker might actually confront information about how regrettable a decision had been. Regret avoidance was found, irrespective of risk avoidance, to be spontaneously adopted by many adults and even most adults in some circumstances (Zeelenberg et al., 1996). Regret avoidance can be easily induced and has behavioral consequences (Richards et al., 1996). Moreover, regret avoidance arises in more abstract decision-making contexts in which decision makers anticipate and avoid regret regarding foregone alternative outcomes that can never be resolved.

In some of the first research presented on the topic, preteens did not spontaneously adopt regret-based decision-making strategies. However, with decision-making support, as many preteens as adults made decisions avoiding the worst possible emotional outcome even if that outcome was associated with a socioculturally desired option. Adolescents' acquisition of rational decision-making strategies, whether based on Regret or EU theory, was connected to the growth of metacognitive knowledge of decision-making strategy effectiveness, which is a characteristic of well-regulated decision makers (Byrnes, 1998). It was further suggested that development of such metacognitive knowledge may be related to the decrease in idiosyncratic or unjustified decisions and an increase in both appropriate responses to contextual variation and the use of more methodical, systematic, and unbiased regret-based decision-making processes (i.e., generating possible outcomes, anticipating feelings about those possible outcomes, and emotionally rank-ordering outcomes).

The suggestion that the acquisition of metacognitive decision-making knowledge may be related to more unbiased regret-based decision making and more appropriate responses to contextual variation is an important one. Other studies have found strong effects of all sorts of contexts on adolescent decision making (cf. Byrnes, 1998; Finken & Jacobs, 1996; Klaczynski, 2001, chap. 2, this volume; Miller & Byrnes, 1997), often resulting in less adequate or appropriate decisions being made. That is, all types of context effects have been shown to induce biased decision making in adolescents, undermining rational processes. For example, the presence of peers is a contextual factor that has been shown to increase adolescents' tendency for risk taking both on athletic performance tasks and questionnaires assessing health-related risk-taking behaviors (Maggs, Almeida, & Galambos, 1995; Miller & Byrnes, 1997; Wallace & Logan, 2001), although in some contexts and for some tasks, peers can actually promote rational reasoning (Moshman & Geil, 1998). Although the influence of peers on risk taking may depend on the nature of the peer relationship (Jones, 1985), characteristics of the social setting (Finken, 2001), and broader aspects of the sociocultural context (Lightfoot, 1997), it is nonetheless a powerful influence. This is particularly noteworthy, as being with peers is a context in which teenagers often find themselves (Larson & Verma, 1999). Miller and Byrnes (1997; also see Finken, chap. 8, this volume) discuss the often-negative influence of peers as due to their role as models of, audiences for, and competitive partners egging on adolescents' poor decision making and risk taking. Perhaps a fourth role of peers is that of an agent who biases the rational assessment of regret. Peers and their (sub)culture create a decision-making context in which certain decision options might be seen as socioculturally desired. We have seen that, without decision-making support, preteens biasedly judge socioculturally desirable options, inadvertently setting into motion a cognitive process that almost "rubber stamps" a socioculturally desired option.

Although biased, adolescent regret assessment involves many of the cognitive processes identified as being acquired during adolescence and necessary for hypothetico–deductive reasoning, including hypothetical and logical reasoning. As with the case of hypothetico–deductive reasoning, where children must learn to coordinate component skills in the service of a strategic approach to problem solving (Amsel & Brock, 1996; Schauble, 1996), so it is with decision making. In both cases, inexperience and lack of metacognitive knowledge produce bias leading to poor scientific conclusions and risky decisions. Support for the process and learning from poor outcomes may debias decision-making processes (Baron, 1993; Byrnes, Miller, & Reynolds, 1999) just as they have shown to debias scientific reasoning (Kuhn et al., 1988, 1995).

The next step in this work will be to explicitly examine at the role of regret-based decision making in risky decisions. Developmental and individual differences in generating, evaluating, and avoiding regret may be more meaningfully studied in contexts where decisions have interesting and important consequences. Evidence of developmental and individual differences in adolescents' regulation of anticipated emotions in decision making might provide a coherent explanation of how adolescents can be so full of intellectual capability and still make some of the kinds of decisions they do.

ACKNOWLEDGMENTS

The data presented in this chapter were based on senior undergraduate theses completed by the junior authors and supervised by the senior author. Our appreciation also goes to the students and teachers of the 4th and 5th grades of Hillcrest (Mr. Thompson, Principal) and Gramercy (Mr. Drainy, Principal) elementary schools and administrators of the Ogden City Schools (Cathy Ortega, Assistant Superintendent). A tremendous amount of gratitude goes to Bill McVaugh, who read and critiqued all the research and sat on each student's proposal and thesis defense committee. Thanks to Paul Klaczynski for making clear just how important the individual differences factors may be. Editorial advice and challenges from Paul Klaczynski and Janis Jacobs made this chapter much better than it was. Finally, thanks to my family: Judi, for a critical and always trustworthy ear and eye, and David and Daniel, whose valuable insights into the thinking and culture of preteens were appreciated, if not always offered consciously.

APPENDIX A: LOTTERY TICKET (LT)
AND TENNIS PLAYER (TP) STORIES USED
IN BOWDEN AND AMSEL (2002)

Danny was just given a raffle ticket to win a wonderful new bike. Sam was also given a ticket. Sam wants to trade his ticket for Danny's ticket. Danny said *no*, so Sam offers Danny $1.00 to trade tickets. In considering the trade, Danny is aware that all the tickets really have an equal chance of winning. Imagine that you are Danny. You want to make a good decision—one that you would not feel so sad about later depending on how the decision turned out.

How likely is it that you will trade raffle tickets with Sam for $1.00 or resist trading them and not get the $1.00?

1	2	3	4	5	6	7
Very likely to trade (and get $1.00)			Equally likely to trade or resist trading			Very likely to resist trading (and not get $1.00)

Explain your choice _____

_____

_____

Sandra was to play an important tennis tournament. She had to pick the name of a partner from a hat. Molly also played in the tournament and she too picked a partner's name from a hat. After drawing names, Molly asked Sandra to trade names for the partner she had picked. Sandra said *no*, so Molly offers Sandra $1.00 to trade partners. In considering the trade, Sandra is aware that neither she nor Molly knows any of the names in the hat and all are equally good tennis players. Imagine that you are Sandra. You want to make a good decision—one that you would not feel so sad about later depending on how the decision turned out.

How likely is it that you would trade partners with Molly for $1.00 or resist trading them and not get the $1.00?

1	2	3	4	5	6	7
Very likely to trade (and get $1.00)			Equally likely to trade or resist trading			Very likely to resist trading (and not get $1.00)

Explain your choice _____

_____

_____

APPENDIX B: STORY AND TASKS ASSESSING REGRET-BASED DECISION MAKING (COTTRELL & AMSEL, 2001)

John, a student, has a very important test in his first class tomorrow, and he wants to get a good grade on it to please himself and his parents. It is the movie's last night in the theaters and John and his friends have wanted to see it for a long time. He thinks that he will have a great time if he goes. John also thinks that by studying tonight he will do very well on the test. He knows he *can't* both go to the movie with friends and study for the exam—he has to decide to do one or the other.

Generating positive and negative outcomes. Pretend John is your friend and he has asked you to help him think through the decision he has to make. He asks you to help him think of possible outcomes associated with the decision he has to make. He has asked you to come up with four possible *outcomes*. Briefly describe these four below.

Anticipating one's feeling about possible outcomes. Please imagine you are John and circle the number corresponding to how it would feel if each of the following four options occurred.

1. If he studied for the exam, he would get a good grade on his test and most likely his parents will be happy with him.

1	2	3	4	5	6	7
Very sad	Pretty sad	A little sad	Not sad or happy	A little happy	Pretty happy	Very happy

2. If he went to the movie, he would be unprepared to take his test and most likely his test performance will negatively affect his GPA, disappointing himself and his parents.

1	2	3	4	5	6	7
Very sad	Pretty sad	A little sad	Not sad or happy	A little happy	Pretty happy	Very happy

3. If he studied for the exam, he would not see the movie and most likely he will feel left out when his friends talk about it.

1	2	3	4	5	6	7
Very sad	Pretty sad	A little sad	Not sad or happy	A little happy	Pretty happy	Very happy

4. If he went to the movie, he would hang out with his friends and most likely they will think he is cool for putting them first and the exam second.

1	2	3	4	5	6	7
Very sad	Pretty sad	A little sad	Not sad or happy	A little happy	Pretty happy	Very happy

Rank ordering outcome options. Please read these possible outcomes below and rank them from 1–4 according to what *you* think is the BEST or MOST POSITIVE possible outcome in terms of how it would make him feel (ranked as 1) to what you think is the WORST or MOST NEGATIVE possible outcome in terms of how it would make him feel (rank as 4). Be sure to rank each possible outcome and give each outcome a 1, 2, 3, or 4.

Rank: Outcome:

_____   If he studied for the exam, he will get a good grade on his test and most likely his parents would be happy with him.

_____   If he went to the movie, he will be unprepared to take his test and most likely his test performance will negatively affect his GPA, disappointing himself and his parents.

_____   If he studied for the exam, he will not see the movie and most likely he will feel left out when his friends talk about it.

_____   If he went to the movie, he will hang out with his friends and most likely they will think he is cool putting them first and the exam second.

Deciding to avoid the worst possible outcome. John ranked the possible outcomes associated with making one decision or the other. He ranked them according to what he thought is the BEST or MOST POSITIVE possible outcome in terms of how he would feel (ranked as 1) to what he thought is the WORST or MOST NEGATIVE possible outcome in terms of how it would make him feel (rank as 4).

Rank: Outcome:

1   If he studied for the exam, he will get a good grade on his test and most likely his parents would be happy with him.

2   If he went to the movie, he will hang out with his friends and most likely they will think he is cool putting them first and the exam second.

3   If he went to the movie, he will be unprepared to take his test and most likely his test performance will negatively affect his GPA, disappointing himself and his parents.

4   If he studied for the exam, he will not see the movie and most likely he will feel left out when his friends talk about it.

To John, each decision outcome seemed equally likely to occur. John wanted to make a good decision—one that he would *not* deeply regret later depending on how it turned out. Imagine you are John, and decide which is the best decision he could make.

John should (circle one):   Study for the exam.   Go to the movie with friends.

REFERENCES

Amsel, E. (1985). Psychologism and the psychology of scientists: A response to Gibson. *New Ideas in Psychology, 3*, 265–272.

Amsel, E., & Brock, S. (1996). Developmental changes in children's evaluation of evidence. *Cognitive Development, 11*, 523–550.

Amsel, E., McVaugh, B., Biggs, A., & Ferguson, T. (2003, April). *Regret and its relation to guilt and shame.* Poster presented at Rocky Mountain Psychology Association, Denver, CO.

Amsel, E., & Smalley, J. (2000). Beyond really and truly: Children's counterfactual thinking about pretend and possible worlds. In K. Riggs & P. Mitchell (Eds.), *Children's reasoning and the mind* (pp. 99–134). Brighton, England: Psychology Press.

Arnett, J. J. (1992). Reckless behavior in adolescence: A developmental perspective. *Developmental Review, 12*, 339–373.

Arnett, J. J. (1999). Adolescent storm and stress, reconsidered. *American Psychologist, 54*, 317–326.

Arnett, J. J., & Balle-Jensen, L. (1993). Cultural bases of risk behavior: Danish adolescents. *Child Development, 64*, 1842–1855.

Bar-Hillel, M., & Neter, E. (1996). Why are people reluctant to exchange lottery tickets? *Journal of Personality and Social Psychology, 70*, 17–27.

Baron, J. (1990). Harmful heuristics and the improvement of thinking. In D. Kuhn (Ed.), *Developmental perspectives on the teaching and thinking reasoning skills: Contributions to human development* (pp. 28–47). Basel, Switzerland: Karger.

Baron, J. (1993). The effects of normative beliefs on anticipate emotions. *Journal of Personality and Social Psychology, 63*, 320–330.

Bell, N., & Bell, R. (1993). *Adolescent risk taking.* Newbury Park, CA: Sage.

Berg, C. (1989). Knowledge of strategies for dealing with everyday problems from childhood to adolescence. *Developmental Psychology, 25*, 607–618.

Beyth-Marom, R., Austin, L., Fischhoff, B., Palmgren, C., & Jacobs-Quadrel, M. (1993). Perceived consequences of risky behaviors: Adults and adolescents. *Developmental Psychology, 29*, 549–563.

Beyth-Marom, R., Fischhoff, B., Quadrel, M. J., & Furby, L. (1991). Teaching decision making to adolescents: A critical review. In J. Baron & R. V. Brown (Eds.), *Teaching decision-making to adolescents* (pp. 19–59). Washington, DC: APA Press.

Bowden, T., & Amsel, E. (2002, April). *The development of regret-based decision making: The role of context.* Poster presented at Rocky Mountain Psychology Association, Park City, UT.

Boydston, R., Goodliffe, N., Hoag, B. J., Money, T., & Amsel, E. (2002, April). *Guilt and regret: The nature of their relation.* Poster presented at Rocky Mountain Psychology Association, Park City, UT.

Braithwaite, R. B. (1957). *Scientific explanation: A study of the function of theory, probability and law in science.* Cambridge, England: Cambridge University Press.

Byrnes, J. P. (1998). *The nature and development of decision making: A self-regulation model.* Mahwah, NJ: Lawrence Erlbaum Associates.

Byrnes, J. P., Miller, D. C., & Reynolds, M. (1999). Learning to make good decisions: A self-regulation perspective. *Child Development, 70,* 1121–1140.

Byrnes, J. P., Miller, D. C., & Schafer, W. D. (1999). Gender differences in risk taking: A meta-analysis. *Psychological Bulletin, 125,* 367–383.

Caffrey, C. M., & Schneider, S. L. (2000). Why do they do it? Affective motivators in adolescents' decisions to participate in risk behaviours. *Cognition & Emotion, 14,* 543–576.

Cottrell, J., & Amsel, E. (2001, April). *The development of reasoning about anticipated regret in adolescents and adults.* Poster presented at Rocky Mountain Psychology Association, Reno, NV.

Fay, A., & Klahr, D. (1996). Knowing about guessing and guessing about knowing: Preschoolers' understanding of indeterminacy. *Child Development, 67,* 689–716.

Finken, C. (2001, April). *Explaining risky adolescent behaviors with the Propensity-Event theory.* Poster presented at Society for Research in Child Development, Minneapolis, MN.

Finken, L. L., & Jacobs, J. E. (1996). Consultant choice across decision contexts: Are abortion decisions different? *Journal of Adolescent Research, 11,* 235–261.

Furby, L., & Beyth-Marom, R. (1992). Risk taking in adolescence: A decision-making perspective. *Developmental Review, 12,* 1–44.

Gardner, W. (1993). A life-span rational-choice theory of risk taking. In N. Bell & R. Bell, *Adolescent risk taking* (pp. 66–83). Newbury Park, CA: Sage.

Gerrard, M., Gibbons, F. X., Benthin, A. C., & Hessling, R. M. (1996). A longitudinal study of the reciprocal nature of risk behaviors and cognitions in adolescents: What you do shapes what you think and vice-versa. *Health Psychology, 15,* 344–354.

Gilovich, T., & Medvec, V. H. (1995). The experience of regret: What, when, and why. *Psychological Review, 102,* 379–395.

Goldinger, S. D., Kleider, H. M., Azuma, T., & Beike, D. R. (2003). Blaming the victim under memory load. *Psychological Science, 14,* 81–85.

Gullone, E., Moore, S., Moss, S., & Boyd, C. (2000). The adolescent risk-taking questionnaire: Developmental and psychometric evaluation. *Journal of Adolescent Research, 15,* 231–251.

Harris, D. (2000). *The work of the imagination.* Oxford, England: Blackwell.

Hastie, R., & Dawes, R. (2001). *Rational choice in an uncertain world.* Newbury Park, CA: Sage.

Inhelder, B., & Piaget, J. (1958). *The growth of logical thinking from childhood to adolescence.* New York: Basic Books.

Irwin, C. E. (1993). Adolescence and risk taking: How are they related? In N. Bell & R. Bell (Eds.), *Adolescent risk taking* (pp. 7–28). Newbury Park, CA: Sage.

Jacobs, J. E., & Ganzel, A. K. (1993). Decision-making in adolescence: Are we asking the wrong question? In P. R. Pintrich & M. L. Maehr (Eds.), *Motivation in adolescents: Advances in achievement and motivation* (pp. 1–31). Greenwich, CT: JAI.

Jones, D. C. (1985). Persuasive appeals and responses to appeals among friends and acquaintances. *Child Development, 56,* 757–763.

Kahneman, D., & Tversky, A. (1982). The simulation heuristic. In D. Kahneman, P. Slovic, & A. Tversky (Eds.), *Judgments under uncertainty: Heuristics and biases* (pp. 201–208). New York: Cambridge University Press.

Kasimatis, M., & Wells, G. L. (1995). Individual differences in counterfactual thinking. In J. Roese & J. M. Olson (Eds.), *What might have been: The social psychology of counterfactual thinking* (pp. 80–102). Hillsdale, NJ: Lawrence Erlbaum Associates.

Klaczynski, P. A. (2001). Framing effects in adolescent task representations, analytic and heuristic processing, and decision making: Implications for the normative/descriptive gap. *Applied Developmental Psychology, 22,* 289–309.

Klaczynski, P. A., Byrnes, J. P., & Jacobs, J. E. (2001). Introduction to the special issue: The development of decision making. *Applied Developmental Psychology, 22*, 225–236.

Klaczynski, P., & Fauth, J. M. (1996). Intellectual ability, rationality, and intuitiveness as predictors of warranted and unwarranted optimism for future life events. *Journal of Youth & Adolescence, 25*, 755–773.

Kuhn, D., Amsel, E., & O'Loughlin, M. (1988). *The development of scientific thinking skills*. Orlando, FL: Academic.

Kuhn, D., Garcia-Mila, M., Zohar, A., & Andersen, C. (1995). Strategies of knowledge acquisition. *Monographs of the Society for Research in Child Development, 60*(4, Serial No. 245).

Landman, J. (1987). Regret and elation following action and inaction: Affective responses to positive versus negative outcomes. *Personality & Social Psychology Bulletin, 13*, 524–536.

Landman, J. (1993). *Regret: The persistence of the possible*. New York: Oxford University Press.

Larson, R., & Verma, S. (1999). How children and adults spend their time across the world: Work, play, and developmental opportunities. *Psychological Bulletin, 125*, 701–736.

Lewis, C. (1981). How do adolescents approach decisions?: Changes over grades seven to twelve and policy implications. *Child Development, 52*, 538–544.

Lightfoot, C. (1997). *The culture of adolescent risk-taking*. New York: Guilford.

Maggs, J., Almeida, D., & Galambos, N. (1995). Risky business: The paradoxical meaning of risky behavior young adolescents. *Journal of Early Adolescence, 15*, 344–364.

Mellers, B. A. (2000). Choice and the relative pleasure of consequences. *Psychological Bulletin, 126*, 910–924.

Miller, D. C., & Byrnes, J. P. (1997). The role of contextual and personal factors in children's risk taking. *Developmental Psychology, 33*, 814–823.

Moore, S., & Gullone, E. (1996). Predicting adolescent risky behavior using a personalized cost–benefit analysis. *Journal of Youth and Adolescence, 25*, 343–259.

Moshman, D. (1999). *Adolescent psychological development: Rationality, morality, and identity*. Mahwah, NJ: Lawrence Erlbaum Associates.

Moshman, D., & Franks, B. (1986). Development of the concept of inferential validity. *Child Development, 57*, 153–165.

Moshman, D., & Geil, M. (1998). Collaborative reasoning: Evidence for collective rationality. *Thinking and Reasoning, 4*, 231–248.

Mueller, U., Overton, W. F., & Reene, K. (2001). Development of conditional reasoning: A longitudinal study. *Journal of Cognition and Development, 2*, 27–49.

Quadrel, M. J., Fischhoff, B., & Davis, W. (1993). Adolescent (in)vulnerability. *American Psychologist, 48*, 102–116.

Reyna, V. F., & Ellis, S. C. (1994). Fuzzy-trace theory and framing effects in children's risky decision making. *Psychological Science, 5*, 275–279.

Richard, R., De Vries, N., & Van Der Plight, J. (1998). Anticipated regret and precautionary sexual behavior. *Journal of Applied Social Psychology, 28*, 1411–1428.

Richard, R., Van Der Plight, J., & De Vries, N. (1996). Anticipated regret and time perspective: Changing sexual risk-taking behavior. *Journal of Behavioral Decision Making, 9*, 185–199.

Ritov, I. (1996). Probability of regret: Anticipation of uncertainty resolution in choice. *Organizational Behavior and Human Decision Processes, 68*, 228–236.

Roese, N. J. (1994). The functional basis of counterfactual thinking. *Journal of Personality and Social Psychology, 66*, 805–818.

Roseman, I., Weist, C., & Swartz, T. S. (1994). Phenomenology, behaviors, and goals differentiate discrete emotions. *Journal of Personality and Social Psychology, 67*, 206–221.

Sanna, L. J., & Turley, K. J. (1996). Antecedents to spontaneous counterfactual thinking: Effects of expectancy violation and outcome valence. *Personality and Social Psychology Bulletin, 22*, 906–919.

Santrock, J. W. (2003). *Adolescence* (9th ed.). New York: McGraw-Hill.

Schauble, L. (1996). The development of scientific reasoning in knowledge-rich contexts. *Developmental Psychology, 32,* 102–119.

Schlottman A., & Anderson, N. H. (1994). Children's judgments of expected value. *Developmental Psychology, 30,* 56–66.

Shimanoff, S. B. (1984). Commonly named emotions in everyday conversations. *Perceptual and Motor Skills, 58,* 514.

Stanovich, K. E. (1999). *Who is rational: Studies of individual differences in reasoning.* Mahwah, NJ: Lawrence Erlbaum Associates.

Steinberg, L., & Cauffman, E. (1996). Maturity of judgment in adolescence: Psychosocial factors in adolescent decision making. *Law and Human Behavior, 20,* 249–272.

Stewart, A., & Vanderwater, E. A. (1999). If I had it to do over again . . . : Midlife review, midcourse corrections, and women's well-being in midlife. *Journal of Personality and Social Psychology, 76,* 270–283.

Sullivan, J. E., & Amsel, E. (2001). *The development of anticipated regret.* Poster presented at Rocky Mountain Psychology Association, Reno, NV.

Tversky, A., & Kahneman, D. (1981). The framing of decisions and the psychology of choice. *Science, 211,* 453–458.

Wallace, J. R., & Logan, M. A. (2001, April). *Peer influence on risk-taking in 7- to 12-year-old children.* Poster presented at Society for Research in Child Development, Minneapolis, MN.

Zeelenberg, M. (1999a). Anticipated regret, expected feedback, and behavioral decision making. *Journal of Behavioral Decision Making, 12,* 93–105.

Zeelenberg, M. (1999b). The use of crying over spilt milk: A note on the rationality and functionality of regret. *Philosophical Psychology, 12,* 325–340.

Zeelenberg, M., & Beattie, J. (1997). Consequences of regret aversion 2: Additional evidence for effects of feedback on decision making. *Organizational Behavior and Human Decision Processes, 72,* 63–78.

Zeelenberg, M., Beattie, J., Van Der Plight, J., & De Vries, N. K. (1996). Consequences of regret aversion: Effects of expected feedback on risky decision making. *Organizational Behavior and Human Decision Processes, 65,* 148–158.

Zeelenberg, M., Van Dijk, W. W., Manstead, A. S. R., & Van Der Plight, J. (1998). The experience of regret and disappointment. *Cognition and Emotion, 12,* 221–230.

5

"Everyone Else Is Doing It": Relations Between Bias in Base-Rate Estimates and Involvement in Deviant Behaviors

Janis E. Jacobs
Kristen E. Johnston
The Pennsylvania State University

"Everyone else is doing it" is a well-known refrain to parents. It is typically used by their offspring as evidence that engaging in a particular behavior or activity is normative (and therefore should be allowed). Although most parents are not swayed by such entreaties (they know that not *everyone* else is doing it), are the adolescents aware of the fallacy? In other words, are adolescents' perceptions of the relevant base rates accurate and their use of the phrase, "everyone else," is simply a strategy employed to wear down their parents *or* do they really believe their own rhetoric?

Several decades of research have pointed to the importance of the use of base rates to make accurate social judgments (e.g., Dawes, 1988; Kahneman, Slovic, & Tversky, 1985) because in many situations, individuals must rely on their estimates of the base rates of behaviors when making inferences about others or when deciding about future behaviors for themselves. Decision-making skills often involve a combination of base-rate judgments and the use of anecdotal heuristics (Zukier & Pepitone, 1984), and it is generally agreed that the use of base rates is associated with more accurate judgments and predictions (Hasher & Chromiak, 1977; Swann, 1984).

Actual base rates, however, are rarely available in most real-life social situations (Bar-Hillel & Fischhoff, 1981; Kruglanski, 1989). Jacobs, Greenwald, and Osgood (1995) suggested that perceivers must rely on their own estimates of the base rates of social behaviors and attitudes from the events that they experience, and when data about actual base rates are not provided, accurate estimates are essential for making appropriate inferences about the meaning of behavior. For adolescents, this means drawing from their own experiences and their interactions with peers to estimate base rates of certain types of behaviors. For example, an adolescent may decide to begin smoking cigarettes based on her or his estimate of how many other teens smoke (Unger & Rohrbach, 2002). Estimates about the base rates of everyday behaviors and attitudes (whether accurate or inaccurate) ultimately serve as the "data" upon which decisions will be made. Such base-rate estimates may be particularly important for decisions about high-risk or problem behaviors.

Parents and intervention programmers often blame adolescent involvement in delinquency and other problem behaviors on lack of planning, failure to use available information (including base rates), and other attributes that have been characterized as poor decision making. Several researchers have linked adolescent risk taking to poor decision-making skills and biased reasoning (e.g., Fischhoff, 1992; Furby & Beyth-Marom, 1992); however, little is known about what decision-making skills are related to deviant behaviors. A number of studies document age-related increases in judgment biases (e.g., Davidson, 1995; Jacobs & Potenza, 1991; Smith, 1993) that might lead to biases in decision making; however, many studies also show that children and adolescents can, in fact, use statistical information to make judgments about a sample (Ferguson, Olthof, Luiten, & Rule, 1984; Jacobs et al., 1995; Johnston & Jacobs, 2003; Klaczynski & Fauth, 1997; Klaczynski & Narasimham, 1998; Shaklee & Paszek, 1985). This apparent contradiction suggests that there are two forms of developmental change going on. Klaczynski (chap. 2, this volume) and Jacobs and Klaczynski (2002) suggested that both experiential and analytic reasoning systems are developing at the same time and that various situational, motivational, and cognitive factors influence whether one or the other will be used.

The fact that children and adolescents exhibit both biased reasoning and the appropriate use of numerical reasoning under different conditions suggests that the accuracy of base-rate estimates may be related to a variety of individual factors, such as prior experience, motivation, or metacognitive skills (see Klaczynski, chap. 2, this volume). Furthermore, although we know that adolescents' estimates of base rates may be biased, we know much less about the ways in which judgment biases, such as inaccuracies in the estimation of base rates for deviant behaviors, might affect decisions to engage in deviant behaviors. The goal of the study described here was to investigate young adolescents' estimation biases for delinquent behaviors and to relate these biases to both their own involvement in such behaviors and to their psychosocial adjustment.

ADOLESCENCE AS AN IMPORTANT PERIOD
FOR ESTIMATION OF PEERS' BEHAVIORS

Social conformity peaks during early and middle adolescence (Berndt, 1979; Krosnick & Judd, 1982; Steinberg & Silverberg, 1986). Furthermore, peers' behaviors and attitudes gain significance as parents' attitudes and opinions decrease in salience (Young & Ferguson, 1979). Not only are peer role models more influential during adolescence, but the desire to conform to the standards of peer role models also increases. Therefore, adolescents' perceptions of their peers' engagement in risky behaviors and delinquent activities may be a powerful predictor of adolescents' own involvement in risky behaviors. Increases in social perspective taking during early adolescence (Steinberg & Cauffman, 1996) are typically seen as positive because these skills allow the adolescent to recognize how the thoughts and actions of one person influence those of another and to imagine how others might perceive them. A downside of this new ability, however, is that adolescents are highly concerned with peer conformity and this may make them susceptible to peer pressure. The majority of studies indicate a positive relationship between susceptibility to peer pressure and risk-taking behavior (such as drinking), although there is clearly variation in the extent to which adolescents succumb to social influence, including pressure to engage in behaviors that are undesirable (see Steinberg & Cauffman, 1996, for a review).

In addition, our previous studies indicate that individuals make more biased estimates when they are reasoning about social rather than nonsocial events (Jacobs & Potenza, 1991); about populations with greater variability (Jacobs & Narloch, 2001); and about unfamiliar others (Jacobs, Greenwald, & Osgood, 1995). Adolescent risk taking and deviance are likely to occur in exactly the kinds of situations in which estimation biases have been documented—social situations with large groups of unfamiliar peers. In these situations, adolescents are left to estimate how others typically behave and what they think. This may result in overestimations of others' deviance and acceptance of such behavior, leading adolescents to believe that the norm is to be involved in problem behaviors and that they, too, should try the same behaviors.

The social situations in which youth find themselves also change during adolescence. Indeed, movement toward autonomy is accompanied by real changes in the social world as adolescents mature. Most move from environments in which they are protected, scheduled, and dominated by adults into environments that are primarily populated with other adolescents and in which they have much more autonomy. On average, middle-class adolescents spend about 20% of their time with parents and other relatives, 25% of their time alone, and the rest with friends and classmates (Larson, 1983; Larson &

Csikszentmihalyi, 1978). Younger adolescents report that television, home- and family-centered activities fill much of their leisure time. This shifts dramatically as they get older and report that peer-focused and solitary activities fill most of their time (Kleiber, Larson, & Csikszentmihalyi, 1986; Larson & Kleiber, 1993). Thus, as adolescents get older, they spend greater periods of their leisure time away from adult supervision, increasing the importance of their estimates of the base rates of deviant behavior as they encounter more opportunities to be involved in such activities themselves.

PREVIOUS RESEARCH
ON ESTIMATION BIASES

Previous research has shown that, although adults are generally accurate in their statistical perceptions of social behaviors, they show a number of systematic biases, including overestimation of the means and dispersion of distributions of social behaviors and the *false consensus effect*, a tendency to assume that others' attitudes and behaviors will resemble their own (e.g., Dawes, 1990; Kruglanski, 1989; Marks & Miller, 1987; Mullen et al., 1985; Nisbett & Kunda, 1985). The term *pluralistic ignorance* has been used in the adult literature to describe individuals' tendencies to overestimate the population base rates for activities in which they, themselves, are engaged (e.g., Miller & Prentice, 1994). Adults also tend to overestimate their own chances of experiencing positive events and underestimate their chances of experiencing negative events (Weinstein, 1980; Weinstein & Lachendro, 1982). In addition, systematic biases have been found for adults' estimates of the frequency of particular causes of death, revealing a tendency to overestimate small and underestimate large base rates (Lichtenstein, Slovic, Fischhoff, Layman, & Combs, 1978). In a series of studies related to the effect of overconfidence on social prediction, the accuracy of adult self-predictions was low, ranging from 59% to 68% accuracy (Dunning, Griffin, Milojkovic, & Ross, 1990). Overall, these studies suggest that adults' base-rate estimates of others' behaviors are often inaccurate.

A contributing factor may be that norms for social decisions are not typically known. Instead, individuals are often forced to make judgments based on their own estimates of the norms of social behaviors or attitudes. This general dilemma, faced by people of all ages, is even greater for adolescents because they must make decisions based on limited amounts of experience and little feedback from earlier decisions (Jacobs, Greenwald, & Osgood, 1995). Indeed, Aas and Klepp (1992) reported that adolescents often overestimate peers' problem behaviors. In their study, adolescents who gave higher estimates of peer problem behavior, such as alcohol and tobacco use, also reported being involved in more problem behavior. Other studies have found similar relations between overestimation and intention to smoke in the future (e.g., Sherman, Preston, Chassin, Corty, & Olshavsky, 1983); actual cigarette smoking (Sussman et al., 1988); increases in alcohol use over time (Marks, Graham, & Hansen, 1992); and other deviant behaviors (e.g., Benthin, Slovic, & Severson, 1993; Nucci, Guerra, & Lee, 1991). These findings indicate the importance of understanding adolescents' social judgment biases in relation to problem behaviors.

Research on children's estimation abilities varies. Some research has found that children are capable of making frequency estimations as accurately as adults (Ellis, Palmer, & Reeves, 1988; Hasher & Chromiak, 1977), although these studies involved estimating the frequency of light flashes or word lists rather than social interactions. In a study by Higgins, Feldman, and Ruble (1980), children as young as age 4 accurately predicted the activities in which their peers were likely to be involved. In addition, there is evidence that young children can accurately estimate base-rate information presented to them in a laboratory (Nicholls, 1978; Shaklee & Mims, 1981). These studies suggest that young children are capable of correctly estimating the relative frequency of words or other visual stimuli shown to them in a laboratory, yet research on estimation of the base rates of social behavior (Jacobs, Greenwald, & Osgood, 1995) suggested that children fail to incorporate base-rate estimates of naturally occurring events. Other studies indicate that children also have problems accurately judging the relations between social events (e.g., rock throwing, classroom misbehavior) and the individual characteristics of actors (e.g., gender, group membership), resulting in what have been labeled *illusory correlations* (Johnston & Jacobs, 2003; Meehan & Janik, 1990; Primi & Agnoli, 2002). Young children's inaccuracy at estimating base rates of social behaviors could be due to a lack of social experience or social cognitive skills needed to make real-life estimates.

In accordance with this argument, Jacobs and colleagues have found that children's base-rate estimation improves with age throughout middle childhood. For example, Jacobs, Greenwald, and Osgood (1995) reported age-related increases in correspondence between base-rate estimates and actual base rates, indicating that as children get older, the base-rate estimates that serve as the basis for many social judgments become more accurate. Furthermore, Jacobs and Potenza (1991) found that base-rate information was used increasingly to make social judgments across the elementary school years. Others have reported similar developmental patterns (Davidson, 1995; Smith, 1993). In addition, research by Klaczynski (2001) suggested that normative responding to problems using deduction, probability, covariation, and other statistical reasoning continues to improve during adolescence.

Thus, by about age 12, young adolescents' estimations may be increasingly accurate, but also show systematic biases similar to those seen in adults. Involvement in problem behavior and delinquency increases during early and middle adolescence (Dryfoos, 1990) and peers have been identified as one of the major influences on involvement in problem behaviors (e.g., R. B. Cairns, B. D. Cairns, Neckerman, Gest, & Gariépy, 1988; Warr, 2002). Therefore, it is likely that understanding the potential biases and individual differences in adolescents' judgments about their peers' behaviors may be important to understanding adolescents' deviant behaviors.

INDIVIDUAL DIFFERENCES IN ESTIMATION ACCURACY AND RELATED OUTCOMES

Although we have concentrated on describing the normative changes that will affect estimation accuracy for almost all adolescents, there are likely to be individual differences as well. One of these may be the level of estimation bias—some individuals may be much better calibrated than others, so that they exhibit only small estimation biases, whereas others may exhibit extreme biases. These individual differences may be related to motivational factors, such as self-interest or self-protection (e.g., Klaczynski & Narasimham, 1998; Kunda, 1990), general cognitive abilities, and other factors.

A second individual difference variable that may be related to estimation accuracy is prior experience. For example, experience with drinking alcohol may serve to reinforce perceptions of widespread alcohol use ("Everybody does it"), contributing to overestimation of the prevalence of drinking. On the other hand, prior experiences may help hone one's estimation abilities, leading to greater accuracy. Adolescents who engage in deviant behaviors are more likely to overestimate the rates of others' involvement in such behaviors and to have friends who engage in similar behaviors (e.g., Benthin et al., 1993; Blanton, Gibbons, Gerrard, Conger, & Smith, 1997; Nucci et al., 1991). If adolescents use their friends as a reference group for judging the behavior of their peers in general, estimates of base rates for deviant behavior may be inflated for adolescents who are involved in such activities themselves.

In addition, gender may make a difference. Most research indicates that females are involved in far less deviant behavior than are males (e.g., Empey, 1982; Johnston, O'Malley, & Bachman, 2003). If experience is related to greater overestimation (as already hypothesized), females would be likely to make more accurate estimations of deviant behaviors than males. If, however, experience is related to greater accuracy, females might be expected to exhibit greater estimation bias on this topic.

Adolescents' accuracy in estimating the base rates of their peers' behaviors may be related to a number of outcomes, as well. These include engagement in deviant behaviors and psychosocial adjustment. As discussed, adolescents who overestimate the frequency of their peers' deviant behaviors may be more likely to engage in deviant behaviors themselves, believing that such behavior is more normative than is actually the case. Likewise, because victimization and deviant behavior are often related, reports of victimization were also examined. Adolescents who overestimate peer victimization may report being victimized more often than more accurate estimators for the same reasons that those involved in deviance believe that others have high involvement (e.g., pluralistic ignorance, self-protection). If individual differences in estimation bias are related to actual behaviors, extreme biases are likely to be more strongly related to outcomes than less extreme biases.

Adolescents who are less accurate at estimating the base rates of behaviors of their peers may also have poorer outcomes in other arenas, such as school performance, self-esteem, and depression. Because deviant behaviors often involve negative school-related behaviors, such as skipping school, adolescents who overestimate their peers' deviant behaviors may engage in more school-related deviant behaviors, leading to poorer grades. Similarly, adolescents who overestimate peers' deviant behaviors may also overestimate the prevalence of poor school performance or academic disengagement, providing a rationale for psychologically disengaging from school or earning bad grades themselves. It is also possible that students who overestimate peers' deviant behaviors overestimate or misjudge other events, thereby leading to poorer school performance. Finally, overestimation of deviant behaviors by peers could also be related to poor psychosocial adjustment, such as lower self-esteem and depression, although these outcomes may be more distally related to estimation inaccuracy, and more proximally related to factors associated with poor base-rate estimation such as participation in deviant behaviors.

The study presented in this chapter was designed to examine the relations between estimation bias for deviant behaviors and various outcomes, including adolescents' involvement in deviance, psychosocial outcomes, and school performance. In addition, we investigated the effects of individual differences in estimation bias and gender on these relationships.

METHOD

Data were collected during the pretest phase of a 10-week intervention study of adolescent decision making, risky behaviors, academic achievement, and adaptive functioning during early and middle adolescence. Data were collected using paper-and-pencil measures that asked adolescents to describe their involvement in risky behaviors, perceptions of the risky behaviors of other students in their grade, and other outcome variables.

Participants

Student participation was solicited through letters sent to parents of seventh- and eighth-grade students in two school districts within a small industrial city in the northeastern United States who were identified by school personnel as "high-risk" adolescents for future involvement in drug abuse, violence, delinquency, school dropout, and teen pregnancy. A total of 273 students (55 seventh graders and 218 eighth graders; 135 girls and 138 boys) returned consent forms from their parents.

Participants in the sample were in the middle adolescent years; the average ages of girls and boys were 14 years, 4 months (range = 13 years to 16 years, 1 month) and 14 years, 6 months (range = 13 years to 15 years, 11 months), respectively. Ninety-two percent of the sample was of White, non-Hispanic ethnicity and 8% of the sample was composed of African American, Hispanic, and Asian American students.

Seventy-three percent of participants reported that they lived in two-parent households, 21% reported that they lived in single-parent households, and the remaining 6% of the sample reported other arrangements (e.g., living with grandparents or aunts and uncles). Because adolescents were not likely to know their parents' income levels, participants were asked to report their parents' highest level of education as a measure of social class. Participants reported that 44% of their mothers and 32% of their fathers had earned a college degree or higher.

Procedure and Measures

Participants who had received consent from their parents to participate in the study completed a set of paper-and-pencil measures at a 2-hour session during school hours. Participants received instructions prior to each task and a 15-minute break during the administration of the questionnaires. Response packets were marked with a random number in order to assure confidentiality. Participants were provided with ice cream later in the day to thank them for their participation in the study.

Deviant Behavior Measure. Participants completed a 37-item measure of deviant behavior that was adapted from the *Monitoring the Future* study (Johnston et al., 2003). This self-report measure asked adolescents to describe the frequency with which they had engaged in a range of high-risk behaviors during the past 30 days. Each item was answered on a 5-point scale:[1] (1) *not at all,* (2) *1 to 2 times,* (3) *once a week,* (4) *a few times a week,* or (5) *once a day or more.* In addition, participants were asked to respond to the same set of questions regarding the frequency with which "all the other students in your grade" engage in the same behaviors. Three subscales were developed from the 37 items: (a) mildly deviant behaviors, (b) very deviant be-

---

[1]For questions pertaining to the frequency of cigarette smoking, an alternative 5-point scale was used: (1) *not at all,* (2) *less than one cigarette per day,* (3) *1 to 5 cigarettes per day,* (4) *about half a pack a day,* and (5) *about one or more packs a day.*

haviors, and (c) victimization. In addition, the neutral behaviors were analyzed as individual items. The subscales are now described:

> *Mildly Deviant Behavior*—The mildly deviant behavior subscale included a subset of four items (smoked cigarettes, drank alcoholic beverages, smoked marijuana, used chewing tobacco) that were averaged to create the mildly deviant behaviors subscale. Mean scores for the averaged items were 1.2 (SD = .4, range = 1.0 to 3.8) for self-reports and 2.5 (SD = 1.0, range = 1.0 to 5.0) for reports of others. Cronbach's alpha for this measure was .65.

> *Very Deviant Behaviors*—Ten items were included in this subscale that represent those behaviors that are illegal at any age and represent more serious offenses (e.g., got in a serious fight at school, got in a serious fight outside of school, took something over $50). The mean self-report score was 1.2 (SD = .3, range = 1.0 to 3.8), and the mean report of others' behavior was 2.3 (SD = .8, range = 1.0 to 5.0). Cronbach's alpha for this measure was .81.

> *Victimization Scale*—Most research indicates that individuals who are involved in acts of crime are likely to report that they are also the victims of crimes; thus, a subscale of three items was developed to measure victimization. Items included questions about damage and theft of property (e.g., "How often has something of yours been stolen?") and threats of violence. The mean scores for these three items were 1.3 (SD = .5, range = 1.0 to 4.3) for self-reports and 2.3 (SD = .9, range = 1.0 to 5.0) for reports of others. Cronbach's alpha was .49. This may be low because there were few items and because victimization in one area may have little relation to victimization in another area.

> *Neutral Behaviors*—Four items asked participants, "How often you have ridden a bike, gotten sick, felt afraid, eaten candy in the past 30 days." Because these items are not related, they were analyzed as individual items rather than attempting to form a scale. Responses were between 1.0 and 4.5 for participant self-reports and from 1.0 to 5.0 for responses about others.

Grade-Point Average. Grade-point average (GPA) was calculated from participants' self-reports of their most recent grades in math, science, English, and history on a scale from 1 (equivalent to A) to 5 (equivalent to F). Scores for each participant were averaged in order to calculate an overall GPA.

Depression. A short-form of the Center for Epidemiological Studies Depression Scale (CES-D) was used to measure current depressive symptoms. This 12-item self-report form demonstrated satisfactory discriminant and convergent validity (Devins & Orme, 1985). Ten items of the scale assess the cognitive, affective, behavioral, and somatic symptoms associated with depression. Two items were included to minimize bias attributable to response sets and their informational value. Respondents used a 4-point scale to indicate how often they felt a certain way during the past week in response to items such as, "I could not get going," and "I talked less than usual." The scale ranged from 1 (*rarely* or *none of the time*, or *less than 1 day*) to 4 (*most* or *all of the time*, or *5 to 7 days*). Items were summed, with higher scores indicating more depressed affect. The Cronbach's alpha for the CES-D for this sample was .83.

Self-Esteem. The 10-item Rosenberg self-esteem scale was used to assess general self-worth (Rosenberg, 1965). Responses were rated on a 4-point scale (1 = *strongly agree* to 4 = *strongly disagree*). Items were summed, and higher scores indicate higher self-esteem. Cronbach's alpha for this sample was .84.

RESULTS

Computation of Accuracy Scores

To determine how accurate participant reports of the behaviors of other students in their grade were, an accuracy score for each participant was calculated for each subscale of the measure of deviant behavior and victimization. First, the mean self-report response and responses about others' behavior were calculated for each item of the Mildly Deviant Behaviors, Very Deviant Behaviors, and Victimization subscales for students in each school. The self-reported subscale mean for each school represented the *criterion*, or actual sample mean frequency for each type of behavior for students in that school, that is, the frequency of respondents' own behaviors averaged across the sample. Each mean report of others' behavior represented the *perceived* frequency of each type of behavior, that is, how often participants thought their peers engaged in each type of behavior.

Second, difference scores were created by subtracting the criterion for the participant's school from the individual's perceived frequency for each subscale to reflect the degree to which a participant was accurate in her or his estimation of the frequency of peers' behaviors (Jacobs, Greenwald, & Osgood, 1995). Thus, the accuracy scores were computed by subtracting the criterion from the perceived frequency estimate for each participant. Because criterion scores were calculated based on average self-reported behaviors for adolescents in each school separately, the difference score more closely represented accuracy in adolescents' perceptions of the behaviors of their peers, that is, the students with whom they attended school. Accuracy scores around zero indicate that participants were highly accurate at estimating the frequency of occurrence for behaviors, whereas numbers greater than zero reflect an overestimation bias and numbers less than zero reflect an underestimation bias.

To determine whether estimation bias was related to deviant behaviors and psychosocial outcomes during adolescence, accuracy scores were combined across the entire sample and used to classify participants into three estimator groups for each subscale separately. Groupings were created for each subscale based on the mean estimations given by the participants so that estimation bias for each type of behavior could be examined in relation to self-reported involvement in that same type of behavior; for example, the grouping variable created for the Very Deviant Behaviors subscale was examined in relation to self-reported behaviors from that subscale. Participants whose scores fell between the minimum score and .5 standard deviation below the mean estimates for the group were classified as *On-Target Estimators*. Because few adolescents underestimated peers' deviant behaviors (9.8% for mildly deviant behaviors, 7.5% for very deviant behaviors, and 11% for victimization), and because the degree of underestimation was minimal (see Table 5.1), adolescents with scores falling below zero were also classified as On-Target Estimators. Participants whose scores fell within .5 standard deviation below and .5 standard deviation above the mean were classified as *Moderate Overestimators*. Finally, participants whose accuracy scores fell more than .5 standard deviation above the mean were classified as *Extreme Overestimators*.

Estimation Bias

To test the accuracy of participants' estimates of behaviors, t tests were used to compare all accuracy scores to zero (see Table 5.1). All scores were significantly different from zero, indicating that on average, adolescents overesti-

TABLE 5.1
Mean and Range of Accuracy Scores

Behavior Type	n	Mean	SD	Minimum	Maximum	t
Neutral[a]						
Ride bike	256	.46	1.2	−1.33	2.67	6.3***
Get sick	256	.55	1.0	−.99	3.01	8.7***
Feel afraid	253	.45	1.0	−.96	3.04	7.0***
Eat candy bar	254	.49	1.3	−1.81	2.19	6.1***
Mildly Deviant[b]	246	1.3	1.0	−.21	3.8	20.2***
Very Deviant[b]	242	1.1	.8	−.16	3.9	20.9***
Total Deviant[b,c]	241	1.2	.8	−.22	3.9	21.7***
Victimization[b]	247	1.0	.9	−.29	3.7	16.9***

Note. t score represents comparison to zero (perfect accuracy).
[a]Single items. [b]Scale. [c]Average of Mildly Deviant and Very Deviant Behaviors.
***$p < .001$.

mated the behaviors of the students in their grade, including neutral behaviors, revealing a general overestimation bias. There were no gender differences in estimation bias, however, indicating that girls and boys were equally likely to overestimate deviant behaviors, victimization, and neutral behaviors. As can be seen in Table 5.1, on average, adolescents were more accurate at estimating neutral behaviors than deviant behaviors or victimization (the neutral estimates were significantly closer to zero than were the estimates for each of the other categories).

Relation Between Estimation Bias and Involvement in Deviant Behaviors

The modal response to questions about deviant behaviors and victimization in the past 30 days was *not at all*. Nevertheless, substantial proportions of students reported engaging in certain deviant behaviors and experiencing victimization in the past month (ranging from 6% who reported stealing something worth more than $50, to 24% who reported drinking alcohol, to 29% who reported that someone threatened to hurt them). To examine whether adolescents who overestimated their peers' deviant behaviors were also more likely to engage in deviant behaviors themselves, adolescents' self-reported mildly deviant behaviors and very deviant behaviors were entered into separate 3 (estimator category) $\times$ 2 (gender) analyses of variance with school as a covariate. Results for *mildly deviant behaviors* indicated a significant main effect for estimator classification, $F(2, 229) = 3.4$, $p < .05$, and a significant main effect for gender, $F(1, 229) = 4.5$, $p < .05$, with boys reporting more deviant behaviors than girls. Planned comparisons indicated that extreme overestimators reported engaging in more mildly deviant behaviors than on-target estimators ($p = .07$). Moderate overestimators did not differ significantly from on-target estimators or extreme overestimators. Means are listed in Table 5.2.

Results for *very deviant behaviors* revealed more striking differences among estimators. There was a significant main effect of estimator, $F(2, 224) = 4.1$, $p < .05$, which was subsumed by a significant estimator $\times$ gender interaction, $F(2, 224) = 3.0$, $p < .05$. Planned comparisons indicated that among boys, extreme overestimators engaged in more deviant behaviors than on-target estimators ($p < .001$) or moderate overestimators ($p < .05$). On-target and moderate overestimators did not differ significantly from one another. Among girls, there were no significant differences among estimator groups. Means are listed in Table 5.3. Overall, these analyses indicate that boys who were extreme overestimators reported engaging in more mildly deviant and very deviant behaviors than boys who were more accurate at estimating their peers' behaviors. Girls who were extreme overestimators engaged in more mildly deviant, but not more very deviant behaviors, perhaps reflecting the tendency for girls to be involved in fewer extremely deviant behaviors than boys.

TABLE 5.2
Mean Frequencies of Deviant Behaviors
and Victimization by Estimator Category

Subscale	Estimator Category	n	M	SD
Mildly Deviant Behaviors	On-target estimators			
	Boys	45	1.2	.3
	Girls	31	1.1	.1
	Combined	76	1.1[a]	.3
	Moderate overestimators			
	Boys	40	1.3	.6
	Girls	43	1.1	.2
	Combined	83	1.2[a,b]	.4
	Extreme overestimators			
	Boys	34	1.3	.6
	Girls	37	1.2	.4
	Combined	71	1.3[b]	.5
Very Deviant Behaviors	On-target estimators			
	Boys	45	1.1[a]	.1
	Girls	29	1.1[a]	.4
	Combined	74	1.1	.2
	Moderate overestimators			
	Boys	41	1.2[a,b]	.2
	Girls	55	1.1[a]	.2
	Combined	96	1.1	.2
	Extreme overestimators			
	Boys	30	1.4[c]	.7
	Girls	25	1.2[a]	.3
	Combined	55	1.3	.5
Victimization	On-target estimators			
	Boys	40	1.1	.3
	Girls	33	1.2	.3
	Combined	73	1.1[a]	.3
	Moderate overestimators			
	Boys	53	1.3	.5
	Girls	60	1.3	.4
	Combined	113	1.3[b]	.5
	Extreme overestimators			
	Boys	27	1.5	.5
	Girls	25	1.5	.6
	Combined	52	1.5[c]	.5

Note. Means that do not share superscripts differ significantly from each other.

Victimization

We used the same analysis strategy to examine whether estimation bias is related to reported victimization and found a significant main effect for estimator category, $F(2, 237) = 8.7$, $p < .001$. Planned comparisons indicated that moderate overestimators ($p < .05$) and extreme overestimators ($p < .001$) re-

TABLE 5.3
Mean Scores for Depression, Self-Esteem,
and Grade-Point Average by Estimator Category

Subscale	Estimator Category	n	M	SD
Depression	On-target estimators			
	Boys	35	13.3	6.0
	Girls	27	11.0	5.5
	Combined	62	12.3[a]	5.9
	Moderate overestimators			
	Boys	38	14.0	6.0
	Girls	51	13.3	5.7
	Combined	89	13.6[a,b]	5.8
	Extreme overestimators			
	Boys	28	15.1	7.7
	Girls	24	17.3	8.1
	Combined	52	16.0[b]	7.9
Self-Esteem	On-target estimators			
	Boys	35	10.5	6.1
	Girls	27	13.1	5.4
	Combined	62	11.6[a,b]	5.9
	Moderate overestimators			
	Boys	38	12.3	4.1
	Girls	51	12.3	5.5
	Combined	89	12.3[b]	4.9
	Extreme overestimators			
	Boys	28	10.6	5.4
	Girls	24	9.0	4.8
	Combined	52	9.9[a]	5.2
Grade-Point Average (5-point scale)	On-target estimators			
	Boys	35	3.8	.8
	Girls	27	4.4	.6
	Combined	62	4.1	.8
	Moderate overestimators			
	Boys	38	3.8	.7
	Girls	51	4.1	.7
	Combined	89	4.0	.7
	Extreme overestimators			
	Boys	28	3.7	1.1
	Girls	24	3.8	.8
	Combined	52	3.8	1.0

Note. Means that do not share superscripts differ significantly from each other.

ported significantly more victimization than on-target estimators. Extreme overestimators also reported more victimization than moderate overestimators ($p < .05$). Means are listed in Table 5.2. Thus, self-reports of victimization differed according to degree of estimation bias, similar to self-reports of mildly and very deviant behaviors.

Relations Between Estimation Bias and Psychosocial Adjustment

In order to examine whether estimation bias was related to psychosocial adjustment, an additional categorical grouping variable was created using self-reports and reports of others' *total deviant behaviors*. These scores were calculated by adding the items included in both the mildly deviant behaviors and very deviant behaviors subscales, which were significantly positively correlated. Separate scores were calculated for self- and other reports, with self-reports serving as the criterion and reports of others' behaviors representing perceived frequency. Once again, the criterion was subtracted from the perceived frequency to yield difference scores. Adolescents were then classified into three groups based on their difference scores, with adolescents whose scores fell below .5 standard deviation from the mean classified as *on-target estimators*, those whose scores fell within .5 standard deviation above or below the mean classified as *moderate overestimators*, and adolescents whose scores fell more than .5 standard deviation above the mean classified as *extreme overestimators*.

Depression scores, global self-esteem scores, and GPA were entered into separate 3 (estimator classification) × 2 (gender) analyses of variance with school as a covariate. Results for depression indicated a main effect for estimator classification, $F(2, 202) = 4.7, p < .01$. Planned comparisons showed that extreme overestimators reported significantly more depressed affect than on-target estimators ($p < .01$), and marginally more depressed affect than moderate overestimators ($p = .07$). Means are listed in Table 5.3.

Similarly, results for self-esteem indicated a main effect of estimator classification, $F(2, 202) = 3.6, p < .05$. Planned comparisons revealed only one group difference: Extreme overestimators showed significantly more depressed affect than moderate overestimators ($p < .05$). Means are listed in Table 5.3.

Finally, the main effect of estimator classification for GPA was not significant, $F(2, 202) = 2.0$, ns, although GPA was highest among on-target estimators, and lowest among extreme overestimators. There was also a main effect for gender, $F(1, 202) = 6.9, p < .01$, with girls reporting higher grades than boys. Means are listed in Table 5.3. These analyses indicate that estimation bias regarding deviance is related to psychosocial indicators, but not related to academic performance.

DISCUSSION

Numerous studies with adolescents and adults (e.g., Aas & Klepp, 1992; Benthin et al., 1993; Nucci et al., 1991; Sussman et al., 1988) reported that individuals who are involved in risk-taking behaviors are more likely to overestimate the participation of others in similar behaviors than those who are not. Our goal in this study was to extend previous work by asking: Do individuals differ in the extent to which they hold estimation biases? Do individual differences relate to involvement in particular risk-taking behaviors? Is estimation bias related to other performance and psychosocial outcomes? We designed this study to answer these questions by measuring adolescents' abilities to estimate the base rates of their peers' deviant behaviors and comparing their estimates to the peers' self-reported involvement in deviant behaviors.

We found, first, that adolescents generally overestimate the base rates of their peers' deviant behaviors and victimization, with relatively few accurately estimating the frequency of their peers' deviant behaviors, and even fewer underestimating peers' deviant behaviors. There was, however, great variability in the degree to which adolescents exhibited this overestimation bias, with close to equal numbers in the on-target, moderate overestimation, and extreme overestimation groups.

We also found that, as expected, adolescents' own involvement in deviant behavior differed according to the degree of bias they showed in estimating their peers' deviant behaviors; adolescents who overestimated their peers' deviant behaviors to a larger degree also reported engaging in more deviant behaviors themselves. We also examined reports of victimization based on findings that involvement in delinquency and victimization are related (Lauritsen, Sampson, & Laub, 1991). As in the case of deviant behaviors, adolescents' self-reported victimization varied according to their degree of estimation bias, with extreme overestimators reporting the most victimization, and more accurate estimators reporting the least victimization. Consistent with previous research showing gender differences in deviant behavior (e.g., Empey, 1982; Johnston et al., 2003), boys reported more involvement in mildly deviant and very deviant behavior than girls.

In addition to examining the relations between bias in estimation of deviant behaviors and victimization and self-reports of those same behaviors, we also examined the relations between biased estimations of deviance and psychosocial adjustment and school performance. We found that depression and self-esteem were indeed related to degree of estimation bias; adolescents who showed the greatest degree of overestimation bias also reported more depressed affect and lower global self-esteem than adolescents who were more accurate in their estimation of their peers' deviant behaviors. We do not have evidence to suggest that the relations between estimation bias and depression and/or self-esteem are causal (in either direction).

We included measures of self-esteem and depression to ascertain whether biased social perceptions might be related to other psychosocial problems. Although we found a strong positive relationship between these variables and overestimation, we are not suggesting that overestimating the frequency of deviant behavior by one's peers leads to increased depression and decreased self-esteem. Rather, it is more likely that mediating factors are responsible for this relation. The same biased social perceptions that are related to involvement in deviant behaviors and in deviant peer groups may lead to these psychosocial effects. It is interesting to note that estimation bias about deviance was not significantly related to school performance, suggesting that such biases are content-specific and are likely to affect only perceptions and behaviors related to the same topic. Klaczynski (chap. 2, this volume) includes the importance of context in his description of experiential processing, one part of his two-process model.

What do these findings mean? First, they underscore the practical importance of understanding estimation bias. It appears that adolescents' beliefs about the frequency of their peers' deviant behaviors are related to their own behaviors and psychosocial well-being. The most troubling finding from this study may be the fact that one group is affected more than others; those students who are extreme overestimators are involved in the most deviant behavior and report the most depression and lowest self-esteem. Thus, in addition to making less accurate social judgments, this group reports greater behavioral and psychosocial problems. If educators and others are interested in interventions related to judgment and decision making, this may be an important group to target.

The positive side of the individual difference findings, however, is that adolescents who accurately perceive the frequency of peers' deviant behaviors are far less likely to engage in deviant behaviors themselves. Indeed, in our sample, self-reported deviant behaviors in the past month were low in frequency, with means of 1.2 for both mildly and very deviant behaviors and modal scores of one, with one representing *not at all* and two representing *1 to 2 times*. Thus, adolescents who accurately match their behavior to their perceptions of peers' behaviors are less likely to be involved in delinquent acts. Our findings also point to the importance of accurate social perception in relation to psychological well-being.

It is important to note that this study does not tell us whether adolescents who have accurate perceptions choose to engage in deviant behaviors because they believe that everyone is doing it or whether they believe that everyone is doing it because they use their own behavior as the anchor and they know that they are involved in such deviant acts. The abundant research on conformity to peers and the influence of peer pressure on adolescents' deviant behaviors (Steinberg & Cauffman, 1996) suggested that adolescents' perceptions of their peers' behaviors may very well influence their decisions about how to behave. However, the relation between base-rate estimation and social deviance could work in the opposite direction. For example, Horney and Marshall (1992) found that prior experiences influenced incarcerated criminals' perceptions of risk of arrest; committing a crime and getting away with it was related to decreased perceptions of the risk of arrest for that type of crime. Others have found that greater involvement in risk-taking behaviors was related to lower perceptions of personal risk (e.g., Goldberg, Halpern-Felsher, & Millstein, 2002; Halpern-Felsher & Cauffman, 2001). Similarly, Finken, Jacobs, and Laguna (1998) found that more experience with drinking and driving without negative consequences was related to lower perceptions of risk. Of course, the relation between perceived frequency of deviant behavior and involvement in deviant behavior may also be bidirectional. Adolescents could be using their own behavior as a reference for estimating the frequency of their peers' behavior, but then increase their own deviant behavior as a result of their overestimation of peers' deviant behavior. Still another possibility is that adolescents who engage in deviant behaviors more often have friends who are involved in the same behaviors. Thus, if these adolescents use their friends as a reference group to a greater extent than they use the wider peer group as a reference, their estimates of deviance may be inflated. It may be the case that everyone else is doing it if one thinks only of one's friends when estimating what everyone does. In this chapter, we have to be content with speculation concerning the potential causes underlying the relation between base-rate estimation and involvement in deviant behaviors because causal effects cannot be determined from nonexperimental data collected at a single time point. The potential causes just listed provide direction for future research, however.

IMPLICATIONS FOR DECISION-MAKING PROGRAMS

Our findings have implications for intervention programs aimed at reducing the risk of deviant behavior among teens. The relation between overestimation of deviant behavior and greater involvement in such behavior suggests the need for programs to increase adolescents' accuracy at estimating the base rates of peers' behavior through presentation of actual base-rate information as well as training in improving social perspective taking, statistical reasoning, and decision making. If adolescents can be taught to more accurately perceive the infrequency of deviant behavior, the perceived pressure imposed by the self or peers to conform to peers' behavior may work to reduce deviance and delinquency, rather than increasing such behaviors. Our findings related to individual differences in estimation bias and the relations between judgment bias, deviance, and greater psychosocial problems suggest that some adolescents may be at greater risk than others. As schools and policymakers consider teaching decision-making skills or other interventions related to risk taking, it might be reasonable to consider targeting particular groups of adolescents who already exhibit biased reasoning and problem behaviors.

Some research, however, suggests that intervention programs based on statistical perception must be implemented with caution and their outcomes tested carefully. For example, Jacobs, Hashima, and Kenning (1995) studied an intervention program aimed at increasing children's knowledge about the prevalence of sexual abuse in order to increase their vigilance against abuse, and found that after receiving information about the prevalence of sexual abuse, children's estimates of the base rates of sexual abuse increased despite the fact that children's perceptions of the base rates for sexual abuse before the intervention were already higher than the national average and higher than the reported rate in their county. Similarly, "social norming" intervention programs implemented on many college campuses to reduce binge drinking have often met with little success. These programs use posters, ads, and education programs to announce that most students only drink four drinks at one time or that most students party only twice each week. Such approaches have produced mixed results, with some programs showing increases in alcohol consumption or no changes (e.g., Kallgren, Reno, & Cialdini, 2000). Thus, presenting children or adolescents with base-rate information does not necessarily mean that they will become more accurate at perceiving base rates in the future or that more accurate perceptions will lead to changes in behavior. As pointed out by Reyna et al. (chap. 3, this volume), behavioral change and long-term effects are hard to come by.

In sum, in a sample of at-risk adolescents, bias toward overestimating peers' deviant behaviors was related to greater involvement in both mildly deviant and very deviant behaviors, higher reports of victimization, greater depressed affect, and lower self-esteem. It is important to note that the relations varied markedly between on-target estimators and extreme overestimators; thus, if we return to the question posed at the beginning, these findings suggest that some adolescents (the on-target group) may be saying "Everyone is doing it" when they realize the actual behaviors would be far less frequent. Other adolescents, however, may believe their own overestimation rhetoric. Although we cannot infer causality from this study, it is clear that real-world experiences were related to judgment biases, highlighting the importance of considering both adolescents' previous experiences and their cognition about social phenomena when examining judgment and decision-making skills. In order to elucidate the causal mechanisms behind these relations, longitudinal and experimental studies are needed, as well as examinations of the effectiveness of intervention programs aimed at reducing deviant behavior by improving social judgment and decision making.

REFERENCES

Aas, H., & Klepp, K. I. (1992). Adolescents' alcohol use related to perceived norms. *Scandinavian Journal of Psychology, 33,* 315–325.

Bar-Hillel, M., & Fischhoff, B. (1981). When do base rates affect predictions? *Journal of Personality and Social Psychology, 41,* 671–680.

Benthin, A., Slovic, P., & Severson, H. (1993). A psychometric study of adolescent risk perception. *Journal of Adolescence, 16,* 153–168.

Berndt, T. J. (1979). Developmental changes in conformity to peers and parents. *Developmental Psychology, 15,* 608–616.

Blanton, H., Gibbons, F. X., Gerrard, M., Conger, K. J., & Smith, G. E. (1997). Role of family and peers in the development of prototypes associated with substance use. *Journal of Family Psychology, 11*(3), 271–288.

Cairns, R. B., Cairns, B. D., Neckerman, H. J., Gest, S. D., & Gariépy, J. L. (1988). Social networks and aggressive behavior: Peer support or peer rejection? *Developmental Psychology, 24,* 815–823.

Davidson, D. (1995). The representativeness heuristic and conjunction fallacy effect in children's decision making. *Merrill-Palmer Quarterly, 41,* 328–346.

Dawes, R. M. (1988). *Rational choice in an uncertain world.* San Diego, CA: Harcourt Brace Jovanovich.

Dawes, R. M. (1990). The potential nonfalsity of the false consensus effect. In R. M. Hogarth (Ed.), *Insights in decision making* (pp. 179–199). Chicago: University of Chicago Press.

Devins, G. M., & Orme, C. M. (1985). Center for Epidemiological Studies depression scale. In D. J. Keyser & R. C. Sweetland (Eds.), *Test critiques* (pp. 144–160). Kansas City, MO: Test Corporation of America.

Dryfoos, J. (1990). *Adolescents at risk: Prevalence and prevention.* New York: Oxford University Press.

Dunning, D., Griffin, D. W., Milojkovic, J. D., & Ross, L. (1990). The overconfidence effect in social prediction. *Journal of Personality and Social Psychology, 58,* 568–581.

Ellis, N. R., Palmer, L. L., & Reeves, C. L. (1988). Developmental and intellectual differences in frequency processing. *Developmental Psychology, 24,* 38–45.

Empey, L. (1982). *American delinquency: Its mean and construction* (Rev. ed.). Homewood, IL: Dorsey.

Ferguson, T. J., Olthof, T., Luiten, A., & Rule, B. G. (1984). Children's use of observed behavioral frequency versus behavioral covariation in ascribing dispositions to others. *Child Development, 55,* 2094–2105.

Finken, L. L., Jacobs, J. E., & Laguna, K. (1998). The role of age, experience, and situational factors in the drinking and driving decisions of college students. *Journal of Youth and Adolescence, 27,* 493–511.

Fischhoff, B. (1992). Risk taking: A developmental perspective. In F. J. Yates (Ed.), *Risk-taking behavior, Wiley series in human performance and cognition* (pp. 133–162). Oxford, England: Wiley.

Furby, L., & Beyth-Marom, R. (1992). Risk-taking in adolescence: A decision-making perspective. *Developmental Review, 12,* 1–44.

Goldberg, J. H., Halpern-Felsher, B. L., & Millstein, S. G. (2002). Beyond invulnerability: The importance of benefits in adolescents' decision to drink alcohol. *Health Psychology, 21,* 477–484.

Halpern-Felsher, B. L., & Cauffman, E. (2001). Costs and benefits of a decision: Decision-making competence in adolescents and adults. *Journal of Applied Developmental Psychology, 22,* 257–273.

Hasher, L., & Chromiak, W. (1977). The processing of frequency information: An automatic mechanism? *Journal of Verbal Learning and Verbal Behavior, 16,* 173–184.

Higgins, E. T., Feldman, N. S., & Ruble, D. N. (1980). Accuracy and differentiation in social prediction: A developmental perspective. *Journal of Personality, 48,* 520–540.

Horney, J., & Marshall, I. H. (1992). Risk perceptions among serious offenders—the role of crime and punishment. *Criminology, 30,* 575–594.

Jacobs, J. E., Greenwald, J. P., & Osgood, D. W. (1995). Developmental differences in base-rate estimates of social behaviors and attitudes. *Social Development, 4,* 165–181.

Jacobs, J. E., Hashima, P. Y., & Kenning, M. (1995). Children's perceptions of the risk of sexual abuse. *Child Abuse and Neglect, 19,* 1443–1456.

Jacobs, J. E., & Klaczynski, P. A. (2002). The development of judgment and decision making during childhood and adolescence. *Current Directions in Psychological Science, 11,* 145–149.

Jacobs, J. E., & Narloch, R. H. (2001). Children's use of sample size and variability to make social inferences. *Journal of Applied Developmental Psychology, 22,* 1–21.

Jacobs, J. E., & Potenza, M. T. (1991). The use of judgment heuristics to make social and object decisions: A developmental perspective. *Child Development, 62,* 166–178.

Johnston, K., & Jacobs, J. E. (2003). Children's illusory correlations: The role of attentional bias in group impression formation. *Journal of Cognition and Development, 4*(2), 129–160.

Johnston, L. D., O'Malley, P. M., & Bachman, J. G. (2003). *Monitoring the future national results on adolescent drug use: Overview of key findings, 2002.* Washington, DC: U.S. Dept. of Health and Human Services.

Kahneman, D., Slovic, P., & Tversky, A. (Eds.). (1985). *Judgment under uncertainty: Heuristics and biases.* Cambridge, England: Cambridge University Press.

Kallgren, C. A., Reno, R. R., & Cialdini, R. B. (2000). A focus theory of normative conduct: When norms do and do not affect behavior. *Personality and Social Psychology Bulletin, 26,* 1002–1012.

Klaczynski, P. A. (2001). Framing effects on adolescent task representations, analytic and heuristic processing and decision making. Implications for the normative/descriptive gap. *Journal of Applied Developmental Psychology, 22,* 289–309.

Klaczynski, P. A., & Fauth, J. (1997). Developmental differences in memory-based intrusions and self-serving statistical reasoning biases. *Merrill-Palmer Quarterly, 43,* 539–566.

Klaczynski, P. A., & Narasimham, G. (1998). Development of scientific reasoning biases: Cognitive versus ego-protective explanations. *Developmental Psychology, 34,* 175–187.

Kleiber, D., Larson, R., & Csikszentmihalyi, M. (1986). The experience of leisure in adolescence. *Journal of Leisure Research, 18,* 169–176.

Krosnick, J. A., & Judd, C. M. (1982). Transitions in social influence at adolescence: Who induces cigarette smoking? *Developmental Psychology, 18,* 359–368.

Kruglanski, A. W. (1989). The psychology of being "right": The problem of accuracy in social perception and cognition. *Psychological Bulletin, 106,* 395–409.

Kunda, Z. (1990). The case for motivated reasoning. *Psychological Bulletin, 108*(3), 480–498.

Larson, R. W. (1983). Adolescents' daily experience with family and friends: Contrasting opportunity systems. *Journal of Marriage and the Family, 45,* 739–750.

Larson, R. W., & Csikszentmihalyi, M. (1978). Experiential correlates of time alone in adolescence. *Journal of Personality, 46,* 677–693.

Larson, R. W., & Kleiber, D. (1993). Daily experience of adolescents. In P. H. Tolan & B. J. Cohler (Eds.), *Handbook of clinical research and practice with adolescents* (pp. 125–145). Oxford, England: Wiley.

Lauritsen, J. L., Sampson, R. J., & Laub, J. H. (1991). The link between offending and victimization among adolescents. *Criminology, 29,* 265–292.

Lichtenstein, S., Slovic, P., Fischhoff, B., Layman, M., & Combs, B. (1978). Judged frequency of lethal events. *Journal of Experimental Psychology: Human Learning and Memory, 4,* 551–578.

Marks, G., Graham, J. W., & Hansen, W. B. (1992). Social projection and social conformity in adolescent alcohol use: A longitudinal analysis. *Personality and Social Psychology Bulletin, 18*, 96–101.

Marks, G., & Miller, N. (1987). Ten years of research on the false-consensus effect: An empirical and theoretical review. *Psychological Bulletin, 102*, 72–90.

Meehan, A. M., & Janik, L. M. (1990). Illusory correlation and the maintenance of sex role stereotypes in children. *Sex Roles, 22*, 83–95.

Miller, D., & Prentice, D. A. (1994). Collective errors and errors about the collective. *Personality and Social Psychology Bulletin, 20*, 541–550.

Mullen, B., Atkins, J. L., Champion, D. S., Edwards, C., Hardy, D., Story, J. E., & Vanderklok, M. (1985). The false consensus effect: A meta-analysis of 155 hypothesis tests. *Journal of Experimental Social Psychology, 21*, 262–283.

Nicholls, J. G. (1978). The development of the concepts of effort and ability, perception of academic attainment, and the understanding that difficult tasks require more ability. *Child Development, 49*, 800–814.

Nisbett, R. E., & Kunda, Z. (1985). Perception of social distributions. *Journal of Personality and Social Psychology, 48*, 297–311.

Nucci, L., Guerra, N., & Lee, J. (1991). Adolescent judgments of the personal, prudential, and normative aspects of drug usage. *Developmental Psychology, 27*, 841–848.

Primi, C., & Agnoli, F. (2002). Children correlate infrequent behaviors with minority groups: A case of illusory correlation. *Cognitive Development, 17*, 1105–1131.

Rosenberg, M. (1965). *Society and the adolescent self-image.* Princeton, NJ: Princeton University Press.

Shaklee, H., & Mims, M. (1981). Development of rule use in judgments of covariation between events. *Child Development, 52*, 317–325.

Shaklee, H., & Paszek, D. (1985). Covariation judgment: Systematic rule use in middle childhood. *Child Development, 56*, 1229–1240.

Sherman, S. J., Preston, C. C., Chassin, L., Corty, E., & Olshavsky, R. (1983). The false consensus effect in estimates of smoking prevalence: Underlying mechanisms. *Personality and Social Psychology Bulletin, 9*, 197–207.

Smith, H. D. (1993). *Cognitive heuristic use in children: The development of representativeness, anchoring and adjustment, and framing.* Unpublished doctoral dissertation, Virginia Commonwealth University, Richmond.

Steinberg, L., & Cauffman, E. (1996). Maturity of judgment in adolescence: Psychosocial factors in adolescent decision making. *Law and Human Behavior, 20*, 249–272.

Steinberg, L., & Silverberg, S. B. (1986). The vicissitudes of autonomy in early adolescence. *Child Development, 57*, 841–851.

Sussman, S., Dent, C. W., Mestel-Rauch, J. M., Johnson, C. A., Hansen, W. B., & Flay, B. R. (1988). Adolescent nonsmokers, triers, and regular smokers' estimates of cigarette smoking prevalence: When do overestimations occur and by whom? *Journal of Applied Social Psychology, 18*, 537–551.

Swann, W. B. (1984). Quest for accuracy in person perception: A matter of pragmatics. *Psychological Review, 91*, 457–477.

Unger, J. B., & Rohrbach, L. A. (2002). Why do adolescents overestimate their peers' smoking prevalence? Correlates of prevalence estimates among California 8th-grade students. *Journal of Youth and Adolescence, 31*, 147–153.

Warr, M. (2002). *Companions in crime.* Cambridge, England: Cambridge University Press.

Weinstein, N. D. (1980). Unrealistic optimism about future life events. *Journal of Personality and Social Psychology, 39*, 806–820.

Weinstein, N. D., & Lachendro, E. (1982). Egocentrism as a source of unrealistic optimism. *Personality and Social Psychology Bulletin, 8*, 195–200.

Young, J. W., & Ferguson, L. R. (1979). Developmental changes through adolescence in the spontaneous nomination of reference groups as a function of decision content. *Journal of Youth and Adolescence, 8,* 239–252.

Zukier, H., & Pepitone, A. (1984). Social roles and strategies in prediction: Some determinants of the use of base-rate information. *Journal of Personality and Social Psychology, 47,* 349–360.

6

Culture and the Construction of Concepts of Personal Autonomy and Democratic Decision Making

Charles C. Helwig

University of Toronto

Recent research has advanced our understanding of how children evaluate their own decision-making autonomy and make judgments about the fairness of social organization in various social contexts, including the peer group, the family, and the school. Research conducted in Western cultural contexts has shown that children develop concepts of *personal autonomy* and *democratic decision making*, which they apply to evaluate procedures for making decisions (e.g., democratic vs. authority-centered) in social groups. However, until now, little was known about children's and adolescents' judgments about these issues in cultures with fundamentally different political systems from those typically found in the West. This chapter reviews research on children's judgments of personal choice, autonomy, and democracy in Western and other cultural contexts; preliminary findings are presented from a new line of research investigating judgments of democratic decision making conducted in mainland China. The implications of these findings for broader questions regarding explanations of similarities and differences in reasoning about personal choice, autonomy, and democracy across cultures are discussed.

CONCEPTS OF PERSONAL DECISION MAKING AND AUTONOMY

Western psychologists have long identified the achievement of autonomy and individuation as important milestones in social development (Erikson, 1968). Autonomy is significant for a variety of life tasks, including individuals' assumptions of adult roles as productive members of society. The development of a sense of autonomy, and especially the formation of the capacity to make independent and informed decisions, is seen as especially central to citizenship and participation in democratic political institutions in modern societies (Kurtines, Berman, Ittel, & Williamson, 1995). One important aspect of individual autonomy is the development of an understanding of the areas over which the self may legitimately make decisions, free from the necessary influence or guidance of adults or other authorities. Children's conceptions of their own decision-making autonomy or personal choice is an area that has received a lot of attention recently in the social-cognitive literature. A large number of studies (reviewed in Turiel, 1998), conducted mostly, but not exclusively, in Western cultural contexts, has found that children identify a domain of "personal issues," or matters considered to be part of children's own discretion and beyond the bounds of legitimate regulation by parents, teachers, or other authorities. American children and adolescents have been found to judge issues such as choice of friends, appearance (hairstyles or choices of clothing), and preferences for leisure activities as up to themselves to decide (Nucci, 1981; Smetana, 1989). Rules or commands by authorities restricting or prohibiting children from making their own decisions over these matters are judged as wrong, even by elementary school children, and these judgments are often justified by explicit appeals to children's rights to freedom, autonomy, and personal choice. Children have been found to begin to define areas of personal discretion even as young as the preschool years (Nucci & Weber, 1995), with the scope of issues over which children are given decision-making autonomy expanding substantially in adolescence (Dornbusch et al., 1985; Yee & Flanagan, 1985).

The development of a personal domain of decision-making autonomy is not always a smooth process, but is often characterized by conflicts, tensions, and negotiations with authority figures such as parents. Observations of interactions between parents and children have found that children are more likely to challenge parental authority over personal issues than other issues, such as moral issues entailing harm to others or issues of fairness, or social conventional issues entailing violation of cultural customs or social organizational rules (Nucci & Weber, 1995). Conflicts between personal discretion and parental authority become especially acute in adolescence, when adolescents are more likely to assert their autonomy over issues that they, but not always their parents, begin to see as personal, such as cleaning one's room or maintaining conventional standards of appearance (Smetana, 1989). Nucci (2001) suggested that conflicts of this sort are essential for the formation of a sense of self and personal agency, with the negotiations and discussions they provoke helping to aid in children's gradual construction of a sense of independence and self-efficacy within an expanding personal domain.

The process of the construction of a personal domain has been found in other cultural contexts besides the United States, such as Brazil (Nucci, Camino, & Sapiro, 1996) and Japan (Killen & Sueyoshi, 1995). For example, Nucci et al. (1996) examined the judgments of middle- and lower-class children and mothers in urban and rural regions of Brazil. Mothers and children across social classes and regions distinguished a domain of personal issues in their judgments and reasoning, but mothers of lower-class and rural children were less likely to grant personal decision making autonomy to younger children. These social class and regional differences in judgments disappeared by adolescence, however. Personal decision making autonomy was granted to adolescents by both Brazilian mothers and their children over similar issues, and reasons of autonomy, choice, and the development of identity and uniqueness were used to justify their judgments.

CONCEPTIONS OF DEMOCRATIC
DECISION MAKING

Conceptions of basic autonomy and personal choice are likely to serve as a foundation for democratic social organization or group decision making, in which each individual is given a voice and opportunity to participate (Kurtines et al., 1995). Early studies examining the development of concepts of *democracy* conducted in the 1960s and 1970s have looked at children's abilities to define democracy or to understand its manifestation in complex political situations (Gallatin, 1985; Greenstein, 1965), and have placed the origins of these understandings in early adolescence. However, recent research has examined younger children's understandings of more basic features of democracy, using a somewhat different paradigm (Helwig, 1998; Helwig & Kim, 1999). Helwig (1998) examined Canadian elementary school children's judgments of the fairness of a variety of government systems, including democratic governments (representative democracy, majority rule, or government by strict consensus) and nondemocratic governments, such as rule by the wealthy, or a meritocracy, in which the "smartest" people rule. The findings of Helwig (1998) indicated that even young children (6-year-olds) judged democratic governments as more fair than nondemocratic governments. Younger children were more likely to prefer democracy by consensus, in which everyone in a nation had to agree on all decisions, whereas older children were more likely to perceive the impracticality of such a system and to prefer decision making by majority rule instead. With the development of more sophisticated perspective-taking skills (Selman, 1980), older children are able to recognize the impossibility of achieving consensus in larger social groups composed of individuals having diverse values and perspectives.

Although democracy is often viewed as a political construct, appropriate at the level of government, it may also apply in more local contexts. For example, researchers have identified democratic family structures (Berkowitz & Grych, 2000) or school environments (Nucci, 2001) in which children are given a voice in decision making and their perspectives are heard and respected. Accordingly, research has begun to examine children's judgments about decision-making procedures involving children themselves. Studies examining children's conceptions of *majority rule* (Kinoshita, 1989; Mann & Greenbaum, 1987; Moessinger, 1981), conducted in Geneva, Israel, Japan, and Australia, have found that children endorse and support majority rule for a number of decisions made by groups of children, including, for example, field trip decisions in the school context.

However, democratic decision making may not be ideal for all decisions made within social contexts. Some forms of social organization are structured more along egalitarian lines, whereas others are more hierarchical and authority-based. Even adults in Western democracies encounter both democratic and authority-based forms of social organization in various aspects of their daily lives, such as the family, the workplace, or the political sphere. Deciding when and where democratic social organization is preferred or appropriate is likely to depend on a number of factors, including judgments about the competence of "agents" to make autonomous decisions and the overall goals of a social system.

Studies of children's conceptions of *authority* (Laupa, Turiel, & Cowan, 1995) have found that children endorse and view as legitimate decision making by adult authority in some situations, such as in the hierarchical context of the school. This research did not, however, examine children's conceptions of democratic decision making in the school setting, or gather information about how children might understand distinctions regarding when and where democratic versus authority-oriented decision making is appropriate. Recent research has examined Canadian elementary school children's (Helwig & Kim, 1999) and adolescents' and young adults' (Helwig, 2001) abilities to distinguish the appropriateness of democratic forms of decision making for 8-year-old child agents in the social contexts of the peer group, the family, and the school. This research included examples that were expected to gravitate toward children's own involvement in decision making, such as decisions about what game a group of children would play, where a family would go on a vacation, and where a school class would go on a field trip. Also included were decisions that were expected to raise concerns over the competence of children to make informed decisions or of potential harm that might ensue if children were granted decision-making autonomy. These examples were expected to gravitate toward decision making by adult authorities. Included here were (a) a decision about what movie a group of children would see, (b) a decision in the family about what school a child would attend, and (c) a decision about the content of the school curriculum. Participants in this study evaluated three decision-making procedures: majority rule, consensus (everyone would have to agree), and decision making by adult authorities alone. Overall, children, adolescents, and adults distinguished the different types of decisions and social contexts in the ways expected, although the judgments of older participants were more differentiated than those of younger children. The majority of older children and adolescents, for example, believed that curriculum decisions should be left up to teachers because the teachers were seen as having the expertise and competence to make better decisions. However, for other decisions, such as school field trips or games, democratic or autonomy-granting procedures such as majority rule or consensus were preferred. In justifying democratic decision making, children, adolescents, and adults appealed to ideas of fairness based on majority rule or consensus, and to the importance of granting children a voice or a say in decision making.

Interestingly, younger children seemed to have a somewhat broader view of their own decision-making autonomy than older children. For example, younger children (6- to 7-year-olds) were more likely than older children to endorse decision-making procedures that gave children greater autonomy, such as consensus, over decision making by adult authorities alone, across a variety of decisions made in the peer group, family, and school. Younger children were about evenly divided over whether curriculum decisions should be made by adult authority or by the consensus of the class, whereas older children clearly preferred such decisions to be made by adults (teachers). Overall, the findings of this study suggest that, as children develop, they become more aware of cognitive limitations on their own decision-making ability, and how these judgments of competence intersect with the goals of different social organizations, such as the school. This allows them to better distinguish the contexts in which democratic decision making may or may not be desired.

The findings of the research reviewed up to this point suggest that concepts of personal autonomy and democratic decision making emerge early in development and are applied to distinguish social contexts and specific areas of decision making. These findings have been interpreted to be consistent with models of social reasoning that describe children's increasing capacity to distinguish social domains and the contexts of social judgment in development (Helwig, 1995; Neff & Helwig, 2002; Turiel, 1998), rather than global stage models ascribing broad constructs such as heteronomy or "blind" obedience to authority to young children (Kohlberg, 1981; Piaget, 1932). Earlier theories of the development of moral judgment have viewed children's social and moral reasoning as moving from a more heteronymous concern with authority, punishment, and a rigid adherence to existing social rules and norms in early childhood, toward a more autonomous orientation found in late childhood based on rights, fairness, and consensus (Piaget, 1932). The achievement of autonomous moral judgment is seen as resulting, in part, from changes in the nature of children's social interactions, reflecting a transition from the unilateral restraint that characterizes young children's relationships with adults, toward more egalitarian relationships with peers encountered in late childhood (Piaget, 1932).

Recent perspectives, however, have presented a different view of children's social development, in which the construction of personal autonomy is more of a gradual process that manifests itself in a variety of social contexts and relationships, including those with adults. For example, Nucci and Weber (1995) documented many instances in which even preschool children challenge and negotiate with parents over issues they believe to involve their own personal jurisdiction, such as choices over wardrobe or recreational activities. Correspondingly, judgments of democratic decision making reveal that even young children develop beliefs about their own involvement in group decision making, and they often tend to prefer and evaluate as more fair democratic procedures that give them greater voice or more say in decisions. However, at the same time, children are responsive to different features of social context, and they sometimes subordinate their own decision-making autonomy to hierarchical social organization, especially for decisions over which children are seen as lacking in competence. Support for hierarchy or individual autonomy in children's social judgments thus should not be seen as representing successive stages of social reasoning, but rather as coexisting in children's (and even adults) social judgments (Neff & Helwig, 2002). Accounts of the development of reasoning about decision-making autonomy and democracy therefore need to take into account the different ways in which autonomy and hierarchy are coordinated throughout development, and how they are applied in different social contexts. One of the most important of such contexts, addressed only indirectly in this chapter up to this point, is that of culture.

DEMOCRACY AND AUTONOMY: "COLLECTIVISM" AND THE CHINESE CULTURAL CONTEXT

The findings of the research described in the previous section suggest that conceptions of personal autonomy and democratic decision making emerge in development in a variety of cultural contexts. Conceptions of democratic decision making based on majority rule appear to cut across the Western/ Asian divide (e.g., Kinoshita, 1989), despite significant cultural variations among these societies. However, all of the cultures studied up to this point are governed by political structures based on modern Western models and are subject to considerable Western influences in the form of cultural and economic exchanges and free flow of information. Little is known about reasoning related to decision-making procedures and personal autonomy in societies with fundamentally different political systems and social structures from those typically found in the West, such as mainland China.

Several features of Chinese society make it an especially appropriate environment in which to investigate the potential universality, or cultural embedment, of concepts of personal autonomy and democratic decision making. China's cultural orientation, like that of many Asian societies, is frequently described as "collectivistic," in contrast to the "individualistic" orientation believed to be found in Western societies (Triandis, 1989). It is maintained by some theorists that in collectivistic societies, such as Asian cultures including China, a sociocentric or interdependent concept of the *self* is held, in contrast to the independent or egoistic self-conception found in individualist cultures such as Western democracies and especially in North America (Markus & Kitayama, 1991; Shweder & Bourne, 1982). It is argued that these different construals of the self are tied to different systems of social organization resulting in culturally dependent and varying moral systems. In collectivist societies, social organization is more hierarchical, and thus moral systems in these societies revolve around strict adherence to duties and role obligations, inequalities among persons, maintenance of the existing social order, and strong support of group goals and obedience to authorities. In contrast, in individualist societies, social organization is more egalitarian and democratic, leading to moral systems focusing on equality among persons, individual rights and autonomy, and consensus and contract (e.g., Shweder, 1990; Shweder, Mahapatra, & Miller, 1987). In subsequent sections of this chapter, questions will be raised about the utility of such global characterizations of cultures implied by the individualism/collectivism construct, but it is useful at this juncture to examine some of the features of Chinese culture and social organization that have led to the characterization of China as a collectivist society.

The collectivist character of social organization and psychology in Communist China is evident in some descriptions provided by Western researchers during their encounters with contemporary Chinese social institutions, including educational systems, which became more frequent following China's opening up to the West during the last 30 years. Sander Breiner (1980), a Western psychiatrist, offers the following description of life in a Chinese nursery and school:

> The most remarkable thing about this nursery day care center was that it was quiet. There was very little crying, practically nonexistent, very little verbal communication, very little sound. . . . As you enter the courtyard of each school, the children from age one and one-half to seven are usually standing in

groups with their teachers, a hand upraised, waving in identical fashion, smil-
ing broadly and singing a chant. The chant continues until they are told to
stop. When you leave, you are treated to the same experience. The kindergar-
ten is more like a primary school than a play area. The children are taught by
rote; they are given learning games of language and counting. . . . All forms of
education had a rote quality. There was no spontaneous drawing in the youngest of classes. Everything was copying, and the child was praised most who
copied the best. There was no evidence of spontaneous individual or group
play in the classrooms or schoolyard. Even the youngest children sit quietly
and, on cue, perform, even turning their faces to the camera. The children
were the most lovely, trained, conforming, quiet, "well-behaved" children I
have seen anywhere in the world but utterly lacking in spontaneity. (pp.
89–90)

These informal and anecdotal observations of the educational system receive some support from recent findings of empirical research conducted on
preschool teachers' beliefs about the curriculum in China and the United
States (Wang, Elicker, McMullen, & Mao, 2001). Chinese teachers were
found to be more likely to endorse teacher-centered, or top–down educational practices, whereas U.S. teachers were more likely to endorse child-
centered practices in which children's autonomy and choice over learning
matters are fostered. For example, Chinese preschool teachers were more
likely than their U.S. counterparts to endorse practices such as using authority through rewards, coloring within predefined lines, and routine group-
learning activities in which flash cards were used. The differences in perspectives between Chinese and U.S. teachers is vividly illustrated in the following
excerpts from open-ended interviews conducted with teachers about their
"naive" theories of learning (Wang et al., 2001):

> U.S. Teachers: "I think the program should be child-centered. The curricu-
> lum should come from children's interest and strengths." . . . "Children
> should be allowed to explore or express themselves as much as possible,
> within certain limits."
> Chinese Teachers: "Teacher's authority is quite important, especially in
> terms of the knowledge-gaining process. If the teacher is knowledgeable
> and has power in what's right and what's wrong, children may admire the
> teacher, or realize the importance of knowledge. Thus they are motivated
> to learn from the teacher." . . . "If in play time, yes (they could choose to
> do things), but in instruction time, we require children to do things ac-
> cording to the teacher's plan."

The examples illustrate some apparent differences in the conceptions of
learning held by Chinese and U.S. teachers. Teachers in the United States
appeared to be more likely to hold a view of learning based on stimulating in-

terest through allowing children choice and active involvement, whereas Chinese teachers were more likely to stress the role of respect for authority in facilitating an interest in learning and in the more passive, rote learning of fixed curricula. Conceptions of learning may be expected to play a part in judgments about children's own involvement in decision making in academic contexts. Insofar as children's active involvement and choice are seen as vital in stimulating their motivation and interest, it can be expected that greater involvement in academic decision making would be seen as desirable, leading to greater endorsement of more democratic forms of social organization. Conversely, if children's role in education is construed as essentially passive, then hierarchical or authority-oriented decision making regarding academic matters may be more likely to be endorsed.

In accord with the characterization of China as a collectivist society, conceptions of family life in China are often described as heavily influenced by traditional Confucian ethics and its central idea of *filial piety*, or the fostering of strict obedience toward and respect for parents and elders (Dien, 1982; Pye, 1992). In Confucian philosophy, the family is conceptualized as a fixed hierarchy, with the father or other male elders especially held in high esteem and reverence. These ideas usually are taught and transmitted to the child through texts and stories, such as *The Classic of Filial Piety*—a text that has been used in the context of socialization and moral education for many generations to convey models of ideal filial behavior. According to Pye (1992), "The prime point of the *Classic of Filial Piety* is that filial obligation is an absolute requirement and exists without regard to the quality of parental behavior" (p. 93). The child is taught to accept the supreme authority of the omnipotent father, and that to oppose or think ill of parental authority is to have committed "a most serious crime" (p. 92). Historically, the strict upholding of rules and duties by the family system in Confucianism was used to relieve the state of some of the burden of enforcement of laws and appropriate social behavior. As well, attitudes toward obedience to authority in the family had analogs in attitudes requiring strict obedience to the rulers or state. Social compliance in the family and in society at large was maintained through severe punishments for infractions or by social "shaming" by fellow citizens (Pye, 1992). The uses of shaming as a socialization process have been identified and studied in contemporary Chinese societies, such as Taiwan (Fung & Chen, 2001).

The political structure of contemporary China also has been seen by many to support a characterization of the Chinese culture as collectivistic. Political life in China is dominated by the political ideology of Communism, interpreted, at least by many in the West, as a political system in which individual rights and autonomy are subordinated to group goals, centralized planning, and the authority of the Communist Party elite. The Party has a monopoly on political power, and administrates and controls every unit of society, from urban centers to villages and the military (Worden, Savada, & Dolan, 1988). Government is based on the Marxist–Leninist principle of democratic centralism, in which lower level bodies consult with the people but must answer to and follow the orders of higher level organizations. The democratic aspect involves debate and discussion within all levels of the Party on key issues, along with decision making by majority rule; however, subordinate organizations must follow the dictates and policies of upper levels, hence the "centralism." Although there is some accommodation within the political system for elected legislative bodies that meet occasionally, such as People's Congresses, the role of these institutions is to play primarily a consultative role while the major political course of the country remains under the direction of the Chinese Communist Party (Mackerras, 2001; Worden et al., 1988).

Taken together, these portrayals of Chinese social life, political institutions, and culture as consistent with the assumption of collectivism, would suggest that support for individual autonomy in decision making—especially for child agents—should be severely attenuated when contrasted with the findings from individualistic societies such as Canada and the United States. Evaluations of decision making and personal autonomy within the family would be expected to follow Confucian ideals of filial piety and respect for and obedience to parental authority (Dien, 1982). Reasoning about decision making in the school would be expected to observe top–down principles of hierarchy and respect for the competence of adult educational authorities, in accordance with the hierarchical teaching styles practiced in the classroom and the highly centralized control over the curriculum exerted by Party educational bodies under democratic centralism.

THE INDIVIDUALISM/COLLECTIVISM
CONSTRUCT REEXAMINED

The aforementioned conclusions are derived from the assumption that cultures and the thinking of individuals can be accurately portrayed within global constructs such as collectivism, and that China represents one such culture. In models of social reasoning that draw on general cultural orientations such as individualism and collectivism, the underlying assumptions supporting the conclusions reached are often left unspecified or are accepted without critical examination. It is instructive here to provide an explicit accounting of these assumptions, and to examine them critically in the light of contemporary Chinese social structures and culture and especially with regard to recent psychological empirical evidence emerging in several relevant areas.

As noted by other theorists (e.g., Spiro, 1982/1987; Strauss, 2000; Turiel, 1998, 2002), broad-based cultural orientations such as individualism and collectivism assume the validity of a number of usually interconnected propositions about cultures in general and about the processes by which individuals acquire social knowledge. Starting at the broadest cultural level, there is the assumption that cultural orientations are monolithic or all-embracing constructs that characterize social organization across diverse social contexts, institutions, and environments existing within cultural settings. Even though subcultures are sometimes identified within a broader nation or culture, cultural orientations are predicated on the assumption that enough homogeneity exists within a bounded culture to make these broad characterizations useful as templates for defining cultures and, by extension, for explaining the psychology of individuals who live within them. Secondly, there is the assumption that cultural orientations or ideologies are transmitted to individuals in rather direct fashion, such that individuals in the course of their natural development absorb or internalize the prevailing features of the broader cultural orientation, and that this orientation will be manifest both in individuals' outward behavior as well as in their internal thoughts, judgments, and affective processes and psychology. Third, there is the assumption that individual compliance with cultural norms is tantamount to acceptance of these norms, and that individuals do not tend to critically evaluate and interpret both cultural practices and ideologies. Finally, there is the assumption that the perspective of individuals in subordinate positions in social hierarchies are the same as those in dominant positions, because individuals in subordinate positions largely internalize the broader cultural perspective, often through direct social transmission of cultural ideology by "local guardians of the moral order" (Shweder et al., 1987, p. 73) or by participation in cultural rituals and socially prescribed forms of behavior.

All of these assumptions, however, may be open to question, both on general terms and as applied to contemporary China. Considered as a whole, they may overestimate the extent to which cultures and the thinking of individuals may be typed according to overarching and general belief systems and cultural ideology, and they may downplay the degree of heterogeneity and diversity that exists within the thinking of individuals (Turiel, 2002).

Some Chinese scholars have responded in turn to the characterizations that abound in the research literature describing Chinese culture as collectivistic, oriented to authority, or dominated by a Confucian ideology based on filial piety. These descriptions, it has been argued, are overly monolithic, outdated, perhaps ethnocentric, and inconsistent with much empirical evidence. For example, Lau and Yeung (1996) argued that "the single-minded focus on one ideology has created a phenomenon whereby researchers tend to overgeneralize the influence of Confucianism" (p. 33). Other philosophies, such as Taoism and Buddhism, also have exerted great influence on Chinese thought, and yet the impact of these philosophies on Chinese psychology remains largely unaccounted for in contemporary psychological research and theorizing. Moreover, these other philosophies frequently contain elements, such as the focus of Buddhism and Taoism on personal freedom, and the attendant notion of transcending earthly connections, that may place them at odds with Confucianism's emphasis on obedience to received social roles and hierarchies and strict observance of filial piety (Lau, 1996; Sen, 1999). As noted by Lau (1996), the tendency to view all of Chinese social practices and thinking entirely through the lens of one ancient philosophy would be as misguided, incomplete, and potentially ethnocentric as using the ideas of Plato or Aristotle as a model for interpreting all aspects of contemporary Western culture and psychology.

Confucianism itself is not as monolithic and unidimensional with respect to its emphasis on filial piety as suggested by some scholars who draw on it as a model for explaining Chinese moral judgments. Yeh (1972) noted that Confucianism was always adapted to prevailing social realities, and that notions of filial piety and obedience to superior kin, although clearly an important feature of the philosophical system, were sometimes subordinated to other social and moral concerns. For example, although the moral standard of honesty can be overridden by the virtue of filial piety, such that it is not believed to be right for a son to bear witness against his father for stealing a sheep, Confucius did regard it as morally exemplary for a political leader to execute his own elder and younger brothers for plotting to overthrow the state (Yeh, 1972). Importantly, however, Sen (1999) pointed out that even Confucius did not advocate blind obedience to the state, and recognized a duty to oppose a bad or unjust government.

Moreover, some contemporary Chinese social practices that appear to support the classification of the culture as collectivist have even come under scrutiny by Chinese commentators themselves. Chinese writers have criticized social practices that they believe place too great a restriction on children's autonomy in social contexts such as the family and the school. For example, increased emphasis on academic achievement by both schools and families has created immense pressures on children in mainland China (Wu, 1996). Chinese researchers have raised alarm about what they perceive as the potentially detrimental effects of recent increases in demands placed on children in one-child families by overinvolved parents. As observed by Wu (1996):

> there may be adverse effects on child development and psychological orientation of parental control in the form of extreme attention, overprotection, constant monitoring of a child's behavior and desires, and high expectations of a child's school performance and future aspirations. (p. 20)

Concern over the potential negative effects of too much control and too little autonomy extends to public discussions about teaching practices in the

Chinese educational system. As already indicated, educational methods in Chinese kindergartens have been described as being oriented toward extreme regimentation, uniformity, rote learning, and as reflecting an absence of spontaneity and creativity (Breiner, 1980; Wu, 1996). These views do not merely represent those of nonmainland Chinese commentators, for as noted by Wu (1996), an article in a leading English language official Chinese publication, *China Today*, "recently admitted that rigid teaching methods demanding order and obedience have made Chinese kindergartens 'lifeless' " (p. 15). Chen and Su (2001), in a recent article on children's rights in China, pointed to the need for reform in educational practices in kindergartens and schools in order to facilitate the development of more egalitarian treatment of children and to further greater expression of children's opinions on matters of importance to them.

Characterizations of Chinese family life and educational systems as overly authoritarian and rigidly hierarchical, it is important to mention, may be relatively true or they may be somewhat or severely exaggerated. Nevertheless, it is evident that debates about the relative merits and consequences of different ways of balancing individual autonomy with authority-based, hierarchical systems of social order do occur in contemporary Chinese discourse over issues pertinent to both school and family contexts. The presence of these debates at various levels of Chinese society (among elites, commentators, and scientific researchers) is not consistent with a global cultural orientation of collectivism, as described by some. Rather, it is more in line with a perspective on social reasoning postulating the coexistence of a variety of social orientations, reflecting both a commitment to individual autonomy along with a commitment to maintaining hierarchical features of the social system, as found in studies of social judgments in both Western and non-Western social contexts (Turiel, 1998; Wainryb & Turiel, 1994). Where social structures take more hierarchical forms, and conformity with social conventional expectations is maintained through both explicit group sanctions and implicit processes like "shaming," the ideological systems promulgated and enforced by elites and social authorities may, correspondingly, be more likely to stress concepts such as respect for authority, honor, and the subordination of self-interest to collective goals. It is important, however, not to generalize the perspectives of elites and authorities to members of the society in general, and especially to those in subordinate positions. Individuals may respond to ideological and belief systems in ways that show both active acceptance as well as tacit disapproval, or even explicit rejection or rebellion, depending on the circumstances (Turiel, 2002).

Support for this perspective has been found in research conducted in another culture fitting the description collectivist, the Druze of Israel. The Druze are a traditional, hierarchically organized Muslim society in which strict prescriptions exist regarding the roles and duties of women, along with inequality in rights and personal autonomy between genders. Wainryb and Turiel (1994) found that concepts of personal entitlements, rights, and individual autonomy were, in many instances, judged to be applicable to Druze men, but not in the same way to Druze women. Even women in this society frequently asserted the rights of husbands and fathers to control their wives and daughters over decisions relating to education, work, and association, and they generally advocated women's obedience to the dictates of male authority figures. However, Druze women often saw obedience in strictly pragmatic terms—as necessary in order to avoid severe social sanctions, such as ostracism or physical punishment. Importantly, when asked about the fairness of restrictions on women's autonomy and rights, the majority of Druze women in that study, however, judged these restrictions to be unjust. This example points up the importance of examining reasoning from diverse perspectives in hierarchical social systems, and the need to move beyond assessments of mere compliance or obedience to examine directly conceptions of the fairness and justice of social practices held by individuals within these systems.

Further support for this view is found in research directly examining the individualism/collectivism construct in mainland China, which has produced paradoxical findings inconsistent with the characterization of Chinese psychology and culture as collectivistic (Lau, 1992; Yuan & Shen, 1998). For instance, Lau (1992) examined support for collectivistic and individualist values, using the Rokeach value survey (Rokeach, 1973), among university students in mainland China, two other Asian cultures (Hong Kong and Singapore), and the United States. The Rokeach value survey requires participants to rank order 36 values on how important they are to them. Lau (1992) found that mainland Chinese students were no less individualistic than even Americans (the prototypical individualistic culture) in their value rankings. For example, mainland Chinese ranked values such as freedom, ambition, and imagination significantly higher than Americans, and both groups did not differ in their rankings of other individualistic values such as equality, and independence. In contrast, Americans ranked collectivist values such as family security higher than mainland Chinese, and the two groups did not differ with respect to rankings of other collectivist values such as politeness, cleanliness, and self-control. Lau (1992) argued that these findings suggest that "the conceptualization of individualism–collectivism and its utility in differentiating cultures and societies have to be reconsidered" (p. 365).

Accounting for discrepancies in values endorsements such as these that seem to run counter to the common or stereotypical characterizations of American and Chinese cultures is, of course, a complex task. One possibility is that these values, as presented in decontextualized fashion in the Rokeach values survey, simply meant different things to each group, because participants were not required to define what they understood these values to mean or to apply them in making judgments about concrete situations. However, Lau (1992) suggested another possibility relating to another aspect of the study that investigated "locus of control," or the degree to which individuals perceive either themselves or external agents or forces as having control over important aspects of their lives (this variable was assessed only among the Asian cultures by Lau, 1992). In comparisons among the Asian groups on individualism–collectivism and locus of control, it was found that mainland Chinese students were higher than students from Hong Kong or Singapore in both their endorsement of individualistic values and in their perception of external (vs. internal) locus of control. Lau (1992) proposed that in environments that impose a higher degree of control over the satisfaction of personal desires, individualistic values would be valued more highly, because "things are more valued when they are out of reach" (p. 362), and data from Lau (1992) largely supported this hypothesis. Of course, one might not expect this relation always to hold true (i.e., individuals also may be fully accepting of high degrees of external control in certain circumstances, as has been found, for example, in studies of American children's and adults' acceptance of social convention and authority in the family and the school; see Laupa et al., 1995, for a review). However, this proposition suggests that value orientations uncovered by general assessments such as the Rokeach value survey are comprised not only of values that are supported by, or are seen as emblematic of, individuals' particular cultural environments, but also those values that may become sensitized because individuals see them as serving important human needs that are insufficiently realized, contested, or problematic within their current social environments or general experience.

This view is consistent with the perspective outlined earlier that relations among the value orientations of individuals, and the cultural belief systems and social organization that they experience, are complex and characterized, at times, by both agreement and disagreement, and equilibrium and disequilibrium. This makes it impossible simply to "read off" the moral understandings of individuals from global, broad brush-stroke descriptions of culture or social organization. Instead, more direct investigations of individuals' judgments of specific features of their social experiences is needed. This is especially important in the context of research in China, where collectivistic characterizations of Chinese culture are often derived from simple descriptions of existing social practices, or from evidence of individuals' compliance and seeming acceptance of these practices, gathered mainly through the examination of outward behavior. Until recently, we have known surprisingly little about the different ways in which individual autonomy and various forms of social organization may be construed by individuals in China, and especially about their judgments of ideal or desired procedures for organizing social life, including democratic decision making. Examining the development of these concepts in the context of Chinese culture may shed light on important questions about their potential universality, as well as differences in their manifestation under varying cultural conditions.

One line of research (Smetana, 2002; Yau & Smetana, 2003) began to examine Chinese children's and adolescents' construals of their own autonomy in the family context. Although collectivist characterizations of Chinese culture based on Confucianism would imply that Chinese children rarely or never challenge parental authority or control, this conclusion has been called into question by the findings of this research. Yau and Smetana (2003) investigated adolescents' reports of disagreements and conflicts they experienced with parents, and their reasoning about these events, in Hong Kong and a city in mainland China (Shenzhen). Yau and Smetana (2003) found that adolescents in both Hong Kong and Shenzhen reported conflicts over similar sorts of issues, including regulation of activities, schoolwork, chores, and interpersonal relationships. In general, adolescents from Shenzhen reported fewer conflicts than those from Hong Kong; however, conflicts over schoolwork were more prevalent in Shenzhen than in Hong Kong. Although the frequency of conflicts in China appears to be somewhat lower than reported among Western adolescents (Smetana, 1989), Chinese adolescents reported conflicts over similar sorts of issues as found in American samples. Moreover, in justifying their own position on family conflicts, Chinese adolescents, like their Western counterparts, frequently appealed to individualistic concepts such as personal choice and the pursuit of individual desires and wants. These types of justifications were found by Yau and Smetana (2003) to increase with age in both Hong Kong and Shenzhen, suggesting that this kind of reasoning may be more indicative of a developmental shift toward increased concern with autonomy in adolescence (Erikson, 1968), rather than being a product of a general cultural orientation. (If, on the other hand, Chinese children are gradually acquiring a dominant cultural orientation of collectivism and filial piety, one would expect appeals to personal choice and individualistic concerns to decline with age, especially in situations of conflict with traditional authorities such as parents.) The findings of this research suggest that conceptions of personal choice and appeals to individual autonomy are features of social reasoning that emerge in a variety of contexts, including so-called collectivistic cultures. Accordingly, autonomy and individual choice may place constraints on the types of social control and restrictions likely to be perceived as ideal, just, or conducive to healthy psychological functioning.

Studies of the actual outcomes of authoritarian parenting in China appear to support this view. For example, Lau, Lew, Hau, Cheung, and Berndt (1990) found that family harmony in mainland Chinese families was related to greater warmth and less control by parents over children, paralleling findings on socialization outcomes in Western cultural contexts. Similarly, studies of parenting in Chinese families (e.g., Chen, Dong, & Zhou, 1997) found that authoritarian parenting styles are associated with negative outcomes for children such as increases in aggression, declines in school achievement, and less acceptance by peers, as also found in Western cultures. Other reviews of research by Chinese scholars (e.g., Ho, 1986; Lau & Cheung, 1987) led to the general conclusion that Chinese children "do resent strict and authoritarian parenting" (Lau & Yeung, 1996, p. 33).

JUDGMENTS OF DEMOCRATIC DECISION MAKING AMONG CHINESE ADOLESCENTS

The research just described suggests that Chinese adolescents possess conceptions of personal autonomy and choice and actively employ these concepts in making social judgments in some situations, at least those entailing conflicts experienced in family settings. In the West, concepts of individual rights, personal decision making, and autonomy are seen as essential underpinnings of democratic social organization, in which individuals are permitted a say or voice in group decision making. Up until now, however, virtually no research has been conducted on judgments about democratic and authoritarian social decision making in China. As noted earlier, the perspectives found among elites (academics, policymakers, and researchers) within China reveal a mixture of views, ranging from acceptance to serious criticism of existing social practices and calls for democratic reform. We know comparatively little, however, about how laypersons in China, including children, evaluate democratic and nondemocratic social practices and procedures. In this section, some results from recent research (Helwig, Arnold, Tan, & Boyd, 2003) examining Chinese adolescents' judgments of democratic and authority-based forms of decision making in the peer, family, and school contexts will be described. This research represents an extension into the Chinese cultural context of previous research on the development of democratic decision making conducted in Canada (Helwig & Kim, 1999) and was carried out with the collaboration of Dr. Dingliang Tan of Nanjing Normal University.

The sample included 574 adolescents drawn from junior high and high schools in each of three age groups/grades: Junior 1 (13-year-olds), Senior 1 (15- to 16-year-olds), and Senior 3 (18-year-olds). Participants were drawn from three sites in China: Nanjing, a modern city; Taizhou, a small, more traditional city currently undergoing development; and a rural, isolated village in Hebei Province. These sites were selected to provide a wide spectrum of environments from which to sample reasoning, and allowed for the examination of the effect of degree of modernization or traditionalism on judgments and reasoning. The sample was balanced such that approximately half

the participants came from the modern urban environment (Nanjing), while
the other half was drawn from the more traditional environments (Taizhou
and Hebei Province).

A written version of the interview instrument used in previous research
(Helwig & Kim, 1999) was developed for use with adolescents. Use of a pen-
and-paper version of the instrument permitted data to be obtained from
larger numbers of participants than by interview methodologies, ensuring
better representativeness and allowing for more extensive comparisons to be
conducted among samples from the different regions. In addition, it allowed
for data collection under conditions of anonymity, enabling participants to
express themselves more freely on these topics than they might in face-to-
face interviews. Data collection was conducted by Chinese research assistants trained by the Chinese collaborator and administered in group classroom settings (with students working individually). After completing the
instrument, participants were asked to place the questionnaire packets into a
nondescript envelope provided for this purpose and to seal the envelope,
thus ensuring anonymity of responses.

The design was derived from Helwig and Kim (1999), as described earlier,
and included examples of decisions in the peer context about games and
movies, and school field trips and curriculum. However, some changes were
made to items used in the family context to make them more appropriate for
the Chinese cultural context. Because families in China are not allowed to
choose their children's school, a family decision about which school a child
should attend used in Helwig and Kim (1999) was changed to an example in
which a family is making a decision about whether a child should receive
special tutoring on weekends to boost the child's grades in school (a common
area of concern among families in contemporary China, as mentioned earlier). Also, a decision about a family vacation in Helwig and Kim (1999) was
changed to a decision about a family day outing, because vacations are not
common in rural environments in China. Moreover, all descriptions of the
family context included a family with a single child, in accordance with
China's official one-child policy. As in Helwig and Kim (1999), all child
characters in the scenarios were described as being around 8 years of age
(participants were reminded of the age of the child story agents before each
of the six decisions was presented). Participants were required to provide ratings of the goodness or badness of each decision-making procedure (majority
rule, consensus, and adult authority) for each decision, and to choose the
procedure they thought was best for each decision. They were also invited to
provide written justifications for their choices. Following is an example of the
scenario for the field trip decision (school context):

> Suppose there's a class of third grade students, all around 8 years of age. Every
> Friday afternoon, the whole class would go on a field trip. Suppose they were

trying to decide where they should go for one of their field trips. Below, you will be given examples of some different ways they could decide where they're going to go for a field trip. We would like you to tell us what you think about each one. You are to indicate whether you think it's a good or a bad way of making this decision.

Participants' preferences (their choice of which procedure would be best) for each decision are presented in Table 6.1, broken down by region (Nanjing, Taizhou, and Hebei Province) and age. The table shows that strong support for the democratic procedure of majority rule was found across all decisions, in both traditional and urban environments and in general across age groups. Support for authority tended to be found most for curriculum decisions in the school, and in decisions about what movie children would see in the peer context. These were decisions in the peer and school contexts that were expected to pull more for decision making by adult authorities, and indeed they did so, although democratic procedures were still preferred even for these decisions. Support for consensus was most likely to be found in the family context. The only age differences found pertained to increasing distinctions made among contexts with age in ratings of procedures; younger participants tended not to distinguish among social contexts when judging majority rule whereas older participants tended to judge consensus as more appropriate for the family context but majority rule as more appropriate for the peer and school contexts.

Interestingly, and contrary to expectations, decisions about whether a child should receive special tutoring did not produce large percentages of authority-based preferences. Chinese adolescents in general believed that such decisions should be made by democratic means, such as consensus or majority rule. These general patterns held up across urban and traditional environments. Indeed, responses were highly similar across all three environments, although participants from the more traditional regions (Hebei and Taizhou) were somewhat more supportive of decision making by adult authority for most decisions (see Table 6.1). These findings suggest that differences among the contexts and particular decisions being contemplated were more important than broader environmental factors such as modernism or traditionalism in accounting for patterns of judgments.

The findings reveal a strong commitment by Chinese adolescents to democratic decision making in a variety of contexts. Justifications for preferences and ratings were consonant with the democratic nature of their choices. The most frequent justifications used referred to individual rights, autonomy, or personal choice, along with democratic principles reflecting appeals to voice or majority rule (these responses accounted for 49% of all justifications). Appeals to children's autonomy, freedom, and the right to make decisions free from the interference of adult authorities tended to be found in instances in

TABLE 6.1

Preferences (Best Choice) for Decision-Making Procedures by Region, Age, Context, and Decision Type

| | Peer Context | | | | | | Family Context | | | | | | School Context | | | | | |
| | Game | | | Movie | | | Outing | | | Tutoring | | | Field Trip | | | Curriculum | | |
Region/Age	M	C	A	M	C	A	M	C	A	M	C	A	M	C	A	M	C	A
Nanjing																		
13 yrs.	71	25	4	67	16	17	64	28	8	55	41	4	66	19	14	58	16	26
15 to 16 yrs.	74	25	1	58	31	12	59	39	2	38	60	2	79	8	14	49	21	30
18 yrs.	78	20	2	78	16	5	61	34	5	47	49	4	88	8	3	65	10	25
Taizhou																		
13 yrs.	49	40	12	37	34	29	41	51	8	41	50	9	28	41	30	40	26	34
15 to 16 yrs.	67	26	6	51	28	21	56	42	2	37	54	9	66	17	17	45	15	40
18 yrs.	75	18	7	68	18	14	63	33	5	45	48	7	80	9	11	47	13	40
Hebei																		
13 yrs.	54	34	12	46	17	37	54	31	15	45	37	18	60	11	30	55	10	35
15 to 16 yrs.	67	30	2	66	25	9	56	44	0	51	42	7	64	26	10	36	30	34
18 yrs.	70	28	2	46	20	35	67	31	2	63	32	5	82	7	11	54	12	34

Note. Table gives percentage of adolescents judging each procedure as best. For decision-making procedures: M = majority rule (voting), C = consensus, and A = authority-based. Percentages may not sum to 100 due to rounding. From "Chinese Adolescents' Reasoning About Democratic and Authority-Based Decision Making in Peer, Family, and School Contexts," by C. C. Helwig, M. L. Arnold, D. Tan, and D. Boyd, 2003, *Child Development, 74*, p. 792. Copyright © 2003 by The Society for Research in Child Development. Reprinted with permission.

which participants rejected decision making by adult authority. Some examples of these responses by Chinese adolescents are given here (an example of a response from the prior research with Canadian adolescents is also given for purposes of comparison):

> *Peer/Game, Hebei, 13 years*: "Adults have no right to interfere into children's free time."
> *Peer/Game, Taizhou, 15 years*: "Parents should not do so. Kids do have awareness of autonomy, and should be allowed to make their own choice."
> *Peer/Movie, Canadian, 16 years*: "Kids should pick what they want to see on their free time not someone else, not someone that is not in their age group."

As mentioned, majority rule was the most frequently endorsed form of decision making overall and in most contexts and decisions. In general, Chinese adolescents evaluated this procedure using democratic principles of voice or "having a say," or the necessity of meeting the interests and needs of the greatest number, similar to the responses of Canadian children and adolescents (Helwig, 2001; Helwig & Kim, 1999). Some examples of Chinese adolescents' responses follow (along with a sample response from a Canadian adolescent):

> *Family/Outing, Nanjing, 18 years*: "This [majority rule] is able to satisfy most people's needs, quite fair."
> *School/Field Trip, Hebei, 13 years*: "Because everybody's opinion should be considered."
> *Family/Vacation, Canadian, 16 years*: "It's alright [majority rule] because everyone has input but they don't necessarily get what they want."

However, Chinese adolescents also frequently expressed concerns about the majority imposing its will on the minority, and correspondingly, that the interests of the minority would not be respected. On the other hand, consensus was often rejected as unfair because the dissent of one individual could lead to the interests of the majority not being met, or because it would be impossible to achieve complete agreement in many situations (responses that were also frequently found among Canadian children and adolescents). Some examples of these kinds of responses:

> *Peer/Movie, Taizhou, 15 years*: "Views of majority don't represent those of all. Why should others have to agree unwillingly with some people's private desires?"

School/Curriculum, Nanjing, 18 years: "It is difficult to make everybody have the same opinion [in consensus]. It is rare that everybody agrees."

These examples illustrate the quality and range of support for individual autonomy, rights, and democratic decision making found among Chinese adolescents. Democratic decision making was supported by appeals to individual rights and autonomy, and by references to basic democratic principles of voice, majority rule, the protection of the rights of minorities, and consensus. Chinese adolescents were quite cognizant of the possibility of individual conflict and disagreement, and appealed to broader democratic decision-making procedures such as majority rule as a means of resolving disputes among individuals who have clashing perspectives or interests. All of these aspects of Chinese adolescents' reasoning are not consistent with a monolithic characterization of Chinese psychology as oriented toward obedience to authority, the subordination of personal autonomy to the group, and assumptions of uniformity of opinion and behavior.

The insufficiency of general collectivist orientations to account for Chinese adolescents' social judgments and reasoning is perhaps most evident in responses to two of the examples: special tutoring in the family and curriculum decisions in the school. The majority of adolescents rejected adult jurisdiction over these issues, even though adults are characteristically highly involved in decisions over academic matters both in the classroom and in the family in China. Regarding special tutoring, adolescents frequently endorsed consensus because they saw it as respecting the right of the child to dissent if he or she did not want to receive the tutoring (rather than as implying that the child should conform to the parents' wishes). Many responses specifically mentioned that the tutoring would not be effective unless the child's assent was obtained first, because otherwise the child would not be motivated to learn:

Family/Tutoring, Nanjing, 18 years: "Tutoring will only be effective when the child wants to learn. Also, the child has the right to arrange her own time. Parents should give the child the right to veto."
Family/Tutoring, Nanjing, 18 years: "Many things, such as natural inclination, creativity and freedom, are strangled because of this."

Similarly, in the curriculum example, Chinese adolescents generally preferred democratic decision making because it was seen as leading to overall agreement and as stimulating children's interest and motivation. At times, adolescents took a critical perspective on curricula decided by educational authorities, perceiving such curricula as boring or lacking relevance to children's interests:

School/Curriculum, Taizhou, 15 years: "Education authorities' decisions are only based on examinations, and make us learn the boring texts. As to today's quality education, it develops one's interest. No to education authorities' decision!"

School/Curriculum, Hebei, 18 years: "This [authority decides] will make kids passive in action. . . . When kids want to learn a subject, they must be interested in it. As it goes, interest is the best teacher. This way [majority rule] will make them learn actively."

These examples are striking for their similarity with American teachers' views of education quoted earlier in the research conducted by Wang et al. (2001). Both Chinese students in our research, and American teachers in Wang et al. (2001), defended a conception of curriculum based on allowing children choice as a means of stimulating and maintaining interest and engagement. The responses of Chinese adolescents appear to be in some tension with the philosophy of an educational system in which respect for hierarchy and authority, memorization, and top–down teaching methods have been prominent features. These examples highlight the varying perspectives held among individuals at different levels of the hierarchy within Chinese culture, and illustrate how individuals may disagree with, challenge, or fail to assimilate cultural belief systems or ideologies.

To be sure, Chinese adolescents, like their Canadian counterparts, sometimes endorsed decision making by adult authorities. This was found most frequently in curriculum decisions and in decisions about the choice of a movie in the peer context. Like their Canadian counterparts, Chinese adolescents were often concerned with the effects that different decision-making procedures might have for children's welfare (these comprised 20% of total responses), or they appealed to the greater expertise and competence of adults to make appropriate decisions (6% of the total). Some examples follow:

Peer/Movie, Hebei, 13 years: "If it's not a proper film for children, it'll have a bad influence on children."

School/Curriculum, Taizhou, 15 years: "Kids of this age group are not so disciplined. They can do it as planned only when they are regulated. They would certainly like to learn what they like. However, some subjects they might not like have to be studied, which should not be decided by the will of the majority. A curriculum is not something that may be learnt or not, depending on who likes it or not."

The following example shows the keen awareness possessed by some adolescents of the conflicting perspectives inherent in such decisions:

School/Curriculum, Taizhou, 15 years: "For us students, we naturally wish to make our decisions on what to learn and what not. However, education authorities will surely have more comprehensive consideration for a decision than students, and we can learn more. Therefore, it is not comfortable for students to say this [authority] is a good way, and it is not realistic to say this is not."

The responses of Chinese adolescents will perhaps surprise some for the degree of support shown for democracy, autonomy, and rights, and for their similarity overall with responses found in the research with Western children and adolescents. However, some responses did appear to draw on specific content of the type described by some as collectivist, such as references to the importance of fostering group solidarity, cooperation, and general harmony. Explicit reference sometimes was made to political concepts such as *Communist* and *Marxist* ideals and principles:

Peer/Game, Nanjing, 18 years: "Children learn to live in a democratic centralist atmosphere at an early age and everybody learns to deal with the relationship between individual and collective. Today's society is a society of cooperation. The spirit of cooperation should be cultivated from an early age."

It must be stressed that responses of this sort were quite rare (comprising approximately 3% of total responses) and appeared much more infrequently than the references to rights, autonomy, and democratic principles discussed earlier. When found, such collectivist notions appeared to be integrated into broader democratic concepts and perspectives, such as decision making by majority rule or consensus. Even explicit appeals to Communist principles such as "democratic centralism" were often made in support of majority rule, rather than centralized or top–down control by the Party or educational authorities. No overarching collectivist orientation comprised of respect for authority or filial piety could be discerned in the reasoning of Chinese adolescents. Instead, overall, Chinese adolescents (a) asserted children's autonomy to make decisions in the peer context; (b) believed that children have (or ought to have) equal rights to contribute to familial decision making and school decisions; and (c) rejected the imposition of hierarchical, adult-oriented decision making for most decisions across all three social contexts.

A full account of the responses of Chinese adolescents requires a consideration of the role of social context, understood in at least two senses. One sense in which social context is relevant pertains to how various features of social context and situations are represented in individuals' judgments and reasoning. For example, although there was a high support for majority rule overall, consensus was more likely to be seen as appropriate in the family than in other social contexts with increasing age, and adult authority was seen as more appropriate to the school context than other social contexts. This pattern is consistent with other research findings suggesting that consensus is more likely to be seen as appropriate in small group settings, where similarities in perspective among members (and informal negotiations to resolve differences) are more easily facilitated (e.g., Helwig, 1998; Helwig & Kim, 1999). The findings from the Chinese research also show that further discriminations were made even within these contexts; for example, decisions that implicated concerns with issues of children's welfare or competence elicited less support for democratic procedures. These findings are consistent with a model of social reasoning in which individuals increasingly take into account, with development, the features of situations when making social and moral judgments (Helwig, 1995; Turiel, 2002), and they contrast with more global accounts of social and moral reasoning describing broad changes from heteronomy to autonomy (Piaget, 1932). Similar developmental and contextual patterns in judgments about decision making appear to be evident in cultures with very different social organizational structures, ideology, and belief systems.

A second sense in which social context is relevant pertains to the practices, belief systems, and cultural norms that are encountered by individuals in particular cultural environments. In some social scientific accounts (e.g., Shweder et al., 1987), these influences are seen as directly determinative of social or moral judgments, in the sense that individuals will encounter different cultural environments or belief systems that are held to account for differences in their thinking. At the broader cultural level, one such characterization is the individualism/collectivism dichotomy described earlier. Another, sometimes used to account for differences within cultures, is that due to more local environmental features such as traditionalism versus modernity. In the present study, it was found that differences in types of environment (e.g., modern urban vs. more traditional) did have some effect on responses in the direction that might be predicted; for example, participants from more traditional environments were somewhat more likely than those from modern urban environments to affirm decision making by adult authority. However, as discussed earlier, the differences due to social contexts and types of decision were much larger, and the same patterns appeared across the three environments sampled in the current study, despite vast differences in degree of traditionalism. Even more striking, however, was the extent to which participants' responses departed from the prevailing general "cultural" orientation. Chinese adolescents not only identified an area of personal discretion for decision making where children are usually given autonomy (e.g., for recreational decisions made in the peer context), but they also frequently supported children's autonomy over more contested areas, such as parental decision making over academic matters and even curriculum decisions made by educational authorities. If anything, Chinese adolescents appeared to extend greater decision making autonomy to children in their judgments of what should be the case than found in studies with Canadian children and adolescents (e.g., as in the case of children's democratic participation in curriculum decisions).

A complete explanation of these interesting divergences between the judgments of Canadian and Chinese adolescents is complex and must await further research. One possibility, consistent with the justifications they gave, is that Chinese adolescents come to perceive some existing cultural practices as having a negative impact on the development of children's autonomy, especially in academic settings. This proposition is in accord with much of the evidence reviewed earlier, including descriptions of the high achievement orientation stressed in Chinese families (Chao & Sue, 1996; Wu, 1996), the greater prevalence of family conflict between parents and adolescents in mainland China over academic issues (Yau & Smetana, 2003), and the presence of stringent university entrance exams and the more uniform educational curriculum in place across Chinese schools. As suggested by Lau's (1992) value survey findings, showing that Chinese college students gave high levels of endorsement of "individualistic" values (e.g., freedom), such values may come to be of heightened significance when it is perceived that they are insufficiently realized within one's current environment or experience. Chinese adolescents' strong support of children's autonomy and their emphasis on the need for intrinsic motivation may be, in part, a reaction to perceptions of severe external pressure and a comparative lack of autonomy over issues of academic achievement in familial and institutional educational contexts. This indicates that in this instance the cultural practices are relevant and must be taken into account, not because they directly determine individuals' judgments and reasoning, but rather because they may provoke a heightened awareness of other values and needs that, in the perception of some, are not sufficiently being met.

Western children and adolescents, in contrast, may be more likely to cede some forms of decision making in academic contexts to educational authorities, because they are otherwise given more autonomy and choice over academic matters, and thus they do not perceive these issues as areas of particular threat to the expression of their autonomy. Indeed, debates over educational reforms in North America have tended to stress more collectivistic concerns, such as good discipline in schools, classroom order, and safety. Corresponding institutional reforms currently popular in North America include school uniforms, dress codes, and mandatory drug testing. North American adolescents may in turn experience these areas, rather than academic matters, as more likely to represent problematic restrictions on expression of their needs for autonomy.

Further research, of course, is necessary to explore these and other issues. It would be interesting, for example, to determine whether Chinese adolescents' perceptions of children's decision-making autonomy change over historical time, especially as Chinese students become more familiar with the consequences (both positive and negative) of giving children more decision-making autonomy over academic issues (assuming that such changes do occur within Chinese cultural institutions and practices). It would also be informative to explore these issues further by including judgments of younger agents, to determine whether and at what point Chinese adolescents would give greater weight to issues such as children's possible lack of competence in making these sorts of decisions. Finally, it might prove fruitful to examine how conceptions of group decision making in hypothetical situations such those investigated in this research relate to real-life processes of group decision making. Research in Western cultures has found that parents sometimes exert greater influence over decision outcomes than children even in decisions made by consensus within families (Jacobs, Bennett, & Flanagan, 1993). One might expect this sort of influence to be even stronger in hierarchical, traditional cultures such as China.

The dialectic between general needs for autonomy experienced by individuals, and the specific constraints on autonomy found in some situational or cultural contexts, may play itself out in different ways at different points in development. There are some surface similarities between the focus on children's own autonomy and involvement in democratic decision making found among young children in the West (Helwig & Kim, 1999) and the similar focus found among Chinese adolescents. The strong support for children's autonomy common to both these groups may reflect a reaction to somewhat similar circumstances encountered by younger children in the West, and by Chinese children and adolescents in general, such as the frequent experience of social situations involving hierarchy, authority, and adult constraint. However, the particular types of democratic decision making that are preferred, and the reasons for these preferences, may vary by development. As noted earlier, the tendency of young children in the West to endorse the procedure of consensus across social contexts has been interpreted to reflect deficiencies in their perspective-taking ability—notably their inability to recognize the difficulty of achieving consensus in large groups with individuals having different perspectives or values (Helwig, 1998; Helwig & Kim, 1999). In contrast, Chinese adolescents, like their Canadian counterparts, tended to endorse the procedure of majority rule—not consensus—for group decisions in the peer and school contexts, and they clearly recognized clashes among individual perspectives, evident in the examples quoted in this chapter. The common need for a formal means of reconciling differences in perspectives may produce a developmental convergence across cultures on majority rule as a valued method of group decision making. However, for reasons discussed earlier, there may be cultural differences in the boundaries of areas over which autonomous or democratic decision making is viewed as legitimate or is seen as needed. These differences may manifest in ways that may be hard to predict, as they may include both areas over which it is agreed that personal autonomy and democratic decision making may be restricted and subordinated to social hierarchy, and other areas in which individuals occupying different positions in social hierarchies (e.g., teachers, students) may disagree or have conflicting perspectives. Taken together, the findings illustrate how both developmental and cultural (socioenvironmental) factors must be considered conjointly in examining how judgments of democratic decision making emerge and vary by age, status, culture, and social context.

In sum, an interactional model is needed that takes into account the features of specific social contexts encountered by individuals within cultures, and how these local environments are seen as affecting the expression of more universal concerns, such as autonomy, likely to be found in some form within any cultural context. This approach stresses the need for a more detailed analysis of features of social contexts within cultures, along with a careful consideration of how social norms and practices are interpreted, evaluated—and at times contested—by individuals.

CONCLUSION

In discussions of individual rights, freedoms, and democracy, many theoreticians and researchers have tended to look mainly at the broader level of political systems or culture, with a corresponding tendency to type societies into individualistic or collectivist cultural orientations. This division has led some to contrast Western and non-Western societies along these dimensions, with individual rights, freedoms, and democracy seen as largely the province of Western societies. This distinction is often taken at face value as both a contemporary and a historical fact. However, the arguments and empirical evidence presented in this chapter suggest that there are several reasons to question this view. First, by focusing on the broader level of cultural or political systems, insufficient attention is given to the heterogeneous environments individuals encounter within cultural contexts. Within any cultural environment, individuals experience social contexts structured along hierarchical lines, where individual autonomy is constrained by existing social norms, authority, and conformity to the duties of social roles, along with some areas in which personal autonomy and choice is granted expression. Although the boundaries of legitimate expression of individual autonomy certainly vary across cultural contexts and social systems, personal autonomy and freedom have been found to be important values in every culture thus far investigated, both traditional and modern, as well as those labeled *individ-*

ualistic and *collectivist*. The findings of the research conducted in China on judgments of decision-making procedures indicate, moreover, that democratic concepts and principles of voice, participation, and majority rule are not restricted to Western cultural contexts.

To fully account for the heterogeneity of both cultural practices and their interpretation by individuals, a much more fine-grained analysis is needed of the particular conditions in which cultures grant, or fail to grant, individual autonomy in decision making, and how these cultural facts are understood. As we have seen, broad cultural orientations, such as individualism and collectivism, are of limited use in illuminating the social judgments of both Chinese and Western children and adolescents. At times, the judgments and reasoning of Chinese and Canadian students went against the prevailing assumptions about cultural orientations. For example, "individualistic" Canadian children and adolescents rejected personal choice and democracy for curriculum decisions in school settings, favoring hierarchical, teacher-centered control over the curriculum—judgments that were supported by the assumption that children may lack the competence to make autonomous decisions. On the other hand, "collectivistic" Chinese adolescents strongly endorsed children's autonomy and control over academic decisions in the school and the family, often appealing to conceptions of learning based on the importance of fostering individual children's autonomy, motivation, and choice. In this research, adolescents from a traditional Asian culture were found to endorse democratic decision-making procedures even when they understood this to be at odds with existing cultural, institutional, or familial practices. All of these subtleties and complexities are obscured or poorly accounted for by broad, cultural-level constructs such as individualism and collectivism, and call for a more detailed analysis of the way particular social contexts and cultural practices are construed and evaluated by individuals throughout their development.

ACKNOWLEDGMENTS

Preparation of this chapter was supported by a grant to the author from the Social Sciences and Humanities Research Council of Canada. I would like to thank Judith Smetana, Elliot Turiel, Rachel Ryerson, and Angela Prencipe for comments on an earlier version of the chapter.

REFERENCES

Berkowitz, M. W., & Grych, J. H. (2000). Early character development and education. *Early Education & Development, 11*, 55–72.
Breiner, S. J. (1980). Early child development in China. *Child Psychiatry and Human Development, 11*, 87–95.

Chao, R. K., & Sue, S. (1996). Chinese parental influence and their children's school success: A paradox in the literature on parenting styles. In S. Lau (Ed.), *Growing up the Chinese way: Chinese child and adolescent development* (pp. 93–120). Hong Kong: The Chinese University Press.

Chen, X., Dong, Q., & Zhou, H. (1997). Authoritative and authoritarian parenting practices and social and school performance in Chinese children. *International Journal of Behavioral Development, 21,* 855–873.

Chen, H., & Su, L. (2001). Child protection and development in China. *International Society for the Study of Behavioral Development Newsletter, 2,* 7–8.

Dien, D. S. (1982). A Chinese perspective on Kohlberg's theory of moral development. *Developmental Review, 2,* 331–341.

Dornbusch, S. M., Carlsmith, J. M., Bushwall, S. J., Ritter, P. L., Leiderman, H., Hastorf, A. H., & Gross, R. T. (1985). Single parents, extended households, and the control of adolescents. *Child Development, 56,* 326–341.

Erikson, E. (1968). *Identity, youth, and crisis.* New York: W. W. Norton.

Fung, H., & Chen, E C. (2001). Across time and beyond skin: Self and transgression in the everyday socialization of shame among Taiwanese preschool children. *Social Development, 10,* 420–437.

Gallatin, J. (1985). *Democracy's children: The development of political thinking in adolescents.* Ann Arbor, MI: Quod.

Greenstein, F. (1965). *Children and politics.* New Haven, CT: Yale University Press.

Helwig, C. C. (1995). Social contexts in social cognition: Psychological harm and civil liberties. In M. Killen & D. Hart (Eds.), *Morality in everyday life: Developmental perspectives* (pp. 166–200). Cambridge, England: Cambridge University Press.

Helwig, C. C. (1998). Children's conceptions of fair government and freedom of speech. *Child Development, 69,* 518–531.

Helwig, C. C. (2001). [Canadian adolescents' and young adults' judgments of decision making procedures]. Unpublished raw data.

Helwig, C. C., Arnold, M. L., Tan, D., & Boyd, D. (2003). Chinese adolescents' reasoning about democratic and authority-based decision making in peer, family, and school contexts. *Child Development, 74,* 783–800.

Helwig, C. C., & Kim, S. (1999). Children's evaluations of decision making procedures in peer, family, and school contexts. *Child Development, 70,* 502–512.

Ho, D. Y. F. (1986). Chinese patterns of socialization: A critical review. In M. H. Bond (Ed.), *The psychology of the Chinese people* (pp. 1–37). Hong Kong: Oxford University Press.

Jacobs, J. E., Bennett, M. A., & Flanagan, C. (1993). Decision making in one-parent and two-parent families: Influence and information selection. *Journal of Early Adolescence, 13,* 245–266.

Killen, M., & Sueyoshi, L. (1995). Conflict resolution in Japanese social interactions. *Early Education and Development, 6,* 313–330.

Kinoshita, Y. (1989). Developmental changes in understanding the limitations of majority decisions. *British Journal of Developmental Psychology, 7,* 97–112.

Kohlberg, L. (1981). *Essays on moral development: Vol. 1. The philosophy of moral development.* San Francisco: Harper & Row.

Kurtines, W. M., Berman, S. L., Ittel, A., & Williamson, S. (1995). Moral development: A co-constructivist perspective. In W. M. Kurtines & J. L. Gewirtz (Eds.), *Moral development: An introduction* (pp. 337–376). Needham Heights, MA: Allyn & Bacon.

Lau, S. (1992). Collectivism's individualism: Value preference, personal control, and the desire for freedom among Chinese in mainland China, Hong Kong, and Singapore. *Personality and Individual Difference, 13*(3), 361–366.

Lau, S. (1996). Self-concept development: Is there a concept of self in Chinese culture? In S. Lau (Ed.), *Growing up the Chinese way: Chinese child and adolescent development* (pp. 357–374). Hong Kong: The Chinese University Press.

Lau, S., & Cheung, P. C. (1987). Relations between Chinese adolescents' perception of parental control and organization and their perception of parental warmth. *Developmental Psychology*, 23, 726–729.

Lau, S., Lew, W. J. F., Hau, K. T., Cheung, P. C., & Berndt, T. J. (1990). Relations among perceived parental control, warmth, indulgence, and family harmony of Chinese in mainland China. *Developmental Psychology*, 26, 674–677.

Lau, S., & Yeung, P. W. (1996). Understanding Chinese child development: The role of culture in socialization. In S. Lau (Ed.), *Growing up the Chinese way: Chinese child and adolescent development* (pp. 29–44). Hong Kong: The Chinese University Press.

Laupa, M., Turiel, E., & Cowan, P. (1995). Obedience to authority in children and adults. In M. Killen & D. Hart (Eds.), *Morality in everyday life: Developmental perspectives* (pp. 131–165). Cambridge, England: Cambridge University Press.

Mackerras, C. (2001). *The new Cambridge handbook of contemporary China*. Cambridge, England: Cambridge University Press.

Mann, L., & Greenbaum, C. W. (1987). Cross-cultural studies of children's decision rules. In C. Kagitcibasi (Ed.), *Growth and progress in cross-cultural psychology* (pp. 130–137). Berwyn, PA: Swets North America.

Markus, H. R., & Kitayama, S. (1991). Culture and the self: Implications for cognition, emotion, and motivation. *Psychological Review*, 98, 224–253.

Moessinger, P. (1981). The development of the concept of majority decision: A pilot study. *Canadian Journal of Behavioral Science*, 13, 359–362.

Neff, K. D., & Helwig, C. C. (2002). A constructivist approach to understanding the development of reasoning about rights and authority within cultural contexts. *Cognitive Development*, 17, 1429–1450.

Nucci, L. P. (1981). The development of personal concepts: A domain distinct from moral and social concepts. *Child Development*, 52, 114–121.

Nucci, L. P. (2001). *Education in the moral domain*. Cambridge, England: Cambridge University Press.

Nucci, L. P., Camino, C., & Sapiro, C. (1996). Social class effects on northeastern Brazilian children's conceptions of areas of personal choice and social regulation. *Child Development*, 67(3), 1223–1242.

Nucci, L. P., & Weber, E. (1995). Social interactions in the home and the development of young children's conceptions within the personal domain. *Child Development*, 66, 1438–1452.

Piaget, J. (1932). *The moral judgment of the child*. London: Routledge & Kegan Paul.

Pye, L. W. (1992). *The spirit of Chinese politics*. Cambridge, MA: Harvard University Press.

Rokeach, M. (1973). *The nature of human values*. New York: Free Press.

Selman, R. L. (1980). *The growth of interpersonal understanding: Developmental and clinical analyses*. New York: Academic.

Sen, A. (1999). *Development as freedom*. New York: Random House.

Shweder, R. A. (1990). In defense of moral realism: Reply to Gabennesch. *Child Development*, 61, 2060–2067.

Shweder, R. A., & Bourne, E. J. (1982). Does the concept of the person vary cross-culturally? In A. J. Marsella & G. M. White (Eds.), *Cultural conceptions of mental health and therapy* (pp. 97–137). Boston: Reidel.

Shweder, R. A., Mahapatra, M., & Miller, J. G. (1987). Culture and moral development. In J. Kagan & S. Lamb (Eds.), *The emergence of morality in young children* (pp. 1–83). Chicago: University of Chicago Press.

Smetana, J. G. (1989). Adolescents' and parents' reasoning about actual family conflict. *Child Development*, 60, 1052–1067.

Smetana, J. G. (2002). Culture, autonomy, and personal jurisdiction in adolescent–parent relationships. In H. W. Reese & R. Kail (Eds.), *Advances in child development and behavior* (Vol. 29, pp. 51–87). New York: Academic.

Spiro, M. E. (1987). Collective representations and mental representations in religious symbol systems. In B. Kilborne & L. L. Langness (Eds.), *Culture and human nature: Theoretical papers of Melford E. Spiro* (pp. 161–184). Chicago: University of Chicago Press. (Original work published 1982)

Strauss, C. (2000). The culture concept and the individualism–collectivism debate: Dominant and alternative attributions for class in the United States. In L. Nucci, G. Saxe, & E. Turiel (Eds.), *Culture, thought, and development* (pp. 85–114). Mahwah, NJ: Lawrence Erlbaum Associates.

Triandis, H. C. (1989). The self and social behavior in differing cultural contexts. *Psychological Review, 96*, 506–520.

Turiel, E. (1998). The development of morality. In W. Damon (Series Ed.) & N. Eisenberg (Vol. Ed.), *Handbook of child psychology: Vol. 3. Social, emotional, and personality development* (5th ed., pp. 863–932). New York: Wiley.

Turiel, E. (2002). *The culture of morality: Social development, context, and conflict.* Cambridge, England: Cambridge University Press.

Wainryb, C., & Turiel, E. (1994). Dominance, subordination, and concepts of personal entitlement in cultural context. *Child Development, 65,* 1701–1722.

Wang, J., Elicker, J., McMullen, M., & Mao, S. (2001, April). *American and Chinese teachers' beliefs about early childhood curriculum.* Poster presented at the biennial meeting of the Society for Research in Child Development, Minneapolis.

Worden, R. L., Savada, A. M., & Dolan, R. E. (Eds.). (1988). *China: A country study.* Washington, DC: Library of Congress.

Wu, D. Y. H. (1996). Parental control: Psychocultural interpretations of Chinese patterns of socialization. In S. Lau (Ed.), *Growing up the Chinese way: Chinese child and adolescent development* (pp. 1–28). Hong Kong: The Chinese University Press.

Yau, J., & Smetana, J. G. (2003). Adolescent–parent conflict in Hong Kong and mainland China: A comparison of youth in two cultural contexts. *International Journal of Behavioral Development, 27,* 201–211.

Yee, D. K., & Flanagan, C. (1985). Family environments as self-consciousness in early adolescence. *Journal of Early Adolescence, 5,* 59–68.

Yeh, E. K. (1972). The Chinese mind and human freedom. *Journal of Social Psychiatry, 18,* 132–136.

Yuan, B., & Shen, J. (1998). Moral values held by early adolescents in Taiwan and Mainland China. *Journal of Moral Education, 27*(2), 191–207.

7

Not All Hurried Children Are the Same: Children's Participation in Deciding on and Planning Their After-School Activities

Mary Gauvain
Susan M. Perez
University of California, Riverside

> *No matter what philosophy of life we espouse, it is important to see childhood as a stage of life, not just the anteroom to life. Hurrying children into adulthood violates the sanctity of life by giving one period priority over another.*
>
> —Elkind (2001, p. 221)

When David Elkind's book, *The Hurried Child*, appeared in 1981, it aroused both professional and public attention. For the first time, psychological stressors identified with adulthood, such as overscheduling one's day, shifting from activity to activity in a day with few breaks in between, and a fixation on achievement, were associated with youth. Much has changed since Elkind's book first appeared, and in many ways, the circumstances of children's everyday lives have become more harried and stressful than what was described in the book. The current state of children's after-school experiences is of rising concern to educators, policymakers, and parents, and over the last 10 years, this topic has entered the arena of national debate. This chapter is concerned with what developmental psychologists can bring to this discussion.

Several societal trends of the late 20th and early 21st centuries have made children's daily lives markedly different from that experienced by the post-World War II generation. These trends include increased numbers of single parents and dual-wage-earning families that necessitate long hours for children in after-school care. Parental anxiety about maximizing future options for children has led to an upsurge in various types of apprenticeship programs outside of school, including sports, youth organizations, and arts programs. Parental dissatisfaction with public schools has led to an abundance of compensatory after-school tutorials for children. Heightened concern about child safety has resulted in greater privatization of play and regulation of children's playtime by parents. Nowhere is the busy life of childhood more evident than in the recent surge in children's day organizers, books in which children record their appointments, homework assignments, and things to do during and after school ("Getting Ahead," 2000). Educators claim that organizers benefit children by helping them keep on schedule and reminding them of their homework. They are also a way for teachers and parents to communicate about the child. More and more schools are requiring that students use organizers. In fact, the *Los Angeles Times* ("Getting Ahead," 2000) reported that sales by the largest company producing these books, *Premier School Agendas*, jumped from 8,000 in 1988 to a whopping 15 million in 1999.

In some ways, these social patterns are not all that new. In the 1930s, after-school programs were introduced to get youth off the street and away from various nefarious influences (Wartella & Mazzarella, 1990). Today, a similar sentiment is echoed. A report by the Department of Health and Human Services (Carmona & Stewart, 1996) discussed alternative programs for "youth-oriented prevention." Ballot measures, like the 2002 California After-School Initiative, are targeted to fund programs that get children into adult-supervised centers between the hours of 3 p.m. and 6 p.m., the peak time for juvenile crime. In the United States today, the number of after-school programs for youth is at a historic high (Cappella & Larner, 1999). Clearly, parents and the public at large are desperate for a greater sense of security and control over children's experiences outside of school.

In the main, the motives behind these efforts are benevolent. These include the protection and well-being of children and other members of society. However, unintended consequences of these efforts include the fact that children have little opportunity over middle childhood to develop skills at deciding how to use their recreational or "free" time. Thus, although these societal trends differ in many ways, they are similar in that they all leave children with little time outside of school that is not controlled or supervised by adults, a historical pattern that Sutton-Smith (1994) called the domestication of play. As a result, this social pattern may undermine what many consider a critical aspect of child development—with increasing age, children will have greater regulation or control of their own activities. In addition, these societal trends run counter to current developmental theory regarding the contribution of peers to healthy psychological growth (e.g., see Schaffer, 1996). Extensive involvement in organized, after-school settings gives children few opportunities to be with small groups of children in informal, unstructured activities in which relationships and activities are developed and negotiated by the children themselves.

This chapter is concerned with one aspect of this process, the relation between children's after-school experiences and cognitive development. We concentrate on the cognitive consequences of these societal trends because, to date, most of the research investigating the link between children's after-school experiences and child development has focused on the impact on social and emotional development. Concentrating on social and emotional development does not account for the full impact of these experiences on children, however. Other important aspects of growth may also be affected by children's after-school activity pattern, such as learning how to manage free time by deciding on and planning activities that will occur in the near or distant future. We concentrate on the school years because they are especially important in the development of future-oriented skills like decision making and planning.

THE DEVELOPMENT OF SKILL
AT DECISION MAKING AND PLANNING
IN MIDDLE CHILDHOOD

Decision making involves the generation or recognition of behavioral options for achieving a goal along with evaluation and selection among these options (Byrnes, 1998). Planning is the next step in the decision-making process. It involves the deliberate organization of a sequence of actions oriented toward achieving a goal (Rogoff, Gauvain, & Gardner, 1987). Skills at decision making and planning emerge gradually over childhood and are important to mature social and cognitive functioning.

When we consider contemporary patterns of children's after-school experiences in conjunction with the fact that a majority of adolescents claim that they have a lack of purpose and direction in their daily and long-range commitments (Carnegie Council on Adolescent Development, 1992), it seems that better understanding of the experiences of middle childhood in relation to the developmental trajectory of skills at decision making and planning is needed. To explore this topic, we draw on an approach to cognitive development that emphasizes the connections between social experience, everyday practices, and the development of thinking (Goodnow, Miller, & Kessel, 1995; Rogoff, 1998). Specifically, we are interested in cultural and social practices, instantiated in parent–child interaction, that support or constrain the development of skill at decision making and planning during middle childhood. Our research concentrates on children's experiences outside of school. Research indicates that children have little opportunity to plan and make decisions on their own at school during middle childhood. In fact, children have more freedom to make decisions in elementary school than they do when they are in junior high and high school (Larson & Verma, 1999).

In this discussion, we treat decision making and planning as components of the same overall cognitive process, referred to as *future-oriented behavior* (Haith, Benson, Roberts, & Pennington, 1994). Although in laboratory research these cognitive skills are often separated, they are intricately linked in everyday behavior. The development of decision making is reviewed in several chapters in this volume. Therefore, the discussion here reviews the development of planning.

Planning is a complex cognitive skill that draws on a wide range of intellectual capabilities, including perception, attention, memory, and conceptual, procedural, and declarative knowledge. Given the range of skills on which planning relies, it is not surprising that it emerges early in life and has a protracted developmental course (Friedman & Scholnick, 1997; Friedman, Scholnick, & Cocking, 1987; Haith et al., 1994). Although infants can make rudimentary plans as early as 9 months of age (Haith, 1994; Willatts, 1990), complex planning that involves social awareness or the organization of a large number of actions or events does not appear until adolescence (Parrila, Aysto, & Das, 1994). The period from middle childhood to early adolescence is an auspicious time in the development of this skill.

Over middle childhood, children participate in increasingly complex activities, many of which rely on the ability to set goals, make decisions, and construct and carry out plans. Children become more involved in activities outside the home, activities that often involve coordination with other people. Children also are increasingly involved in activities that are intellectually complex. And, finally, as children get older there are more options available to them as to how to spend their time. Social coordination, carrying out complex acts, and choosing among a range of alternatives all benefit from decision making and planning skills. As children approach adolescence, their plans include more awareness of contextual constraints, greater flexibility, more elaborate strategies, and more formalized approaches (S. Kreitler & H. Kreitler, 1987). For instance, Dreher and Oreter (1987) asked participants ranging from age 11 to college age to plan a series of errands in a model town. They found that with increasing age, participants were more likely to use certain strategies like delegating tasks to others, selecting among alternative actions, and using resources in the environment to improve their plan. During group planning, younger adolescents relied on an action-specific approach whereas older adolescents used a more conceptual approach in which hypothesized solutions were evaluated in relation to an overall plan based on some general principle, like cost–benefit analysis or maximum possible speed. A conceptual plan is more comprehensive than an action-specific plan in that it includes the action sequence, the reasoning behind the plan, and how specific actions fit with this reasoning. Thus, conceptual plans reflect the structure of knowledge that the participants create about the task (Berg, Strough, Calderone, Meegan, & Sansone, 1997). This suggests that early in adolescence, planning improves as children develop better understanding of the hierarchical structure of goals and means to reach them.

Like most areas of development, both biology and experience account for these age-related changes (Haith et al., 1994). In terms of experience, research has demonstrated that decision making and planning are influenced by both task structure (Scholnick, Friedman, & Wallner-Allen, 1997) and social context (Gauvain, 2001). In other words, what a person is trying to do (the task) and with or for whom the task is being done (the social context) influence the thinking that occurs. For instance, tasks can be designed to support children's performance by providing opportunities for children to develop and practice components of decision making or planning before they reach full competence at these skills. Klahr and Robinson (1981), who created a modified version of the Tower of Hanoi task,[1] demonstrated this point. Their modification, which substituted a set of nested cans for the rings traditionally used, made the task easier for children to follow the rule that a larger piece cannot be placed on a smaller piece. Young children were more successful on the modified than the traditional version of the task because the modified version provided support for or scaffolded the children's cognitive performances by lessening task demands. The term *scaffolding*, which is typically associated with contributions from social partners, is used deliberately here even though children in this study worked on their own. Despite solitary performance, the children were aided socially, that is, they were assisted by the investigators who designed the task in a way that was cognitively accessible to young children. This is a form of social assistance, albeit an indirect form. Research on more direct social assistance, especially social interaction, suggests that children can learn about and practice decision making and planning when working with others (Gauvain, 2001).

Social interaction, which composes a large part of children's everyday experience, may play an especially important role in the development of skills like decision making and planning. Much of children's everyday decision making and planning is a social process, as other people elicit and model these behaviors for children. Observations of children planning with adults and with peers demonstrate that children learn about planning as they coordinate plans and observe and interact with others who are more experienced planners (Gauvain & Rogoff, 1989; Radziszewska & Rogoff, 1988). Because of the different roles that adults and peers play in children's lives and the different skills that adults and children bring to social interaction, experiences

---

[1]The Tower of Hanoi is a game involving three identical pegs aligned on a board. On each peg, different size rings or disks are arranged. The object of the game is to rearrange the rings so that they are all stacked in order of size on one peg, usually with the smallest ring on the top. Task rules, which include that only one ring can be moved at a time, only transfers between adjacent pegs are allowed, and a larger ring cannot be placed on top of a smaller ring, require planning out moves in advance of action.

with these two types of partners contribute in different ways to cognitive development. Adults, relative to peers, provide more overt and explicit opportunities for children to learn about task structure and strategies (Gauvain, 1992; Radziszewska & Rogoff, 1988). Adults are also more likely to verbalize their thinking process during joint cognitive activity, which may model executive functioning by explicating how and what is being deliberated. Adults also have more skill at social coordination than peers do. This skill is important for regulating the distribution of labor and resources, as well as recognizing, supporting, and building on the contributions of the child during joint cognitive activity. Parent–child interaction may be especially instrumental in the socialization of cognitive skills like decision making and planning due to the protracted nature of the development of these skills and the long-term, regular, and emotionally significant nature of the parent–child relationship.

As a sustained socialization context, the family frequently decides on and plans future activities (Benson, 1994; Ochs, Smith, & Taylor, 1989). These cognitive activities are woven into the family process and involve co-construction by the participants as they attempt to coordinate and direct future activities in ways that satisfy mutual interests and needs. The different cognitive status of family members allows for the social transmission of cognitive skills through processes like scaffolding (Wood & Middleton, 1975) and modeling (Bandura, 1989) that are associated with cognitive development in these areas of growth (Gauvain, 2001). Thus, by its nature and its structure, the family context is a primary site for the development of future-oriented cognitive skills. Consider some examples of how parents may help children learn how to decide on and plan their actions. Parents may ask children what game they would like to play or if they have all the pieces of a game before play begins. Or parents may ask children which homework assignment they want to do first or they may draw lines or numbers on children's homework pages that help them arrange the presentation of their answers in advance. Parents may externalize their own decision making and planning when they are with their children, such as when parents verbally rehearse activities or errands scheduled for the day. By identifying or arranging future actions to meet goals, parents provide children with opportunities to learn about and participate in the process of decision making and planning. Both parents and children contribute to this process and the child's contribution is expected to change as he or she becomes increasingly skilled at venturing into and shaping these experiences (Rogoff, 1998).

In sum, research suggests that regardless of whether the social contribution comes in the task structure or via social interaction, other people often assist children in the development of decision-making and planning skills. Because interaction with parents may be especially important in this process, our research concentrates on the opportunities that children have at home to decide on or plan how they spend their time. Although deciding on or setting a goal is critical to the planning process, its development is not well understood. This is largely due to an emphasis in developmental research on other aspects of planning, particularly the sequencing of action steps. Limited understanding of goal formulation during planning is also an artifact of efforts in laboratory research to standardize tasks across participants (Das, Kar, & Parrila, 1996). Some research does exist on goal setting in adolescence and findings indicate improvement from the early to late teen years (Klaczynski, Laipple, & Jurden, 1992). These observations, along with the well-established link between goal setting, task engagement, and psychological well-being (Carver & Scheier, 1998), underscore the need for more research on the development of goal setting, and the period of middle childhood is particularly interesting in this regard.

CHILDREN'S AFTER-SCHOOL ACTIVITIES AND THE DEVELOPMENT OF DECISION MAKING AND PLANNING IN THE FAMILY DURING MIDDLE CHILDHOOD

Research in Western communities suggests that healthy psychological development during middle childhood is driven by satisfaction of the basic psychological needs of competence, autonomy, and relatedness (Connell, 1990; Eccles, 1999). Parental encouragement and support for the development of these capabilities during middle childhood plays a formative role in this process (Jacobs & Eccles, 2000). In fact, much of the foundation of adolescent competence and autonomy is played out in the family during middle childhood. During middle childhood, parents expect children to act more independently and parents provide children with opportunities to do so either on their own or under parental tutelage. These changes necessitate adjustments in parenting strategies and the involvement of children in regulating their everyday experiences, a process Maccoby (1994) called *co-regulation*. Thus, effective parenting in middle childhood involves nurturing the child's self-regulatory skills along with more opportunities for independent action. Research suggests that parents provide different types of support and encouragement for this transition (Jacobs & Eccles, 2000).

Figure 7.1 contains a hypothesized set of relations between children's after-school experiences and the development of skill at decision making and planning in the family during the years of middle childhood. Each component of the model is discussed, but first a comment about assumptions of causality in the model. As initial features of the model, several parental and child contributions are identified. Socialization is a bidirectional process, that is parents and children influence each other. It occurs over time, and influences external to the family system, even influences in place before the child was born (Cole,

220

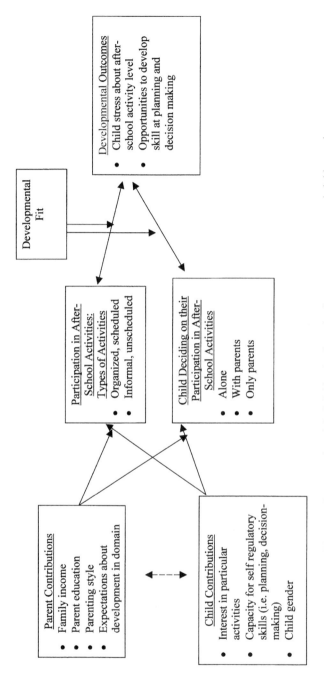

FIG. 7.1. Conceptual model of children's after-school experience, parent and child contributions, and developmental outcomes in the years of middle childhood.

1992), play a role in the socialization process. Socialization involves changing patterns of participation by parents and children as they experience life together and adjust to their mutually developing capabilities (Rogoff, 1998). Therefore, the identification in a model of any particular point in time or contribution from the parent or child as the origination of this ongoing developmental process is an arbitrary decision. As presented, the model begins by describing a set of parental and child contributions that we consider relevant to the process under study. For psychologists familiar with studying individual human behavior, these serve as useful starting points for the developmental process depicted in the model. However, given the nature of this process and of human development more generally, we do not consider these contributions to be the origins or causes of the process. Rather, the model describes some of the key psychological factors operative in the family that pertain to the decision-making and planning experiences that children have regarding their after-school activities in middle childhood.

Contributions of Parents

In keeping with recent theory in cognitive development that emphasizes the social contributions to the development of intellectual skill, we are interested in the role that parents play in this process. Research, some of which we just described, suggests that social experiences provide a formative base for the development of future-oriented cognitive skills like decision making and planning.

Factors such as family income and parental education may influence how parents and children interact with each other as well as the nature and extent of children's participation in after-school activities. For instance, Kohn (1977) hypothesized a link between parental occupation and socialization goals of self-direction that may be related to how much parents encourage independent planning and decision making in children. He proposed that working-class parents would socialize children to value compromise and conformity and middle-class parents would socialize children to value self-direction. However, recent research by Tudge and colleagues (Tudge et al., 1999) that included samples from the United States, Russia, Estonia, and Korea did not find differences between working- and middle-class parents in their concern with child self-direction. Tudge and colleagues suggest that, although working-class parents may have historically valued compromise and conformity, in modern postindustrial societies in which children's future occupations are less certain, parental emphasis on child initiative and independence may be shared by working- and middle-class families. Parent education has also been identified as a contributor to socialization practices. This contribution may be especially critical in areas of development that are aided by guidance and instruction from parents, like decision making and planning.

Other contributions from parents, such as parenting style and parental expectations or beliefs, may be related to the opportunities that children have to plan their after-school activities in and around the home. Parenting style (Baumrind, 1972), which describes the emphasis that parents place on maturity demands, warmth, and control, may account for systematic variation in children's engagement in planning-related behaviors during the school years. An emphasis on maturity demands may increase opportunities at home for children to develop planning skills, and a climate of warmth or responsiveness may help support children in the development of these abilities in interactions with parents. In contrast, an emphasis on control may restrict these opportunities for children. Parental expectations or beliefs as to when children are able to decide on their own activities may also influence children's participation at home in deciding on and planning their activities. Research demonstrates that such expectations reflect broader cultural values (Goodnow, Cashmore, Cotton, & Knight, 1984; Gutierrez & Sameroff, 1990; Rosenthal & Bornholt, 1988) and influence the ways in which parents interpret children's behaviors and interact with their children (Goodnow, 1985; Sigel, 1982). One way to examine the influence of parental expectations on child development is to study communities in which parental expectations relevant to the topic under study are likely to differ. For example, in some of our research discussed now, we studied the after-school experiences of children in families of European American and Latino American ancestry, communities that differ in their expectations regarding the timing of independent behavior in children (Savage & Gauvain, 1998).

Contributions of the Child

The model includes children's interest in particular activities (Renninger, 1990) and their capacity for self-regulatory skills (Saarni, 1999). These factors may influence the selection of activities in which children engage, as well as the opportunities that parents provide for children to decide on these activities on their own. Child gender is also included in the model. Although it is known that child gender explains individual variation in activity involvement during middle childhood and adolescence (Jacobs, Vernon, & Eccles, in press), it is not known how gender relates to children's opportunities to decide on their nonschool activities at these ages.

Type of After-School Activities

A sociocultural approach to cognitive development, based on activity theory, introduces a unique level of analysis into research in which socially organized activity is considered the primary unit of psychological study (Wertsch, 1981). By concentrating on children's activity as the locus of cognitive development, the focus of research is shifted from exclusive attention to individual cognitive performance and toward the activities in which children participate and in which thinking develops and is expressed. In this approach, children's participation in activities is considered an index of cognitive growth (Rogoff, 1998).

In the model, two types of after-school activities are identified—organized and informal activities. These two types of activities offer different contexts for learning about and developing skill at decision making and planning. Organized activities are typically scheduled in advance and include more adult supervision and control than informal activities. Children's participation in organized activities involves more planning on the part of the family, and this type of participation also tends to include a time commitment from family members as well as monetary costs. Informal activities usually require less planning by the family and tend to be less costly than organized activities in terms of family time and money. These structural differences may afford different opportunities for children to learn about and practice decision making and planning. Whereas children's involvement in organized after-school activities may make parental decision making and guidance more available to children, deciding on and planning informal activities may be done mostly by children on their own.

Theory and research suggest that child participation and skill at deciding on and planning both organized and informal activities will change over middle childhood. We assume that children will gradually assume or appropriate planning or decision making that was previously done by the parent (Rogoff, 1998). Consistent with Vygotsky's (1978) idea of the zone of proximal development, we expect that children, given the appropriate amount of parental support for their developmental needs (developmental fit), will have greater ease assuming planning-related responsibilities than will children who have too little or too much support from parents.

Developmental Fit

The model includes the idea of developmental readiness or fit (Eccles et al., 1993). *Developmental fit* refers to the connection between the child's capacity to engage in certain behaviors and the opportunities the child has to enact these behaviors. Developmental fit reflects a combination of normative maturational abilities, typically indexed by child age, and individual variation in these abilities. The notion of fit is important for understanding child development and adjustment. Developmental fit is difficult to measure, however, and it is often assessed by inference, for example, by examining the developmental consequences or outcomes for the child of a particular set of experiences. These outcomes may indicate whether the match between the child's abilities and the experiences he or she has are developmentally appropriate. We use an inferential approach to developmental fit in the model and focus on two particular developmental outcomes.

Developmental Outcomes

The two developmental outcomes identified in the model are child satisfaction about the number of activities the child does outside of school and the availability of age-appropriate opportunities for the child to learn about and practice decision making and planning in the family. These two outcomes attempt to capture children's reactions to their after-school experiences and how these experiences relate to age-related expectations in activity level and decision-making participation. We fully expect that these outcomes will feed back into the process described in the model and help set the stage for further opportunities for development in this area of growth.

Children's Satisfaction With the Amount of After-School Activities in Which They Are Engaged.   Children often communicate their understanding of and satisfaction with their parents' socialization efforts by their affective responses (Bugental & Goodnow, 1998). Therefore, the model includes children's feelings about the number of activities in which they are engaged after school. This is consistent with Elkind's (1981/2001) concern about the potential effects on children of a busy after-school life.

There is surprisingly little research on children's determination of and reaction to their everyday experiences outside of school (Weiss, 2001). Several excellent reports on children's activities outside of school focus on programmatic and policy issues and the concerns of parents regarding after-school care (e.g., see Eccles & Gootman, 2002; The Packard Foundation, 1999). However, there is little discussion in these or related reports (e.g., see U.S. Bureau of the Census, 2000) about the contribution and changing role over development that children have in deciding how they spend their time outside of school and how children feel about these experiences. This information is an important part of the overall picture of children's experiences outside of school. Healthy or positive development in middle childhood through adolescence is rooted in getting youth excited about their futures, along with helping children develop the complex set of dispositions and skills that are needed for them to take charge of their own lives. These dispositions and skills, referred to collectively as *initiative* (Larson, 2000), have direct bearing on the development of behavioral autonomy (Steinberg & Silverberg, 1986), which includes the capacity to engage in autonomous acts and decisions about one's own life (Ryan, 1993). For Larson (2000), initiative arises largely from experiences in which children are expected to make decisions about how they use their time. However, Larson wonders whether children in contemporary Western society are given sufficient opportunity to develop initiative. He cites anthropological observations that suggest that youth in the United States and Europe have less responsibility for choosing their own activities than their counterparts in other societies around the world (Schlegel & Barry, 1991).

Developmentally Related Opportunities for Children to Make Decisions About and Plan Their After-School Activities. In the model, developmental fit is also examined by considering children's participation in deciding on their own activities outside of school in relation to normative developmental expectations regarding increased opportunity for children's involvement. During middle childhood, greater participation is expected by children in deciding on their involvement in organized and informal activities outside of school. This gradual change reflects increased capabilities and responsibilities of the child, and serves as a step toward the expectations associated with early adolescence. This outcome is based on Rogoff's (1998) view that developmental change "can be fruitfully studied as transitions in people's participation in sociocultural activities" (p. 291).

The following sections describe findings from two research projects from our laboratory. Each project addresses some of the issues raised in the conceptual model regarding opportunities for children to develop skill at decision making and planning in the family context. The first project used archival longitudinal data and examined whether children's participation in planning-related interactions in the family changes from childhood to adolescence, with particular attention to the role that parenting style may play in this process. The second project, also longitudinal, examined children's changing participation in deciding on their after-school activities over the period of middle childhood. The main questions we asked in this research were whether children have opportunities to plan or decide on their own activities outside of school and how parents are involved in this process. Because of our interest in cultural contributions to this process, we also examined whether parental expectations about development in this area of growth related to the opportunities that parents provided for their children to plan or decide on their own activities outside of school. In response to Elkind's (1981/2001) concerns, we also explored children's satisfaction with the amount of activities they did outside of school and if there were any relations between children's satisfaction and their opportunities to decide on or plan these activities, either on their own or with their parents.

ARCHIVAL ANALYSIS OF PLANNING IN THE FAMILY

An initial question we wanted to answer is whether children's participation in planning-related interactions in the family changes from childhood to adolescence. To answer this question, Gauvain and Huard (1999) analyzed archival data from the Family Socialization and Developmental Competence Project (Baumrind, 1972). Home observations of 68 families when the children were 4, 9, and 15 years of age were coded for the nature and extent of planning-related discussions in the family. We examined children's participation in these discussions and whether this participation was related to parenting style, the main focus of Baumrind's research. We operationalized planning as the anticipation of future events, indexed by parents and children talking about these events. In social contexts, planning often occurs when individuals make their future goals public by talking about them. Such communicative junctures may serve as opportunities for devising, refining, and coordinating plans, and, thereby, provide opportunities for children to learn about the planning process.

Results indicated that future-oriented discussions occurred regularly in the family from early in the child's life, and that mothers and children were more involved in planning talk than fathers and children were. This pattern is consistent with research that shows that mothers are more involved in the day-to-day experiences of children, which tend to include many planning-related decisions (Parke, 1996). Regarding development, we found that as children got older, they initiated more future-oriented discussions in the family. Developmental continuity in children's participation was evident. The frequency with which children initiated planning-related discussions in adolescence was predicted by the frequency of their planning-related initiations at age 9.

Parenting style also played an important role in the planning-related behaviors observed. Authoritarian parents used more directives in organizing their children's future behaviors. For example, one mother, identified as authoritarian, told her child that he had to pick up all his toys before dinner. In contrast, authoritative parents were more likely to use reminders to organize their children's future behaviors. For example, one father, identified as authoritative, told his child that bedtime was near and that she might want to get in some piano practice soon. When we examined planning-related initiations by the children when they reached adolescence, we found that adolescents with authoritarian parents initiated fewer planning-related discussions than adolescents with authoritative, permissive, or uninvolved parents, who did not differ in this regard. Further analysis revealed that adolescents with authoritative parents initiated more planning-related discussions regarding family coordination, whereas adolescents with permissive and uninvolved parents mainly reported to their parents on their own plans.

Although these results may, in part, be due to differences in the children's verbal ability, the systematic patterns that emerged over time suggest that the family is a setting in which children are learning about and practicing planning. They also indicate that children's participation in initiating planning-related talk changes from early in childhood to adolescence. Finally, results suggest that characteristics of the family, specifically parenting style, may influence children's opportunities to learn about and practice these cognitive skills at home.

CHILDREN'S PARTICIPATION
IN AFTER-SCHOOL ACTIVITIES IN RELATION
TO PARENTAL EXPECTATIONS

In this study, we investigated how parental expectations or beliefs about the development or timing of planning and decision making skills relate to the opportunities that children have in the family to practice these skills (Goodnow, 1985; Sigel, 1982). Because parental expectations tend to reflect broader cultural values regarding the patterning and pace of development, these expectations were used to examine the influence of cultural values in this process. In line with a participation view of development (Rogoff, 1998), we assume that over the years of middle childhood, children gradually take on or appropriate planning or decision-making responsibility that was previously done solely by or in collaboration with parents. This research involved 81 European American and 40 Latino American children (63 girls) and their mothers from working and middle-class families over a 3-year period beginning when the children were 7 to 8 years of age. All the Latino American mothers spoke English primarily or solely at home, and the two ethnic groups were similar in social status, which was predominantly lower middle class, as measured by the Hollingshead (1957) two-factor index of social position. We purposely selected a sample of children who spent little or no time in day care after school. On average, 85% of the children went home every day after school and the remainder of the children went to day care or their parents' workplace a few days a week. There were no differences in these patterns over the three time periods or between the ethnic groups.

European Americans and Latino Americans were the focus of the research because they are the two largest ethnic groups in Southern California and they offer patterns of similarity and difference that make them interesting to study in relation to child socialization in the areas of decision making and planning. Both groups stress academic achievement, reflecting a shared belief that education is crucial to children's economic and social success. Like European American parents, Latino American parents exhibit a range of parenting styles (Martinez, 1999). However, Latino American parents tend to be stricter than European American parents are, and European American parents tend to place greater emphasis on child self-control than Latino American parents do. These communities also differ in terms of gender socialization, which may influence the opportunities that boys and girls have to plan and make decisions in the family (Parke & Buriel, 1998). Increased emphasis on independence for boys in European American communities may lead to earlier opportunities for boys to plan and make decisions about how to spend their time on their own. This, in turn, may impact the emergence of autonomy in this group. In contrast, Latino American parents have high and increasing expectations over middle childhood for their daughters to be involved in household and caregiving responsibilities. At this same time, Latino American parents show increased protectiveness toward their daughters due to their impending maturity. Together, these changes may restrict the participation of Latino American girls in planning their activities outside of school.

To find out what these children did after school and who decided on these activities, mothers and children independently completed their own versions of the "Daily Activities Survey" (Gauvain & Huard, 1993) each year of the project. Mothers completed the form in writing and children were interviewed. This survey asks about children's regular after-school activities and who decided that the child would participate in these activities—the parent, the child, or both parent and child. Questions distinguish the child's participation in organized activities (e.g., sports teams, music lessons) and informal activities both inside and outside the home (e.g., reading, watching television, playing in the yard or in the neighborhood). At each data collection period, mothers and children were also asked about how the child felt about the amount of things he or she did after school (1 = *not enough*, 5 = *too much*), which was used to index children's satisfaction regarding their after-school activity level. Children answered this question by choosing among five drawings of thermometers that ranged from not very full to exploding.

In general, the children in this study participated in a diverse range of activities after school, with a rate and pattern similar to other samples of this age (Posner & Vandell, 1999). Regarding after-school responsibilities, 99% of children completed chores, 7% ran errands for their parents (e.g., go to the store), and 10% worked at their parent's business. There were no differences by ethnicity or child gender in these behaviors. In terms of activities, the children regularly, that is, every day or several days a week, participated in an average of 2.88 organized activities and 8.39 informal activities. No group differences appeared for participation in organized activities, but European American children participated in more informal activities ($M = 8.62$) than Latino American children ($M = 8.16$), $F(1, 113) = 15.21$, $p < .01$, and boys participated in more informal activities ($M = 8.55$) than girls ($M = 8.22$), $F(1, 113) = 8.32$, $p < .05$. Children participated in significantly more organized activities over the years of the study, but participation rates for informal activities did not change.

When we examined who decided on children's participation in after-school activities, we found that type of activity was important. For organized activities, parents and children together made the majority (67%) of the decisions about child participation; children alone decided on 23% of these activities and parents alone decided on 10%. This pattern, which did not differ by ethnicity or child gender and did not change over the 3 years of the study, suggests that children receive substantial assistance from parents in making decisions about future organized activities. These types of activities often involve expense to the family, both in time and money, and this may explain why shared decision making dominates. Compared to organized activities, a substantial proportion of decisions about children's participation in informal activities was made by children on their own. Over the 3 years of the study, children made an average of 46% of these decisions, and parents and children together made an average of 45% of these decisions. Only 8% of these decisions were made by parents alone; however, Latino American parents made more of these decisions on their own ($M = 11\%$) than European American parents did ($M = 4\%$), $F(1, 113) = 12.77$, $p < .01$. The rate for children deciding on informal activities on their own increased from 41% to 50% over the 3 years of the study, a shift in responsibility that may represent a developmental transition related to the 5 to 7 shift in cognitive abilities (Sameroff & Haith, 1996).

In the first and third years of the study, mothers completed the "Parental Expectations Questionnaire" that asked them to identify the age at which they expect that most children should be able to decide to do 11 different types of activities (Savage & Gauvain, 1998). The measure assesses two factors, with one factor representing decisions about organized activities (alpha = .80) and one factor representing decisions about informal activities (alpha = .90; see Table 7.1). We used this measure to investigate whether parental expectations about the age at which children should be able to decide on their after-school activities are related to children's participation in and decision making about their activities.

Consistent with socialization values of independence in European American communities, mothers in this group expected children to be able to de-

TABLE 7.1
Items in Parental Expectations Questionnaire Regarding When Children
Are Able to Decide on Their Own to Participate in Various
Organized and Informal Activities and Their Factor Loadings

Type of Activity and Items	Factor 1	Factor 2
Organized activities (alpha = .80)		
Decide to be on a sports team.	.868	.118
Decide to participate in a club or organization.	.815	.185
Decide to take music or dance lessons.	.810	.255
Informal activities (alpha = .90)		
Decide what to do after school.	.328	.811
Decide what to watch on TV.	.344	.788
Decide what to do in the evening before bedtime.	.171	.780
Decide what to eat for breakfast and lunch.	.256	.757
Decide what chores to do around the house.	.082	.750
Decide what to wear to school.	.170	.716
Decide when to go to bed.	.021	.712
Decide how to spend allowance.	.172	.591

cide on organized, $F(1, 114) = 25.04$, $p < .01$, and informal, $F(1, 114) = 25.46$, $p < .001$, activities at earlier ages than Latino American mothers did. Child gender emerged as an important factor in parental expectations regarding informal but not organized activities, and these relations changed over the 3 years of the study. When the children were in Grade 2, mothers of boys and girls reported the same age expectations for when children are able to decide on their own informal activities. However, when the children were in Grade 4, mothers' age expectations for girls, but not boys, increased. In other words, as their daughters got older, mothers' expectations for when girls are able to decide on or plan their activities also increased. This pattern may be indicative of greater protectiveness toward daughters than sons as children approach adolescence. This gender difference is interesting in that girls tend to exhibit more mature behaviors in a wide range of responsibilities over the years of middle childhood than boys do. Thus, if child behavior was influencing parental expectations, one might predict the opposite gender pattern. However, an emphasis on independence for boys, suggested by younger age expectations for boys for independent decision making and planning of informal activities, reflects stereotypical gender-related beliefs and these beliefs appear to be similar across the two communities.

Although parental expectations about when children have the ability to decide on or plan their own activities are interesting in and of themselves, we also wanted to know if these expectations related to children's experiences in the family to decide on and plan their own activities. We found no such relations for organized activities. However, parental expectations and children's participation in informal activities were negatively related at each grade level (rs ranged from $-.16$ to $-.19$, $p < .05$). That is, mothers who reported older ages for when they expected children to be able to decide on their own informal activities had children who, each year of the study, participated in lower rates of informal activities.

Next we examined whether children's opportunities to make decisions about their after-school activities were related to parental expectations. We found that mothers' expectations about when children are able to decide on organized activities were positively related to parents deciding on their own on children's participation in these activities, and this relation was strongest at Grade 4, the oldest age group studied ($r = .22$, $p < .05$). Likewise, mothers' age expectations for informal activities were positively related to parents alone deciding on children's participation in these activities (rs ranged from $.24$ to $.30$, $p < .01$ over the three grade levels) and negatively related to parents and children deciding together on children's participation in these activities (rs ranged from $-.22$ to $-.29$, $p < .05$, over the 3 years). There were no gender-related findings or ethnic differences in these patterns.

These results indicate that parental expectations about the development of children's planning and decision-making skills affect the opportunities that parents provide for children to participate in after-school activities. Moreover, these expectations are related to the opportunities children have at home to make decisions about and plan their participation in these activities.

The final question we asked pertained to children's satisfaction with their activity level outside of school. Recall that both mothers and children were asked about children's satisfaction. There were no differences in the mothers' and children's ratings when the children were in Grade 2 and Grade 3, both rated children as moderately satisfied. However, their ratings differed when children were in Grade 4, $t(90) = -2.42$, $p < .02$. Children said they were less satisfied with their activity level at this time than their mothers reported they were.

An interaction between ethnicity and child gender appeared for both mothers' and children's ratings, $F(1, 109) = 4.24$, $F(1, 109) = 5.95$, respectively, both $p < .05$. Ratings by Latino American mothers of their sons' satisfaction increased over the 3 years of the study, whereas these mothers' ratings of their daughters' satisfaction decreased over this same time period. Latino American girls also reported less satisfaction with their activity level compared with any of the other groups of children in the study. Perhaps for Latino American girls, developmental fit is at issue in that maturational changes may be colliding with culturally related and gender-specific expectations in this community. However, it may also be the case that these girls are extremely busy after school because of a combination of the types of activities we assessed and high rates of household responsibilities, which have been widely reported for Latino American girls as they approach adolescence (Parke & Buriel, 1998).

When we examined the ratings of children's satisfaction and children's actual participation in activities, the only relation that appeared was for mothers' rating when the children were in Grade 2 and it was positive, $r(148) = .20$, $p < .03$. When young children participated in more activities, their mothers perceived their children to be less satisfied about the amount of activities they did after school. Given that this same relation was not found for children's ratings of satisfaction, it may actually reflect mothers', not children's, satisfaction with children's activity level. For children in Grade 2, participation in after-school activities often requires substantial assistance from mothers in making sure children attend these activities.

The lack of relations between children's satisfaction and children's actual participation rates is interesting. The supposition that more activities would be related to less satisfaction due to children being too busy was not upheld. What appears to be more important to children's satisfaction than the amount of activities in which they are engaged is their participation in deciding on or planning these activities. When the children were in Grade 3, a negative relation was found between children's satisfaction with their activity level and parents deciding on children's informal activities, $r(134) = .27, p < .01$, and a positive relation was found between children's satisfaction and shared decision making by parents and children about these activities, $r(134) = -.23, p < .01$. This pattern suggests that when children are 9 years of age, they are less satisfied with their activity level when parents decide on the children's participation. However, if parents and children decide together, children are more satisfied with their activity level. Finally, we found some interesting relations between children's satisfaction with their activity level and parental expectations regarding when children are able to decide on these activities on their own. For both ethnic groups, the younger the age expectations that parents had for when children are able to decide on their activities on their own, the more satisfied children were about the amount of organized and informal activities they did after school, $r(118) = .19$ and .20, $p < .05$, respectively.

In summary, results from this project suggest some of the ways in which the social and cultural context, instantiated in parent–child interaction, may contribute to the development of decision making and planning skills in the school years. Over middle childhood, parents maintained high levels of involvement in helping children decide on their participation in organized activities. In contrast, children's opportunities to decide on informal activities on their own increased over this time. These patterns were related to parental expectations regarding child development in this area of growth, with European American and Latino American parents on slightly different timetables. Consistent with socialization goals in these two communities, European American parents provided earlier opportunities for children's autonomous decision making than Latino American parents did. We also found that these patterns were related to child gender. In general, girls had less opportunity over middle childhood to decide on informal activities on their own than boys did. Daughters in Latino American families were the least satisfied with the amount of activities they did after school, perhaps due to developmental fit or to a large and increasing number of household responsibilities for these girls when they near adolescence.

Having established that the children in our study were engaged in a sizable number of activities after school, we return to the question inspired by Elkind's (1981/2001) writings: Are all hurried children the same? Our results indicate that they are not. Children who reported the most satisfaction with the amount of activities they did after school were those who had more opportunity to decide on or regulate their involvement in these activities. This pattern appeared when children were in Grade 3, around 9 years of age. Thus, as middle childhood progressed, children who had more opportunity in the family to decide on their own after-school activities, and thereby exercise their changing needs for competence and autonomy, appeared to fare better than children who had similar activity levels but whose parents made more of these decisions for the children. These data echo Elkind's (1981/2001) more recent ideas that some children may be resilient in the face of a hurried childhood. He suggests several psychological factors that may contribute to children's ability to cope with this pressure, such as social competence, self-confidence, independence, and achievement orientation. Our findings suggest that some other factors, both internal and external to the child, may also contribute to this process. These include the balance of shared and independent decision making in the family, parental expectations regarding child development in this area of growth, and child gender. Consideration of these factors broadens the scope of the social and psychological contributions to the development of children's skill at decision making and planning over middle childhood.

CONCLUSIONS

The two studies discussed in this chapter stemmed from our theoretical interest in cultural practice views of cognitive development. Despite increasing attention and interest in this perspective, there is presently little systematic research on children's everyday cognitive experiences in particular areas of cognitive functioning, the very types of experiences that cultural practice theories assume occur. Given the importance of skills at decision making and planning coupled with the protracted nature of their development, examining these abilities as they emerge in children's everyday experiences in the family seemed ideal for investigating the contributions of cultural practices. One uncertainty we had in launching this research, however, was whether the current social climate of childhood, described in the introduction, actually affords any opportunities for children to make decisions about and plan activities that have some importance or consequence for their lives.

Some positive news on this front emerged from our data. Yes, we did find that children are very busy after school. But we also discovered that not all children are dissatisfied with being busy and that children's satisfaction with their activity level is linked to a gradual increase over middle childhood in children's participation in deciding on or planning their own after-school activities. The data also indicated that many children are getting substantial opportunity to develop and practice these skills in the context of informal activities. In addition, parents play a significant role in this development by helping children decide on and plan their participation in organized activities. Such parent–child interactions open opportunities for children to learn about and practice these emerging cognitive abilities under their parents' tutelage. Not all parent–child interactions that pertain to decision making and planning are the same, however. Parenting style influences the types of op-

portunities that parents provide for children along these lines, as do culturally related expectations that parents have about child development in this
area of growth. Finally, parental expectations appear particularly relevant
when they are considered in relation to gender socialization. This connection
is not surprising in that decision making and planning skills are directly related to child independence, a factor which we know has importance in cultural value systems and their associated gender socialization practices.

Although our research is preliminary in its examination of the conceptual
model presented, we hope that it directs attention to ways in which the development of cognitive skill may relate to children's everyday social experiences. This type of inquiry is an important contribution of a sociocultural approach to developmental science (Gauvain, 2004). Despite long-standing
interest in the everyday lives of children (Barker, 1968; Bronfenbrenner,
1979), we are still far from understanding how these experiences fit with development. Three points are worth noting about this approach in relation to
the conceptual model proposed and the research discussed:

1. A sociocultural approach is centrally concerned with issues of context
   and, therefore, offers an ecologically valid framework for studying cognitive development.
2. By focusing on sociocultural processes as integral to the development of
   cognitive skill, researchers are better able to address issues of cultural
   variability without appealing to a deficit model. Variation in cognitive
   skill across communities is expected in that different groups have different goals, needs, and resources, and therefore provide different opportunities for child development.
3. Our aim was to include a broad range of factors in the study of the development of a specific cognitive skill.

Our findings suggest that opportunities for children to make decisions about
their future behaviors and to receive assistance from parents in this regard
are important aspects of the development of planning and decision making
skills from childhood through adolescence.

There are several assumptions and limitations of our research that are important to mention. First, we assume both generality, or universality, and
cultural specificity of cognitive functioning and its development in this area
of growth. Investigators who adopt a sociocultural approach to cognitive development hold different positions on the universality of cognitive skill. In
our research, we consider both the processes of cognitive development, specifically guided participation (Rogoff, 1998) and independent practice, as
well as the cognitive skills themselves (i.e., future-oriented behaviors) to be
universal human characteristics. Though, as our research demonstrates, even
in cultural communities that are quite similar in many ways, there are still

some culturally related patterns that have consequences for the development of decision-making and planning skills. Second, our data are limited in that they do not include "thick" ethnographic descriptions of cognitive behaviors, an approach adopted by many who use a sociocultural view. As a first step for examining the issues discussed in the introduction, we opted for empirical techniques that are unconventional in this approach. We agree that ethnographic analysis of children's after-school experiences is needed to enrich understanding of the development of the cognitive abilities studied here. Work by Heath (1991) serves as an excellent model for such research. Third, our research lacks the rigor and control of laboratory experimentation. Perhaps future research on this topic will combat this limitation. However, given the scope of the questions raised in the introduction, laboratory investigation will be useful for some questions and other methods will be needed to address others.

In closing, it bears reiteration that the current social climate of childhood in the United States is largely and increasingly invested in controlling children's time rather than in helping children learn how to use their time. Despite the understandable and well-intentioned goals that most parents have in this regard, the potential consequences of this pattern from the perspective of current theory and research in developmental psychology are, in our view, rather bleak. Many psychologists are attending to this issue and are making important contributions to policy, especially in the areas of social and emotional development (e.g., see Eccles & Gootman, 2002). Our aim is to broaden this discussion to include how children's after-school experiences, including family practices, may relate to cognitive development. In the end, we hope that these collective efforts will demonstrate how theories and concepts of developmental psychology may help in addressing a real-life issue facing children today.

ACKNOWLEDGMENT

The research described in this chapter was supported by a grant from the National Institute of Health and Child Development (R01-HD33998-04) awarded to the first author.

REFERENCES

Bandura, A. (1989). Cognitive social learning theory. In R. Vasta (Ed.), *Annals of child development* (Vol. 6, pp. 1–60). Greenwich, CT: JAI.

Barker, R. (1968). *Ecological psychology.* Stanford, CA: Stanford University Press.

Baumrind, D. (1972). The development of instrumental competence through socialization. In A. Pick (Ed.), *Minnesota symposium on child psychology* (Vol. 7, pp. 349–378). Minneapolis: University of Minnesota Press.

Benson, J. B. (1994). The origins of future orientation in the everyday lives of 9- to 36-month-old infants. In M. M. Haith, J. B. Benson, R. J. Roberts, & B. F. Pennington (Eds.), *The development of future-oriented processes* (pp. 375–407). Chicago: University of Chicago Press.

Berg, C. A., Strough, J., Calderone, K., Meegan, S. P., & Sansone, C. (1997). Planning to prevent everyday problems from occurring. In S. L. Friedman & E. K. Scholnick (Eds.), *The developmental psychology of planning: Why, how, and when do we plan?* (pp. 209–236). Mahwah, NJ: Lawrence Erlbaum Associates.

Bronfenbrenner, U. (1979). *The ecology of human development: Experiments by nature and design.* Cambridge, MA: Harvard University Press.

Bugental, D. B., & Goodnow, J. J. (1998). Socialization processes. In W. Damon (Series Ed.) & N. Eisenberg (Vol. Ed.), *Handbook of child psychology: Vol. 3. Social, emotional, and personality development* (pp. 389–462). New York: Wiley.

Byrnes, J. P. (1998). *The nature and development of decision making: A self-regulation model.* Mahwah, NJ: Lawrence Erlbaum Associates.

Cappella, E., & Larner, M. B. (1999). America's schoolchildren: Past, present, and future. In R. E. Behrman (Ed.), *The future of children: When school is out* (Vol. 9, No. 2, pp. 21–29). Los Altos, CA: The Packard Foundation.

Carmona, M., & Stewart, K. (1996). *A review of alternative activities and alternative programs in youth-oriented prevention* (CSAP Tech. Rep. No. 13). Washington, DC: Department of Health and Human Services.

Carnegie Council on Adolescent Development. (1992). *A matter of time: Risk and opportunity in the nonschool hours.* New York: Carnegie Corporation.

Carver, C. S., & Scheier, M. F. (1998). *On the self-regulation of behavior.* New York: Cambridge University Press.

Cole, M. (1992). Context, modularity, and the cultural constitution of development. In L. T. Winegar & J. Valsiner (Eds.), *Children's development within social context* (Vol. 2, pp. 5–31). Hillsdale, NJ: Lawrence Erlbaum Associates.

Connell, J. P. (1990). Context, self, and action: A motivational analysis of self-system processes across the life-span. In D. Cichetti (Ed.), *The self in transition: From infancy to childhood* (pp. 61–97). Chicago: University of Chicago Press.

Das, J. P., Kar, B. C., & Parrila, R. K. (1996). *Cognitive planning: The psychological basis of intelligent behavior.* New Delhi, India: Sage.

Dreher, M., & Oreter, R. (1987). Action planning competencies during adolescence and early adulthood. In S. L. Friedman, E. K. Scholnick, & R. R. Cocking (Eds.), *Blueprints for thinking: The role of planning in cognitive development* (pp. 321–355). New York: Cambridge University Press.

Eccles, J. S. (1999). The development of children ages 6 to 14. *The Future of Children, 9*(2), 30–44.

Eccles, J., & Gootman, J. A. (2002). *Community programs to promote youth development.* Washington, DC: National Academy Press.

Eccles, J. S., Midgely, C., Buchanan, C. M., Wigfield, A., Reuman, D., & MacIver, D. (1993). Development during adolescence: The impact of stage/environment fit. *American Psychologist, 48,* 90–101.

Elkind, D. (2001). *The hurried child: Growing up too fast too soon* (3rd ed.). Reading, MA: Addison-Wesley. (Original work published 1981)

Friedman, S. L., & Scholnick, E. K. (1997). *The developmental psychology of planning.* Mahwah, NJ: Lawrence Erlbaum Associates.

Friedman, S. L., Scholnick, E. K., & Cocking, R. R. (1987). *Blueprints for thinking: The role of planning in cognitive development.* New York: Cambridge University Press.

Gauvain, M. (1992). Social influences on the development of planning in advance and during action. *International Journal of Behavioral Development, 15,* 377–398.

Gauvain, M. (2001). *The social context of cognitive development.* New York: Guilford.

Gauvain, M. (2004). Bringing culture into relief: Cultural contributions to the development of children's planning skills. In R. Kail (Ed.), *Advances in child development and behavior* (Vol. 32, pp. 37–71). San Diego, CA: Academic.

Gauvain, M., & Huard, R. D. (1993, April). *What do children do when they have nothing to do?* Paper presented at the meeting of the Society for Research in Child Development, New Orleans.

Gauvain, M., & Huard, R. D. (1999). Family interaction, parenting style, and the development of planning: A longitudinal analysis using archival data. *Journal of Family Psychology, 13,* 1–18.

Gauvain, M., & Rogoff, B. (1989). Collaborative problem solving and children's planning skills. *Developmental Psychology, 25,* 139–151.

Getting ahead by getting organized. (2000, March 22). *Los Angeles Times,* p. B2.

Goodnow, J. J. (1985). Change and variation in parents' ideas about childhood and parenting. In I. E. Sigel (Ed.), *Parental belief systems* (pp. 235–270). Hillsdale, NJ: Lawrence Erlbaum Associates.

Goodnow, J. J., Cashmore, J., Cotton, S., & Knight, R. (1984). Mothers' developmental timetables in two cultural groups. *International Journal of Psychology, 19,* 193–205.

Goodnow, J. J., Miller, P. J., & Kessel, F. (1995). *Cultural practices as contexts for development.* San Francisco: Jossey-Bass.

Gutierrez, J., & Sameroff, A. (1990). Determinants of complexity in Mexican-American and Anglo-American mothers' conceptions of child development. *Child Development, 61,* 384–394.

Haith, M. M. (1994). Visual expectations as the first step toward the development of future-oriented processes. In M. M. Haith, J. B. Benson, R. J. Roberts, & B. F. Pennington (Eds.), *The development of future-oriented processes* (pp. 11–38). Chicago: University of Chicago Press.

Haith, M. M., Benson, J. B., Roberts, R. J., & Pennington, B. F. (1994). *The development of future-oriented processes.* Chicago: University of Chicago Press.

Heath, S. B. (1991). "It's about winning!" The language of knowledge of baseball. In L. B. Resnick, J. M. Levine, & S. D. Teasley (Eds.), *Perspectives on socially shared cognition* (pp. 101–124). Washington, DC: American Psychological Association.

Hollingshead, A. B. (1957). *Two-factor index of social position.* Unpublished manuscript, Yale University.

Jacobs, J. E., & Eccles, J. S. (2000). Parents, task values, and real-life achievement-related choices. In C. Sansone & J. M. Harackiewicz (Eds.), *Intrinsic and extrinsic motivation: The search for optimal motivation and performance* (pp. 405–439). San Diego, CA: Academic.

Jacobs, J. E., Vernon, M. K., & Eccles, J. S. (in press). Activity choices in middle childhood: The role of gender, self-beliefs, and parents' influence. In J. L. Mahoney, R. Larson, & J. S. Eccles (Eds.), *Organized activities as contexts of development: Extracurricular activities, after-school and community programs.* Mahwah, NJ: Lawrence Erlbaum Associates.

Klaczynski, P. A., Laipple, J. S., & Jurden, F. H. (1992). Educational context differences in practical problem solving during adolescence. *Merrill-Palmer Quarterly, 38,* 417–438.

Klahr, D., & Robinson, M. (1981). Formal assessment of problem solving and planning processes in preschool children. *Cognitive Psychology, 13,* 113–148.

Kohn, M. L. (1977). *Class and conformity: A study in values* (2nd ed.). Chicago: University of Chicago Press.

Kreitler, S., & Kreitler, H. (1987). Conceptions and processes of planning: The developmental perspective. In S. L. Friedman, E. K. Scholnick, & R. R. Cocking (Eds.), *Blueprints for thinking: The role of planning in psychological development* (pp. 205–272). New York: Cambridge University Press.

Larson, R. W. (2000). Toward a psychology of positive youth development. *American Psychologist, 55,* 170–183.

Larson, R. W., & Verma, S. (1999). How children and adolescents spend time across the world: Work, play, and developmental opportunities. *Psychological Bulletin, 125,* 701–736.

Maccoby, E. E. (1994). The role of parents in the socialization of children: An historical overview. In R. D. Parke, P. A. Ornstein, J. J. Rieser, & C. Zahn-Waxler (Eds.), *A century of developmental psychology* (pp. 589–615). Washington, DC: American Psychological Association.

Martinez, E. A. (1999). Mexican American/Chicano families. In H. P. McAdoo (Ed.), *Family ethnicity* (pp. 121–134). Thousand Oaks, CA: Sage.

Ochs, E., Smith, R., & Taylor, C. (1989). Dinner narratives as detective stories. *Cultural Dynamics, 2,* 238–257.

The Packard Foundation (1999). *The future of children: When school is out* (Vol. 9, No. 2). Los Altos, CA: The Packard Foundation.

Parke, R. D. (1996). *Fatherhood.* Cambridge, MA: Cambridge University Press.

Parke, R. D., & Buriel, R. (1998). Socialization in the family: Ethnic and ecological perspectives. In W. Damon (Series Ed.) & N. Eisenberg (Vol. Ed.), *Handbook of child psychology: Vol. 3. Social, emotional, and personality development* (pp. 463–552). New York: Wiley.

Parrila, R. K., Aysto, S., & Das, J. P. (1994). Development of planning in relation to age, attention, simultaneous and successive processing. *Journal of Psychoeducational Assessment, 12,* 212–227.

Posner, J. K., & Vandell, D. L. (1999). After-school activities and the development of low-income urban children: A longitudinal study. *Developmental Psychology, 35,* 868–879.

Radziszewska, B., & Rogoff, B. (1988). Influence of adult and peer collaborators on children's planning skills. *Developmental Psychology, 24,* 840–848.

Renninger, K. A. (1990). Children's play interests, representation, and activity. In R. Fivush & J. Hudson (Eds.), *Knowing and remembering in young children* (Vol. 3, pp. 127–165). New York: Cambridge University Press.

Rogoff, B. (1998). Cognition as a collaborative process. In W. Damon (Series Ed.), & D. Kuhn & R. S. Siegler (Vol. Eds.), *Handbook of child psychology: Cognition, perception, and language* (pp. 679–744). New York: Wiley.

Rogoff, B., Gauvain, M., & Gardner, W. (1987). The development of children's skill in adjusting plans to circumstances. In S. L. Friedman, E. K. Scholnick, & R. R. Cocking (Eds.), *Blueprints for thinking: The role of planning in psychological development* (pp. 303–320). New York: Cambridge University Press.

Rosenthal, D. A., & Bornholt, L. (1988). Expectations about development in Greek- and Anglo-Australian families. *Journal of Cross-Cultural Psychology, 19,* 19–34.

Ryan, R. M. (1993). Agency and organization: Intrinsic motivation, autonomy, and the self in psychological development. In J. Jacobs (Ed.), *Nebraska Symposium on Motivation* (Vol. 40, pp. 1–56). Lincoln: University of Nebraska Press.

Saarni, C. (1999). *The development of emotional competence.* New York: Guilford.

Sameroff, A. J., & Haith, M. M. (1996). *The five to seven year shift: The age of reason and responsibility.* Chicago: University of Chicago Press.

Savage, S., & Gauvain, M. (1998). Parental beliefs and children's everyday planning in European American and Latino families. *Journal of Applied Developmental Psychology, 19,* 319–340.

Schaffer, H. R. (1996). *Social development.* Oxford: Blackwell.

Schlegel, A., & Barry, H. (1991). *Adolescence: An anthropological inquiry.* New York: Free Press.

Scholnick, E. K., Friedman, S. L., & Wallner-Allen, K. E. (1997). What do they really measure? A comparative analysis of planning tasks. In S. L. Friedman & E. K. Scholnick (Eds.), *The developmental psychology of planning: Why, how, and when do we plan?* (pp. 127–156). Mahwah, NJ: Lawrence Erlbaum Associates.

Sigel, I. E. (1982). *Parental belief systems.* Hillsdale, NJ: Lawrence Erlbaum Associates.

Steinberg, L., & Silverberg, S. B. (1986). The vicissitudes of autonomy in early adolescence. *Child Development, 57,* 841–851.

Sutton-Smith, B. (1994). Does play prepare the future? In J. H. Goldstein (Ed.), *Toys, play, and child development* (pp. 130–145). New York: Cambridge University Press.

Tudge, J., Hogan, D., Lee, S., Tammeveski, P., Meltsas, M., Kulahova, N., Snezhkova, I., & Putnam, S. (1999). Cultural heterogeneity: Parental values and beliefs and their preschoolers' activities in the United States, South Korea, Russia, and Estonia. In A. Goncu (Ed.), *Children's engagement in the world: Sociocultural perspectives* (pp. 62–96). Cambridge, UK: Cambridge University Press.

U.S. Bureau of the Census. (2000). Current population reports. Washington, DC: U.S. Government Printing Office, U.S. Department of Education.

Vygotsky, L. S. (1978). *Mind in society.* Cambridge, MA: Harvard University Press.

Wartella, E., & Mazzarella, S. (1990). A historical comparison of children's use of leisure time. In R. Butsch (Ed.), *For fun and profit: The transformation of leisure into consumption* (pp. 173–193). Philadelphia: Temple University Press.

Weiss, H. (2001, April). *Commentary in the Symposium Children's Lives After School: Opportunities for Development.* Presented at the meetings of the Society for Research in Child Development, Minneapolis, MN.

Wertsch, J. V. (1981). *The concept of activity in Soviet psychology.* Armonk, NY: E. Sharpe.

Willatts, P. (1990). Development of problem solving strategies in infants. In D. F. Bjorkland (Ed.), *Children's strategies* (pp. 23–66). Hillsdale, NJ: Lawrence Erlbaum Associates.

Wood, D. J., & Middleton, D. (1975). A study of assisted problem solving. *British Journal of Psychology, 66,* 181–191.

Commentary:
Lessons From a Life-Span
Perspective to Adolescent
Decision Making

Cynthia A. Berg
University of Utah

The chapters in Part II address important aspects of adolescent decision making that have received little attention in the literature to date. Decision making is examined as adolescents make decisions regarding their after-school activities (Gauvain & Perez, chap. 7), make decisions utilizing democratic versus authority-based justifications (Helwig, chap. 6), make judgments regarding the frequency with which peers in general engage in deviant behaviors (Jacobs & Johnston, chap. 5), and utilize regret to avoid making bad decisions (Amsel, Bowden, Cottrell, & Sullivan, chap. 4). These chapters address crucial issues in the field concerning how to characterize the adolescent decision maker (e.g., competent vs. incompetent), the domain of decision making (from the more everyday task of making decisions regarding which after-school activity to be involved in to decisions regarding at-risk behaviors), and the development of decision making across adolescence (gaining autonomy to make independent decisions). Cutting across these chapters are three themes: (a) adolescent decision making occurs in a rich context of parental, peer, and cultural influences; (b) individual autonomy guides much of the decision making of adolescents; and (c) adolescents are both competent and cognitively mature as well as incompetent and risky decision makers. These themes are consonant with a broader life-span developmental perspective to decision making. In my comments, I elaborate on how lessons learned within a life-span perspective to adolescent decision making may prove useful in the next steps in this literature as researchers continue to broaden the scope of models and tasks to capture the complexity of decision-making processes as they occur in adolescents' daily lives.

ADOLESCENT DECISION MAKING OCCURS
IN A SOCIAL AND CULTURAL CONTEXT

A central tenet of a life-span perspective to development is that development occurs in a rich network of interconnected contexts that change across age and historical time (Baltes, 1987; Bronfenbrenner, 1979). The chapters point out three factors in adolescents' contexts that are important for understanding decision making: parents, peers, and the broader culture. The importance that parents play in adolescents' lives (Steinberg & Silk, 2002) is no more apparent than when making decisions that have been characterized as "risky" or "deviant" (Brown, Mounts, Lamborn, & Steinberg, 1993; Herman, Dornbusch, Herron, & Herting, 1997). Adolescents benefit when parents monitor adolescent behavior while allowing adolescents to exercise their independence in decision making (Steinberg & Morris, 2000). However, often during adolescence, parents' involvement can be characterized as too intensive and potentially intrusive (Barber, 2001; Pomerantz & Ruble, 1998). Parents' use of controlling involvement is associated with important aspects of parental style (e.g., authoritarian vs. authoritative). Parental style may also affect the opportunity for democratic versus authority-based decision making in the family (Steinberg, Lamborn, Darling, Mounts, & Dornbusch, 1994).

The different ways that parents can interact with their children (control, showing warmth and acceptance, collaboration) may inform some of the research results in Part II of this volume. For instance, Gauvain and Perez (chap. 7) found that the children who experienced the most distress over their after-school activities were those whose parents believed that adolescent independence in making those decisions should come at a later age. Children's distress may not necessarily have come about because parents were simply involved in making those activity decisions, but because the form of that involvement was intrusive, controlling, and unsolicited. Adolescents often interpret from such intrusive parental involvement the message that they [adolescents] are incompetent and cannot make competent decisions, thereby producing distress (Pomerantz & Eaton, 2001). An important direction for work on adolescent decision making will be to gain a more specific understanding of the ways in which parents are involved in the decision making of their adolescents. In addition, this literature may profit from work on the socialization of memory (Nelson & Fivush, 2000) and coping (Kliewer, Fearnow, & Miller, 1996) to understand how families may provide more direct modeling, coaching, and instruction in decision-making processes. Families differ in terms of their direct experience with deviant behaviors engaged in either by parents or siblings (Capaldi, Pears, Patterson, & Owen, 2003; Thornberry, Freeman-Gallant, Lizotte, Krohn, & Smith, 2003), and in the style with which they engage in decision making with their adolescents (Steinberg et al., 1994). The different experiences that families provide children may be useful in understanding the development of adolescent decision making.

A contextual factor only hinted at in these studies is the influence of peers. Across adolescence, individuals spend increasing amounts of time with their peers (Larson & Richards, 1991) and peer influence on behavior also increases. The potential importance of the peer group is most apparent in the work of Jacobs and Johnston (chap. 5). In their work, adolescents were to make judgments concerning base rates of peers' deviant behaviors and victimization. Unpacking "peers" in their methodology will be important. That is, if adolescents interpret peers as "those adolescents at my school whom I know engage in risky behaviors versus those in my own network of friends," estimation of deviant behaviors may be different. Peers may also contribute to the stress and satisfaction with activity choices examined in chapter 7 by Gauvain and Perez. That is, children's satisfaction with their activities may be different when activity frequency is low compared to one's peers (i.e., "I only get one after school activity but my friends are doing five") versus on par with one's peers.

In chapter 6, Helwig points out how cultural beliefs (e.g., independence vs. interdependence) may affect the types of justifications adolescents make concerning authority versus autonomous decisions. However, his work cautions us from overinterpreting culture as overriding more normative needs for autonomous decision making by adolescents. Culture was clearly important in Gauvain and Perez's (chap. 7) study of activity choices and expectations in European American versus Latino American parents. Unpacking the meaning of *culture* (e.g., parental style, expectations concerning adolescent independence vs. interdependence) will be important in understanding when culture is useful in predicting aspects of adolescent decision making.

A life-span developmental perspective would remind us that such contextual influences may change across historical time. A central tenet of life-span developmental psychology (Baltes, 1987; Schaie, 1984) is that development is influenced by the historical time in which one lives (i.e., cohorts may differ in their development) as much as by age. This is immediately apparent to me as I now experience adolescence from my children's perspective. Some relevant aspects of the changing context of adolescence for decision making include the following: (a) earlier onset of puberty (Herman-Giddens et al., 1997); (b) adolescence as a time period is now drawn out such that it may not end until the late 20s; (c) changing frequency of "risky" adolescent behaviors in the peer groups (increase in violent weapons in our schools; National Center for Education Statistics, 1998); (d) burgeoning availability of out-of-school activities (Cappella & Larner, 1999; e.g., availability of sports for girls); and (e) changes in cultures that have been traditionally characterized as collective (reviewed by Helwig, chap. 6). Such factors may influence the age by which adolescents expect to make autonomous decisions, when

society views children as "adolescent" decision makers, and the frequency
with which adolescents are faced with difficult domains of decision making.
As I read the chapters in this part, I asked myself what the results would
have been like when I was an adolescent or what the results will be 40 years
from now. As researchers work toward identifying key aspects of adolescent
decision making, we must acknowledge that these aspects may change with
changes in the sociocultural and biological contexts of adolescence.

INDIVIDUAL AUTONOMY AS AN IMPORTANT COMPONENT OF ADOLESCENT DECISION MAKING

In several of the chapters, the importance of individual autonomy and independence is highlighted as a critical component of adolescent decision making (most notably, Helwig, chap. 6, and Gauvain & Perez, chap. 7). From a
life-span perspective (Erikson, 1968), gaining a separate identity from one's
parents is a key developmental life task of adolescence. Helwig's results indicate that individual autonomy is even important in "collectivistic" cultures
that are oriented toward authority and obedience to family. Gauvain and
Perrez's results indicate that children are less satisfied with their activity
choices when they are less independent in making those choices. These
characterizations of adolescence as a time for independent, autonomous behavior are consistent with long-standing notions of adolescence as a time
when children renegotiate the influence of parents in their lives to become
more self-reliant (Erikson, 1968; Greenberger, Josselson, R. Knerr, & B.
Knerr, 1974; Steinberg & Morris, 2000). However, most conceptualizations
of autonomy emphasize that healthy autonomy development occurs when
adolescents gain self-reliance while maintaining emotional bonds and connections to parents (Steinberg & Morris, 2000; Steinberg & Silverberg,
1986).

This conceptualization of optimal adolescence as self-reliant but connected
to parents is an important one for understanding adolescent decision making.
How can adolescents gain independent control over their behavior and decisions while maintaining connections to parents? In our own work examining
how adolescents with type 1 diabetes make decisions regarding successful management, we have found that it is crucial for adolescents to feel that their parents are "collaborators" in the decisions they make, even though the adolescents' behavior looks quite independent (Palmer et al., 2004; Wiebe et al., in
press). That is, across adolescence, children become much more independent
in the behaviors that make up the management of diabetes (e.g., determining
insulin doses, checking blood glucose levels). However, for successful management to occur, adolescents must perceive that parents are available as collabo-

rators or support-providers when difficult management episodes occur. Viewing parents as uninvolved in these difficult episodes is associated with poorer metabolic control and psychosocial outcomes.

This view of adolescent decision making as autonomous but connected works well for the types of decision making examined in the present chapters. Healthy adolescent development can be construed as children gaining autonomy in making decisions regarding activity choices, decisions to avoid deviant behaviors, decisions involving regret, and those involving authority. However, when problematic situations arise with respect to these decisions, adolescents must view that parents are available as collaborators to help them generate solutions, evaluate the efficacy of those decisions, and to anticipate regret from making various decisions.

A life-span perspective, however, would caution us from making generalizations about what characterizes "adolescent" behavior from cross-sectional data. All of the researchers in this part wish to identify what uniquely characterizes adolescent development from later childhood and adulthood. However, most of the studies presented examine a fairly narrow age range (Gauvain & Perez examine 7- to 10-year-olds in chap. 7; Jacobs & Johnston examine 14- to 16-years-olds in chap. 5), do not compare adolescents with children or adults (Helwig, chap. 6), or involve large age-group differences (Amsel et al. compare fourth- to fifth-grade students with college students). Much more systematic consideration of age and the corresponding changes that are thought to occur with age (marked by puberty, autonomy granting, etc.) are needed. In addition, this literature would greatly benefit from longitudinal research where the multiple changes that are occurring can be tracked with much greater precision. Longitudinal research will assist in understanding what demarcates adolescent from adult decision making and from middle-childhood development. The field may also benefit from an understanding of the commonalities across development in decision-making performance (e.g., use of heuristics, influence of emotion-driven processes, priming).

A second life-span principle proposed by Baltes (1987) that will be useful in understanding the development of adolescent decision making is that throughout the life span, development consists of the joint occurrence of gain (growth) and loss (decline). The authors of these chapters seek to understand what characterizes the development of decision making from a gain (or growth) model only. For instance, a key change that is noted in the present chapters that occurs across development is reported in chapter 4 by Amsel and colleagues, who characterize adolescent decision making as gaining the potential for utilizing regret to avoid poor decisions. Although this clearly is a gain, I wondered what an adolescent would lose with this gain. Given that regret may evoke "negative emotions," would adolescents lose the broadening of attention and cognition that positive emotions may trigger

(Fredrickson & Joiner, 2001)? A closer examination of both the gains and losses involved in the development of adolescent decision making would assist in the development of models of decision making across the life span.

ARE ADOLESCENTS COMPETENT
AND MATURE DECISION MAKERS
OR INCOMPETENT RISKY DECISION MAKERS?

In chapter 4, Amsel et al. nicely describe the conundrum in the adolescent literature between characterizing adolescents as "thoughtful and impulsive, deliberative and impetuous, or reflective and foolhardy" (p. 119). This conundrum comes about largely because of the normative models (expected utility; information-processing-based rational models) on which all decision making is based. As I read the chapters on adolescent decision making, I wondered how different adolescent decision making really is from adult decision making. Could not the same characterizations of adolescents (i.e., thoughtful and impulsive, deliberative and impetuous) characterize adults' decisions regarding whether to engage in potentially risky behaviors (e.g., investing in a volatile stock market, having an affair that may cause the dissolution of one's marriage, trying diet supplements to lose weight)? Both adolescent and adult decision making can be characterized by competence and incompetence, rationality and irrationality, depending on the specific domain of decision making and the activation of one's emotional, cognitive, and motivational systems (Berg & Klaczynski, 2002; Klaczynski, 2000).

I will illustrate what I perceive as the overly "cold cognitive and rational" side of current decision-making models with some personal experiences. My 11-year-old daughter and I have fairly heated discussions on an increasingly regular basis about numerous decisions (e.g., whether she can sit in the front seat of my vehicle—an Explorer with the older generation air bag, go to the mall with her friends unattended, skip her group lesson for violin, participate in competitive soccer on top of all of her other activities). She has a difficult time utilizing her developing cognitive competencies as we engage in joint decision making with respect to any of these decisions (as her mother I, too, do not always utilize my cognitive competencies alone to make such decisions). The model that underlies our decision-making process is much more complex than the componential models utilized traditionally in the decision-making literature (see Byrnes, 2002; Klaczynski, Byrnes, & Jacobs, 2001), whereby individuals set goals, compile and evaluate decision-making options, and enact a particular strategy. Instead, I am struck by how we utilize our cognitive competencies in a self-serving fashion (Klaczynski, 2000), draw on different pools of knowledge, experience strong emotions that influence our memories of past decision-making events (Levine & Stein, 1999), and utilize different comparisons. (My daughter utilizes strong self–other comparisons—"Everyone else is doing it," I use present–past comparisons—"When I was your age, I only had one after-school activity.") Throughout our decision making I see the different developmental life tasks that organize our approach: her autonomy-based needs and my generativity goals. Such factors have received sparse attention in the literature on adolescent decision making. Models such as Klaczynski's (2000) dual-process model of cognition that seeks to understand how adolescents and adults can appear to be rational and self-serving across problems, depending on motivation, are important in understanding how adolescents (and adults) can be both competent and incompetent, rational and heuristic. Such models will be important in capturing the richness of decisions that dominate the adolescent literature (e.g., avoiding risk taking behaviors) as well as more typical decisions adolescents must make on a more daily basis (e.g., whether to take on another after-school activity, take the science book home to study for the test tomorrow, etc.).

The development of models of decision making will benefit from a broadening of the types of tasks used to assess decision making. The literature on adolescent decision making has focused nearly exclusively on "risky" decisions (Beyth-Marom & Fischhoff, 1997). However, there are numerous domains of decision making that could be examined, utilizing the extensive work done on adolescents' activities (e.g., Larson & Richards, 1991), everyday problem solving (e.g., Berg, Strough, Calderone, Sansone, & Weir, 1998), and stress and coping (Compas, Connor-Smith, Saltzman, Thomsen, & Wadsworth, 2001) to guide their development. For instance, just a few of the decision tasks that come to mind include decisions as to whether to spend additional time on a project at school, to try out for the school play, deciding to try out for advanced classes or competitive sports teams, or a decision to take an oral contraceptive. By enlarging the realm of tasks that researchers examine, we may be able to bring factors into our models (e.g., emotion, social understanding, etc.) that better represent the richness and complexity of adolescent decision making. Although there is always the tendency to simplify tasks so as to exert control, the design of tasks will need to match the complexity of the processes involved (e.g., researchers should not necessarily abstract from decisions regarding regret over trading lottery tickets to regret over engaging in risky sexual behavior).

SUMMARY AND CONCLUSIONS

The chapters in Part II represent an important advance in the field of adolescent decision making as researchers address crucial questions concerning how to characterize the adolescent (competent vs. incompetent), the domain of decision making (estimation of risks regarding hypothetical tasks vs.

actual decisions) and the processes of decision making (focused on componential rational processes or irrational ones). These chapters push the field to broaden the scope of adolescent decision making, incorporating factors such as autonomy and the sociocultural context into current models. In my comments, I have described how lessons learned from a life-span perspective to development may assist in understanding the context of adolescent decision making, developmental factors in decision making, and the rational and irrational side of adolescent decision makers. A crucial next step in this literature is to embrace the diversity present in adolescent decision making across adolescents, tasks, and contexts. The chapters in this part provide an excellent basis for this expansion.

REFERENCES

Baltes, P. B. (1987). Theoretical propositions of life-span developmental psychology: On the dynamics between growth and decline. *Developmental Psychology, 23,* 611–626.
Barber, B. K. (2001). *Intrusive parenting: How psychological control affects children and adolescents.* Washington, DC: American Psychological Association.
Berg, C. A., & Klaczynski, P. (2002). Contextual variability in the expression and meaning of intelligence. In R. J. Sternberg & E. L. Grigorenko (Eds.), *The general factor of intelligence: How general is it?* (pp. 381–412). Mahwah, NJ: Lawrence Erlbaum Associates.
Berg, C. A., Strough, J., Calderone, K. S., Sansone, C., & Weir, C. (1998). The role of problem definitions in understanding age and context effects on strategies for solving everyday problems. *Psychology and Aging, 13,* 29–44.
Beyth-Marom, R., & Fischhoff, B. (1997). Adolescents' decisions about risks: A cognitive perspective. In J. Schulenberg, J. Maggs, & K. Hurrelmann (Eds.), *Health risks and developmental transitions during adolescence* (pp. 110–135). New York: Cambridge University Press.
Bronfenbrenner, U. (1979). *The ecology of human development.* Cambridge, MA: Harvard University Press.
Brown, B. B., Mounts, N., Lamborn, S. D., & Steinberg, L. S. (1993). Parenting practices and peer group affiliation in adolescence. *Child Development, 64,* 467–482.
Byrnes, J. P. (2002). The development of decision-making. *Journal of Adolescent Health, 31,* 208–215.
Capaldi, D. M., Pears, K. C., Patterson, G. R., & Owen, L. D. (2003). Continuity of parenting practices across generations in an at-risk sample: A prospective comparison of direct and mediated associations. *Journal of Abnormal Child Psychology, 31,* 127–143.
Cappella, E., & Larner, M. B. (1999). America's schoolchildren: Past, present, and future. In R. E. Buhrman (Ed.), *The future of children: When school is out* (pp. 21–29). Los Altos, CA: The Packard Foundation.
Compas, B. E., Connor-Smith, J. K., Saltzman, H., Thomsen, A. H., & Wadsworth, M. E. (2001). Coping with stress during childhood and adolescence: Problems, progress, and potential in theory and research. *Psychological Bulletin, 127,* 87–127.
Erikson, E. H. (1968). *Identity, youth, and crisis.* New York: Norton.
Fredrickson, B. L., & Joiner, T. (2001). The role of positive emotions in positive psychology: The broaden-and-build theory of positive emotions. *American Psychologist, 56,* 218–226.
Greenberger, E., Josselson, R., Knerr, C., & Knerr, B. (1974). The measurement and structure of psychosocial maturity. *Journal of Youth and Adolescence, 4,* 127–143.

Herman, M. R., Dornbusch, S. M., Herron, M. D., & Herting, J. R. (1997). The influence of family relations, connection, and psychological autonomy on six measures of adolescent functioning. *Journal of Adolescent Research, 12,* 34–67.

Herman-Giddens, M. E., Slora, E. J., Wasserman, R. C., Bardonay, C. J., Bhapkar, M. V., Koch, G. G., & Hasemeier, C. M. (1997). Secondary sexual characteristics and menses in young girls seen in office practice: A study from the Pediatric Research in Office Settings Network. *Pediatrics, 99,* 505–512.

Klaczynski, P. A. (2000). Motivated scientific reasoning biases, epistemological beliefs, and theory polarization: A two-process approach to adolescent cognition. *Child Development, 71,* 1347–1366.

Klaczynski, P. A., Byrnes, J. P., & Jacobs, J. E. (2001). Introduction to the special issue: The development of decision making. *Applied Developmental Psychology, 22,* 225–236.

Kliewer, W., Fearnow, M. D., & Miller, P. A. (1996). Coping socialization in middle childhood: Tests of maternal and paternal influences. *Child Development, 67,* 2339–2357.

Larson, R., & Richards, M. H. (1991). Daily companionship in late childhood and early adolescence: Changing developmental contexts. *Child Development, 62,* 284–300.

National Center for Education Statistics. (1998). *Violence and discipline problems in U.S. public schools.* Washington, DC.

Nelson, K., & Fivush, R. (2000). Socialization of memory. In E. Tulving & F. I. M. Craik (Eds.), *The Oxford handbook of memory* (pp. 283–295). London, England: Oxford University Press.

Palmer, D., Berg, C., Wiebe, D., Beveridge, R., Korbel, C., Upchurch, R., Swinyard, M., Lindsay, R., & Donaldson, D. (2004). The role of autonomy and pubertal status in understanding age differences in maternal involvement in diabetes responsibility across adolescence. *Journal of Pediatric Psychology, 29,* 35–46.

Pomerantz, E. M., & Eaton, M. M. (2001). Maternal intrusive support in the academic context: Transactional socialization processes. *Developmental Psychology, 37*(2), 174–186.

Pomerantz, E. M., & Ruble, D. N. (1998). The multidimensional nature of control: Implications for the development of sex differences in self-evaluation. In J. Heckhausen & C. S. Dweck (Eds.), *Motivation and self-regulation across the life-span* (pp. 159–184). New York: Cambridge University Press.

Schaie, K. W., (1984). Historical time and cohort effects. In K. A. McCloskey & H. W. Reese (Eds.), *Life-span developmental psychology: Historical and generational effects* (pp. 1–15). New York: Academic.

Steinberg, L., Lamborn, S. D., Darling, N., Mounts, N. S., & Dornbusch, S. M. (1994). Over-time changes in adjustment and competence among adolescents from authoritative, authoritarian, indulgent, and neglected homes. *Child Development, 65,* 754–770.

Steinberg, L., & Morris, A. S. (2000). Adolescent development. *Annual Review of Psychology, 52,* 83–110.

Steinberg, L., & Silk, J. S. (2002). Parenting adolescents. In M. Bornstein (Ed.), *Handbook of parenting: Vol. 1. Children and parenting* (pp. 103–133). Mahwah, NJ: Lawrence Erlbaum Associates.

Steinberg, L., & Silverberg, S. (1986). The vicissitudes of autonomy in early adolescence. *Child Development, 57,* 841–851.

Thornberry, T. P., Freeman-Gallant, A., Lizotte, A. J., Krohn, M. D., & Smith, C. A. (2003). Linked lives: The intergenerational transmission of antisocial behavior. *Journal of Abnormal Child Psychology, 31,* 171–185.

Wiebe, D. J., Berg, C. A., Korbel, C., Palmer, D. L., Beveridge, R. M., Upchurch, R., Lindsay, R., Swinyard, M. T., & Donaldson, D. L. (in press). Children's appraisals of maternal involvement in coping with diabetes: Enhancing our understanding of adherence, metabolic control, and quality of life across adolescence. *Journal of Pediatric Psychology.*

III

DECISION MAKING
IN THE REAL WORLD

The authors of previous chapters in this volume have, either implicitly or explicitly, suggested how their theories and research have implications for decision making in everyday contexts. The three chapters in Part III take an additional, and critical, step forward. Specifically, each author addresses decision making in specific contexts that have serious implications for adolescent wellbeing and treatment. The authors in this part were asked to go beyond describing their own work, to place research on adolescent decision making within the "real world" of legal, medical, and educational institutions. They have highlighted both the ways in which adolescent decision makers are viewed by these institutions and the ways in which their judgments and decisions are affected by the choices they have to make. In each chapter, implications and suggestions for policymakers and educators are explored in detail.

In chapter 8, Finken addresses decisions about abortions and the role of consultants (e.g., romantic partners, friends, family) in making those decisions. The author begins by detailing the policy debates surrounding adolescent abortion and differences among states in laws regarding the permissibility of adolescent's making abortion decisions with or without parental consent. Subsequently, age-related patterns of the use of consultants in making critical decisions, and abortion in particular, are reviewed. Finken then explores the implications of extant research on adolescent's consultation with peers and adults, asking two key questions: Are parental involvement laws necessary to ensure that parents play some role in adolescents' abortion decisions? Is parental involvement actually beneficial for an adolescent attempting to make a pregnancy resolution decision?

In her review, Finken (chap. 8) notes that significant decisions by children and adolescents are often made in consultation with others. Consultants influence numerous components of the decision-making process. For example, consultants can affect (a) the particular alternatives adolescents consider, (b) adolescents' awareness of possible consequences, and (c) adolescents' assessments of possible consequences (e.g., their likelihood and desirability). Determining whom adolescents consult with and about which issues they consult is therefore a critical topic for both uncovering contextual influences on decision making and—in the case of abortion decisions—examining and, perhaps challenging, laws that compel adolescents to consult with their parents. In the latter section of her chapter, Finken reviews research indicating that most adolescent girls do indeed consult with their parents (mothers in particular), as well as best friends and (almost universally) romantic partners, about their pregnancies and abortion decisions. Questions Finken raises and that must be addressed by future researchers are: How productive are these consultations? How valuable and realistic is the input pregnant girls receive from their various consultants? What role does psychosocial maturation play in deciding whether to involve consultants and which consultants should pregnant girls value most highly?

In chapter 9, Cauffman and Woolard also address the importance of psychosocial maturation in adolescent decision making. They begin their chapter by discussing the historical changes in the judicial system's perceptions of adolescent decision-making competence, as well as theory and research that challenge assumptions often made in the legal system about adolescent competence. A key point of their thesis is that "the assumptions of law are not necessarily guided by developmental reality" (p. 280). Specifically, whereas, juvenile offenders were once treated as too socially and cognitively immature to make reasoned autonomous decisions about participation in illegal activities, the current judicial system is likely to assume that even young adolescent offenders (e.g., 13-year-olds) are (or can be held) accountable for their crimes. This historical trend has been guided by (a) the media's depictions of juvenile offenders as "predators"; (b) increases in high-profile murders by adolescents (e.g., Columbine); and (c) reliance on outdated research on adolescent cognitive development.

Cauffman and Woolard (chap. 9) propose that reliance on traditional tests of intellectual competence (e.g., standardized intelligence tests; Piagetian measures) fail to provide a complete picture of adolescent decision-making competence. They suggest that assessments of competence should also include measures of psychosocial competence. Although definitions of psychosocial competence vary among theorists, they converge on the notion that this competence involves (a) responsibility (e.g., resistance to conformity pressures and autonomy); (b) perspective (e.g., perceptions of risk, understanding the complexity of situations); and (c) temperance (e.g., temporal perspective, ability to inhibit impulses). These authors review research on the relationships among psychosocial maturity, age, and decisions about engagement in illegal activities. They go on to present research in support of their contention about the importance of psychosocial maturity for determining whether adolescents can be held culpable for their actions. Their work illustrates age trends in psychosocial maturity and the importance of level of psychosocial maturation in predicting decisions to engage in prosocial activities. This research thus serves as a challenge to those who believe that young adolescents can be held responsible for their crimes and as an opportunity for policymakers to review their assumptions concerning the meaning of competence and its development.

In chapter 10, Galotti focuses on the development of goal setting, the relationship between goal setting and decision making, and implications for research on goal setting for educators. In most theories of decision making, goals serve to motivate individuals to formulate plans and, more generally, to give individuals a sense of purpose. Unfortunately, most research on goal setting has either focused on adults or, when children and adolescents have been participants, has involved artificial tasks. As a foundation for her research, Galotti discusses *image theory*, in which individuals begin with a multitude of possible goals and eventually "winnow" these down to one or two optimal candidates. This is accomplished by comparing each goal to each of three images: A value image (e.g., moral principles), a trajectory image (e.g., future aspirations), and a strategic image (means by which goals can be achieved. Goals incompatible with one or more of these images are discounted.

In her research with children and adolescents, Galotti (chap. 10) found considerable support for her developmental hypotheses in which adolescence is seen as a period in which goal setting and planning become more flexible, more systematic, and more future-oriented. Specifically, relative to children, 8th-grade and 12th-grade adolescents not only had more goals in more diverse settings, but also had more complex and controllable goals that were temporally extended into the future (specifically, over the entire life span). Even in the adolescent groups, however, large differences were found between 8th and 12th graders. Galotti speculates that the dramatic difference observed between these two age groups could have arisen because of (a) cognitive developmental differences; (b) sociocultural influences (e.g., adolescents may feel compelled to develop more complex and temporally extended goals as the end of high school approaches); and (c) an interaction between these potential influences. From an educational standpoint, Galotti's work suggests the need for interventions to improve early adolescents' goal-setting abilities to better prepare them for the plethora of important decisions they will need to make by the end of high school.

The three chapters in this part converge on the importance of examining decision making, its components, and correlates in real-life situations. This convergence suggests, as emphasized throughout this volume, a need for more interaction and collaboration among "basic" and "applied" researchers interested in decision making and its development. These chapters highlight developmental and contextual influences on important, real-life decisions and draw attention to some of the factors (e.g., media, peers, parents) that both influence decision making and point policymakers toward the possibility of changes in educational and legal practices.

8

The Role of Consultants in Adolescents' Decision Making: A Focus on Abortion Decisions

Laura L. Finken

Creighton University

Although rates have been declining significantly in recent years, nearly 1 million adolescent girls become pregnant in the United States every year (Alan Guttmacher Institute, 1999). Out of all of the developed Western countries, an adolescent girl from the United States has the highest risk of becoming pregnant (Ambuel, 1995). Almost 4 out of 10 teenage pregnancies end in selected abortion (Alan Guttmacher Institute, 1999) and adolescents account for nearly one fifth of the abortions performed in the United States (Alan Guttmacher Institute, 2003). Since the Supreme Court's legalization of abortion in 1973, there has been a whirlwind of state legislation designed to progressively restrict access to abortion (for a review, see Limber & Pagliocca, 2000). Currently, the most intense controversy about adolescent abortion revolves around consultation: that is, whether or not minors should be legally required to consult with their parents prior to obtaining an abortion. Thirty-two states have mandatory parental involvement laws in effect for adolescent abortions and another 10 states have laws on the books, although they are not currently enforced (Alan Guttmacher Institute, 2001). Mandatory parental involvement policies indicate that courts do not trust adolescents to choose appropriate consultants (Limber, 1992) and that the courts perceive adolescents as being incapable of making abortion decisions on their own (Adler, Smith, & Tschann, 1998).

As highlighted by the policy debates surrounding adolescent abortion, a central issue surrounding children's and adolescents' judgment is whether or not they are competent to make major life decisions on their own. Curiously,

255

the courts' presumption of the incapacity of adolescents as a justification for parental involvement policies is both flawed and antithetical to its own arguments (see Ambuel & Rappaport, 1992, and Soper, 1999, for reviews). Not surprisingly then, the legislative policies surrounding adolescent abortion vary chaotically from state to state; a pregnant teenager in Washington, DC, has the explicit legal right to make the decision on her own, whereas a pregnant teenager in Biloxi, Mississippi, is required by law to involve *both* of her parents before she may seek an abortion (Alan Guttmacher Institute, 2001). Although laws are commonly perceived as being inconsistent, even social scientists do not agree on the issue of adolescents' competency. On one hand, researchers argue that adolescents should be considered mature and therefore competent to make decisions (e.g., decisions regarding treatment— Weithorn, 1983; intellectual freedoms—Moshman, 1993, 1999; and abortion—Melton, 1986; Ambuel & Rappaport, 1992). Yet, on the other hand, researchers argue that adolescents should not be considered mature and thus not culpable for their crimes (e.g., Cauffman & Steinberg, 2000; Steinberg & Cauffman, 1996). These discrepancies arise, in part, from differences in how maturity is operationally defined and analyzed (e.g., focusing on cognitive factors, such as identifying alternatives, vs. focusing on psychosocial factors, such as temperance), and in part, these discrepancies are related to how adolescents are grouped (e.g., early adolescents vs. later adolescents). However, what is eminently clear from the incongruous judicial rulings, disparate legislative policies, and existing literature is that the issue of adolescents' decision-making competency is complex and far from being resolved.

Many of the significant decisions facing today's children and adolescents that elicit such concern from society are decisions that require the minor to decide whether or not to participate in a certain behavior (e.g., use drugs, have sex, seek an abortion). Research indicates that these "whether to do" decisions are subjectively very difficult ones for adolescents to resolve and that when faced with these hard decisions, adolescents seek information and support from others (Fischhoff, 1996). Accordingly, many of the consequential decisions that children and adolescents make involve consultation with others (e.g., friends). Investigating the role of consultants is a legitimate and potentially beneficial approach to decision making. The examination of developmental consultation patterns can provide researchers with insight into adolescents' level of cognitive functioning and competence, as well as provide policymakers and educators with practical information about potential sources of advice and the design of effective interventions for children and adolescents (Wintre, Hicks, McVey, & Fox, 1988).

Indeed, understanding the role of consultants is essential for an appreciation of the social influences that underlie decision making in the real world. The purpose of the present chapter is to examine the role of consultants in decision making. First, this chapter outlines the relevant research regarding adolescent decision making and consultants in general, then it addresses adolescents' significant relationships that serve as the basis for consultation, and finally, this chapter highlights the role of consultants in adolescents' decisions by focusing specifically on pregnancy-resolution decisions.

DECISION MAKING AND CONSULTANTS

Consultant choice is an essential facet for understanding the decision-making process because the input that children and adolescents receive from other people has the potential to influence so many of the components considered requisite for competent decision making. Theorists have identified a variety of factors considered to be fundamental in traditional models of decision making. In reviewing the literature, Furby and Beyth-Marom (1992) concluded that among the normative models of decision making, several steps were considered necessary for good decision making: (a) identifying potential options, (b) identifying the potential consequences of each option, (c) evaluating the desirability of each potential consequence, (d) gauging the likelihood of each consequence, and (e) combining all of the previous steps to devise a guideline or rule for making the decision. Furby and Beyth-Marom (1992) further suggested that the reason that adolescents may make decisions that adults consider to be risky is that adolescents may approach these five steps from a different perspective than do adults (e.g., adolescents may assess the likelihood of the possible consequences differently).

Consultants play an essential role in the development of children's and adolescents' competent decision making, according to Byrnes' (1998) self-regulation model of decision making. The self-regulation model incorporates advice-seeking from knowledgeable sources as characteristic of the generation phase of self-regulated decision making. Moreover, competent decision makers (e.g., parents, teachers) can foster children's decision-making skills by identifying the connection between children's actions and specific outcomes, as well as by interpreting the desirability or undesirability of these outcomes (Byrnes, 1998). In a series of empirical studies (e.g., Byrnes & McClenny, 1994; Byrnes, Miller, & Reynolds, 1999), Byrnes and his colleagues have compared adolescents' and adults' approaches to making decisions. This research indicates that there are, in fact, developmental differences in various components of decision making (e.g., adults use different strategies and are able process more information than young adolescents when faced with complex decision tasks). Thus, involving experts or other adults in adolescents' decisions has the potential to improve the quality of the decision making.

It is not from adults alone, though, that adolescents can advance their decision-making skills. Collaboration, or consultation, with peers can improve the quality of adolescents' reasoning. Moshman and Geil (1998) demonstrated that interaction with peers when trying to solve a problem led to dramatic improvement in older adolescents' reasoning. Indeed, social interaction with peers is proposed to have a special function in the development of adolescents' rational thinking by encouraging reflection, reconstruction, and the justification of ideas (Moshman, 1995). Along this line, Hunter (1984) revealed that adolescents' interactions with their parents and interactions with their peers serve different socializing functions. Although adolescents' interactions with their parents were characteristically unilateral, adolescents interacted reciprocally with their friends through co-construction. Thus, interaction with peers also has the potential to improve the quality of adolescents' decision making.

On the other hand, previous studies demonstrate that consultants, whether adolescent or adult, do not simply act as passive sounding boards; they actively participate in decisions and attempt to sway the outcome according to their own preferences (Farber, 1991). Furthermore, there is a well-established line of literature illustrating that simply adding more voices does not necessarily improve the quality of thinking nor the outcome (e.g., Dishion, McCord, & Poulin, 1999; Esser & Lindoerfer, 1989; Janis, 1989). Therefore, depending on the situation and depending on the choice of advisors, consultants have the potential both to aid in the decision-making process, as well as to impede it.

Clearly then, within traditional decision-making frameworks, consultation plays a considerable role in the process of decision making. When children and adolescents seek advice from people regarding a decision, their consultants are in the position to identify particular options and consequences, to give their own subjective opinions about the desirability and likelihood of those consequences, and even to promote a particular approach that minors should follow when making the decision. As a result, consultants are crucial to understanding the decision-making process because they have the potential to directly influence so many components of decision making. In fact, after a decision has been made, the consultation that occurred during the time surrounding the decision can affect how people adjust to their decisions later (e.g., M. B. Bracken, Klerman, & M. Bracken, 1978b; Major & Cozzarelli, 1992).

Even alternative models of decision making (i.e., those that accentuate the role of heuristics as opposed to the components of decision making) are recognizing the significance of social factors in the process of making decisions. In uncertain situations, such as an unexpected pregnancy, individuals are more likely to utilize heuristics to simplify the cognitive demands placed on them. As outlined by Chen and Chaiken (1999), the application of heuristics is dependent on social factors. In fact, specific heuristics outline the role that consultants may play in decision making. For example, if adolescents perceive a consensus among their peer group about a topic, they may use this to formulate their own attitudes regarding that issue. Interestingly, this consensus heuristic has even been demonstrated when the issue has high personal relevance for the decision maker (Chen & Chaiken, 1999).

Traditionally, much of the concern about adolescents' and children's consultants is that minors will depend too heavily on the advice of their peers who themselves are potentially lacking in competent decision-making skills (e.g., Mann, Harmoni, & Power, 1989). Indeed, in their rulings (e.g., *Lee v. Weisman*, 1992), the courts have even referred to the perceived susceptibility of adolescents to peer influence as a justification for protective legal policies that limit adolescents' autonomy (Scott, Reppucci, & Woolard, 1995; see C. Crosby & Reppucci, 1993, for an extended review of the legal system's treatment of adolescents). When examining the myriad changes that occur in how and with whom adolescents spend their time, it is evident that major transformations occur in children's relationships beginning in early adolescence (Fuligni & Eccles, 1993) and that these changes have implications for how consultants may influence adolescents' decision making.

ADOLESCENT RELATIONSHIPS

Although it is a normal and a necessary part of growing up, adolescents' desire to establish their autonomy can be unsettling for adults. As adolescents struggle to define their identity, they begin to assert themselves as individuals separate from their parents (Steinberg & Silk, 2002). The search for identity has implications for adolescents' decision making. Adolescents' concept of their identity will impact the choices that they make, and these decisions, in turn, will help to solidify their identity. It is to be expected that there will be fluctuations in adolescents' goals, decision-making strategies, and even in their choice of consultants (Jacobs & Ganzel, 1993). Not surprisingly then, there exists a developmental trend for adolescents to seek additional sources for support and guidance. In childhood, parents are the most frequent source of support; in early adolescence (approximately ages 11 to 13), parents and same-gender friends provide equivalent amounts of support; in middle adolescence (ages 14 to 16), same-gender peers become the dominant source of support; and finally in late adolescence/early adulthood (ages 17 to 19), there exists a three-way tie between romantic partners, same-gender friends, and mother (Furman & Buhrmester, 1992). Thus, romantic partners, peers, and family are all potentially important consultants for adolescents contemplating decisions.

The Role of Romantic Partners

Romantically, adolescence is a time of meaningful changes. The number of opposite-gender "friends" increases significantly in early adolescence (Feiring & Lewis, 1991) and younger adolescents express a strong interest in romantic relationships, even if they have not directly experienced them (Connolly, Craig, Goldberg, & Pepler, 1999). Intimacy with romantic partners contributes to adolescents' self-esteem in a way that is unique from the effect of intimacy with same-gender friends on adolescents' self-esteem (Connolly & Konarski, 1994). By middle adolescence, approximately half of all adolescents report having a current romantic relationship (Feiring, 1996). During adolescence, romantic relationships grow increasingly supportive (Furman & Simon, 1998). By late adolescence, the romantic partner is typically the first person named on a list of significant people in adolescents' lives (Buhrmester, 1996; Furman & Wehner, 1994). Surprisingly though, very little attention has been given to the role of adolescents' romantic relationships (Furman & Simon, 1998; Steinberg & Morris, 2001). Indeed, false conceptualizations about the insignificance of adolescent romantic relationships have impeded the progress of research in this area (Collins, 2003).

Theoretically, the romantic partner may play a crucial role in the attachment, caregiving, supportive, and affiliative needs of adolescents. In times of distress then, the romantic partner may be sought as an attachment figure and a source of support (Furman & Simon, 1998). Collins (2003) maintained that adolescent romantic relationships have meaningful implications for adolescents' development and that these relationships play a distinct role in adolescents' lives that is not encompassed by other types of relationships (i.e., relationships with family or friends). A few studies reveal that adolescents consistently seek advice from their romantic partners about situations as diverse as career/educational choices, how to handle interpersonal/friendship conflicts, which medical treatments to seek, and whether or not to visit a family-planning clinic (Finken & Jacobs, 1996; Limber, 1992). In sum, there is both theoretical and empirical evidence to indicate that romantic partners may be influential in adolescents' decisions. However, current reviews of the adolescent literature highlight the paucity of research addressing the role of romantic relationships in adolescents' lives and call for expanded investigation into this area (e.g., Collins, 2003; Steinberg & Morris, 2001).

The Role of Peers

Although the desire for companionship and intimacy with peers exists across all ages in childhood (Buhrmester & Furman, 1987), the form and function of friendships undergo dramatic changes in adolescence. Beginning in early adolescence, the establishment of close and intimate relationships becomes increasingly desired (Berndt & Perry, 1986; Buhrmester, 1990) and in general, friendships become more meaningful (Berndt, 1992). The amount of contact with same-gender friends continues to increase throughout childhood until, for the first time in early adolescence, contact with same-gender friends surpasses contact with adults (Feiring & Lewis, 1991). In fact, adolescents spend more time with their friends than they do alone or with family members (Savin-Williams & Berndt, 1990). Moreover, the perceived importance of same-gender friends increases from middle childhood to early adolescence (Buhrmester & Furman, 1987). During adolescence, peers' influence on a child's self-esteem gradually overtakes parents' influence until by the end of adolescence, the impact of peers' beliefs vastly overwhelm parents' influence on self-esteem (Harter, 1990). With all of these changes, adolescents may begin to depend more on the guidance and advice of their peers (Fuligni, Eccles, Barber, & Clements, 2001).

Understandably, these normative transformations may raise red flags for concern; however, a high degree of apprehension about peers' influence may be unwarranted. To begin with, the influence that friends have in adolescence has been greatly overestimated (Berndt, 1992). Previous research showing a high susceptibility of adolescents to negative peer pressure comes from extremely contrived methods usually involving hypothetical scenarios and self-report (Berndt, 1992; Brown, 1990). In real life, friends' influence on each other is rarely coercive, but is instead reciprocal (Berndt, 1992); as teens are being influenced by their friends, they also exerting influence on their friends. Furthermore, most of the disconcerting developmental trends about peers' influence fade after early adolescence. Older adolescents, as compared to younger adolescents, view group membership as less important (Brown, Eicher, & Petric, 1986; Gavin & Furman, 1989), show lower levels of peer orientation (Fuligni & Eccles, 1993), report more flexibility for individuality with the group (Gavin & Furman, 1989; Shulman, Laursen, Kalman, & Karpovsky, 1997), and perceive less pressure to conform to group norms (Clasen & Brown, 1985). It is worth noting, however, that this research as well is based on self-report data that by design cannot measure implicit pressures.

Although the influence that peers have over one another may have been overstated by earlier research, there is no question about the importance of peers in the lives of adolescents. Adolescents clearly place great value on their friendships, and as a result, when making decisions, adolescents are likely to turn to their friends for advice and reassurance. Yet, each adolescent's response to peer influence is, in fact, mediated by several factors (e.g., individual personality traits, age, socialization), not the least of which is the role of the family in the adolescent's life (Brown, 1990; Steinberg & Morris, 2001).

The Role of Family

Companionship with family members starts to decrease significantly in early adolescence (Buhrmester & Furman, 1987). Larson and Richards (1991) found that as adolescents grow older, they spend less time at home and less time interacting with family members even when they are at home; indeed, ninth graders spend only half of the time with family members as do preadolescents. Moreover, this trend continues into late adolescence (Csikszentmihalyi & Larson, 1984). There is also evidence that adolescents and their parents become more emotionally detached (Larson & Richards, 1991). In fact, Steinberg and Silverberg (1986) suggested that in the development of autonomy, adolescents replace their previous dependency on their parents with a dependency on their peers. In early adolescence, parents become a less important provider of intimate disclosure (Buhrmester & Furman, 1987), and there is a peak in the tension between teens and parents during early and middle adolescence (Furman & Buhrmester, 1992). Also, recent meta-analyses suggest that although the rate of conflict declines in middle and late adolescence, the affect surrounding conflict continues to increase with age and pubertal maturation (Steinberg & Silk, 2002). These developmental trends within the family, taken in concert with the increasing importance of peers for adolescents, can facilitate the concern that peers' influence will usurp the parents' place in their adolescent's life.

However, the assumption that the lost centrality of the family is taken over by adolescents' friends is simplistic and premature. This misconception has been created, in part, by hypothetical studies that artificially pit parental influence against peer influence. This approach fails to represent the more realistic picture of both influences impacting adolescents' behaviors (Youniss & Haynie, 1992). Although it is true that the family recedes as the major portion of daily interactions, only certain portions of family time decline, specifically, time with the unit as a whole (i.e., parents and siblings together), time with the extended family members, and time with the siblings. The amount of time adolescents spend with their mother and father individually does not decrease nor does the amount of time spent talking with their parents (Larson & Richards, 1991). Complimentary findings are provided by Feiring and Lewis (1991), who reported that although contact with adults in general declines in early adolescence, contact with the family remains the same as in middle childhood.

Furthermore, the subjective quality of the adolescents' time spent with the family does not erode with age, with the minor exception of less positive affect during family interactions between middle childhood and early adolescence (Larson & Richards, 1991). Larson and Richards characterize this as merely a transitional process rather than as a dramatic division between adolescents and their parents. Finally, although teens report increasingly more positive interactions with their friends, there are only limited increases in the amount of time spent with friends that do not completely account for the reduced time spent with family members. Instead, among boys, family time is replaced with time alone, and among girls, family time is replaced with a combination of time alone and time with friends (Larson & Richards, 1991).

Adolescents' identification with their peers does not lead to the disintegration of relationships within the family. Adolescents who are closely affiliated with their peer group are more likely to turn to their parents, as well as to their friends, for guidance when faced with problems. Specifically, adolescents who identify highly with a peer group are more inclined to talk about their problems, ask for help from both peers and parents, accept offers of aid, view interactions positively, and to resolve their problems (Pombeni, Kirchler, & Palmonari, 1990). Moreover, adolescents' relationships with their families actually impact their interactions with their peers. Brown (1990) reported that adolescents' reactions to peer influence varies among family structures and parenting styles. Similarly, Whitaker and Miller (2000) found that adolescents' communication with their parents moderates the influence of peer norms for risky behaviors. Even adolescents' selection of a peer group is connected to the parenting styles within adolescents' families (Durbin, Darling, Steinberg, & Brown, 1993).

During adolescence, families continue to be a salient source of guidance and support for adolescents. Adolescents do listen to their parents' counsel and, at least to some extent, moderate their behavior accordingly. For example, an extensive literature affirms the effect of communication between parents and adolescents about sexual issues on adolescents' sexual attitudes and behaviors (e.g., DiIorio, Kelley, & Hockenberry-Eaton, 1999; Karofsky, Zeng, & Kosorok, 2001; Miller, Norton, Fan, & Christopherson, 1998; for a detailed review, see Miller, Benson, & Galbraith, 2001). Parents' influence on their adolescents is especially strong when there is a good underlying relationship between the parent and the child. White (1996) found that when the parent–child relationship is open and relatively harmonious, parents are perceived as having considerable influence regarding their adolescents' social activities (which is typically conceptualized as a peer-dominated realm of influence).

The research is also clear that mothers, in particular, are central to the social support system of adolescents. Mothers report having more open and positive communication with adolescents than do fathers (White, 1996), mothers' advice is more frequently sought than fathers' advice on how to handle situations with peers, mothers are often approached earlier in the decision-making process than are fathers (Finken & Jacobs, 1996), mothers' opinions are rated as more important (Limber, 1992), and communication with mothers is more influential on adolescents' behavior than communication with fathers (e.g., DiIorio, Kelley, & Hockenberry-Eaton, 1999; Karofsky et al., 2001).

Social interactions between adolescents and their peers and between adolescents and their parents take on different forms and serve different functions, but both are important for adolescent development (Hunter, 1984; Tokuno, 1986; Youniss & Haynie, 1992). Hunter (1984) compared the interactions of parents and friends during adolescence and revealed that peers interact more mutually (i.e., utilizing negotiation and co-construction), whereas parents act more unilaterally (i.e., power based on authority and expertise). Rather than directly trying to influence the adolescent's behavior, the most frequent form of interacting for both peers and parents is social verification, or reassurance, that is initiated by the adolescent. Parents and peers provide different types of support and influence; parents interact based on greater experience and knowledge in a nurturing manner, whereas peers share mutual experiences and understanding (Hunter, 1984). Indeed, Fuligni et al.'s (2001) longitudinal study found that adolescents maintain healthy, interdependent relationships with both their parents and their friends. Within the context of these relationships, adolescents seek guidance from both their parents and their peers on everyday concerns, as well as on future-oriented decisions.

Research indicates that children and adolescents seek and/or follow the advice of parents and friends based appropriately on the type of decision being considered. Wintre et al. (1988) found that even children as young as 8 years old seek different sources of advice for hypothetical problems, depending on the domain of the problem (i.e., what purchase to make, a disagreement with a friend, and a problem with a parent). Furthermore, even general findings, such as the fact that adolescents seek more advice from friends and less from adults with age, are dependent on the topic. Tokuno (1986) found that older adolescents who were making the transition to young adulthood also discriminate in the value that they placed on varying sources of advice depending on the situation. Specifically, Tokuno observed that friends' advice is considered the least influential on career decisions, as compared to self-identity issues and intimate relationships, and that even young adults continue to seek their parents' guidance on future-oriented, or career, decisions.

Wilks (1986) examined a wide variety of decision domains and found that there are clear differences in the patterns of consultation depending on the type of decision. In this study, Wilks surveyed parents, their adolescents, and the adolescents' friends. There was consistency from all three groups in that parents' advice was the most important for educational and vocational decisions (i.e., attending a university, what classes to take, and choosing a career), money managing decisions, and decisions regarding a potential spouse. All three groups also agreed that for certain "current" decisions (i.e., how to dress, what social events to attend, what clubs to join, what books to read, what magazines to buy, and which hobbies to participate in), friends' guidance was more relevant. On other types of decisions, the groups did not agree on whose advice was the most important (e.g., attending drinking parties, personal problems, whom to date). They concluded that adolescents are more likely to turn to their friends for advice on short-term issues, but for future-oriented decisions that have the potential for a long-term impact on their lives, adolescents are more likely to seek their parents' guidance. Similarly, Biddle, Bank, and Marlin (1980) reported that adolescents consider their friends' input as more important for decisions regarding drinking, and their parents' advice as more important for decisions about school issues. Taken together, this research indicates that the context of the decision is salient to children and adolescents in determining whom they will turn to for advice.

ABORTION DECISION MAKING

Finken and Jacobs (1996) demonstrated how essential the context (i.e., the nature of the decision) is for understanding adolescents' consultant choice regarding abortion decision making. Until more recently, empirical studies that directly addressed the role of consultants in adolescent abortion decisions had been quite limited. Consequently, research findings regarding adolescents' use of consultants and other areas of decision making, such as medical decisions, were being extrapolated to describe adolescents' abortion decisions (e.g., Lewis, 1987). Although there are elements of other types of decisions intertwined in an unintentional pregnancy (e.g., health implications, implications for the future), a pregnancy resolution decision is unique and carries with it a potential stigma (e.g., Major & Gramzow, 1999) that other decisions do not possess. Thus, the role of consultants in other types of decisions may not extend to abortion decisions.

Finken and Jacobs (1996) presented 169 older adolescents (ages 18 to 20) with multiple decisions across four contexts of decisions (i.e., interpersonal, future-oriented/career, medical, and pregnancy resolution) to compare the consultation patterns of abortion decision making with the other three decision domains. They examined both the order of consultation and the frequency of consultation of a large number of consultants (e.g., parents, friends, romantic partner, siblings, extended family members, teachers, professionals) across these different types of decisions. Many of their findings confirm the role of consultants in decision making in general; romantic partners, friends, and parents are all perceived as meaningful sources of advice and support for adolescents facing decisions.

Specifically, parents play a substantial role for important life decisions. When presented with anticipated decisions regarding medical treatments and vocational choices, adolescents listed their mothers and fathers as the two most frequent consultants. In the order of how adolescents would approach individuals for guidance, mothers and fathers were also the first people whom adolescents reported that they would turn to for advice when faced with these decisions. In comparison, the role of peers as consultants was more generalized. Across all of the different types of decisions, the majority of the adolescents indicated that they would seek their best friend's advice about what to do. Although other individuals had higher frequencies of anticipated consultation for a particular decision, no other consultant received this consistent of an endorsement across all types of decisions. However, what the major finding of this study indicated, and what this study was specifically designed to test, was that abortion decisions do, as described subsequently, produce unique consultation patterns that cannot be adequately summarized by other types of decisions. So, although there may be similarities among decisions in a generalized sense, the aforementioned research indicates that we must look at the research specifically investigating whom adolescents turn to for advice when considering an abortion, and what impact this advice has on their decisions.

Whom Do Adolescents Consult?

When faced with a decision about whether or not to have an abortion, most adolescents do seek guidance (Adler et al., 1998; Limber & Pagliocca, 2000). Figure 8.1 summarizes the information regarding whom adolescents typically

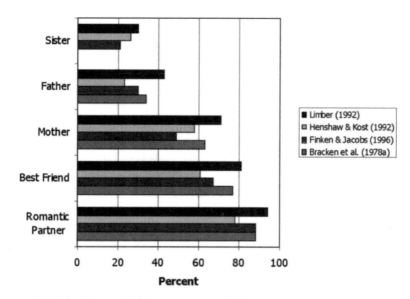

FIG. 8.1.   Percent of adolescents who sought the advice of various consultants about an abortion decision across different studies.

consult about an abortion decision from the studies that have provided the most complete data. The variation that exists among the exact percentage of adolescents who would consult specific individuals across studies likely results from methodological differences in (a) the nature of the decisions (i.e., actual vs. hypothetical); (b) the ages of the participants; (c) the origin of the sample (e.g., clinic vs. school); (d) the ethnic make-up of the samples (e.g., predominantly African American vs. predominantly European American); and (e) the time during which the data were collected (i.e., ranging from 1978 to 1996). Given the vast differences in the design of these studies, the similarity of the overall consultation patterns is striking. The research converges to reveal that adolescents consistently seek input from certain key consultants when faced with an unexpected pregnancy.

Without exception, the romantic partner is the most frequently consulted person for adolescents contemplating abortion. In fact, Finken and Jacobs (1996) reported that not only is the romantic partner the most frequently consulted (selected by 88%), but the romantic partner is also typically the first person to be approached in the process of making the decision. Limber (1992) revealed that adolescents and young adults rate the partner's input about this decision as the most important. M. B. Bracken, Klerman, and M. Bracken (1978a) surveyed never-married pregnant women and found, not surprisingly, that young women who choose to have an abortion are significantly less likely to discuss their decision with their partner than those who complete the pregnancy. Yet, even among those who obtain an abortion, the overwhelming majority (83%) still includes their partner in the decision. Undoubtedly, the romantic partner is a pivotal consultant in adolescents' pregnancy resolution decisions.

Also clearly important as a source of support for adolescents is their best friend; across studies, the best friend is the next most likely consulted person. Additionally, following the romantic partner in the order of consultation, the best friend is usually the second person to whom adolescents would turn for advice when faced with a decision about abortion (Finken & Jacobs, 1996). However, M. B. Bracken et al. (1978a) found that young women do make a distinction based on their resolution intention; whereas 86% of women who intend to deliver the baby discuss their decision with their best friend, only 68% of women who intend to seek an abortion discuss it with their best friend, possibly due to the stigmatization surrounding abortion. Furthermore, Limber (1992) identified a developmental trend in which adolescents are more likely than young adults to discuss their pregnancy resolution decisions with their friends.

Given its relevance to social policies, a greater number of studies have focused on the issue of parental involvement in adolescents' abortion decisions and consistent trends appear across the various studies. First, a majority of adolescents discuss their pregnancy with at least one parent (e.g., Blum,

Resnick, & Stark, 1987; Henshaw & Kost, 1992; Resnick, Bearinger, Stark, & Blum, 1994; Rosen, 1980). Again, depending upon samples and methodological designs, studies of adolescents in this situation vary as to the percentage of adolescents who voluntarily inform their parents of the pregnancy, ranging from 51% (Griffin-Carlson & Mackin, 1993) to 91% (Zabin, Hirsch, Emerson, & Raymond, 1992). Second, adolescent girls are much more likely to seek out their mothers' advice about an abortion than their fathers' advice (Blum et al., 1987; Finken & Jacobs, 1996; Henshaw & Kost, 1992; Limber, 1992; Resnick et al., 1994; Zabin et al., 1992). Third, there is a developmental trend in which younger adolescents are more likely than older adolescents to include their parents in their decision about an abortion (Griffin-Carlson & Mackin, 1993; Henshaw & Kost, 1992).

Fourth, adolescents clearly consider their mother's input to be meaningful for their pregnancy resolution decision (e.g., M. B. Bracken et al., 1978b; Limber, 1992; Ortiz & Nuttall, 1987). Rosen (1980) found that most adolescent girls facing an unwanted pregnancy rate their mothers' influence as more important than their girl friends' influence and in fact, even rate their mothers' input as being as important as their male partners' input. Resnick et al. (1994) also reported that 1 year after the abortion, adolescents consider their mothers to have been the most helpful source of advice during the time surrounding their decision. Along this line, Young, Berkman, and Rehr (1975) found that adolescents overwhelmingly indicated that the most important person for helping them cope with an unexpected pregnancy is their mother.

Finally, whether or not an adolescent seeks her parents' advice about abortion is determined in large part by the nature of the relationship between the teen and her parents. In a large sample of over 1,500 adolescents who obtained abortions, Henshaw and Kost (1992) found that if adolescents have a good relationship with their mother (i.e., they can discuss their feelings, problems, and fears with her), they are more likely to tell at least one parent about their pregnancy. Similarly, Zabin et al. (1992) reported adolescents are more likely to inform their mothers of a pregnancy when they live at home with their mother and when they feel that they are able to talk about sexual issues with their mother. Simply stated, when adolescents perceive their parents to be supportive, adolescents will involve their parents in a pregnancy resolution decision (Resnick et al., 1994).

In some cases, however, adolescents do not inform their parents of an abortion decision. Adolescents who do not involve their parents in their pregnancy resolution decisions tend to be older (Griffin-Carlson & Mackin, 1993; Henshaw & Kost, 1992; Resnick et al., 1994), and they often exhibit other signs of autonomy or maturity, such as living apart from their parents, or being employed (Henshaw & Kost, 1992). Unfortunately, some adolescents may have valid concerns against involving their parents because, for example, they fear being forced into a decision against their wishes, or even because they fear a violent reaction (e.g., Adler et al., 1998; Limber & Pagliocca, 2000). Indeed, 45% of adolescents experience negative consequences when their parents find out about their pregnancies (e.g., being punished, problems between their parents); a small percentage report severely negative consequences—physical violence within the home or being forced to leave home (Henshaw & Kost, 1992). It is noteworthy that if adolescents do not feel comfortable discussing their pregnancy resolution decision with a parent, the vast majority will then seek advice from another adult who may act as a parental surrogate for them (Resnick et al., 1994; Zabin et al., 1992).

Beyond the romantic partner, best friend, and parents, adolescents list several other people as potential consultants and sources of support when they are faced with an unexpected pregnancy. The father, siblings, stepparent, other peers/friends, physicians, aunts, grandparents, counselors, teachers, coaches, ministers, and other adult friends have all been identified by adolescents as possible sources for advice on decisions regarding abortion (M. B. Bracken et al., 1978a; Finken & Jacobs, 1996; Resnick et al., 1994; Zabin et al. 1992).

The Impact of Consultation

Given that adolescents do in fact typically turn to others for advice about abortion decisions, it is crucial to understand what the effect of this consultation is on their decision-making process. Surprisingly though, relatively little research has directly investigated what impact consultation has on adolescents' thinking and decision about their pregnancy resolution (Limber & Pagliocca, 2000). Yet, the evidence that exists suggests that the influence of consultants is potentially very significant.

It is clear that the people with whom adolescents discuss their situation attempt to influence the adolescents' pregnancy resolution decision. Henshaw and Kost (1992) found that adolescents' consultants often pressure minors toward a particular choice. In fact, 54% of the pregnant adolescents report that someone has tried to persuade them to have an abortion, whereas 40% report that someone has tried to persuade them to continue the pregnancy. Farber (1991) observed that across all groups, regardless of socioeconomic status or ethnicity, the people who are consulted by pregnant adolescents "actively participated in and shaped the decision process according to their [own] preferences" (p. 714). Moreover, it is important to note that this pressure from advisors can influence the adolescents' decision making. Limber (1992) found that pressure from parents against adolescents' preferences weakens the strength of the adolescents' original decisions. Similarly, Eisen, Zellman, Leibowitz, Chow, and Evans (1983) reported that over one third of adolescents who initially wanted to complete the pregnancy later had an abortion. The vast majority of these young women reported experiencing strong pressure from their romantic partners or from their mothers to have an abortion. In fact, the second most frequently listed consequence of adolescents' parents being informed about their daughter's pregnancy was that the daughter reported that her parent(s) were forcing her to have an abortion (Henshaw & Kost, 1992).

Interestingly, adolescents do not appear to always be aware of the influences on their pregnancy resolution decisions. Evans (2001) interviewed over 1,300 pregnant Australian adolescents. The majority of teens reported that they had made their decision completely on their own without influence from anyone, and yet, there is evidence of the indirect influence of other people (i.e., their mother and sister) in their decision to continue or terminate the pregnancy. Among those adolescents who report experiencing direct influence from other people about their decision, only the partner's urging (either to have the abortion or to have the baby) significantly predicts the adolescents' decision. These findings suggest that the path of influence may vary by consultants; although romantic partners seem to have a direct influence on adolescents' abortion decisions, the influence of mothers and sisters may be more subtle.

Beyond the issue of what choice is made, consultation plays a central role in how adolescents cope with their pregnancy resolution decision. Ideally, talking with other people about stressful situations can facilitate the coping process. Along this line, Major and Gramzow (1999) followed 442 women who obtained an abortion for 2 years and revealed that emotional disclosure to others is related to women's coping over this period of time. M. B. Bracken et al. (1978b) also investigated the coping methods of unmarried pregnant women and found that consultation with others is one of the major ways of coping with their decision. Specifically, they observed that support from important people (e.g., parents, partners, friends) is associated with earlier acceptance of their decision, greater ease in making the decision, and increased happiness.

However, if consultants are not supportive, their input can actually lead to greater difficulty in coping. Major and Cozzarelli (1992) reported that young women who receive a negative response from their family, partners, or friends about their decision to have an abortion have higher depression scores initially following the procedure, as compared to young women who perceive their consultants to be completely supportive, even as compared to young women who do not consult with anyone prior to the abortion. Adolescents' sense of autonomy is also related to the acceptance of their pregnancy resolution decision. Zabin et al. (1992) observed that minors who make the decision for themselves are more satisfied with their choice than minors who feel that others have made the decision for them. Similarly, adolescents who alter their initial choice about their pregnancy resolution are significantly less satisfied with the outcome than those adolescents whose initial preference matches their final decision (Zabin et al., 1992).

IMPLICATIONS

Consultation is considered to be such an essential facet of decision making that legislatures are passing laws designating whom people should consult with prior to making certain decisions; the policies surrounding adolescent abortion decisions illustrate this point. Parental involvement laws require that adolescents consult with their parent(s) prior to obtaining an abortion. To evaluate these policies, two key questions need to be answered: first, whether these policies are necessary to ensure parental involvement and second, whether this involvement is beneficial for adolescents facing a pregnancy resolution decision (Adler & Tschann, 1993). A plethora of studies have addressed the first question; the majority of adolescents do, in fact, seek a parent's advice when deciding how to handle an unexpected pregnancy. Those minors who do not discuss a decision to obtain an abortion almost always discuss their situation with at least one other adult, and these adolescents are typically older and more independent. There are also valid reasons, such as a realistic fear of retribution, why some adolescents should not involve their parents (e.g., Ambuel, 1995).

The parental involvement policies are simply not practical for increasing parents' role in adolescent abortion decisions. If the family environment is a supportive one, adolescents do not typically need a law to encourage them to seek their parents' guidance; in fact, due to judicial bypass, parental involvement laws do not even increase consultation in dysfunctional families (M. C. Crosby & English, 1991). A judicial bypass is a required option under federal law, and it allows a minor to seek the court's authorization for an abortion in lieu of involving her parents (Limber & Pagliocca, 2000). Courts almost uniformly grant a bypass to minors seeking an abortion (Pliner & Yates, 1992), given that it is counterintuitive to argue that a minor is too immature to make a decision about abortion, and yet, that this same minor is, by default then, mature enough to assume the responsibilities of becoming a teenage parent (Stotland, 1996).

The answer to the second question, of whether parental involvement is beneficial to adolescents, is more complicated. Ideally, support from parents could indeed assist the adolescent in making her decision and coping with the outcome (e.g., M. B. Bracken et al., 1978b; Major & Cozzarelli, 1992; Worthington et al., 1991). However, the quality of parent–child interactions regarding an abortion decision is not guaranteed and the nature of these interactions varies depending upon the functioning of the family (Griffin-

Carlson & Schwanenflugel, 1998). Indeed, there is evidence from other domains, such as decisions about alcohol use and sexuality, that discussion with
parents may actually lead to greater risk taking among adolescents (Ennett,
Bauman, Foshee, Pemberton, & Hicks, 2001; O'Sullivan, Meyer-Bahlburg,
& Watkins, 2001). Family dynamics evolve and coalesce long before a child
becomes an adolescent, and parental involvement laws cannot magically
transform dysfunctional families into healthy ones (e.g., Resnick et al.,
1994). Furthermore, the relationships between adolescents and their families
are diverse and constantly changing. Laws intending to govern family interactions cannot accommodate such complex and individualistic considerations and, as a result, may lead to more harm than benefit (Moshman,
1993).

The empirical evidence provides no support for the assumption that parental involvement laws regarding adolescents' abortion decisions are beneficial or even necessary (Adler, Ozer, & Tschann, 2003), and they may even
cause harm. Thus, to understand why these policies are so popular, one
needs to be aware of the not-so-subtle agenda that remains unstated offi-
cially: These policies are designed to curtail abortions (Altman-Palm &
Tremblay, 1998; O'Keefe & Jones, 1990; Tomal, 2001). Ironically, these policies appear to be largely ineffective for this purpose as well. When parents
become involved, they often pressure minors to have an abortion (e.g., Eisen
et al., 1983; Henshaw & Kost, 1992). Moreover, studies comparing the abortion rates prior to and following the enactment of parental involvement laws
offer only mixed evidence, at best, of any direct impact on abortion rates
(e.g., Adler et al., 1998; Rogers & Miller, 1993).

On a broader note, to fully understand the process of adolescents' decision making, it is essential that researchers consider the role of consultants
within all contexts. Artificially conceptualizing the adolescent decision
maker as an isolated individual, analytically calculating and evaluating the
benefits and costs of a given decision, fails to capture the social and psychological complexity that is involved in real-life decisions (Farber, 1991; Jacobs
& Ganzel, 1993). Consultants actively participate in and influence the decision process, and although consultants have the potential to aid in decision
making (e.g., provide information, options, and support), there are also potential costs associated with consultation. The quality of the information
that is gleaned from consultants is strongly dependent on the quality and
agenda of the advisors themselves. Therefore, the persons to whom adolescents turn for advice is critical in determining the outcome of their decisions.

A step beyond this is to consider the impact of consultants' consultants.
For example, the existing literature verifies that adolescent girls almost unilaterally seek out their romantic partner's input about an unplanned pregnancy and that these partners have a direct influence on the resolution decision. But to whom do these adolescent boys themselves turn to for advice

and support—and how does this consultation, in turn, influence their decision about how the situation should be resolved? There is likely a wide web of social interplay that spins outward from the initial circle of consultants. Although Finken and Jacobs (1996) included adolescent males in their examination of consultation patterns and a few studies have examined the qualitative experiences of males involved with abortion (e.g., Buchanan & Robbins, 1990; Holmberg & Wahlberg, 2000), research addressing these broader consultation issues is essentially nonexistent.

Unfortunately, we know relatively little about the role of consultants in most of the decisions that adolescents face in today's society. What are the particular mechanisms through which consultants have their influence? Given what we know about the role of peers and family in adolescents' lives, it is likely that different consultants have varying paths of impact. For example, friends may influence the perceived desirability of possible consequences, whereas older consultants, especially those perceived as authority figures, may affect adolescents' confidence in their own preferences. With the exception of Evans (2001), the role of indirect or tacit consultant influence has not received much attention in decision-making research.

Also, we need to identify under which circumstances discussion with consultants will actually be beneficial for adolescents. For example, Sargent and Dalton (2001) found that parents' communication of disapproval prevented adolescent smoking, whereas Ennett et al. (2001) found that parent–child communication actually escalated adolescent tobacco use. The linkages involved in these relationships are intricate and undoubtedly interacting, and traditional approaches to decision making do not address these complexities of real-life decisions. Newer approaches are becoming more responsive to this need; Byrnes' (1998) self-regulation model incorporates moderating factors and can therefore encompass the psychosocial factors that are typically ignored by traditional decision-making models (e.g., heuristics, emotion, stress). For example, are the potential benefits of consultation (e.g., alternative perspectives, support) moderated by whether the consultation was voluntarily sought versus legally imposed?

Finally, there is a great need for future research to utilize mediational models to identify which intervening factors influence the impact of consultants on adolescents' behavior and to evaluate potential causal links among the factors involved. Much of the research on adolescents' decision making to date has focused on only one to two components in isolation. Yet, research is emerging that highlights the need to examine the role of multiple factors simultaneously to fully understand their impact on adolescents' risky behaviors (e.g., Lansford, Criss, Pettit, Dodge, & Bates, 2003). In order to gain insight into the interplay between these factors and to discover their relative importance for adolescents' decisions, future research needs to be ambitious by incorporating the multitude of factors and by employing sophisticated statistical techniques (e.g., structural equation modeling). To capture the complex and realistic picture of the process underlying adolescents' decisions, we must include the wider social environment of consultation in our models for understanding decision making.

REFERENCES

Adler, N. E., Ozer, E. J., & Tschann, J. M. (2003). Abortion among adolescents. *American Psychologist, 58*, 211–217.
Adler, N. E., Smith, L. B., & Tschann, J. M. (1998). Abortion among adolescents. In L. J. Beckman & S. M. Harvey (Eds.), *The new civil war: The psychology, culture and politics of abortion* (pp. 285–298). Washington, DC: American Psychological Association.
Adler, N. E., & Tschann, J. M. (1993). The abortion debate: Psychological issues for adult women and adolescents. In S. M. Matteo (Ed.), *American women in the nineties: Today's critical issues* (pp. 193–212). Boston, MA: Northeastern University Press.
Alan Guttmacher Institute. (1999). *Facts in brief: Teen sex and pregnancy.* New York: Author.
Alan Guttmacher Institute. (2001). *State policies in brief: Parental involvement in minors' abortions.* New York: Author.
Alan Guttmacher Institute. (2003). *Facts in brief: Induced abortion.* New York: Author.
Altman-Palm, N., & Tremblay, C. H. (1998). The effects of parental involvement laws and the AIDS epidemic on the pregnancy and abortion rates of minors. *Social Science Quarterly, 79*, 846–862.
Ambuel, B. (1995). Adolescents, unintended pregnancy, and abortion: The struggle for a compassionate social policy. *Current Directions in Psychological Science, 4*(1), 1–5.
Ambuel, B., & Rappaport, J. (1992). Developmental trends in adolescents' psychological and legal competence to consent to abortion. *Law and Human Behavior, 16*, 129–154.
Berndt, T. J. (1992). Friendships and friends' influence in adolescence. *Current Directions in Psychological Science, 1*(5), 156–159.
Berndt, T., & Perry, B. T. (1986). Children's perceptions of friendships as supportive relationships. *Developmental Psychology, 22*, 640–648.
Biddle, B. J., Bank, B. J., & Marlin, M. M. (1980). Parental and peer influence on adolescents. *Social Forces, 58*, 1057–1079.
Blum, R. W., Resnick, M. D., & Stark, P. (1987). The impact of a parental notification law on adolescent abortion decision making. *American Journal of Public Health, 77*, 619–620.
Bracken, M. B., Klerman, L. V., & Bracken, M. (1978a). Abortion, adoption, or motherhood: An empirical study of decision-making during pregnancy. *American Journal of Obstetrics and Gynecology, 130*, 251–262.
Bracken, M. B., Klerman, L. V., & Bracken, M. (1978b). Coping with pregnancy resolution among never-married women. *American Journal of Orthopsychiatry, 48*, 320–333.
Brown, B. B. (1990). Peer groups and peer cultures. In S. S. Feldman & G. R. Elliot (Eds.), *At the threshold: The developing adolescent* (pp. 171–196). Cambridge, MA: Harvard University Press.
Brown, B. B., Eicher, S. A., & Petrie, S. (1986). The importance of peer group ("crowd") affiliation in adolescence. *Journal of Adolescence, 9*, 73–96.
Buchanan, M., & Robbins, C. (1990). Early adult psychological consequences for males of adolescent pregnancy and its resolution. *Journal of Youth and Adolescence, 19*, 413–424.
Buhrmester, D. (1990). Intimacy of friendship, interpersonal competence, and adjustment during preadolescence and adolescence. *Child Development, 61*, 1101–1111.

Buhrmester, D. (1996). Need, fulfillment, interpersonal competence, and the developmental contexts of early adolescent friendship. In W. Bukowski, A. Newcomb, & W. Hartup (Eds.), *The company they keep: Friendship in childhood and adolescence* (pp. 158–185). New York: Cambridge University Press.

Buhrmester, D., & Furman, W. (1987). The development of companionship and intimacy. *Child Development, 58,* 1101–1113.

Byrnes, J. P. (1998). *The nature and development of decision making: A self-regulation model.* Mahwah, NJ: Lawrence Erlbaum Associates.

Byrnes, J. P., & McClenny, B. (1994). Decision-making in young adolescents and adults. *Journal of Experimental Child Psychology, 58,* 359–388.

Byrnes, J. P., Miller, D. C., & Reynolds, M. (1999). Learning to make good decisions: A self-regulation perspective. *Child Development, 70,* 1121–1140.

Cauffman, E., & Steinberg, L. (2000). (Im)maturity of judgment in adolescence: Why adolescents may be less culpable than adults. *Behavioral Sciences and the Law, 18,* 741–760.

Chen, S., & Chaiken, S. (1999). The heuristic-systematic model in its broader context. In S. Chaiken & Y. Trope (Eds.), *Dual-process theories in social psychology* (pp. 73–96). New York: Guilford.

Clasen, D. R., & Brown, B. B. (1985). The multidimensionality of peer pressure in adolescence. *Journal of Youth and Adolescence, 14*(6), 451–468.

Collins, W. A. (2003). More than myth: The developmental significance of romantic relationships during adolescence. *Journal of Research on Adolescence, 13,* 1–24.

Connolly, J., Craig, W., Goldberg, A., & Pepler, D. (1999). Conceptions of cross-sex friendships and romantic relationships in early adolescence. *Journal of Youth and Adolescence, 28*(4), 481–494.

Connolly, J. A., & Konarski, R. (1994). Peer self-concept in adolescence: Analysis of factor structure and of associations with peer experience. *Journal of Research on Adolescence, 4*(3), 385–403.

Crosby, C., & Reppucci, N. D. (1993). The legal system and adolescents. In P. Tolan & B. Coher (Eds.), *Handbook of clinical research and practice with adolescents* (pp. 281–304). New York: Wiley.

Crosby, M. C., & English, A. (1991). Mandatory parental involvement/judicial bypass laws: Do they promote adolescents' health? *Journal of Adolescent Health Care, 12,* 143–147.

Csikszentmihalyi, M., & Larson, R. (1984). *Being adolescent: Conflict and growth in the teenage years.* New York: Basic.

DiIorio, C., Kelley, M., & Hockenberry-Eaton, M. (1999). Communication about sexual issues: Mothers, fathers, and friends. *Journal of Adolescent Health, 24*(3), 181–189.

Dishion, T. J., McCord, J., & Poulin, F. (1999). When intervention harms: Peer groups and problem behavior. *American Psychologist, 54,* 755–764.

Durbin, D. L., Darling, N., Steinberg, L., & Brown, B. B. (1993). Parenting style and peer group membership among European-American adolescents. *Journal of Research on Adolescence, 3,* 87–100.

Eisen, M. G., Zellman, L., Leibowitz, A., Chow, C. W. K., & Evans, E. J. R. (1983). Factors discriminating pregnancy resolution decisions of unmarried adolescents. *Genetic Psychology Monographs, 108,* 69–95.

Ennett, S. T., Bauman, K. E., Foshee, V. A., Pemberton, M., & Hicks, K. A. (2001). Parent–child communication about adolescent tobacco and alcohol use: What do parents say and does it affect youth behavior? *Journal of Marriage and Family, 63,* 48–62.

Esser, J. K., & Lindoerfer, J. S. (1989). Groupthink and the space shuttle *Challenger* accident: Toward a quantitative case analysis. *Journal of Behavioral Decision Making, 2,* 167–177.

Evans, A. (2001). The influence of significant others on Australian teenagers' decisions about pregnancy resolution. *Family Planning Perspectives, 33*(5), 224–230.

Farber, N. B. (1991). The process of pregnancy resolution among adolescent mothers. *Adolescence, 26,* 697–716.

Feiring, C. (1996). Concept of romance in 15-year-old adolescents. *Journal of Research on Adolescence, 6,* 181–200.

Feiring, C., & Lewis, M. (1991). The transition from middle childhood to early adolescence: Sex differences in the social network and perceived self-competence. *Sex Roles, 24,* 489–508.

Finken, L., & Jacobs, J. (1996). Consultation choice across decision contexts: Are abortion decisions different? *Journal of Adolescent Research, 11*(2), 235–260.

Fischhoff, B. (1996). The real world: What good is it? *Organizational Behavior and Human Decision Processes, 65,* 232–248.

Fuligni, A. J., & Eccles, J. S. (1993). Perceived parent–child relationships and early adolescents' orientation towards peers. *Developmental Psychology, 29,* 622–632.

Fuligni, A. J., Eccles, J. S., Barber, B. L., & Clements, P. (2001). Early adolescent peer orientation and adjustment during high school. *Developmental Psychology, 37,* 28–36.

Furby, L., & Beyth-Marom, R. (1992). Risk-taking in adolescence: A decision-making perspective. *Developmental Review, 12,* 1–44.

Furman, W., & Buhrmester, D. (1992). Age and sex differences in perceptions of networks of personal relationships. *Child Development, 63,* 103–115.

Furman, W., & Simon, V. A. (1998). Advice from youth: Some lessons from the study of adolescent relationships. *Journal of Social and Personal Relationships, 15*(16), 723–739.

Furman, W., & Wehner, E. A. (1994). Romantic views: Toward a theory of adolescent romantic relationships. In R. Montemeyer, G. Adams, & T. Gullotta (Eds.), *Personal relationships during adolescence* (pp. 168–195). Beverly Hills, CA: Sage.

Gavin, L. A., & Furman, W. (1989). Age differences in adolescents' perceptions of their peer groups. *Developmental Psychology, 25*(5), 827–834.

Griffin-Carlson, M. S., & Mackin, K. J. (1993). Parental consent: Factors influencing adolescent disclosure regarding abortion. *Adolescence, 28,* 1–11.

Griffin-Carlson, M. S., & Schwanenflugel, P. J. (1998). Adolescent abortion and parental notification: Evidence for the importance of family functioning on the perceived quality of parental involvement in U.S. families. *Journal of Child Psychology and Psychiatry, 39*(4), 543–553.

Harter, S. (1990). Self and identity development. In S. S. Feldman & G. R. Elliot (Eds.), *At the threshold: The developing adolescent* (pp. 277–307). Cambridge, MA: Harvard University Press.

Henshaw, S. K., & Kost, K. (1992). Parental involvement in minors' abortion decisions. *Family Planning Perspectives, 24*(5), 196–207, 213.

Holmberg, L. I., & Wahlberg, V. (2000). The process of decision-making on abortion: A grounded theory study of young men in Sweden. *Journal of Adolescent Health, 26,* 230–234.

Hunter, F. T. (1984). Socializing procedures in parent–child and friendship relations during adolescence. *Developmental Psychology, 20,* 1092–1099.

Jacobs, J. E., & Ganzel, A. K. (1993). Decision-making in adolescence: Are we asking the wrong question? In P. Pintrich & M. Maehr (Eds.), *Advances in motivation and achievement* (Vol. 8, pp. 1–31). New York: JAI.

Janis, I. L. (1989). *Crucial decisions: Leadership in policymaking and crisis management.* New York: Free Press.

Karofsky, P. S., Zeng, L., & Kosorok, M. R. (2001). Relationship between adolescent–parental communication and initiation of first intercourse by adolescents. *Journal of Adolescent Health, 28,* 41–45.

Lansford, J. E., Criss, M. M., Pettit, G. S., Dodge, K. A., & Bates, J. E. (2003). Friendship quality, peer group affiliation, and peer antisocial behavior as moderators of the link between negative parenting and adolescent externalizing behavior. *Journal of Research on Adolescence, 13,* 161–184.

Larson, R., & Richards, M. H. (1991). Daily companionship in late childhood and early adolescence: Changing developmental contexts. *Child Development, 62,* 284–300.

Lee v. Weisman, 112 S. Ct 2649 (1992).

Lewis, C. C. (1987). Minors' competence to consent to abortion. *American Psychologist, 42,* 84–88.

Limber, S. P. (1992). *Parental notification in cases of adolescent abortion: Parental consultation and the effects of parental influence upon adolescents' pregnancy decisions.* Unpublished doctoral dissertation, Department of Psychology, University of Nebraska–Lincoln.

Limber, S. P., & Pagliocca, P. M. (2000). Psychological and legal issues in abortion. In F. W. Kaslow (Ed.), *Handbook of couple and family forensics: A sourcebook for mental health and legal professionals* (pp. 142–163). New York: Wiley.

Major, B., & Cozzarelli, C. (1992). Psychosocial predictors of adjustment to abortion. *Journal of Social Issues, 48,* 121–142.

Major, B., & Gramzow, R. H. (1999). Abortion as a stigma: Cognitive and emotional implications of concealment. *Journal of Personality and Social Psychology, 77,* 735–745.

Mann, L., Harmoni, R., & Power, C. (1989). Adolescent decision-making: The development of competence. *Journal of Adolescence, 12,* 265–278.

Melton, G. B. (Ed.). (1986). *Adolescent abortion: Psychological and legal issues.* Lincoln: University of Nebraska Press.

Miller, B. C., Benson, B., & Galbraith, K. A. (2001). Family relationships and adolescent pregnancy risk: A research synthesis. *Developmental Review, 21*(1), 1–38.

Miller, B. C., Norton, M. C., Fan, X., & Christopherson, C. R. (1998). Pubertal development, parental communication, and sexual values in relation to adolescent sexual behaviors. *Journal of Early Adolescence, 18*(1), 27–52.

Moshman, D. (1993). Adolescent reasoning and adolescent rights. *Human Development, 36,* 27–40.

Moshman, D. (1995). Reasoning as self-constrained thinking. *Human Development, 38,* 53–64.

Moshman, D. (1999). *Adolescent psychological development: Rationality, morality, and identity.* Mahwah, NJ: Lawrence Erlbaum Associates.

Moshman, D., & Geil, M. (1998). Collaborative reasoning: Evidence for collective rationality. *Thinking and Reasoning, 4,* 231–248.

O'Keefe, J. O., & Jones, J. M. (1990). Easing restrictions on minors' abortion rights. *Issues in Science and Technology, 7,* 74–80.

Ortiz, C. O., & Nuttall, E. V. (1987). Adolescent pregnancy: Effects on family support, education, and religion on the decision to carry or terminate on Puerto Rican teenagers. *Adolescence, 22,* 898–917.

O'Sullivan, L. F., Meyer-Bahlburg, H. F. L., & Watkins, B. X. (2001). Mother–daughter communication about sex among African American and Latino families. *Journal of Adolescent Research, 16*(3), 269–292.

Pliner, A. J., & Yates, S. (1992). Psychological and legal issues in minors' rights to abortion. *Journal of Social Issues, 48,* 203–216.

Pombeni, M. L., Kirchler, E., & Palmonari, A. (1990). Identification with peers as a strategy to muddle through the troubles of the adolescent years. *Journal of Adolescence, 13,* 351–369.

Resnick, M. D., Bearinger, L. H., Stark, P., & Blum, R. W. (1994). Patterns of consultation among adolescent minors obtaining abortion. *American Journal of Orthopsychiatry, 64,* 310–316.

Rogers, J. L., & Miller, A. M. (1993). Inner-city birth rates following enactment of the Minnesota parental notification law. *Law and Human Behavior, 17,* 27–42.

Rosen, R. H. (1980). Adolescent pregnancy decision-making: Are parents important? *Adolescence, 15,* 43–54.

Sargent, J. D., & Dalton, M. (2001). Does parental disapproval of smoking prevent adolescents from becoming established smokers? *Pediatrics, 108*(6), 1256–1262.

Savin-Williams, R. C., & Berndt, T. J. (1990). Friendship and peer relations. In S. S. Feldman & G. R. Elliot (Eds.), *At the threshold: The developing adolescent* (pp. 277–307). Cambridge, MA: Harvard University Press.

Scott, E. S., Reppucci, N., & Woolard, J. (1995). Evaluating adolescent decision making in legal contexts. *Law and Human Behavior, 19,* 221–244.

Shulman, S., Laursen, B., Kalman, Z., & Karpovsky, S. (1997). Adolescent intimacy revisited. *Journal of Youth and Adolescence, 26,* 597–617.

Soper, J. (1999). Straddling the line: Adolescent pregnancy and questions of capacity. *Law and Psychology Review, 23,* 195–216.

Steinberg, L., & Cauffman, E. (1996). Maturity of judgment in adolescence: psychosocial factors in adolescent decision making. *Law and Human Behavior, 20*(3), 249–272.

Steinberg, L., & Morris, A. S. (2001). Adolescent development. *Annual Review of Psychology, 52,* 83–110.

Steinberg, L., & Silk, J. S. (2002). Parenting adolescents. In M. H. Bornstein (Ed.), *Handbook of parenting* (pp. 103–133). Mahwah, NJ: Lawrence Erlbaum Associates.

Steinberg, L., & Silverberg, S. B. (1986). The vicissitudes of autonomy in early adolescence. *Child Development, 57,* 841–851.

Stotland, N. L. (1996). Conceptions and misconceptions: Decision about pregnancy. *General Hospital Psychiatry, 18,* 238–243.

Tokuno, K. A. (1986). The early adult transition and friendships: Mechanisms of support. *Adolescence, 21*(83), 593–606.

Tomal, A. (2001). The effects of religious membership on teen abortion rates. *Journal of Youth and Adolescence, 30*(1), 103–116.

Weithorn, L. A. (1983). Involving children in decisions affecting their own welfare: Guidelines for professionals. In G. B. Melton, G. P. Koocher, & M. J. Saks (Eds.), *Children's competence to consent* (pp. 235–260). New York: Plenum.

Whitaker, D. J., & Miller, K. S. (2000). Parent–adolescent discussions about sex and condoms: Impact on peer influences of sexual risk behavior. *Journal of Adolescent Research, 15*(2), 251–273.

White, F. A. (1996). Parent–adolescent communication and adolescent decision-making. *Journal of Family Studies, 2,* 41–56.

Wilks, J. (1986). The relative importance of parents and friends in adolescent decision making. *Journal of Youth and Adolescence, 15,* 323–334.

Wintre, M. G., Hicks, R., McVey, G., & Fox, J. (1988). Age and sex differences in choice of consultant for various types of problems. *Child Development, 59,* 1046–1055.

Worthington, E. L., Larson, D. B., Lyons, J. S., Brubaker, J. D., Colecchi, C. A., Berry, J. T., et al. (1991). Mandatory parental involvement prior to adolescent abortion. *Journal of Adolescent Health, 12,* 138–142.

Young, A. T., Berkman, B., & Rehr, H. (1975). Parental influence on pregnant adolescents. *Social Work, 20,* 387–391.

Youniss, J., & Haynie, D. (1992). Friendship in adolescence. *Developmental and Behavioral Pediatrics, 13,* 59–66.

Zabin, L. S., Hirsch, M. B., Emerson, M. R., & Raymond, E. (1992). To whom do inner city minors talk about their pregnancies? Adolescents' communication with parents and parent surrogates. *Family Planning Perspectives, 24*(4), 148–154, 173.

9

Crime, Competence, and Culpability: Adolescent Judgment in the Justice System

Elizabeth Cauffman
University of California, Irvine

Jennifer Woolard
Georgetown University

Basic scientific knowledge about adolescent development and decision making has numerous implications for the development and implementation of a wide range of social policies that govern the behavior and treatment of youth. One such policy context is the justice system, where developmentally based assumptions about adolescent capacities and decision making historically have provided an explicit rationale for the maintenance of a separate justice system for adolescents. Although the founding assumptions behind the juvenile justice system may have been based more on philosophy than science, they were consistent with the notion of the psychologically immature adolescent who, with the right "guidance," could be encouraged to desist from antisocial behavior and grow into a productive, law-abiding adult. Legal reforms of the last half of the 20th century, however, have changed the characterization of juveniles—even juveniles as young as age 10—from wayward youth, who lack the skills necessary for mature judgment, to adultlike criminals with mature capacities for decision making. Although recent legal and policy changes, like those that led to the formation of the juvenile justice system initially, were not based solely or even primarily on science, the changing landscape of juvenile justice represents an opportunity to bring existing research on adolescent behavior to bear on legal reform, as well as to shape new research that can evaluate the legal system's assumptions regarding important differences, or lack thereof, between adolescents and adults.

In this chapter, we attempt to integrate developmental research on adolescent judgment and decision making with the legal system's assessments of and assumptions about adolescent capacities. Such a task is difficult because the assumptions of law are not necessarily guided by developmental reality. At the same time, developmental research has not consistently examined relevant issues in a manner that can inform legal and policy debates. There is a need for more and better research that applies the scientific study of adolescent decision making to the sorts of legal questions asked by policymakers and practitioners about the appropriate treatment of adolescents in the justice system.

This chapter proceeds as follows: First, we briefly discuss adolescent involvement in crime and justice through two legal concepts of *competence* and *culpability*. Then, we examine theory and research on legally relevant developmental aspects of judgment and decision making. Although we do not provide a comprehensive review of this literature, we identify work that either has specifically examined decision making in legal contexts or that has clear implications for the same. Finally, we highlight several new studies that attempt to integrate the legal and scientific aspects of adolescent decision making in legal contexts and identify future directions for research.

ADOLESCENT DEFENDANTS
AND THE LEGAL SYSTEM

The notion that adolescents are immature, have less decision-making capacity, and therefore should be treated differently than adults has permeated the juvenile justice system since its inception in 1899. The original philosophy of such a separate system relied heavily on the belief that minors should be treated differently than adults because they are less mature and more malleable, or changeable (Platt, 1999; Simpson, 1976). Because this belief traditionally worked for the benefit of the child through rehabilitation rather than punishment, the juvenile court had the broad discretion to gather all sorts of relevant information about the child's life in order to determine what treatment would work best, and the juvenile court's activities were relatively unconstrained by procedural protections found in the criminal system (Woolard, in press). Adolescents' "choices" to engage in delinquent acts were viewed as a function of multiple developmental phenomena; as such, their immaturity was both the source of and the solution to the problem. The system presumed that delinquent behavior was a symptom of broader developmental (and familial) dysfunction, yet those same active developmental processes meant that juveniles would be more easily "pushed" in the right direction than adults through court intervention that emphasized treatment and rehabilitation (Woolard, Fondacaro, & Slobogin, 2001).

In recent years, however, the underlying presumption of adolescent immaturity has been called into question as states have enacted more punitive legal reforms. Overall rates of juvenile violence have in fact declined since a

1994 peak, but total arrests remain significantly higher than 1980's rates (Puzzanchera, 1998). Such trends combined with the media's depiction of remorseless and ultraviolent adolescent "predators," "superpredators," and "thrill-killers," have fueled public concern and legislative interest. The accuracy of public perception is largely irrelevant because sentiment that the juvenile court is too "soft" on violent delinquents accelerated 1990's reforms toward a retributive model of justice traditionally reserved for adult offenders (see Zimring, 1998, for an analysis that questions whether the youth violence epidemic is myth or reality). Changes in legal jurisdiction have moved increasing numbers of juvenile offenders as young as age 10 into the criminal justice system for adult prosecution and into the adult correctional system for punishment, and sentencing changes have resulted in minimum mandatory terms and determinate sentences for many who remain in juvenile court (Griffin, Torbet, & Szymanski, 1999; Sickmund, Snyder, & Poe-Yamagata, 1998). No national figures exist on the number of youth now tried in adult court but early estimates of approximately 12,600 in 1978 (Hamparian, Schuster, Dinitz, & Conrad) are dwarfed by recent numbers suggesting over 180,000 juveniles face adult prosecution (Sickmund et al., 1997).

Although public perceptions and political pressures may have been the driving force behind these legislative transformations, they represent changes in our fundamental assumptions about adolescents' capacities to act as defendants in the legal system. We should acknowledge that the current trend of viewing adolescents as adults in the juvenile justice system occurs in a broader legal context that demonstrates inconsistency and ambivalence in its portrait of adolescent decision-making capacities, rights, and responsibilities (e.g., Melton, 1989; Moshman, 1993). In other areas of the law, the concepts of *immaturity* and *lack of judgment* have often been the basis for not granting adolescents equal rights with adults (Woolard, Fried, & Reppucci, 2001). (See, e.g., several Supreme Court decisions: *Parham v. J.R.* (1979), "Most children, even in adolescence, simply are not able to make sound judgments"; *Bellotti v. Baird* (1979), "minors often lack the experience, perspective, and judgment to recognize and avoid choices that could be detrimental to them"; and *Thompson v. Oklahoma* (1988), "[Adolescents under 16] are less mature and responsible than adults.") Yet, juvenile justice appears on an inexorable path toward presumptions of adultlike capacities for decision making and judgment that will expose young people to more punitive and potentially harmful practices. Indeed, legal trends making children as young as 16 eligible for the death penalty have made the determination of what can and cannot be expected of juveniles at various ages, quite literally, a matter of life and death (*Stanford v. Kentucky* (1989) upheld the death penalty for juveniles age 16 and older).

There are two specific areas within juvenile (and criminal) justice for which an understanding of adolescent judgment and decision making is particularly important: adjudicative competence and culpability. *Adjudicative competence*, of which competence to stand trial is one facet, generally refers to the ability of a defendant to consult with counsel, have a rational and factual understanding of the court proceedings, and make decisions about the case (see Bonnie, 1993). A constitutional requirement of participation in the U.S. justice system, competence is presumed for adult defendants unless severe mental illness or mental retardation results in unremediable impairment of these minimal abilities. *Culpability* refers to the extent to which an individual is responsible for his or her actions, and by extension, the degree he or she is held accountable through punishment or other responses (Scott, 2000). Adults are presumed to operate as rational, autonomous actors who are of sufficient maturity to be held fully culpable for their actions unless they have markedly diminished capacity for decision making (e.g., due to mental illness) or engaged in criminal conduct amid circumstances that would elicit such behavior from "ordinary" persons (e.g., when acting in self-defense).

Determinations of adjudicative competence and culpability are based on implicit or explicit assessments of the decisional capacities of defendants. Because these determinations have historically come into question only for adults in criminal court, developmental issues have not been raised as a concern. However, the recent trends toward prosecuting juveniles as adults bring developmental issues into stark relief. In particular, we posit that questions of whether an adolescent is competent to stand trial as an adult, or is as blameworthy as an adult, are both fundamentally concerned with assumptions about the extent to which the adolescent's judgment has matured; that is, how "adultlike" these adolescents truly are (Woolard, in press). Because legal questions of competence and culpability can be reframed as empirical questions about decision making and judgment, we review relevant research in the next section.

DECISION MAKING AND MATURITY OF JUDGMENT IN ADOLESCENCE

The term *decision making* is generally used in research studies of the actual choices that individuals make, whereas *judgment* refers to the underlying cognitive, emotional, and social processes involved in making these choices. *Maturity of judgment* refers to the degree of complexity and sophistication of these underlying processes (Scott, Reppucci, & Woolard, 1995; Steinberg & Cauffman, 1996). To the extent that adolescents' decision making or judgment is comparable to that of adults, one might argue that youthful offenders should be subject to similar legal procedures and punishments. However, if adolescents' decision-making abilities are less than fully developed, or their judgment is immature, the appropriateness of adultlike procedures and consequences could be questioned.

Decision Making and Cognitive Competence

Most psychological research on legally relevant decision making has typically examined maturity in terms of adolescents' abilities to make decisions about their own actions and has focused on cognitive capacity to consent or make a choice. Applied researchers turned to legal doctrine for factors that contribute to those choices. When this research began in earnest in the 1970s, well established legal doctrine of informed consent indicated that consent for treatment must be made knowingly, competently, and voluntarily (Meisel, Roth, & Lidz, 1977). Early attention to medical (e.g., Ambuel & Rappaport, 1992; Grisso & Vierling, 1978; Lewis, 1980; Weithorn & Campbell, 1982) and mental health decision making (e.g., Belter & Grisso, 1984; Kaser-Boyd, Adelman, & Taylor, 1985; Kaser-Boyd, Adelman, Taylor, & Nelson, 1986) emphasized cognitive factors implicated by the legal standard of informed consent, such as abilities to reason, understand, and appreciate decisions, often purposefully excluding social and emotional influences as less legally relevant.

Most studies of cognitive development that have used the informed consent framework have found few major differences between adults and youths about 15 years of age and older (Ambuel & Rappaport, 1992; Belter & Grisso, 1984; Grisso & Vierling, 1978; Lewis, 1980; Weithorn & Campbell, 1982). However, this conclusion is tempered by methodological limitations, including reliance on the use of small, unrepresentative, usually White, middle-class samples of youth taking part in laboratory studies rather than in studies that compare adolescent and adult performance under more ecologically valid conditions (Woolard & Reppucci, 2000). One exception is Grisso's (1980) investigation of Miranda waivers (i.e., waiver of rights during custodial interrogation by police; *Miranda v. Arizona*, 1966), which included delinquent adolescents and criminal adults. Adolescents age 15 and older of average intelligence were able to understand their Miranda rights as well as adults, but younger adolescents performed more poorly. Moreover, the similarities between older adolescents and adults held only for those of average intelligence; adolescents with below average intelligence did not perform as well as adults with similarly deficient IQs.

Beyond the few studies cited, a much wider range of developmental research evaluating cognitive aspects of decision making among adolescents was not specifically intended to examine legal concepts but can be informative, however. Although a comprehensive review of the decision-making literature is beyond the scope of this single chapter, and is indeed well represented by a number of authors in this volume (e.g., see Byrnes, chap. 1;

Jacobs & Johnston, chap. 5; Klaczynski, chap. 2), we focus here on the study of risk behavior and aspects of rational and strategic decision making for two reasons. First, although all risky behavior is neither illegal nor limited to adolescence, the proclivity to engage in such behavior could implicate both competence-related abilities (e.g., "Should I risk going to trial or take a certain plea agreement?") and culpability (e.g., "Should I go along with my friends in their plan to hold up a convenience store?"). Second, the legal system operates on the presumption that adults are rational, thoughtful, autonomous actors who make individually driven choices about their behavior. Information on the decision-making process, use of heuristics, and reasoning could support or undercut the extension of this assumption to juveniles. Both risky behavior and faulty reasoning are undoubtedly found among many adults as well as adolescents, but our focus here is on a developmental framework (e.g., Jacobs & Klaczynski, 2002). What do we know about the decision-making capacities of adolescents as a class of individuals, and about whether their decision making and judgment will predictably improve with development (individual differences notwithstanding)?

The belief that adolescents exhibit immature judgment and make poor choices is, in all likelihood, linked to their frequent participation in dangerous activities. When compared with other age groups, adolescents are the most likely to be involved in automobile accidents, drug use, and unprotected sex (Arnett, 1992), and arrest rates peak between the ages of 15 and 18 (Gottfredson & Hirschi, 1990). However, contrary to the stereotype of adolescents as markedly egocentric, for example, or as handicapped by deficiencies in logical ability, studies show that older adolescents (e.g., those age 15 and above) are no more likely than adults to suffer from the *personal fable* (the belief that one's behavior is somehow not governed by the same rules of nature that apply to everyone else, as when a cigarette smoker believes that he is immune to the health effects of smoking) and no less likely than adults to employ rational algorithms in decision-making situations (Jacobs-Quadrel, Fischhoff, & Davis, 1993). In fact, there is substantial evidence that adolescents are well aware of the risks they take (Alexander et al., 1990), although there are data to suggest more fine-grained differences in risk perception and risk preference between adolescents and adults (Scott et al., 1995). Furthermore, there is ample evidence suggesting that increasing adolescents' awareness of various risks has little impact on their real-world decision making (Office of Technology Assessment, 1991; Rotheram-Borus & Koopman, 1990), suggesting that a lack of information in and of itself does not account for higher rates of dangerous behavior among teens.

Why, then, do adolescents make so many decisions that adults, and the legal system, categorize as poor choices? The very fact that young people engage in risky behaviors at a higher rate than adults is often taken as prima facie evidence of the inherent immaturity of adolescent judgment. The problem with drawing developmental inferences about judgment solely from evidence about risk-taking is that it ignores why and how bad decisions are made. Plenty of adults make poor choices, but we do not consider those choices the products of immaturity; rather, we presume they are the expression of individual preferences and values. We assume that adults have had the opportunity to develop mature decision-making capacities, regardless of whether they are exercised at any given moment; this in part justifies a criminal justice system based on retribution and deterrence. In theory, adolescents are still developing those very capacities, and the efficacy of deterrent and retributive approaches has been questioned (e.g., Lipsey, 1992; Slobogin, Fondacaro, & Woolard, 1999). Demonstrating that adolescents take more risks than adults is straightforward. Demonstrating that adolescents' higher incidence of risk taking is due to developmental differences in judgment is not.

Developmental differences in judgment are difficult to ascertain for two main reasons. First, most of the work on judgment and decision making has relied on theories of adult cognition and decision making, which have remained separate from theories of cognitive development (Jacobs & Klaczynski, 2002). Second, the adult literature demonstrates that, while adults are reasonable decision makers, their behaviors commonly rely on heuristics, biases, and other shortcuts that deviate from the ideal or optimal decision process underlying many theoretical models of decision making. Noting the relative dearth of studies on children and adolescents, recent reviews of developmental aspects of decision making have tentatively concluded that two somewhat competing developmental trends are at work: Age-based improvements in reasoning and decisional capacities occur simultaneously with increased availability and use of adultlike biases and shortcuts that may undermine the effectiveness of judgment and decision making (Byrnes, 1998; Jacobs & Klaczynski, 2002).

Much research remains to be done even at the basic level of documenting the developmental trajectories of biased judgment and decision making. Moreover, there is tremendous potential in taking a developmental approach to research on factors that moderate the decision-making process, and on strategies for overcoming those barriers. For example, Byrnes' (1998) self-regulation model of decision making identifies nine moderating factors that help explain why adults make poor decisions. These include memory limitations, inadequate knowledge, lack of calibration between self-assessment and ability, heuristics and biases, encoding errors, emotion, stress and coping, use of psychoactive substances, and personality traits. For each of these, Byrnes notes that few studies have examined the potential for differential impact on adolescents as compared to adults. Even within a relatively well-studied area such as memory, in which the data suggest that working memory capacity is likely fully developed by adolescence, some research indicates that adults may make better use of the capacity than children and adolescents. Working memory utilization could be a critical factor in an adolescent defendant's ability to manage information and make decisions about testifying during a complex felony murder trial, or to consider all the ramifications of a plea agreement that might involve (a) pleading guilty to one of several charges (each with different potential sentence ranges, confinement outcomes, future consequences for life chances); (b) providing information about accomplices (and subsequent impact on friends, family, personal safety); and (c) remaining in juvenile court versus being transferred to adult court.

The design of most basic research has limited value for the legal context. For example, most of the developmental research cited in recent reviews has not included legally relevant age ranges or tasks. Many studies focus on younger children (through age 10), or include preadolescents and adults, but do not include middle (age 13 to age 15) and older (age 16 to age 17) adolescents, for whom most of the modern legal reforms are in play. Admittedly, this research was not designed to address legal questions, but as the corpus of empirical work grows, it has the potential to be quite informative so long as it focuses on relevant issues.

Implications for Legal Processing

One line of reasoning that has been proposed to explain adolescent risk taking in light of their mature cognitive capacities is derived from behavioral decision theory (Beyth-Marom, Austin, Fischhoff, Palmgren, & Jacobs-Quadrel, 1993). According to this view, adolescent and adults employ the same logical processes when making decisions, but differ in the sorts of information they use and the priorities they hold; adolescents may make bad decisions, but they do not make decisions badly, or at least any differently than would an adult with the same priorities. According to this view, for example, adolescents engage in unprotected sex more often than adults not because adolescents suffer from a "personal fable" that permits them to deny the possibility of pregnancy, or because they are misinformed about the risks of the activity, but because in the calculus of a 16-year-old, the potential benefits of unprotected sex (spontaneity, physical pleasure, etc.) simply outweigh in value the potential costs (pregnancy, infection, etc.). Within this model, age differences in decision making stem from differences in decision calculus, or performance on the decision task, not the capacities for decision making itself (Beyth-Marom et al., 1993; Furby & Beyth-Marom, 1992).

The distinction between capacities and performance has important applied, as well as theoretical, implications (Woolard, Redding, & Reppucci, 1996). It also is directly relevant to the present discussion of adolescent competence and culpability. Indeed, the failure of researchers to document systematic differences between adolescents and adults on measures of the cognitive processes underlying decision making has led many in the policy arena to challenge the long-standing view of adolescents as inherently less competent or culpable than adults (Moshman, 1993), a view that, as we have noted, undergirds the maintenance of a separate juvenile justice system. Although the research base is limited, the absence of systematic data showing that adults outperform adolescents on assessments of cognitive abilities has fueled concerns about the appropriateness of laws and legal decisions that historically have been grounded in this perspective.

Particularly with respect to competence-relevant research, these findings about a relative lack of cognitive differences between adolescents and adults bolstered arguments by youth advocates in the 1980s for expanded rights afforded to minors. In particular, independent access to abortion was at the center of a vigorous moral, political, and legal debate. Based in large part on the lack of differences found in the informed consent literature, a number of psychologists supported the adolescent autonomy advocates' position in *amicus curiae* briefs to the United States Supreme Court (Interdivisional Committee on Adolescent Abortion, 1987). Their assessment of the research was not unanimously supported, however, as critics warned that the limitations of extant research failed to justify strong policy arguments about adolescents' equivalence to adults (Gardner, Scherer, & Tester, 1989).

During the 1990s, youth advocates who had rallied around the "no differences in competence" view in order to support adolescent autonomy in health-care decisions discovered that this view proved to be a double-edged sword. How could adolescents be mature enough to make their own decisions about abortion, but not mature enough to face the consequences of committing armed robbery or using marijuana? If adolescents and adults are equally capable decision makers, the argument that adolescents suffer from diminished responsibility is called into question. Indeed, the very same evidence that had been used to advocate for young people's autonomy in medical decision making could provide—and has provided—fuel for recent calls to treat juvenile delinquents as adults.

Although there are some gaps in the research, there is currently little evidence from legally relevant studies of cognitive development to support the assertion that adolescents, once they have reached age 16, should be viewed as much different than adults. This is not the end of the story, however, nor should it mean the end of the juvenile justice system. Although the early assumptions about qualitative differences between adolescents and adults has generally not been supported, recent research has demonstrated age progressions in decision-relevant abilities, such as conditional reasoning and use of heuristics (e.g., Byrnes & McClenny, 1994; Byrnes, Miller, & Reynolds, 1999; Klaczynski, 2001a, 2001b). These advances are promising but limited in their generalizability to the legally relevant contexts; further work should examine the implications of these age-based trends for juvenile offending and justice-system processing.

The justice system was based not only on ideas about juveniles' cognitive capacities, however, but also on the notion that their judgment was less mature. Indeed, a different perspective on the question of age differences in risk decision making has been suggested by several writers, including the present authors, who have argued that there may be developmental differences between adolescents and adults in noncognitive (or psychosocial) realms that account for age differences in behavior and that may have important implications for assessments of adjudicative competence and culpability (Cauffman & Steinberg 1995; Grisso, 1997; Scott et al., 1995; Steinberg & Cauffman, 1996; Woolard & Reppucci, 2000).

Differences in decision making between adolescents and adults may well reflect differences in capacities that are neither traditionally considered by the justice system nor assessed by measures of logical reasoning. Psychosocial factors may affect the sorts of decisions individuals make, follow a developmental progression between adolescence and adulthood, and bear on the questions of adolescent competence and culpability. Although adolescents and adults may have similar cognitive abilities and perform similarly on abstract reasoning tasks, there may be other characteristics that develop more gradually and prevent adolescents from making decisions in the same manner that they would on reaching the maturity of adulthood. We have made this argument specifically with respect to competence and culpability but it is consistent with the work of several other decision-making researchers on noncognitive aspects of decision making (e.g., Byrnes, 1998; Jacobs & Ganzel, 1993; Klaczynski, 1997, 2001a, 2001b; Klaczynski, Byrnes, & Jacobs, 2001).

Psychosocial Factors and Maturity of Judgment

It is our position that the presumption of equivalence between adolescent and adult judgment that apparently undergirds the punitive response to juvenile offenders characteristic of recent reforms (e.g., "adult time for adult crime") is premature for policy and inconsistent with theory and research. We posit that if psychosocial factors are taken into consideration in addition to the cognitive factors that are typically assessed, significant differences between adolescents and adults will emerge. Moreover, we hypothesize that the putative differences in adolescent and adult judgment are real; that such differences reflect genuine differences in capacities, not merely differences in values and priorities; and that these differences in psychosocial capacities provide a psychological basis for drawing legal distinctions between adolescents and adults.

Scott, Reppucci, and Woolard (1995) proposed a framework of adolescent competence and maturity that includes not only the cognitive factors such as understanding, reasoning, and appreciation, but also several psychosocial factors that would be irrelevant or excluded under an informed-consent framework. In parallel, Steinberg and Cauffman (1996) proposed a model of maturity of judgment that comprised a set of psychosocial factors. The Scott, Reppucci, and Woolard framework comprises factors related to (a) conformity and compliance in relation to peers and parents; (b) attitude toward and perception of risk; and (c) temporal perspective, each of which developmental theory suggests change during adolescence, is hypothesized to influence adolescent decision making, and is acknowledged in legal writings as a factor that likely differentiates adolescents from adults. Similarly, the Steinberg and Cauffman formulation identifies three relevant categories of psychosocial factors: (a) *responsibility*, which encompasses such characteristics as self-reliance, clarity of identity, and healthy autonomy; (b) *perspective*, which refers to the ability to understand the complexity of a situation and place it in a broader context; and (c) *temperance*, which refers to the ability to limit impulsivity and to evaluate situations before acting. Although these approaches differ somewhat in the details emphasized, they both identify similar sets of psychosocial factors that are likely to affect how cognitive capacities are put to use in real-world situations.

Although systematic data on the developmental course of each of these factors, their interrelations, and their joint and cumulative impact on legally relevant decision making are lacking, each of these psychosocial factors has been linked generally to behavior and decision making, and each has been shown to change over the course of adolescent development (Cauffman & Steinberg, 2000; Redding, 1997; Scott et al., 1995). More important, there is reason to suspect that developments in these areas may potentially affect individuals' decision making and risk taking in ways that ought to be taken into account when making determinations regarding competence or culpability (or any other legal issue for which maturity of judgment is relevant). In other words, there is reason to believe that adolescents, as a class, may warrant characterization as less mature than adults, not because of cognitive immaturity or otherwise impaired reasoning, but because of deficiencies in the psychosocial characteristics necessary for exercising mature judgment in real-world situations.

A number of individual and environmental factors are likely to interact with the course of development to affect maturity of judgment. Grisso (1996) suggested that cultural, intellectual, and social disadvantages can have a negative impact on the completion of cognitive and moral developmental stages. Family dynamics and structure also have been shown to affect adolescents' participation in violent activities (Gorman-Smith, Tolan, Zelli, & Huesmann, 1996). The exact mechanisms have not been identified, but social and cultural contexts shape adolescent experience and combine with other developmental factors to affect adolescent decisions and behavior.

Expanding the conceptualization of judgment to include the many noncognitive factors that potentially influence the decision-making process highlights considerable evidence suggesting that individuals do not achieve adult-like levels of maturity until late in adolescence. In the following sections, we examine the issues of adjudicative competence and culpability in relation to the psychological evidence regarding the development of mature judgment during adolescence.

ADJUDICATIVE COMPETENCE AND EFFECTIVE PARTICIPATION AS DEFENDANTS

A fundamental notion of fairness and due process in the criminal system is embedded in the notion of competence to stand trial, which Bonnie (1993) described under the rubric of adjudicative competence. This reformulation includes the standard aspects of competence to assist counsel, such as the capacity to understand the proceedings, appreciate their significance for one's own situation, and communicate relevant information to counsel. It also incorporates notions of decisional competence, which include the ability to engage in a reasoning process and make judgments with input from counsel. For adults, mental illness and mental retardation, to the degree that they impair these abilities, are the primary reasons for incompetence.

A few empirical studies of juvenile competence have used assessments developed under the framework for evaluating adult competence to stand trial. Cowden and McKee (1995) found that the majority of 136 juveniles age 15 and older referred for evaluations met the adult standard of competence; a majority of those below 15 did not. Savitsky and Karras (1984) found that neither 12-year-olds nor 15- to 17-year-olds scored as well as adults on measures of competence. Ninety percent of a juvenile delinquent sample scored below the suggested competence cutoff in Cooper's (1997) study of the Georgia Court Competency Test. In each of these studies, the assessments used to examine juveniles' abilities to meet adult competence standards had been developed for adults and focused on cognitive abilities.

Although it is important to determine how adolescents compare to adults on measures ordinarily used in adult criminal court, it is imperative that empirical research also investigates the developmental implications of applying adult assessment standards to juveniles. In the criminal system, adults are presumed to be mature and to have finished developing their decisional capacities; as such, they are held accountable for their behavior unless severe mental impairment precludes their ability to be competent and they cannot be restored to competence through treatment. However, the juvenile justice system was based not only on ideas about adolescents' cognitive capacities, but also on ideas that their judgment and decision making is less mature (e.g., *Bellotti v. Baird*, 1979; *Parham v. J.R.*, 1979). It is quite possible that, for developmental reasons, the nature of juveniles' capacities for competence specifically, or effective participation as defendants more broadly, may be qualitatively different from that of adults. There may be developmental constructs that are not captured by traditional legal competence assessments that influence the nature of juveniles' understanding and participation in court proceedings. A recent review of the literature with respect to competence to stand trial emphasizes the need to review developmental factors that may differentially influence competence-related capacities in juveniles (Grisso, 1997).

A recent study of adolescent and adult males awaiting trial was designed to assess adjudicative competence, judgment in legal settings, and psychosocial factors relating to parent and peer influence, risk taking, and perspective (Woolard, 1998). Three samples of males were interviewed: 100 young adolescents (10 to 14 years old) and 100 older adolescents (15 to 17 years old) detained in a juvenile pretrial detention facility, and 100 incarcerated adults (18 to 35 years old) held pretrial in a local jail. Participants completed a 2-hour interview that included measures of judgment and decisional capacity as well as adjudicative competence. Judgment and decisional capacity were measured using the Judgment Assessment Tool for Adolescents (Woolard, Reppucci, & Scott, 1996), a three-part interview that describes a male facing a series of decisions: talking with police, consulting with an attorney, and considering a plea bargain in the context of transfer to adult court. Respondents' answers were coded for the choices they made as well as the temporal perspective and valence (risk or benefit). Adjudicative competence was measured with the MacArthur Competence Assessment Tool—Criminal Adjudication (MacCAT-CA; Poythress, Hoge, Bonnie, & Monahan, 1996). Responses to 22 questions administered in interview format generate three subscale scores of Understanding, Reasoning, and Appreciation.

Preliminary results suggest few differences between the groups on adult measures of adjudicative competence, indicating that many adolescents, particularly older adolescents, may perform comparably to adults on questions of understanding, reasoning, and appreciation. No significant age differences were found in the cognitive measure of adjudicative competence, but significant age differences were found in the measures of legal judgment and decision making. For example, the number of respondents who reported that they would waive their right to silence in the police vignette decreased significantly with age—younger juveniles were twice as likely as adults to waive their rights. There were also some differences in the psychosocial factors. For example, adults reported a significantly higher proportion of long- to short-term consequences than older juveniles when evaluating the consequences of refusing a plea bargain and going to trial.

A recent multisite national study of adolescents' competence to stand trial using the MacCAT-CA and the MacArthur Judgment Evaluation Narrative (MacJEN) extended these findings in a large sample of adolescents and adults within the justice system and a comparison sample within comparable communities (Grisso et al., 2003). Approximately one third of 11- to 13-year-olds and one fourth of 14- to 15-year-olds demonstrated deficiencies in competence-relevant abilities that were comparable to the performance of mentally ill adults found incompetent to stand trial. Moreover, adolescents were more likely than adults to make choices that reflected compliance with authority, such as confessing to police or taking a plea agreement. Adolescents also demonstrated more immature judgment through increased emphasis on short term consequences and lesser perception of risks.

Findings that adolescents' responses to and reasoning about legal decision-making scenarios may be significantly different from those of adults, despite comparable performance on traditional measures of competence to stand trial, underscore the importance of considering psychosocial factors in evaluations of the decision-making capacities of adolescents. Further study of the factors most closely related to adjudicative competence is necessary before policy-relevant recommendations can be made. However, it is clear that the default extension of adult competence assessments to juveniles will not capture aspects of judgment that differentiate adolescent decision making from that of adults. Continued research with larger and more racially and ethnically diverse samples of both male and female adolescents and adults facing legal decisions will provide the foundation from which policy and practice recommendations can be made. The developmental aspects of competence and judgment will have implications for practitioners conducting competence evaluations of juveniles and for the manner in which competence is conceptualized for juveniles in criminal and juvenile court.

CULPABILITY IN ADOLESCENTS

While competence involves a defendant's ability to participate in an adversarial court proceeding, culpability concerns the degree to which a defendant can and should be held accountable for his or her actions. In this context, immature judgment is considered as a possible mitigating circumstance, which would render the defendant less blameworthy for transgressions committed. As Cauffman and Steinberg (2000) stated, youths' offenses may stem in part from deficiencies in psychosocial factors that adversely affect judgment. If true, then the presumptions of autonomy, free will, and rational choice, on which adult criminal responsibility is based, become weaker. Under such circumstances, the criminal actions of juveniles could be considered less blameworthy than similar acts committed by adults (Scott & Grisso, 1997). If this is so, then youths should be subject to less severe punishment (or the punishment could be aimed at correcting the offender's behavior, rather than at exacting vengeance). Zimring (1998) argued that adolescence should be conceptualized as a probationary period during which decision makers learn to make responsible choices without bearing the full costs of their mistakes. A legal response that holds youthful offenders accountable, while recognizing that they are less culpable than their adult counterparts, could provide criminal punishment without violating the underlying legal principle of *proportionality*, which suggests that punishment should be based, in part, on the blameworthiness of the offender.

Despite these very important theoretical and practical concerns, there is little empirical research on the psychological attributes most relevant to issues of culpability, especially among juvenile populations. Among juveniles, studies linking psychological factors directly to criminal accountability are virtually nonexistent. Although our understanding of how a number of potentially relevant cognitive and psychosocial factors evolve during adolescence has grown considerably in recent years, the implications of these findings in legal contexts remain largely theoretical.

A recent study explored the relations between judgment and several aspects of psychosocial maturity within a sample of over 1,000 individuals ranging in age from 12 to 48 (Cauffman & Steinberg, 2000). This study examined age differences in individuals' performance on a series of hypothetical judgment tasks designed to assess their likelihood in engaging in antisocial behavior (e.g., shoplifting, smoking marijuana, joy riding in a stolen car), as performance on such tasks has been shown to be predictive of actual antisocial behavior (Brown, Clasen, & Eicher, 1986; Steinberg & Silverberg, 1986). For example, "You're out shopping with some of your close friends and they decide to take some clothing without paying for it. You don't think it's a good idea, but they say you should take something too." Subjects were then presented with three possible scenarios. First, "suppose nothing bad would happen to you (such as getting arrested) if you took the clothing. Would you shoplift or would you refuse to take the item?" The next scenario indicates that something bad would happen, and the third scenario suggests that the subject doesn't know what would happen. For each of these scenarios, subjects were asked to indicate whether or not they would do the irresponsible action on a 4-point scale ranging from (for the above example), *definitely shoplift* to *definitely refuse to shoplift*. This measure was somewhat modified from Ford et al.'s (1989) original measure by adding the *don't know what would happen* scenario, because this more accurately reflects real-life decision-making situations. In addition, age differences in responsibility, perspective, and temperance, as well as relations between decision making and psychosocial maturity, both within and across age groups, were also explored.

Three overall patterns of findings from this study are relevant to the present discussion of culpability and maturity of judgment. First, clear and significant age differences were observed on the measure of decision making in antisocial situations, with adults significantly less likely than adolescents to respond to the hypothetical dilemmas in ways indicative of antisocial inclinations. Second, consistent age differences were found on a wide array of measures of responsibility, perspective, and temperance. Compared with adults, for example, adolescents scored lower on measures of self-restraint, consideration of future consequences, and self-reliance, three widely cited components of psychosocial maturity. Third and most importantly, individuals who scored higher on the measures of psychosocial maturity were more likely to make socially responsible decisions in the hypothetical situations than those who were less psychosocially mature. Once the differences in responsibility, perspective, and temperance were accounted for, age was no longer a significant predictor of judgment. That is to say, although adults tended to make more socially responsible decisions than adolescents, this difference in decision making was accounted for by differences in psychosocial maturity. On average, adolescents make poorer (more antisocial) decisions than adults do because they are more psychosocially immature.

In a study by Halpern-Felsher and Cauffman (2001), comparisons between adolescents' (6th, 8th, 10th, and 12th graders) and adults' decision-making competence was assessed using three open-ended decision-making tasks. Using the decision-making scenarios developed by Lewis (1981), participants were asked to help a peer of the same age and gender decide how to solve a problem. Participants were asked to listen to an audiotaped description of three open-ended dilemmas: (a) whether to seek cosmetic surgery (medical domain); (b) whether to participate in an experimental study for the use of a new acne medicine (informed consent domain); and (c) which parent to live with after a divorce (family domain). All of the scenarios were presented as problems faced by actual people in order to minimize the hypothetical nature of the decision-making tasks. In addition, participants were told that the interview was related to peer counseling rather than decision making. This enforced the premise that the decisions were real, with the expected effect that participants would be less likely to perceive the interview as a test.

The results indicate that, overall, adults outperform adolescents on decision-making competence, as defined by their spontaneous consideration of options, risks, long-term consequences, and benefits associated with each decision. The age differences in the present study were particularly pronounced between younger adolescents (sixth and eighth graders) and the adults. Results also indicate that there is situation-specificity in decision-making competence. That is, across all five age groups, the percentage of participants spontaneously mentioning options, risks, and benefits varied by the type of decision scenario. It is possible that a greater percentage of the participants, across all cohorts, mentioned options and benefits associated with the family scenario than the other two scenarios because divorce is a situation in which most people of all ages have either personal or vicarious experience and can therefore relate to and provide sound advice on the topic. In contrast, the medical and informed-consent domains are less familiar to individuals, especially adolescents. Finally, adults were more likely than the adolescents to suggest seeking consultation from others, providing some evidence that adolescents may be less likely to seek second opinions when appropriate and thus their medical decision-making abilities may not be comparable to those of adults.

It is clear that important progress in the development of psychosocial maturity continues to occur during late adolescence, well beyond the point in development when age differences in purely logical abilities seem to disappear. Moreover, these changes in psychosocial maturity affect adolescents' abilities to make consistently mature decisions when tempted in antisocial situations, supporting the view that, in comparison with adults, adolescents are significantly more likely to suffer from diminished decision-making capacity, and that such diminished capacity should be taken into consideration in the assessment of juvenile culpability.

Psychological research cannot determine the specific level of culpability that should be assigned to a given level of maturity of judgment; decisions about whether an individual is mature enough to be held culpable for his or her actions are moral decisions, not scientific ones. We do believe, however, that the studies we have described challenge the widely reported presumption derived from recent work on the development of logical decision-making that adolescents are just as competent as adults, as well as the popular opinion that teens who commit "adult" crimes must necessarily exhibit adult levels of maturity. With regard to important aspects of psychosocial functioning that affect judgment—such things as self-reliance, the consideration of future consequences, and self-restraint—adolescents, even those who are age 16 or age 17, are not equivalent to adults. Much more, and better, research is certainly needed, but it surely appears as if a great deal of development continues to take place during middle and late adolescence within the realm of judgment that is not picked up in research that equates the study of judgment with the study of logical reasoning.

CONCLUSIONS

The study of developmental factors that affect adolescents' competence and culpability is one example of a field with significant potential to influence both policy and practice in the treatment of juvenile offenders. In recent years, changes in policy and practice have been made in response to fears about violent juvenile crime, often without consideration of what is generally understood about adolescent development. The application of existing knowledge about adolescent development in the formulation of policy is hampered by numerous factors. These factors can all be overcome, but should be borne in mind when planning future research to address legal issues such as competence and culpability.

First, many studies have focused on characteristics that are relevant to issues of competence and culpability, but have not demonstrated this relevance directly (e.g., by empirically relating psychological constructs like "perspective" to legal criteria like "competence to stand trial"). Until more studies are conducted to address legal questions directly, most conclusions regarding competence and culpability must therefore be extrapolated, to some extent, from studies of theoretically relevant psychosocial factors.

Second, many of the studies on which our understanding of adolescent development is based rely on data from populations that may not accurately reflect the characteristics of offenders in particular. Such studies are certainly appropriate in mapping normative development, but if "adult" samples consist of college psychology majors and adolescent samples consist of high-school student volunteers, one may legitimately question whether the results of such studies can be readily applied to delinquent populations. Studies that target populations of offenders are critical for determining how these populations differ from nonoffending populations, and for determining whether conclusions based on nonoffending subjects can be applied to offenders.

Third, many studies of decision making examine particular types of decisions. Given that studies have established that competencies can vary with subject matter, great care must be taken in extrapolating the results of decision making in a given context (such as medical consent) to another (such as waiver of counsel). In addition to appropriate subject selection (as already noted), the types of decision making examined in future studies should be as similar as possible to the legal decisions in question.

Finally, and in the long run perhaps most importantly, the formulation of policy is predominantly a philosophical and social exercise, so even a perfectly designed study may fail to influence policy unless its conclusions can be brought to bear on the philosophical issues in question. For example, the age criteria for the death penalty has been lowered in most states, not because legislators feel that 13-year-olds are as mature as adults, but in response to social pressure to "do something" about violent juvenile crime and in conjunction with a philosophy that adultlike crimes deserve adultlike punishments. However, studies showing that 13-year-olds are inherently less competent decision makers and therefore less accountable for the consequences of their poor judgment may not, by themselves, change legislators' minds on either of these issues. To change policy, the results must be framed in the context of the various philosophical assumptions (about deterrence, about retribution, about the relative importance of competence in the assignment of blame) on which policy is based.

In bringing research findings to bear on policy matters, a good place to start is the identification of the developmental assumptions that underlie existing policy. These assumptions can be compared with empirical evidence, and in cases where the evidence disproves the assumptions, the effect on the philosophical justification for the policy can be argued. Researchers should identify the theories of developmental psychology that underlie various policy choices in part because developmental differences and similarities can have implications for legal constructs, such as adjudicative competence. Clarity in operationalizing legal standards may be difficult to achieve because the legal system itself is frequently unclear regarding juvenile standards. Does adjudicative competence allow for the consideration of developmental factors described in judgment theory? Can culpability assessments incorporate developmental differences in decision-making capacities? The lack of clarity in legal standards for juveniles is compounded by the sometimes contradictory assumptions on which different laws or procedures are based (e.g., requiring parental consent for juveniles to obtain tattoos, while holding them to adultlike levels of accountability for criminal behavior). Identifying the specific assumptions that underlie such policies is a first step toward removing such inconsistencies.

Identifying the assumptions behind legal policies helps to ensure that subsequent research is designed to answer the appropriate questions. In addition to an appreciation for the policy context, attention to ecological validity is also vital to ensure that the results are applicable. This validity may come at the expense of some laboratory-based control, particularly with the study of decision making. Law and policy should be considered at multiple levels, including framing the research question to have policy relevance, sampling in a manner that is both theoretically sound and practically meaningful, and considering the implications and limitations of the findings.

Modeling the complexity of choice and decision making in policy contexts is an iterative process that depends on the integration and testing described in this chapter. Committing a crime or participating in a legal case does not reduce to a rational time-bounded decision; rather these activities reflect a series of decision points made in complicated circumstances, often by more than one person. For example, the decision to accept a plea agreement may involve a juvenile, his or her parents, and an attorney, each with different information, motivations, and biases. It may be shaped by prior interactions with police, probation officers, judges, and accomplices. All of these forces interact with the developmental status and capabilities of the adolescent to ultimately determine how a plea decision is made. We do not mean to imply that decisions outside the legal context are any less complicated; rather, that legally relevant decisions entail specific sets of capacities and inputs across time that may be different from those in other contexts, so research should be designed to maximize applicability to the context in question.

Contextually relevant research on children's capacities in specific legal contexts has much potential to have an impact on law and policy. Although research on decision making and its evolution during adolescence has a long history, and has established a sizeable body of knowledge, the application of this knowledge to specific real-life contexts (such as decision making in various legal settings) requires research specifically tailored to the context and the legal issues in question. Such research will not only advance our understanding of decision making in legal contexts, but has the potential to have a profound impact on the treatment of juvenile offenders in the legal system, where assumptions about adolescent decision-making competencies have taken on life-and-death significance in a very literal sense. For example, findings from adolescents' competence to stand trial using the MacCAT-CA and the MacJEN suggest that juveniles age 15 and younger are significantly more likely than older adolescents and young adults to be impaired in ways that compromise their ability to serve as competent defendants in a criminal proceeding (Grisso et al., 2003). Research on age differences in the composite index of psychosocial maturity suggests that the steepest inflection point in the developmental curve occurs sometime between 16 and 19 years (Cauffman & Steinberg, 2000). Thus, the period between age 15 and age 19 marks an important transition point in psychosocial development that is potentially relevant to debates about the drawing of legal boundaries between adolescence and adulthood. Although psychological research is rarely designed to serve as the sole basis for legal line drawing, researchers can enhance the likelihood that their findings contribute to the policy date by familiarizing themselves with current and anticipated legal issues and policy questions, designing ecologically valid research that can address them, and communicating their results in academic and practitioner-oriented outlets. If scientists do so, political and legal debates on fundamental issues such as a retributive or rehabilitative emphasis in juvenile justice might be informed by sound science rather than by supposition.

ACKNOWLEDGMENTS

The authors wish to thank Dickon Reppucci and Laurence Steinberg for their support and assistance with this chapter.

REFERENCES

Alexander, C., Kim, Y., Ensminger, M., Johnson, K., Smith, B. J., & Dolan, L. (1990). A measure of risk taking for young adolescents: Reliability and validity assessments. *Journal of Youth and Adolescence, 19*, 559–569.

Ambuel, B., & Rappaport, J. (1992). Developmental trends in adolescents' psychological and legal competence to consent to abortion. *Law and Human Behavior, 16*, 129–154.

Arnett, J. (1992). Reckless behavior in adolescence: A developmental perspective. *Developmental Review, 12*, 391–409.

Bellotti v. Baird, 443 U.S. 622 (1979).

Belter, R., & Grisso, T. (1984). Children's recognition of rights violations in counseling. *Professional Psychology: Research and Practice, 15*, 899–910.

Beyth-Marom, R., Austin, L., Fischhoff, B., Palmgren, C., & Jacobs-Quadrel, M. (1993). Perceived consequences of risky behaviors: Adults and adolescents. *Developmental Psychology, 29*(3), 549–563.

Bonnie, R. (1993). The competence of criminal defendants: Beyond *Dusky* and *Drope. University of Miami Law Review, 47*, 539.

Brown, B. B., Clasen, D. R., & Eicher, S. A. (1986). Perceptions of peer pressure, peer conformity dispositions, and self-reported behavior among adolescents. *Developmental Psychology, 22*, 521–530.

Byrnes, J. P. (1998). *The nature and development of decision making: A self-regulation model.* Mahwah, NJ: Lawrence Erlbaum Associates.

Byrnes, J. P., & McClenny, B. (1994). Decision-making in young adolescents and adults. *Journal of Experimental Child Psychology, 58*, 359–388.

Byrnes, J. P., Miller, D. C., & Reynolds, M. (1999). Learning to make good decisions: A self-regulation perspective. *Child Development, 70*, 1121–1140.

Cauffman, E., & Steinberg, L. (1995). The cognitive and affective influences on adolescent decision-making. *Temple Law Review, 68*, 1763–1789.

Cauffman, E., & Steinberg, L. (2000). (Im)maturity of judgment in adolescence: Why adolescents may be less culpable than adults. *Behavioral Sciences & the Law, 18*, 741–760.

Cooper, D. K. (1997). Juveniles' understanding of trial-related information: Are they competent defendants? *Behavioral Sciences and the Law, 15*, 167–180.

Cowden, V., & McKee, G. (1995). Competency to stand trial in juvenile delinquency proceedings: Cognitive maturity and the attorney–client relationship. *University of Louisville Journal of Law, 33*, 629.

Ford, M. E., Wentzel, K. R., Wood, D., Stevens, E., & Siesfeld, G. A. (1989). Processes associated with integrative social competence: Emotional and contextual influences on adolescent social responsibility. *Journal of Adolescent Research, 4*(4), 405–425.

Furby, L., & Beyth-Marom, R. (1992). Risk taking in adolescence: A decision-making perspective. *Developmental Review, 12*, 1–44.

Gardner, W., Scherer, D., & Tester, M. (1989). Asserting authority: Cognitive development and adolescent legal rights. *American Psychologist, 44*, 895.

Gorman-Smith, D., Tolan, P., Zelli, A., & Huesmann, R. (1996). The relation of family functioning to violence among inner-city minority youths. *Journal of Family Psychology, 10*, 115.

Gottfredson, M., & Hirschi, T. (1990). *A general theory of crime.* Stanford, CA: Stanford University Press.

Griffin, P., Torbet, P., & Szymanski, L. (1999). *Trying juveniles as adults in criminal court: An analysis of state transfer provisions.* Washington, DC: U.S. Department of Justice, Office of Justice Programs, Office of Juvenile Justice and Delinquency Prevention.

Grisso, T. (1980). Juveniles' capacities to waive Miranda rights: An empirical analysis. *California Law Review, 68*, 1135–1166.

Grisso, T. (1997). The competence of adolescents as trial defendants. *Psychology, Public Policy, and Law, 3*, 3–32.

Grisso, T., Steinberg, L., Woolard, J. L., Cauffman, E., Scott, E., Graham, S., Lexcen, F., Reppucci, N., & Schwartz, R. (2003). Juveniles' competence to stand trial: A comparison of adolescents' and adults' capacities as trial defendants. *Law and Human Behavior, 27*, 333–363.

Grisso, T., & Vierling, L. (1978). Minors' consent to treatment: A developmental perspective. *Professional Psychology, 9*, 412–427.

Halpern-Felsher, B. L., & Cauffman, E. (2001). Costs and benefits of a decision. Decision-making competence in adolescents and adults. *Journal of Applied Developmental Psychology,* 22(3), 257–273.

Hamparian, D. M., Schuster, R., Dinitz, S., & Conrad, J. P. (1978). *The violent few: A study of dangerous juvenile offenders.* Lexington, MA: Lexington Books.

Interdivisional Committee on Adolescent Abortion. (1987). Adolescent abortion: Psychological and legal issues. *American Psychologist, 42,* 73.

Jacobs, J. E., & Ganzel, A. K. (1993). Decision-making in adolescence: Are we asking the wrong question? *Advances in Motivation and Achievement, 8,* 1–31.

Jacobs, J. E., & Klaczynski, P. A. (2002). The development of judgment and decision making during childhood and adolescence. *Current Directions in Psychological Science, 11,* 145–149.

Jacobs-Quadrel, M., Fischhoff, B., & Davis, W. (1993). Adolescent invulnerability. *American Psychologist, 482,* 102–116.

Kaser-Boyd, N., Adelman, H. S., & Taylor, L. (1985). Minors' ability to identify risks and benefits of therapy. *Professional Psychology: Research and Practice, 16,* 411–417.

Kaser-Boyd, N., Adelman, H. S., Taylor, L., & Nelson, P. (1986). Children's understanding of risk and benefits of psychotherapy. *Clinical Child Psychology, 15,* 165–171.

Klaczynski, P. A. (1997). Bias in adolescents' everyday reasoning and its relationship with intellectual ability, personal theories, and self-serving motivation. *Developmental Psychology, 33,* 273–283.

Klaczynski, P. A. (2001a). Analytic and heuristic processing influences on adolescent reasoning and decision-making. *Child Development, 72,* 844–861.

Klaczynski, P. A. (2001b). Framing effects on adolescent task representations, analytic and heuristics processing, and decision making: Implications for the normative/descriptive gap. *Journal of Applied Developmental Psychology, 22,* 289–309.

Klaczynski, P. A., Byrnes, J. P., & Jacobs, J. E. (2001). Introduction to the special issue: The development of decision making. *Applied Developmental Psychology, 22,* 225–236.

Lewis, C. (1980). A comparison of minors and adults pregnancy decisions. *American Journal of Orthopsychiatry, 50*(3), 446–453.

Lewis, C. C. (1981). How adolescents approach decisions: Changes over grades 7 to 12 and policy implications. *Child Development, 52*(2), 538–544.

Lipsey, M. W. (1992). Juvenile delinquency treatment: A meta-analytic inquiry into the variability of effects. In T. D. Cook, H. Cooper, D. S. Cordray, H. Hartman, L. V. Hedges, R. J. Light, T. A. Louis, & F. Mosteller (Eds.), *Meta-analysis for explanation: A casebook* (pp. 83–128). New York: Russell Sage.

Meisel, A., Roth, L. H., & Lidz, C. W. (1977). Toward a model of the legal doctrine on informed consent. *American Journal of Psychiatry, 134,* 285–289.

Miranda v. Arizona, 384 U.S. 436 (1966).

Moshman, D. (1993). Adolescent reasoning and adolescent rights. *Human Development, 36,* 27–40.

Office of Technology Assessment. (1991). *Adolescent health—Vol. 2: Background and the effectiveness of selected prevention and treatment services.* Washington, DC: U.S. Government Printing Office.

Parham v. J.R., 422 U.S. 584 (1979).

Platt, A. (1999). The triumph of benevolence: The origins of the juvenile justice system in the United States. In B. Feld (Ed.), *Readings in juvenile justice administration* (pp. 20–35). New York: Oxford University Press.

Poythress, N., Hoge, S. K., Bonnie, R. J., & Monahan, J. (1996). *The MacArthur Competence Assessment Tool—Criminal Adjudication.* Unpublished manuscript.

Puzzanchera, C. M. (1998). *The youngest offenders: 1996.* Washington, DC: U.S. Department of Justice.

Redding, R. (1997). Juveniles transferred to criminal court: Legal reform proposals based on social science research. *Utah Law Review, 3*, 710–763.

Rotheram-Borus, M., & Koopman, C. (1990). AIDS and adolescents. In R. Lerner, A. Peterson, & J. Brooks-Gunn (Eds.), *Encyclopedia of adolescence* (pp. 29–36). New York: Garland.

Savitsky, J., & Karras, D. (1984). Competency to stand trial among adolescents. *Adolescence, 19*, 349.

Scott, E. (2000). Criminal responsibility in adolescence: Lessons from developmental psychology. In T. Grisso & B. Schwartz (Eds.), *Youth on trial: A developmental perspective on juvenile justice* (pp. 291–324). Chicago: University of Chicago Press.

Scott, E., & Grisso, T. (1997). The evolution of adolescence: A developmental perspective on juvenile justice reform. *Journal of Criminal Law and Criminology, 88*, 137–189.

Scott, E. S., Reppucci, N. D., & Woolard, J. L. (1995). Evaluating adolescent decision making in legal contexts. *Law and Human Behavior, 19*, 221–230.

Sickmund, M., Snyder, H., & Poe-Yamagata, E. (1998). *Juvenile offenders and victims: 1997 update on violence.* Washington, DC: U.S. Department of Justice.

Simpson, A. L. (1976). Rehabilitation as the justification of a separate juvenile justice system. *California Law Review, 64*, 984–1017.

Slobogin, C., Fondacaro, M., & Woolard, J. L. (1999). A prevention model of juvenile justice: The promise of *Kansas v. Hendricks* for children. *University of Wisconsin Law Review, 1999*, 186–226.

Steinberg, L., & Cauffman, E. (1996). Maturity of judgment in adolescence: Psychosocial factors in adolescent decision-making. *Law and Human Behavior, 20*, 249–272.

Steinberg, L., & Silverberg, S. (1986). The vicissitudes of autonomy in early adolescence. *Child Development, 57*, 841–851.

Weithorn, L. A., & Campbell, S. B. (1982). The competency of children and adolescents to make informed treatment decisions. *Child Development, 53*, 1589–1598.

Woolard, J. L. (1998, March). *Adolescent judgment and adjudicative competence in legal contexts.* Paper presented at the Biennial Conference of the American Psychology–Law Society, San Francisco, CA.

Woolard, J. L. (in press). Capacity, competence, and the juvenile defendant: Implications for research and policy. In B. L. Bottoms, M. B. Kovera, & B. D. McAuliff (Eds.), *Children and the law: Social science and policy.* New York: Cambridge University Press.

Woolard, J. L., Fondacaro, M., & Slobogin, C. (2001). Informing juvenile justice policy: Directions for behavioral science research. *Law and Human Behavior, 25*, 13–24.

Woolard, J. L., Fried, C. S., & Reppucci, N. D. (2001). Toward an expanded definition of adolescent competence in legal contexts. In R. Roesch, R. Corrado, & R. Dempster (Eds.), *Psychology in the courts: International advances in knowledge* (pp. 21–40). London: Routledge.

Woolard, J. L., Redding, R. E., & Reppucci, N. D. (1996). Theoretical and methodological issues in studying children's capacities in legal contexts. *Law and Human Behavior, 20*, 219.

Woolard, J. L., & Reppucci, N. D. (2000). Researching adolescents' capacities as defendants. In T. Grisso & R. Schwartz (Eds.), *Youth on trial* (pp. 173–191). Chicago: University of Chicago Press.

Woolard, J. L., Reppucci, N. D., & Scott, E. (1996). *Judgment assessment tool for adolescents.* Unpublished manual.

Zimring, F. (1998). *American youth violence.* New York: Cambridge University Press.

10

Setting Goals and Making Plans: How Children and Adolescents Frame Their Decisions

Kathleen M. Galotti
Carleton College

Research on the development of decision-making skills and attitudes rests on the premise that good decisions are those that furthers one's own goals (Bandura, 1989, 2001; Byrnes, 1998; Byrnes, Miller, & Reynolds, 1999; Galotti, 2002; von Winterfeldt & Edwards, 1986; Zimmerman, 2001). Yet, quite little is known about how goal setting actually develops. Much of the existing literature on goal setting and planning (e.g., Ellis & Siegler, 1997; Friedman & Scholnick, 1997; Gauvain & Rogoff, 1989; Hudson, Shapiro, & Sosa, 1996; Kahle & Kelley, 1994) presents children with tasks in which goals are given, or constrained to a particular domain, such as doing home-work. In contrast, little is known about the types of goals elementary and secondary aged students set for themselves, or about their approaches to, and successes at, planning to meet their goals. In this chapter, I describe two investigations that address some of these questions.

THE SIGNIFICANCE OF GOAL SETTING

The processes by which people formulate and attempt to attain goals has received much attention in the psychological literature. Miller, Galanter, and Pribram (1960) created the widely regarded seminal work on goal-directed behavior, but the centrality of goals to other psychological constructs goes back much further. William James (1890/1983) argued that "the pursuance of future ends and the choice of means for their attainment are thus the mark and criterion of the presence of mentality" (p. 21), thus thrusting the topic center stage in psychology, the science of mind. Pinker (1997) argued that the presence of goals defines a person's (or animal's, or extraterrestrial's) intelligence, arguing that "Intelligence . . . is the ability to attain goals in the face of obstacles by means of decisions based on rational . . . rules" (p. 62). Bandura (2001) noted that "Forethoughtful, generative, and reflective capabilities are, therefore, vital for survival and human progress" (p. 3).

Kruglanski (1996) saw goals as energizers of behavior, entities that "lend meaning and direction to our existence" (p. 599). Little (1998) agreed that well-being and personal meaning come from both the setting and the accomplishment of personal goals, or, as he calls them, "personal projects." He argues that personal projects "provide a sense of structure to human lives, a source of continuing personal identity, and a point of active interchange between people and their surrounding contexts" (p. 194).

These quotations speak to the fact that many psychologists with different specialties have seen goal setting as playing an essential role in human experience. Goals are seen as a motivator of behavior, and as the source of life's meaning. However, it is my purpose here to examine specifically the role that goals play in directing and constraining decision making.

GOAL SETTING AND DECISION MAKING

Decision-making researchers often concern themselves with issues of rationality—that is, in trying to create ways of assessing the overall goodness of a decision. For example: Have I made a good decision in my choice of a career? In my decision to work for this specific employer? To build a house? To have children?

In assessing the goodness or rationality of a decision, we cannot use the outcome of the decision as the yardstick. Too often, outcomes are influenced by bad luck, unforeseen and unforeseeable factors, and/or uncontrollable elements. I could have chosen to work for Company A as opposed to Companies B or C. My decision could be based on my interactions with prospective supervisors at each company—I "clicked" best with the one at Company A, and wanted to work for her. However, just after I accepted Company A's offer and turned down the other two, the supervisor at Company A calls to tell me that she has just quit, and will now be working at Company C (which has already filled the position I turned down). Does this make my initial decision wrong? No. To the contrary, it may well have been the best decision I could have made, given the information I had at the time.

Moreover, the choice that is best for me might not be best for someone else. My career choice might be great for me, but bad for you—due to differences in our temperaments, our work styles, our values for job-related or family-related issues. Faced with the same options of working for Companies A, B, or C, you might rationally choose Company B because you value more highly certain aspects or features of that company than I do. In other words, for many real-life decisions, the outcomes cannot be objectively ranked on an overall scale of goodness that will hold true for every decision maker. Any set of choices must somehow be considered relative to something about the individual decision maker. That elusive "something" is likely to be a person's overall goals.

For example, imagine I make a career decision to be a lifeguard. If my only goals are to be near the seashore and get a tan while collecting a paycheck, then this decision might be the perfect, most rational choice for me to select. If, instead, my goals include using state-of-the-art technology on a daily basis, experiencing a great deal of intellectual challenge, attaining a high level of societal prestige, and having ability to move up the corporate ladder, then lifeguarding is not really good choice for me. And if I hate sand or getting any part of my clothing or skin wet, then lifeguarding is definitely a wrong and irrational decision. The point is that the overall goodness of a decision can only be evaluated with respect to a person's goals.

A recent and influential descriptive theory of people's real-life decision making, *Image Theory*, locates a person's goals at the heart of the decision making process. Image Theory posits that most of the work of decision making is done during a phase known as the "prechoice screening of options" (Beach, 1993, 1998), during which decision makers typically winnow down the number of options under active consideration to a small number, sometimes one or two. They do this by asking themselves whether a new goal, plan, or alternative is compatible with three images, roughly described as mental representations of three constellations. These are (a) the value image (containing the decision maker's values, morals, principles); (b) the trajectory image (containing the decision maker's goals and aspirations for the future); and (c) the strategic image (the ways in which the decision maker plans to attain her or his goals). Options judged incompatible with one or more of these three images are screened out and given no further consideration.

In summary, a person's goals have several important functions in the process of making decisions. First, the goals can be used to establish the overall rationality or worth of each option. Second, they can be used to screen out unacceptable options from further consideration, thus helping a decision maker focus his or her energies on viable options. Goals can also direct the decision maker as to what information she should gather, what the possible options are, and what plans need to be made to achieve them.

THE NATURE AND STRUCTURE OF GOALS

Goals have been defined as internal representations of desired states (Austin & Vancouver, 1996). Goals can be thought of as ideal outcomes that people would like to achieve in some realm of their life. When a discrepancy exists between a goal and the current state, people are often motivated to take actions to reduce that discrepancy (Carroll, Durkin, Hattie, & Houghton, 1997). So, for example, my goal is to finish this chapter within the next week—but at the moment I have much left to do. That gap in where I am versus where I want to be is an influential motivator in how I choose to spend my time this week.

Goals do not need to be conscious or explicit. In fact, some have argued that physiological mechanisms of homeostasis, such as regulation of internal body temperature, function as goals that are nonconscious. The more commonly thought of case, of course, involves goals that we have set intentionally. A student sets a goal, for example, of achieving an overall B grade point average. That student gets a C on a midterm in one course. This feedback, in light of her goal, might cause her to redouble her efforts in the course, or to change courses, or to do things to improve her grades still more in other courses. The student's goals in this instance define for her an acceptable level of academic performance, and inspire her to achieve in this realm (Carroll et al., 1997).

Obviously, goals differ in content—what they are about. One taxonomy of goals comes from Wadsworth and Ford (1983), who divided personal goals into six different content areas, including work/school, family life, social life, leisure, personal growth and maintenance, and material/environmental. Of course, other taxonomies are possible, and to give just one other example, Williams and Long's (1991) taxonomy includes the following categories: academic achievement, personal health, friendships, job success, intimate relationships, and personal. Other researchers categorize goals according to the functions they are intended to fulfill (Strough, Berg, & Sansone, 1996), for example, goals that help establish independence, goals that promote a sense of being superior to others, goals that promote attachment to others.

Some psychologists distinguish between *learning* or *mastery* goals, intended to help the individual gain a new skill or develop knowledge, and *performance* goals, intended to allow the individual to demonstrate her or his proficiency or talent, to receive praise, and/or to please others (Dweck, 1999; Elliott & Dweck, 1988; Meece, Blumenfeld, & Hoyle, 1988; Pintrich, 2000; see Covington, 2000, for a review of the achievement goal theory literature).

Goals differ in a number of other dimensions. One such dimension is complexity—the degree to which goals are simple (e.g., sweep the floor) or involve lots of parts and subgoals (e.g., write a textbook). Another is difficulty—the chances of actually succeeding in fully meeting the goal. A third dimension is the level of specificity of the goal—the degree to which it is clear when the goal has been accomplished. It is much clearer to know, for example, whether one has or has not attended a meeting than it is to know whether one has developed the strongest proposal possible. Much evidence in the industrial/organizational literature suggests that people who set more difficult and more specific goals perform better and achieve more than do people who do not set any goals or people who set very general ("I'll just try to do my best") goals (Locke & Latham, 1990). Goals also differ in how much control an individual has over them (e.g., sweeping the floor vs. winning an election; Skinner, 1996), and in how realistic they are.

The time frame of each goal also varies. Some goals span a lifetime, whereas others span only a day or even an hour.

To summarize, then, goals have been described as differing in the following dimensions: explicitness, content, general function, complexity, difficulty, specificity, controllability, realism, and time frame. It will be important to assess which aspects differ developmentally. We return to this question after a general review of background on developmental achievements relevant to goal setting.

DEVELOPMENTAL DIFFERENCES IN GOAL SETTING AND PLANNING

Many of the studies described in the goal-setting literature focused on goals that were given to research participants, or else on goals specific to particular tasks that research participants were asked to perform (e.g., Earley, 1985, Locke, 1982). Moreover, most of the studies reviewed involved adult (mainly undergraduate) research participants. In contrast, the objective of the research described here was to examine also the goals that children and adolescents set for themselves in their everyday lives. I turn here to a brief review of what is known about goal setting and planning in children and adolescents.

That even young children set goals for themselves is demonstrated in a study by Lysyuk (1998), who observed 166 children ages 2 to 4 as they played with various objects: clay, paper and colored pencils, blocks, and dolls. Children's spontaneous comments about what they were going to do were recorded, and categorized as to whether or not they indicated a specific intention to use the materials in a particular way (e.g., a goal). It was found that by age 3, most (87.4%) of the children announced at least one goal, and/or at least one evaluation of an activity as productive.

Children as well as adults hold different types of goals. Dweck and her colleagues (Dweck & Leggett, 1988; Elliott & Dweck, 1988) demonstrated the existence of stable individual differences among fourth- and fifth-grade children. These children could be reliably classified as holding or choosing either performance or learning goals. Children with learning goals were more willing to risk error and to persist longer in the face of failed attempts than children with performance goals. The source of individual differences in the type of goals a child (or adult) holds in a given domain is yet to be fully identified. However, a child's self-efficacy and his or her own sense of how mastery of a certain skill or domain is attained have been predicted to change with development, which in turn affects the approach to goal setting, although as yet in ways undocumented by research (Dweck & Leggett, 1988; Eccles, Wigfield, & Schiefele, 1998). Schunk (2001) reviewed work suggesting that self-set goals are particularly important in the development of a sense of self-efficacy.

Children's view of themselves as agents also undergoes a great deal of development during childhood and adolescence (Harter, 1998). For example, while young (preschool) children tend to be unrealistically positive about their abilities to succeed on very difficult tasks, school-agers become increasingly oriented toward information about their performance relative to their peers (Ruble & Frey, 1991). In turn, this depresses their predictions about their future performance, meaning that self-judgments become more negative, albeit more realistic.

School-aged children also become more able and likely to recognize that others (parents, teachers, peers) are evaluating them, and come to internalize at least some of the expectations of others in their own evaluations. Children's behavior becomes more self-regulated as the standards and rules of important others are internalized (Harter, 1998). As these changes occur, they may well affect goal setting. Older children might be more realistic in their goal setting, more able to assess how controllable a goal is, and more able to think about themselves and their activities in a broader number of realms.

Planning abilities also develop over childhood and early adolescence. Children have been shown to become more effective planners, that is, better able to generate ideas, sequence activities, prioritize, and use a bigger and more varied repertoire of existing plans (Baker-Sennett, Matusov, & Rogoff, 1993; Gardner & Rogoff, 1990; Gauvain & Rogoff, 1989). Predictably, children are better planners when they are in more familiar contexts where they have greater knowledge of events (Hudson, Sosa, & Shapiro, 1997). Berg, Strough, Calderone, Meegan, and Sansone (1997) showed that preadolescents were less likely than older groups (college students, middle-aged adults, and older adults) to anticipate problems in their real-life activities. As planning and goal setting seem closely intertwined, one might expect concomitant changes in the way children and adolescents set goals as their planning skills unfold.

Further cognitive and affective developments during adolescence are likely to affect goal setting and planning once more. Adolescents are a particularly important population to study with respect to the activity of setting goals. Adolescence is a developmental period defined by rapid changes in the physical, cognitive, emotional, and social realms. As adolescents leave middle childhood behind, they confront a wide variety of new tasks and challenges and are granted more autonomy with which to face them. As described by Havighurst (1972), Erikson (1968), and Marcia (1966), a major developmental task for adolescents is to establish their identity: a unified vision of their values, aspirations, goals, and roles, both current and future. Nurmi (1991; see also Nurmi, Poole, & Kalakoski, 1994) demonstrated that adolescents do in fact think a great deal about their own futures, especially their own occupation and education and future family.

It seems reasonable to believe that the cognitive changes occurring in adolescence affect and add new dimensions to the task of goal setting. Adolescents are described by Piagetian and neo-Piagetian theorists alike as being able to think hypothetically, to see reality as only one possibility (Keating, 1980, 1990; Moshman, 1999). Adolescents are argued to gain more conscious control over the inferences they make and the ways in which they coordinate hypothetical possibilities and their implications. They are also thought to be more adept at reasoning from principles, as opposed to concrete rules, than are younger children. Thus, the picture that emerges is that of adolescents developing flexibility and power in their thinking and imagination. This development allows them greater control and direction, which in turn enables more systematic generation of possibilities along with the capacity to think ahead, to plan and anticipate consequences (Keating, 1980).

Strough et al. (1996) asked older elementary students, college students, middle-aged (age 40 to age 59) adults, and older adults (60+ years old) to describe a recent problem (hassle, conflict, challenge) they had experienced within the past year, then to state their goal in dealing with the problem. Responses to this question were categorized according to a taxonomy they developed. Results showed that interpersonal elements were most salient to middle-aged adults and least salient to the preadolescents, who in turn were more focused on task improvement and school-related goals. The authors attributed the age differences in goal types to the fact that individuals at different ages were experiencing different age-related life tasks (e.g., finishing school vs. managing a career).

Klaczynski, Laipple, and Jurden (1992) conducted a study in which high-school students (either those college-bound or those in a vocational-training track) were surveyed about their developmental goals, their interpretation of practical problems, and their plan for addressing those problems. The listed goals were classified into three categories: (a) adult anticipation (e.g., getting married, having children, finding an apartment); (b) career anticipation (e.g., be successful, get straight As, find a good job); and (c) social (e.g., party, go to a dance, hang out). Goals were scored for how far in the future the adolescent projected accomplishing them.

There were effects found for both developmental level and track. High-school sophomores, for example, listed a significantly higher percentage of career anticipation goals than did high-school seniors. Vocational-training students listed a greater frequency of adult anticipation goals than did college-bound students. Vocational sophomores, in particular, were more likely to list goals that were projected less into the future than were all other students. These results replicated previous ones that also reported that college-preparatory students focus more on career preparation, whereas vocational students emphasize adult preparation (Klaczynski & Reese, 1991).

Studies by Verstraeten (1980) and Klineberg (1967) suggested that children and adolescents have different views of the future. Younger children have been described as seeing the future as "a refuge for unrealistic fantasies" (Verstraeten, 1980, p. 179), so that the goals they list are not as likely to be meant to influence behavior. A child who states "I want to be an astronaut," on this account, does not use that goal to guide current behavior, but instead states a dream that he may or may not really intend to accomplish. In contrast, adolescents are thought to realistically project their futures further out in time and with more realism.

Nuttin (1985) used the term *time perspective* to be composed of a dimension in which a person locates objects—either memories (located in the past) or goals (located in the future). Presumably, older adolescents will have a more elaborated future time perspective, one that stretches further out in time (as adolescents become better able to use their cognitive skills to mentally model their future lives).

STUDY 1: DEVELOPMENTAL DIFFERENCES IN SELF-SET GOALS

Most of the studies already described have focused on a specific age group, for example, preschoolers or adolescents. Thus, psychologists do not have a broad picture of how goal setting develops. The first goal of this research was to present descriptions of how children and adolescents from a broad age range describe and set personal goals.

The studies just reviewed allowed various predictions to be made. Specifically, these were:

1. *Older adolescents will have more goals than do younger children.* Presumably, the cognitive and psychosocial changes occurring in adolescence, combined with a stronger future orientation, would enable an older adolescent to think about goals more carefully and to be more aware of different realms of life (e.g., school, work, friends, family). This in turn should lead to a more nuanced and more numerous set of goals.

2. *Older adolescents will have different kinds of goals than do younger children.* The work of Klaczynski and colleagues as well as Strough et al. suggests the existence of age-related changes in goals set.

3. *Older adolescents will have goals that span a longer time frame in comparison with the goals of younger children.* A stronger future orientation and ability to think hypothetically ought to allow adolescents to "project" themselves into the future more comfortably and thus, to generate goals with longer time horizons.

4. *Older adolescents will have goals of greater complexity, controllability, and realism in comparison with the goals of younger children.* Both due to cognitive changes (e.g., the ability to reason systematically and to consider more options) and psychosocial changes (a more realistic sense of self-appraisal), the nature of personal goals set ought to differ.

The first study was therefore a descriptive study of the nature of goals that children and adolescents set for themselves. A prior question was whether children and adolescents see the general nature of goals in similar or different ways. So, we began by first asking our respondents to describe their understanding of what a goal is. They were then invited to describe their own goals. At first, they were asked to describe their goals over different time frames (yesterday, tomorrow, next week, next month, next year, lifetime) in an effort to minimally direct or interfere with the kinds of goals they would list. For ease of reference, I refer to these goals hereafter as *time-cued goals.* After generating this list of goals, participants were then asked to consider a number of categories of goals (school or camp; friends; family; hobbies, activities, or sports; jobs or chores; and personal goals) and asked if there were any other goals in these categories they had forgotten to mention. Again for ease of reference, I call this list of goals the *category-cued goals.*

Finally, students were asked to describe the plans they had for achieving each of the goals they had listed (both time-cued and category-cued). Interviewers made reference to a written list of goals they kept during the interview to conduct this latter part of the interview.

We interviewed children in Grades 1, 3, and 5—a broad sampling of elementary school-ages, as well as early adolescents (8th graders), and middle to late adolescents (12th graders). In total, 110 children were interviewed, with the number of each age group and gender shown in Table 10.1. Although specific ages were not recorded, the typical age for the grades is 7, 9, 11, 14, and 18 in the summer after 1st, 3rd, 5th, 8th, and 12th grades, respectively.

Participants were recruited over the summer months from local day-care programs, signs at local stores, recreation centers, and libraries, and through word of mouth. Students received gift certificates to the local Dairy Queen or bagel store as remuneration for their time. It may be worth noting that for the large majority of participants recruited, they "graduate" from elementary, middle, and high school at the conclusion of Grades 5, 8, and 12, respectively.

Interviews were recorded on microcassette recorders that were visible to the child. In addition, interviewers kept handwritten track of the goals each

TABLE 10.1
Number of Participants by Grade and Gender

Grade	Girls	Boys	Total Number of Participants
1st	15	10	25
3rd	8	15	23
5th	12	10	22
8th	11	10	21
12th	10	9	19
TOTAL	56	54	110

child listed on a sheet listing the time horizons of spontaneous goals and the categories of cued goals.

To help organize the results we found, I structure the discussion around the four hypotheses just listed.

Hypothesis 1: Older Adolescents Will Have More Goals Than Do Younger Children

The data showed clear support for this prediction. Older children and adolescents listed more goals than did younger children, as shown in Fig. 10.1. The total number of time-cued and category-cued goals listed was analyzed using a 2 (gender) $\times$ 5 (grade) $\times$ 2 (type of cue) mixed ANOVA, with repeated measures on the last factor. This analysis revealed a main effect of grade, $F(4, 100) = 19.15, p < .001, MSE = 23.61$, and a main effect for type of cue, $F(1, 100) = 84.52, p < .001, MSE = 6.80$. There were also two 2-way interactions: one between gender and type of cue, $F(1, 100) = 10.97, p < .001, MSE = 6.80$, and one between grade and type of cue, $F(4, 100) = 13.88, p < .001, MSE = 6.80$.

Post-hoc Tukey tests ($p < .01$) showed that the means for males and females differed on the number of time-cued goals listed (7.57 vs. 10.05 for males and females), but not for the category-cued goals (5.67 vs. 5.75 for males and females). The means for the grade by type of cue interaction are presented in Fig. 10.1. Post-hoc Tukey tests ($p < .01$) showed that for time-cued goals, the means for 1st and 3rd graders differed significantly from the means for 5th and 8th graders, which were in turn significantly lower than that of the 12th graders. For category-cued goals, the means for 1st, 3rd, and 8th graders differed significantly from that of 12th graders.

Notice in Fig. 10.1 that the most striking age differences in number of goals listed occurs for the time-cued goals. Recall that these were the goals first asked about, and for which the cues were less structured. Although the number of category-cued goals also rose with age, the differences were less pronounced and less linear. Presumably, cuing by category types provided al-

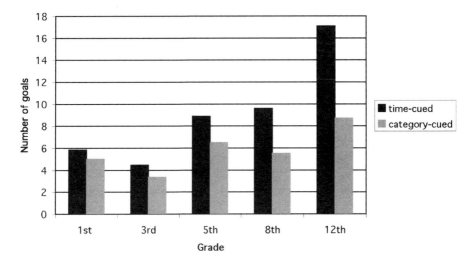

FIG. 10.1. Number of goals by cue and grade.

most the same degree of assistance to participants of all ages. Also, the category-cued goals were always generated in addition to the ones previously listed in response to time cues. These may therefore be of lesser importance to the participants.

Another explanation for the age differences may stem from age-related differences in understanding what a goal is. Recall that all participants were first asked to describe what a goal is. We coded these using the themes shown in Table 10.2, which also presents the overall interrater reliabilities

TABLE 10.2
Themes in Goal Definitions

Theme and Brief Definition	Interrater Reliability[a]
Achievement, accomplishment	.97
Desire, wish (something you want to do)	.85
Plan (activity or event that one plans for, budgets time or allocates resources to)	.86
Effort/Striving: (something one tries hard to do, devotes effort to)	.84
Promise/commitment/expectation of self	.63
Future (activity for the future, for one's lifetime)	.89
Time Frame (activity with a set or defined time frame)	.85
Challenge/standard/objective	.54
Improvement (something one wants to get better at)	.93
Important (something with significance to self or others)	.88
Specific example (student offers a specific "e.g.")	.92
Don't know/no definition	.95

Note. [a]Reliabilities were computed over three independent raters using coefficient alpha.

for each theme. A definition could incorporate any number (0, 1, 2, . . . or all) of themes.

I looked first to see whether older children incorporated more themes into their definitions. Total number of themes used was subjected to a 5 (grade) × 2 (gender) ANOVA. This yielded a main effect for grade, $F(4, 101) = 2.87, p < .001, MSE = .58$. Mean number of themes were 1.20 for 1st graders, 1.65 for 3rd graders, 1.77 for 5th graders, 2.29 for 8th graders, and 2.74 for 12th graders. Post-hoc Tukey tests showed that the mean for 12th graders differed from the means for 1st, 3rd, and 5th graders, as did the mean for 8th graders from the mean for 1st graders ($p < .01$). No other means differed. No gender differences were found.

I also looked to see whether the *content* of children's definitions of what a goal is changed with age, by subjecting the usage of each theme (1 = *used*, 0 = *not used*) to a 2 (gender) × 5 (grade) × 12 (theme usage) mixed ANOVA, with repeated measures on the last factor. This analysis revealed a main effect for grade, $F(4, 100) = 12.87, p < .001, MSE = .05$; a main effect for theme usage, $F(11, 1100) = 9.86, p < .001, MSE = .12$; and an interaction between these two factors, $F(44, 1100) = 3.27, p < .001, MSE = .12$. No other main effects or interactions were statistically significant.

Post-hoc Tukey tests indicated that there were significant grade differences only for Theme A (Achievement, accomplishment), with the mean usage for 8th and 12th graders significantly higher than that for 1st graders ($p < .01$). Although not reaching statistical significance, it is worth noting that the response *don't know* in response to the invitation to offer a definition of what a goal is was 36% for 1st graders, 17% for 3rd graders, but 0% for 5th, 8th, and 12th graders. Moreover, several more could only provide a specific example (e.g., "a goal thing . . . like in golfing when you hit it into a goal," as one 1st-grade girl explained it). Other (statistically nonsignificant) trends showed that older children and adolescents were more likely to see goals as involving the future, as expressing a desire or wish, and as involving a challenge or standard.

Thus, there is at least some evidence for a significant developmental pattern of understanding what the abstract notion of a goal is, which may in turn account, at least in part, for the fact that younger children articulate fewer personal goals than do older children and adolescents.

Hypothesis 2: Older Adolescents Will Have Different Kinds of Goals Than Do Younger Children

To examine the mix of the types of goals listed spontaneously, I examined the percentage of time-cued goals listed that fell into various categories. Recall that the time-cued goals were categorized into the following: school/

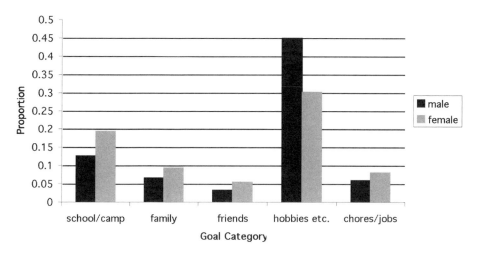

FIG. 10.2.   Percentage of time-cued goals by category and gender.

camp; friends; family; hobbies, activities, sports; job/chores; personal. The dependent measure for the first analysis was the percentage of time-cued goals in each of these categories. A 2 (gender) × 5 (grade) × 5 (category)[1] mixed ANOVA, with repeated measures on the last factor was run on this dependent measure. It revealed a main effect for grade, $F(4, 98) = 3.15$, $p < .05$, $MSE = .01$, although post-hoc Tukey tests did not reveal any pair of means as being significantly different. There was also a main effect of category, $F(4, 392) = 52.35$, $p < .001$, $MSE = .03$, as well as two significant interactions between category and gender, $F(4, 392) = 5.21$, $p < .001$, $MSE = .03$, and category and grade, $F(4, 392) = 4.69$, $p < .001$, $MSE = .03$. Figures 10.2 and 10.3 present the means for these two interactions.

Post-hoc Tukey tests ($p < .01$) revealed a significant gender difference for the category *hobbies, sports, activities* only (see Fig. 10.2). Boys listed more goals in the *hobbies/sports/activities* category than did girls, who instead listed proportionately more *school/camp, family, friends,* and *chores/jobs* goals. It is worth noting that the *hobbies, and so on* category perhaps allows goal setters the most autonomy and independence in the goals. This may in turn reflect a gender difference in autonomy or sense of independence from others.

For the interaction between grade and category, post-hoc Tukey tests ($p < .01$) revealed a significant difference in proportion of use of the category *hobbies, sports, activities* among 1st and 3rd graders, on one hand, and 12th graders, on the other hand (see Fig. 10.3). That is, older adolescents were less

---

[1]Most goals (99.5%) were able to be coded into one of the six categories. Because the data were proportions, and thus summed to one for every respondent, I omitted the category *personal* from the ANOVA.

316

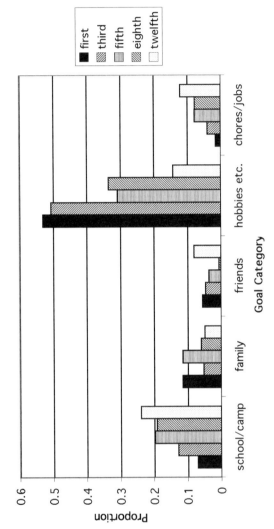

FIG. 10.3. Percentage of time-cued goals by category and grade.

likely than younger children to have as high a proportion of their goals in this category.

In these data, we again see that for at least three of the categories (*school/ camp, hobbies, activities and sports, and chores/jobs*), some familiar age-related discontinuities. Once again, the 1st and 3rd graders' proportion of goals of these types are similar, as are the corresponding ones for 5th and 8th graders. Twelfth graders once again seem to be performing differently from all other participants.

Hypothesis 3: Older Adolescents Will Have Goals That Span a Longer Time Frame in Comparison With the Goals of Younger Children

I next looked at the category-cued goals. Recall that category-cued goals were categorized into the following time horizons: *next day, next week, next month, next year*, and *lifetime*. A 2 (gender) × 5 (grade) × 4 (time horizon)[2] mixed ANOVA, with repeated measures on the last factor, was run on the dependent measure of proportionate use. This analysis revealed a main effect for time horizon grade, $F(3, 294) = 70.74$, $p < .001$, $MSE = .09$, as well as a significant interaction between grade and time horizon, $F(3, 294) = 2.25$, $p < .01$, $MSE = .09$. Figure 10.4 presents the means for this interaction. Post-hoc Tukey tests ($p < .01$) revealed no significant differences in proportion of use of any time horizon by participants of different grades, despite the appearance of a trend for 12th graders to list goals with longer time horizons. Almost no one described next-day, category-cued goals.

It may be that 12th graders, surveyed the summer after completing high school, are particularly aware of their own goals and particularly focused on the long term (e.g., thinking in terms of the next year or the rest of their life). This result certainly echoes Nurmi's (1991) idea that adolescents are strongly future oriented. To see whether this focus is related to graduation or to attaining a specific level of cognitive development, more work would be needed.

Hypothesis 4: Older Adolescents Will Have Goals of Greater Complexity, Controllability, and Realism in Comparison With the Goals of Younger Children

Four research assistants and I independently coded each goal listed along five dimensions. These were: (a) *complexity* (having lots of parts or subgoals);

---

[2]Because the data were proportions, and thus summed to one for every respondent, I omitted the category *next day* from the ANOVA.

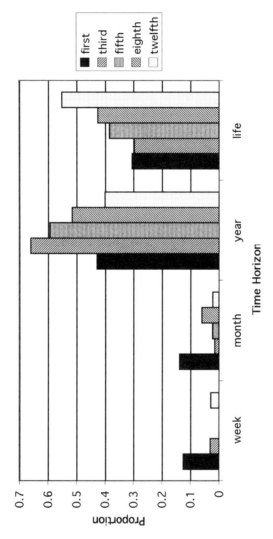

FIG. 10.4. Percentage of category-cued goals by time horizon and grade.

(b) *difficulty* (degree of effort required to achieve the goal); (c) *specificity* (how clear it is when the goal has been achieved); (d) *controllability* (degree to which the achievement of the goal is under the sole control of the participant); and (e) *realism* (plausibility of achieving the goal). The overall inter-rater reliabilities, computed with coefficient alpha over five raters, ranged from .38 to .87, with a median of .76.

Mean ratings for each dimension for each participant were computed, separately for time-cued and category-cued goals. These mean ratings were subjected to a 2 (gender) × 5 (grade) × 2 (cue type) × 5 (rating scale) mixed ANOVA, with repeated measures on the last two factors. This analysis showed main effects for both rating, $F(4, 380) = 319.43$, $p < .001$, $MSE = .96$, and cue type, $F(1, 95) = 20.57$, $p < .001$, $MSE = .66$, as well as several interactions.

The first interactions of interest are between rating and cue type, $F(4, 380) = 11.22$, $p < .001$, $MSE = .54$, and a 3-way interaction between these two factors and grade, $F(16, 380) = 1.84$, $p < .001$, $MSE = .54$. Complexity ratings rose with age for both time-cued and category-cued goals. Difficulty ratings seem to follow this general trend (except for 12th graders). Specificity ratings and ratings of realism of goals show no discernable pattern with age. The controllability ratings showed an increasing pattern with age for time-cued goals, but not for category-cued goals. Post-hoc Tukey tests ($p < .01$) showed reliable differences between time- and category-cued goals only in the specificity ratings, and only for students completing Grades 3, 5, and 8.

These results provide mixed support for Hypothesis 4. In particular, ratings of specificity and realism show little developmental trend, contrary to prediction, whereas ratings of complexity and difficulty do support the prediction, and ratings of controllability vary by type of cue.

Taken as a whole, the results of this study suggest that the number of goals generated rises with age, particularly when the prompts to generate goals are not content specific. The kinds of goals generated also changes as a function of age, with older children generating proportionately fewer leisure time goals such as hobbies or sports. Older children and adolescents generate more complex goals and goals that require more effort to achieve, but not more specific or realistic goals. There are mixed results as to an increase with age of controllability of goals generated.

STUDY 2: INDIVIDUAL DIFFERENCES
IN PLANNING TO MEET GOALS

Generating goals in an interview tells us something about children's and adolescents' goals in everyday life. However, it leaves open the question of whether goals are actually met. In a second set of studies, individual differences in older adolescents' goal setting and scheduling were examined.

I began by looking at the ways in which different adolescents described their own planning abilities, that is, their ability to budget their time and other resources in the service of fulfilling their goals. In part, I was guided by the common image of the "overcommitted" adolescent, an oft-reported persona found frequently on college and high school campuses. I used a previously developed instrument (Simons & Galotti, 1992) that assesses common planning practices and abilities such as budgeting time, keeping written lists of things to do, generating alternative ways of accomplishing a given goal, or attending to details. To examine individual differences in goal setting, I divided samples of participants into three groups, according to their score on this "planning behaviors" instrument. The top third of the group were designated "good" planners; the middle, "average" planners; and the bottom, "poor" planners, although it must be kept in mind that the designations are relative to one another, and not absolute.

In addition to describing behavioral differences in self-reported good and poor planners in setting and achieving goals, I also examined the ways in which they described the purposes of their goals. I wondered whether, for instance, poorer planners focus more on short-term, immediate concerns, attempting to fulfill the "urgent" but "unimportant" tasks in front of them (Covey, A. R. Merrill, & R. R. Merrill, 1994) whereas good planners take a longer view. Alternatively, I looked at whether better planners describe their goals more specifically (Locke & Latham, 1990), or set more or less complex goals than do less good planners.

Undergraduate participants described their goals for the upcoming week one Sunday night. That Thursday, they were asked to describe their goals for the following day (Friday). On Saturday, each participant was given a typed list of both sets of goals they had previously listed and asked to indicate which goals they had accomplished. They were also asked to rate each of their goals on different rating scales, including whether the goal was a long- or short-term one, how specific the goal was, how complex the goal was, and how important the goal was. Of particular interest were three other ratings: (a) to what extent the goal reflected a desire to show themselves that they possessed certain abilities and qualities; (b) to what extent the goal reflected a desire to show others that they possessed certain abilities and qualities; and (c) to what extent the goal reflected a desire to learn about and develop certain abilities and qualities. These ratings were derived from Dweck's work on learning and performance goals (Dweck & Leggett, 1988; Elliott & Dweck, 1988).

Surprisingly, self-reported good planners did not set more goals than did self-reported poor planners, either for the week or for the day. Nor did good planners complete more goals or a higher percentage of goals. Moreover, students with different overall planning scores did not differ in their ratings of their goals' complexity, importance, specificity, or time horizon for completion.

However, goal ratings of the learning and/or performance aspects of the goals did correlate significantly with planning scores. Moreover, the correlations were particularly strong (about .45) with both the "show yourself you possess certain abilities and qualities" and the "learn about and develop certain abilities and qualities" items. This in turn suggests that better planners put their goals into a broader context, and focus on mastery more so than do less good planners.

CONCLUSIONS

I take six points from these studies. The first is that older children set more goals than do younger children. This finding is rather unsurprising, given what we know about the large changes both in cognition and in psychosocial development between middle childhood and adulthood. Teasing apart how much of the increase is due to which developmental source will be left for future work.

The second point is that older adolescents, relative to elementary school children, set fewer goals having to do with leisure activities. Perhaps this is because more of their time is consumed with school, work, or chores. Roles within a family or within the work force differ for the two populations, and it may be that leisure time differences themselves explain this difference.

A third point is that there is an increasing trend for older students to focus much more heavily on lifetime goals than do younger students. Given the findings of Verstraeten (1980) and Klineberg (1967), this result is to be expected, and confirms the results they report.

More interesting is the fourth point, that in many measures (e.g., number of goals set, categories of goals set, some of the ratings of goals) the points of biggest difference seem to be between 3rd graders and 5th graders, and again between 8th and 12th graders. Large differences lead one to wonder about discontinuities, which are often regarded as a symptom of underlying qualitative change. Of course, a cross-sectional study cannot address this, but the trends in the data warrant examination in future studies. The first discontinuity does not correspond to any known developmental stage theory. It may, however, correspond to the distinction made by educators between primary elementary school grades (K to 3) and intermediate grades (4 to 6). We could speculate that there may be increased academic responsibilities placed on intermediate students, either in the classroom, or at home by parents, or both, and that these responsibilities affect one's goal setting. Further work would be needed to explore this account.

The second discontinuity, between 8th and 12th graders might be explained by a general cognitive change occurring in adolescence. Alternatively, it may be that 12th graders, having recently experienced a major life transition (the end of high school), are especially preoccupied with future life goals such as career and family. Again, future work would be needed to explore this question.

The fifth point is that only selected aspects of goals change with age. Specifically, ratings of specificity and realism do not change with age over the range of ages studied. What does increase are complexity, difficulty, and (to a lesser degree), controllability.

Presumably, achieving more complex and more difficult goals requires a more sophisticated ability to marshal resources in the service of a goal. This would imply that increases in planning abilities correlate with changes in goal setting, although in ways not yet specified. However, the sixth point I take from the data is that in the end, better planners are ones who set goals with broader purposes—especially ones having to do with mastery and self-improvement. However, better planners do not necessarily set more goals, or different kinds of goals, or goals with different time horizons.

Some of these findings are broadly reminiscent of popular press accounts of what it takes to lead a well-balanced and organized life. Covey et al. (1994) argued that such a life requires that people identify their core goals and values—their "mission" statement—and then align activities, appointments, and so on, with such values. Obvious next steps in the research program are to investigate how children and adolescents come to create such a mission statement. If they do, when they do, what are the correlates of doing so? A second objective would be to investigate the fit between goal setting, planning, and one's mission statement, and to see how understanding of the interrelationships among the three develops. Such studies would be best performed longitudinally and in a variety of domains—academic, social, leisure, religious, to name a few.

What light does this picture of goal setting in children and adolescents shed on their decision making? Again, the interpretations I offer are preliminary and speculative, and will need testing in future work. It seems, though, that having more personal goals would make personal decision making more complicated. The more different goals I have, the more different objectives might be relevant in considering options for any major decision. This may account for why the decision making of an 8-year-old, who wants only to "have a fun time over the summer," is so much less complicated than that of a college student who wants to "explore a possible career, earn enough to pay for books and board for fall semester, live in an air-conditioned apartment in the hip part of a city, and see a lot of my friends." What one chooses to do in the first case is guided by only one set of criteria, whereas in the second case, there are multiple sets of criteria.

Future time perspective differences also may cause one to frame a personal decision differently. If one is only looking for a summer job that will provide a good salary, then one does not try to consider the options in terms of one's career goals, the chances to network with future employers, or the ability to acquire skills that shore up a resume. However, if a decision maker is thinking ahead to the rest of his or her life (or even ahead to a first "real" job), then the framing of the summer job decision could be very different.

Cognitive developmental researchers need to understand better the relationships between goal setting and making decisions. Although the first is seen as a guide to the second (Beach, 1993), we need to understand how that relationship unfolds over different developmental periods, and whether there are stable individual differences in the relationship (e.g., as a function of cognitive style or ability, cultural background, level of education, personality, or temperament). I hope that decision-making researchers will begin to recognize the importance of these relationships, and to integrate study of them into their research programs.

ACKNOWLEDGMENTS

Grateful acknowledgment is made to the following individuals for their help in data collection, transcription, coding, and/or analysis in one or both of the studies described: Kathryn Ainsworth, Hope Altenbaumer, Sarah Angstrom, Rebecca Hurwitz, Karen Jacobs, Beth Lavin, Dianna Murray-Close, Megan Robb, Jason Schickli, and Dan Simons. I thank Janis Jacobs, Paul Klaczynski, and Hope Altenbaumer for comments on earlier drafts.

REFERENCES

Austin, J. T., & Vancouver, J. B. (1996). Goal constructs in psychology: Structure, process, and content. *Psychological Bulletin, 120*, 338–375.

Baker-Sennett, J., Matusov, E., & Rogoff, B. (1993). Planning as developmental process. In H. W. Reese (Ed.), *Advances in child development and behavior, 24*, 253–281.

Bandura, A. (1989). Human agency in social cognitive theory. *American Psychologist, 44*, 1175–1184.

Bandura, A. (2001). Social cognitive theory: An agentic perspective. *Annual Review of Psychology, 52*, 1–26.

Beach, L. R. (1993). Broadening the definition of decision making: The role of prechoice screening of options. *Psychological Science, 4*, 215–220.

Beach, L. R. (Ed.). (1998). *Image theory: Theoretical and empirical foundations*. Mahwah, NJ: Lawrence Erlbaum Associates.

Berg, C. A., Strough, J., Calderone, K., Meegan, S. P., & Sansone, C. (1997). Planning to prevent everyday problems from occurring. In S. L. Friedman & E. K. Scholnick (Eds.), *The developmental psychology of planning* (pp. 209–236). Mahwah NJ: Lawrence Erlbaum Associates.

Byrnes, J. P. (1998). *The nature and development of decision making: A self-regulation model*. Mahwah, NJ: Lawrence Erlbaum Associates.

Byrnes, J. P., Miller, D. C., & Reynolds, M. (1999). Learning to make good decisions: A self-regulation perspective. *Child Development, 70*, 1121–1140.

Carroll, A., Durkin, K., Hattie, J., & Houghton, S. (1997). Goal setting among adolescents: A comparison of delinquent, at-risk, and not-at-risk youth. *Journal of Educational Psychology, 89,* 441–450.

Covey, S. R., Merrill, A. R., & Merrill, R. R. (1994). *First things first: To live, to love, to learn, to leave a legacy.* New York: Simon & Schuster.

Covington, M. V. (2000). Goal theory, motivation, and school achievement: An integrative review. *Annual Review of Psychology, 51,* 171–200.

Dweck, C. S. (1999). *Self theories: Their role in motivation, personality, and development.* Philadelphia, PA: Psychology Press.

Dweck, C. S., & Leggett, E. L. (1988). A social-cognitive approach to motivation and personality. *Psychological Review, 95,* 256–273.

Earley, P. C. (1985). Influence of information, choice and task complexity upon goal acceptance, performance, and personal goals. *Journal of Applied Psychology, 70,* 481–491.

Eccles, J. S., Wigfield, A., & Schiefele, U. (1998). Motivation to succeed. In W. Damon (Series Ed.) & N. Eisenberg (Vol. Ed.), *Handbook of child psychology: Vol. 3. Social, emotional, and personality development* (5th ed., pp. 1017–1095). New York: Wiley.

Elliott, E. S., & Dweck, C. S. (1988). Goals: An approach to motivation and achievement. *Journal of Personality and Social Psychology, 54,* 5–12.

Ellis, S., & Siegler, R. S. (1997). Planning as a strategy choice, or why don't children plan when they should? In S. L. Friedman & E. K. Scholnick (Eds.), *The developmental psychology of planning* (pp. 183–208). Mahwah, NJ: Lawrence Erlbaum Associates.

Erikson, E. H. (1968). *Identity: Youth and crisis.* New York: Norton.

Friedman, S. L., & Scholnick, E. K. (Eds.). (1997). *The developmental psychology of planning.* Mahwah, NJ: Lawrence Erlbaum Associates.

Galotti, K. M. (2002). *Making decisions that matter: How people face important life choices.* Mahwah, NJ: Lawrence Erlbaum Associates.

Gardner, W., & Rogoff, B. (1990). Children's deliberateness of planning according to task circumstances. *Developmental Psychology, 26,* 480–487.

Gauvain, M., & Rogoff, B. (1989). Collaborative problem solving and children's planning skills. *Developmental Psychology, 25,* 139–151.

Harter, S. (1998). The development of self-representations. In W. Damon (Series Ed.) & N. Eisenberg (Vol. Ed.), *Handbook of child psychology: Vol. 3. Social, emotional, and personality development* (5th ed., pp. 553–617). New York: Wiley.

Havighurst, R. J. (1972). *Developmental tasks and education.* New York: McKay.

Hudson, J. A., Shapiro, L. R., & Sosa, B. B. (1996). Planning in the real world: Preschool children's scripts and plans for familiar events. *Child Development, 66,* 984–998.

Hudson, J. A., Sosa, B. B., & Shapiro, L. R. (1987). Scripts and plans: The development of preschool children's event knowledge and event planning. In S. L. Friedman & E. K. Scholnick (Eds.), *The developmental psychology of planning: Why, how, and when do we plan?* (pp. 77–102). Mahwah, NJ: Lawrence Erlbaum Associates.

James, W. (1983). *The principles of psychology.* Cambridge, MA: Harvard University Press. (Original work published 1890)

Kahle, A. L., & Kelley, M. L. (1994). Children's homework problems: A comparison of goal setting and parent training. *Behavior Therapy, 25,* 275–290.

Keating, D. P. (1980). Thinking processes in adolescence. In J. Adelson (Ed.), *Handbook of adolescent psychology* (pp. 211–246). New York: Wiley.

Keating, D. P. (1990). Structuralism, deconstruction, reconstruction: The limits of reasoning. In W. F. Overton (Ed.), *Reasoning, necessity, and logic: Developmental perspectives* (pp. 299–319). Hillsdale, NJ: Lawrence Erlbaum Associates.

Klaczynski, P. A., Laipple, J. S., & Jurden, F. H. (1992). Educational context differences in practical problem solving during adolescence. *Merrill-Palmer Quarterly, 38,* 417–438.

Klaczynski, P. A., & Reese, H. W. (1991). Educational trajectory and "action orientation": Grade and track differences. *Journal of Youth and Adolescence, 20*, 441–462.

Klineberg, S. L. (1967). Changes in outlook on the future between childhood and adolescence. *Journal of Personality and Social Psychology, 7*, 185–193.

Kruglanski, A. W. (1996). Goals as knowledge structures. In P. M. Gollwitzer & J. E. Bargh (Eds.), *The psychology of action* (pp. 599–618). New York: Guilford.

Little, B. R. (1998). Personal project pursuit: Dimensions and dynamics of personal meaning. In P. T. P. Wong & P. S. Fry (Eds.), *The human quest for meaning: A handbook for research and clinical applications* (pp. 193–212). Mahwah, NJ: Lawrence Erlbaum Associates.

Locke, E. A. (1982). Relation of goal level to performance with a short work period and multiple goal levels. *Journal of Applied Psychology, 67*, 512–514.

Locke, E. A., & Latham, G. P. (1990). *A theory of goal setting and task performance.* Englewood Cliffs, NJ: Prentice Hall.

Lysyuk, L. G. (1998). The development of productive goal setting with 2- to 4-year-old children. *International Journal of Behavioral Development, 22*, 799–812.

Marcia, J. E. (1966). Development and validation of ego-identity status. *Journal of Personality and Social Psychology, 3*, 551–558.

Meece, J. L., Blumenfeld, P. C., & Hoyle, R. H. (1988). Students' goal orientations and cognitive engagement in classroom activities. *Journal of Educational Psychology, 80*, 514–523.

Miller, G. A., Galanter, E., & Pribram, K. H. (1960). *Plans and the structure of behavior.* New York: Henry Holt & Company.

Moshman, D. (1999). *Adolescent psychological development: Rationality, morality, and identity.* Mahwah, NJ: Lawrence Erlbaum Associates.

Nurmi, J. (1991). How do adolescents see their future? A review of the development of future orientation and planning. *Developmental Review, 11*, 1–59.

Nurmi, J., Poole, M. E., & Kalakoski, V. (1994). Age differences in adolescent future-oriented goals, concerns, and related temporal extension in different sociocultural contexts. *Journal of Youth and Adolescence, 23*, 471–487.

Nuttin, J. (1985). *Future time perspective and motivation: Theory and research method.* Leuven, Belgium: Leuven University Press.

Pinker, S. (1997). *How the mind works.* New York: W. W. Norton.

Pintrich, P. R. (2000). Multiple goals, multiple pathways: The role of goal orientation in learning and achievement. *Journal of Educational Psychology, 92*, 544–555.

Ruble, D. N., & Frey, K. S. (1991). Changing patterns of comparative behavior as skills are acquired: A functional model of self-evaluation. In J. Suls & T. A. Wills (Eds.), *Social comparison: Contemporary theory and research* (pp. 70–112). Hillsdale, NJ: Lawrence Erlbaum Associates.

Schunk, D. H. (2001). Social cognitive theory and self-regulated learning. In B. Zimmerman & D. Schunk (Eds.), *Self-regulated learning and academic achievement* (pp. 125–151). Mahwah, NJ: Lawrence Erlbaum Associates.

Simons, D. J., & Galotti, K. M. (1992). Everyday planning: An analysis of time management. *Bulletin of the Psychonomic Society, 30*, 61–64.

Skinner, E. A. (1996). A guide to constructs of control. *Journal of Personality and Social Psychology, 71*, 549–570.

Strough, J., Berg, C. A., & Sansone, C. (1996). Goals for solving everyday problems across the life span: Age and gender differences in the salience of interpersonal concerns. *Developmental Psychology, 32*, 1106–1115.

Verstraeten, D. (1980). Level of realism in adolescent future time perspective. *Human Development, 23*, 177–191.

Von Winterfeldt, D., & Edwards, W. (1986). *Decision analysis and behavioral research.* Cambridge, England: Cambridge University Press.

Wadsworth, M., & Ford, D. H. (1983). Assessment of personal goal hierarchies. *Journal of Counseling Psychology, 30*, 514–526.

Williams, R. L., & Long, J. D. (1991). *Manage your life* (4th ed.). Dallas, TX: Houghton Mifflin.

Zimmerman, B. J. (2001). Theories of self-regulated learning and academic achievement: An overview and analysis. In B. Zimmerman & D. Schunk (Eds.), *Self-regulated learning and academic achievement* (pp. 1–37). Mahwah, NJ: Lawrence Erlbaum Associates.

Commentary:
The Development of Thinking

David Moshman
University of Nebraska–Lincoln

From the titles alone, we can see that the three chapters in Part III address judgment (Cauffman & Woolard, chap. 9), decision making (Finken, chap. 8), goal setting (Galotti, chap. 10), and planning (Galotti). But Galotti alerts us in her title that goal setting and planning are central to decision making, and upon reading the chapters, it becomes clear that judgment, decision making, goal setting, and planning cannot be sharply distinguished, and that all of these chapters are about all of them.

Unsurprisingly, there is less said about problem solving and reasoning. The study of problem solving and reasoning has tended to focus on the cognitive processes involved in responding to laboratory tasks, whereas the study of judgment, decision making, and planning has tended to focus on longer term, naturally occurring processes that are as much social and emotional as cognitive. Given this distinction, the present chapters and others in this volume might be said to fall in the latter, and more contemporary, camp.

Let me suggest, however, that the distinction I have just made has more to do with a historical divergence between two psychological research traditions than with the minds of real people. How can one rationally judge, make decisions, set goals, or plan without engaging in problem solving and reasoning? But how can one solve problems or engage in reasoning without making judgments and decisions? And aren't we more likely to reason correctly and solve our problems if we plan what we are doing and set relevant goals?

Consider, following Finken (chap. 8), an adolescent faced with an unwanted pregnancy. Obviously, she has a problem, and we can say that in solving it, she is engaged in problem solving.

Solving this problem will require, among other things, a series of decisions: Whom should I tell? What should I say? From whom should I seek advice? Should I get an abortion? Should I arrange for adoption? With whom should I make these arrangements? Should I keep and raise the child? Should I get married? Should I quit school? Some options may be out of the question for some adolescents but virtually all adolescents can be expected to make multiple decisions in the course of solving the problem. For some, abortion may be such an obvious choice that it is not really a decision, but there are still decisions to be made on the way to the abortion. For others, abortion may be unavailable or morally out of the question, but there are still decisions to be made about the pregnancy and the child to be born. For many, there may indeed be a genuine decision as to whether to have an abortion, but there are other decisions as well.

The decision making is most likely to solve the problem effectively, moreover, if it is planful, and this is likely to involve setting goals. Ideally, I might determine that if I am to have an abortion, I should have it by a particular date. I might devise a plan to obtain information and advice and make a decision prior to the target date, perhaps with contingency plans for implementing whatever decision I make. By planning my decisions and committing myself to associated goals, I seek to solve my problem.

But my best friend may not react as expected. My mother may try to force a particular solution. My boyfriend may deny he is the father. I may start to feel sick or depressed. Implementing a plan usually leads to unexpected problems, and solving those problems requires additional decisions and planning.

And there is more. How can I solve a problem without making judgments about the relative merits of various solutions and strategies? How can I make a decision without making a judgment? Why commit to a plan unless I have judged it superior to alternatives? To resolve the problem of an unwanted pregnancy, I may need to judge a variety of persons, ideas, options, and consequences. Judgment is deeply intertwined with problem solving, decision making, and planning.

And then there is reasoning, which has multiple facets and multiple connections with all of the aforementioned. In the course of solving the problem of my unwanted pregnancy and engaging in the associated judgments, decisions, planning, and goal setting, I test hypotheses about my pregnancy by seeking relevant information, try to make justifiable inferences, try to correct or transcend contradictions, and try to determine what is morally required, permitted, or forbidden. That is, I engage in scientific, logical, metalogical, and moral reasoning.

Solving the problem of an unwanted pregnancy, then, is not just a matter of problem solving but equally involves decision making, judgment, planning, and multiple forms of reasoning. The rather insular literatures in these areas can be seen as products of the proverbial blind men construing the various parts of an elephant in idiosyncratic ways because they do not see the larger whole.

What, then, is the elephant? Judgment, decision making, goal setting, planning, problem solving, and reasoning are all forms or aspects of *thinking*, a concept and term prevalent in the psychological and educational literatures throughout the 20th century, from Dewey (1910/1997) through the behaviorist-dominated mid-century (Bartlett, 1958; Bruner, Goodnow, & Austin, 1956; Thomson, 1959) and on through the cognitive revolution (J. Baron, 2001; J. B. Baron & Sternberg, 1987; Johnson-Laird & Wason, 1977; Kuhn, 1990; Lipman, 1991; Neimark, 1987; Osherson & Smith, 1990). By *thinking*, I mean "the deliberate application and coordination of one's inferences to serve one's purposes" (Moshman, 2005, p. 23). Thinking, then, is a broad category of cognitive processes, but not so broad as to include all of cognition. Rather, thinking is best seen as a deliberate use of *inference*, which in turn is a subset of cognition involving the transformation of knowledge:

> The term "inference" is generally applied in cases in which new cognitions are derived from prior information. One may or may not be aware of the prior information or the inferential process. To the extent that one is conscious of both, new beliefs are likely to be represented as specific propositions and construed as conclusions. Often, however, the prior information is not encapsulated as a specific set of premises, and/or the process of inference is automatic and unconscious. In such cases, there may be no awareness of having reached a conclusion. Observing a smile on someone's face, for example, one may proceed to interact with her on the assumption that she is in a happy mood without being aware of having made an inference based on her facial expression.
>
> The term "thinking" is generally applied to a self-conscious act of cognition that is intended to serve some purpose. We think in order to solve a problem, devise an option, make a decision, formulate a plan, evaluate a proposal, reach a conclusion, or justify a claim. As defined here, then, thinking does not include cognitive phenomena such as dreaming, daydreaming, or free associating that do not involve a purposeful act. Thinking is inferential in that it goes beyond the information given, but not all inferences are sufficiently purposeful to constitute thinking. An act of thinking may coordinate a variety of automatic inferences; an automatic inference, however, is not an act of thinking. (Moshman, 1995, p. 54)

This conception of thinking as the deliberate and purposeful transformation of knowledge suggests that the development of thinking consists, at least in part, of increasing consciousness and control of one's knowledge and inferences. In fact, the development of thinking may be largely the development of advanced forms of metacognition. Metacognitive development begins early in childhood and continues, for many or most individuals, at least through adolescence and early adulthood (Hofer & Pintrich, 2002; Kuhn, 2000; Moshman, 1998, 2003, 2004b, 2005).

Advanced development is more subtle than the developmental changes of early childhood, less tied to age, less the predictable outcome of genes, experience, and time. Nevertheless there appear to be ongoing changes beyond childhood that are sufficiently self-regulated, qualitative, and progressive to be deemed developmental (Hofer & Pintrich, 2002; Kuhn, 2000; Moshman, 1998, 2003, 2005). A challenge for research and theory on the development of thinking is to find developmental change amid the complexity of thinking in diverse social and cultural contexts, a task that is especially difficult with regard to adolescents and adults.

Why is developmental change more difficult to identify beyond childhood? Even in childhood, the quality of thinking varies substantially across contexts. The same child may think well in some circumstances but fall prey to serious biases in other circumstances. A younger child at her best may show better thinking than an older child under less favorable circumstances.

Nevertheless, there are skills and understandings common among 4-year-olds that are rarely seen in children recently turned 3, and among 12-year-olds that are rarely seen in children as old as 9 or 10. For example, 4-year-olds have a theory of mind that enables them to comprehend false beliefs, whereas 3-year-olds have different, and less adequate, ways of thinking about mental phenomena (Flavell, Miller, & Miller, 2002). Similarly, most 12-year-olds show a capacity for reflective or hypothetico–deductive reasoning rarely seen just a few years earlier (Moshman, 1998, 2004b, 2005). Thus children of different ages can be categorically distinguished.

But what happens beyond the developmental transition from age 10 to age 12? Let us distinguish three possibilities. First, perhaps age 12 represents a state of mature thinking. Of course, we expect specific patterns of problem solving, decision making, judgment, and so forth to change over the lifespan, but changes beyond age 12 would be a matter of ongoing adaptations to evolving task demands and circumstances rather than progress to qualitatively higher levels of thinking. In this case, we might find diverse thinking patterns among adolescents and adults correlated with a variety of variables, including age, but there would be no reason to construe such changes as developmental.

Alternatively, perhaps development continues beyond childhood until maturity is reached at some later age. To make a theoretical and empirical case for this, we must specify two or more levels in the development of thinking and show, at a minimum, that most or all adolescents or adults beyond some specifiable age think in ways rarely or never seen among 12-year-olds. A fully worked-out theory of advanced development might describe the developmental levels of 12-year-olds (who are deemed similar to each other in fundamental ways), and of, say, 15-year-olds (who are seen as similar to each other and qualitatively different from 12-year-olds), and might then go on to describe successive developmental levels and their ages of occurrence up through maturity. In this case, age would predict levels of thinking right through adolescence and perhaps beyond.

Finally, there is an intermediate possibility. Perhaps there are self-regulated, qualitative, and progressive changes in adolescence and beyond but such changes are individual and multidirectional. In this case, we could still identify advanced levels of thinking but, due to variability in the rate and extent of development across individuals and across multiple domains of thinking, attainment of such levels would correlate only modestly with age rather than being strongly predictable from age. Adults, on average, would show better thinking than adolescents, on average, but many adolescents would show better thinking than many adults, and many adults would show worse thinking than many adolescents. That is, for individuals beyond age 12, quality of thinking would show a positive correlation with age but variability across age groups would be small compared to the variability within each age group.

None of the present chapters present evidence for a universal state of rationality or maturity that is attained beyond the age of 12, nor do I know of any such evidence in the diverse literatures of human thinking. Nevertheless, in chapter 9, Cauffman and Woolard make a persuasive case, on both theoretical and empirical grounds, that 12- to 14-year-olds should not be said to have achieved maturity of judgment. I would go further and suggest that various sorts of thinking continue to develop, in most people, long beyond childhood. Indeed, the evidence for this is overwhelming (Moshman, 1998, 2003, 2004b, 2005).

Postchildhood development, however, is not a matter of moving through some age-related series of stages culminating in a state of maturity at the threshold of adulthood. Where Cauffman and Woolard (chap. 9) question the maturity of adolescents, I question the maturity of adults. The point is not that adults are immature, but that adults have not, in general, attained some final stage in the development of thinking, if indeed there is such a stage. Development beyond childhood, it appears, is not a matter of universal progress toward some endpoint routinely achieved at some specifiable age. Rather, developmental progress beyond childhood is more subtle and multifaceted, along the lines of the third option suggested.

What accounts for advanced developmental changes in thinking? Let me suggest two relevant aspects of advanced development. One of these, already noted, is *metacognition*. Thinking, as I defined it, involves consciousness and control with regard to one's knowledge and inferences, and is thus intrinsically metacognitive. There is no evidence for levels of metacognition that appear at particular ages in adolescence or beyond, but there is considerable evidence for metacognitive development beyond childhood in at least some, and probably most or all, individuals (Hofer & Pintrich, 2002; Kuhn, 2000; Moshman, 1998, 2003, 2004b, 2005). With increasing metacognition, we are more likely to really be thinking when we face problems, make decisions and judgments, and formulate plans.

Another aspect of development is suggested by Galotti's research (chap. 10). Setting goals and planning for their achievement involves a sense of yourself as an ongoing rational agent who can work toward a future state of affairs. Some kinds of long-term planning, moreover, may profit from an explicit theory of who you are—an identity (Moshman, 2004a, 2005). Our ability to plan might be expected to develop as we formulate our beliefs, values, and commitments, and Galotti does indeed find evidence for developmental change in this regard.

Our ability to make important decisions, such as whether to have an abortion, might also be expected to develop as we reflect on and coordinate our beliefs, values, and goals in the course of identity formation. Correspondingly, our level of responsibility for our choices (including culpability for immoral and criminal acts) is arguably a function of our level of identity formation. Research reported by Cauffman and Woolard (chap. 9) supports the view that the development of identity is related to the ongoing development of thinking.

But identity is not achieved at the age of 18, or 21, or 30, or indeed at any particular age. Even preadolescents have complex networks of self-conceptions that might be said to be proto-identities. Some individuals form identities during adolescence, some in early adulthood, and some later in adulthood, and some, strictly speaking, never form identities at all. We can distinguish children under age 12 from adolescents and adults in that children cannot construct identities in the Eriksonian sense of the term, whereas adolescents and adults can (Moshman, 2005), but beyond age 12, individual variability in identity formation makes it impossible to tie identity to age. Developmental changes in planning, decision making, judgment, and culpability beyond age 12 are correspondingly real and important without being a matter of age-related progress toward some predestined state of maturity.

What are the policy implications of all this? There are surely cases where immaturity justifies limits on freedom and entails corresponding limits on culpability. Even in childhood, however, the relation of maturity to age is imperfect; beyond age 12, categorical distinctions based on age derive mostly from cultural stereotypes about teens. It is difficult, then, to see how laws restricting the reproductive choices of adolescents can be justified. The point is not that adolescents should be left to make such choices on their own. As Finken shows in chapter 8, adolescents routinely consult with others in making important decisions, as do adults. There is no reason to expect governmental intrusions into these processes to be more helpful, or less harmful, in the case of adolescents than in the case of adults.

This conclusion, however, is not based on the assumption that adolescents have attained some state of maturity, and thus does not entail the outcome that adolescents in the criminal justice system should be treated as if they were adults with fixed criminal identities. Adolescents should be treated as developing individuals with the potential to make progress in their rationality, morality, and identity. Research shows, moreover, that many or most adults are no different from adolescents in this regard. Rather than draw back from a developmental perspective on adolescence, we should extend that perspective into adulthood.

In sum, the development of judgment and decision making—and of planning, goal setting, problem solving, reasoning, and more—is the development of *thinking*, which is largely a matter of increasing consciousness and control of one's knowledge and inferences. This is likely influenced by increasing awareness and control of one's self—that is, by the development of identity. There is plenty of evidence for developmental changes in thinking beyond childhood but, in contrast to the more closely age-graded changes of childhood, there are dramatic individual differences in the rate and extent of development beyond the age of about 12. Many adolescents surpass many adults in their reasoning, problem solving, decision making, judgment, and planning.

This is not to say, however, that the development of thinking does not continue beyond childhood. Development continues well into adulthood but advanced development differs in important ways from earlier development. Childhood changes are more universal and more closely tied to age. The changes of adolescence and adulthood are more individual and diverse. We know where childhood cognition is headed, but it is much more difficult, and less meaningful, to posit universal states of maturity with respect to advanced development.

Some forms of thinking are qualitatively superior to some others but this does not mean there is some state of maturity toward which all of cognitive development tends. The challenge for developmentalists is to identify qualitative progress in the complex and ongoing patterns of change, and to promote development in individuals of all ages.

REFERENCES

Baron, J. (2001). *Thinking and deciding* (3rd ed.). New York: Cambridge University Press.

Baron, J. B., & Sternberg, R. J. (Eds.). (1987). *Teaching thinking skills.* New York: Freeman.

Bartlett, F. (1958). *Thinking: An experimental and social study.* New York: Basic Books.

Bruner, J. S., Goodnow, J. J., & Austin, G. A. (1956). *A study of thinking.* New York: Wiley.

Dewey, J. (1997). *How we think.* Mineola, NY: Dover. (Original work published 1910)

Flavell, J. H., Miller, P. H., & Miller, S. A. (2002). *Cognitive development* (4th ed.). Upper Saddle River, NJ: Prentice Hall.

Hofer, B. K., & Pintrich, P. R. (Eds.). (2002). *Personal epistemology.* Mahwah, NJ: Lawrence Erlbaum Associates.

Johnson-Laird, P. N., & Wason, P. C. (Eds.). (1977). *Thinking*. Cambridge, England: Cambridge University Press.

Kuhn, D. (Ed.). (1990). *Developmental perspectives on teaching and learning thinking skills*. Basel, Switzerland: Karger.

Kuhn, D. (2000). Theory of mind, metacognition, and reasoning: A life-span perspective. In P. Mitchell & K. J. Riggs (Eds.), *Children's reasoning about the mind* (pp. 301–326). Hove, England: Psychology Press.

Lipman, M. (1991). *Thinking in education*. Cambridge, England: Cambridge University Press.

Moshman, D. (1995). Reasoning as self-constrained thinking. *Human Development, 38*, 53–64.

Moshman, D. (1998). Cognitive development beyond childhood. In W. Damon (Series Ed.), & D. Kuhn & R. Siegler (Vol. Eds.), *Handbook of child psychology: Vol. 2. Cognition, perception, and language* (5th ed., pp. 947–978). New York: Wiley.

Moshman, D. (2003). Developmental change in adulthood. In J. Demick & C. Andreoletti (Eds.), *Handbook of adult development* (pp. 43–61). New York: Plenum.

Moshman, D. (2004a). False moral identity: Self-serving denial in the maintenance of moral self-conceptions. In D. K. Lapsley & D. Narvaez (Eds.), *Moral development, self, and identity* (pp. 83–109). Mahwah, NJ: Lawrence Erlbaum Associates.

Moshman, D. (2004b). From inference to reasoning: The construction of rationality. *Thinking & Reasoning, 10*, 221–239.

Moshman, D. (2005). *Adolescent psychological development: Rationality, morality, and identity* (2nd ed.). Mahwah, NJ: Lawrence Erlbaum Associates.

Neimark, E. D. (1987). *Adventures in thinking*. San Diego: Harcourt Brace Jovanovich.

Osherson, D. N., & Smith, E. E. (Eds.). (1990). *Thinking*. Cambridge, MA: MIT Press.

Thomson, R. (1959). *The psychology of thinking*. Baltimore, MD: Penguin.

Afterword:
Development of and
in Behavioral Decision Research

Baruch Fischhoff
Carnegie Mellon University

HALCYON DAYS

In Ward Edwards's original formulation, behavioral decision research has three interrelated components: *Normative* analysis characterizes the choices that decision makers actually face. *Descriptive* analysis addresses how decision makers intuitively conceptualize those choices. *Prescriptive* analysis proposes ways to bridge the gap between the normative ideal and the descriptive reality (Edwards, 1954, 1961; von Winterfeldt & Edwards, 1986).

The complete treatment of any decision requires all three components. Without normative analysis, one cannot know what behavior is worth describing as decision relevant. Indeed, without it, the concept of *bias*, so central to behavioral decision research, is meaningless. Without prescriptive analyses, the field becomes a purely academic exercise, uninterested in bettering the human condition. It is also a somewhat cowardly exercise, unwilling to face the test of demonstrating that it knows enough to change behavior for the better (or, perhaps, to exploit it).

The prospect of an integrated epistemology contributed to the excitement of the field's early days. A once-legendary research program tried to do it all. Edwards and colleagues devised an experimental task, designed to capture the essential features of the practical task facing radar operators on the Cold War's DEW (Distant Early Warning) Line, in northern latitudes. That task included interpreting uncertain signals, in the context of varying prior probabilities (of attack), with explicit incentives for correct and incorrect summary judgments.

Fortuitously, for prescriptive purposes, the performance deficits, observed in these experimental studies, seemed relatively amenable to engineered solutions. Participants could extract signals from uncertain displays. However, they stumbled in combining these signals with one another, and with the assigned priors. Such *misaggregation* could be addressed by applying Bayes' theorem mechanically to assessments of the components. Life would be much more complicated if the problems lay with *misperception* of the signal value, where human judgment was essential. Edwards (1968) offered a brilliant (if admittedly partisan) staged debate between hypothetical proponents of misaggregation and misperception. Slovic and Lichtenstein (1971) summarized the research in a landmark review. In it, they drew parallels with the concurrent study of clinical versus statistical judgment, stimulated by the seminal mid-century research of Donald Fiske (Kelly & Fiske, 1951) and Paul Meehl (1954).

As with any noteworthy research program, each component came under scrutiny. Normatively oriented researchers sought better characterization of the signals and the conditions determining the priors. Descriptively oriented researchers sought better understanding of the mental arithmetic that might produce misaggregation and the cognitive processes that might produce misperceptions. Prescriptively oriented researchers focused on decision aids and training programs, as well as on the costs and benefits of leaving people to their own devices. Recognizing that no single project could do it all, some of the same researchers participated in a loose coalition, assembled by the Defense Advanced Projects Agency (DARPA) decision analysis research program, of the mid-1970s.

Many of these researchers continued to listen to one another, most notably through Edwards' long-running (and just concluded) series of Bayesian Research Conferences. Nonetheless, the complexity of the problems—and the growth of the field—encouraged specialization. To some extent, this meant accepting the risks of isolation in small self-referential communities, whose members learned to live with shared conventions about which elements of reality to ignore. To some extent, though, specialization was essential to intellectual growth. No project could meet all potentially relevant evidentiary standards. This volume could not have happened without specialization. It is difficult enough to extract the decision-making[1] implications of basic research into cognitive, social, or emotional development without having to render them comprehensible to hard-core normative modelers or to offer prescriptive solutions.

---

[1]An orthographic note: Historically, "decision making" has been hyphenated when used as a compound adjective, but not when used as a noun. A recent revision in Microsoft Word's dictionary fails to make that distinction. I recommend the historical practice, as a minor act of defiance (also, Strunk & White, 1979, pp. 34–35).

Nonetheless, something is lost when the pieces separate. As mentioned, the existence of bias is only meaningful in the context of a proper normative analysis. The practical importance of a phenomenon can only be determined through a prescriptive analysis of its implications. Without the common conceptual framework of decision theory's normative perspective, biases can proliferate, with multiple names for a given phenomenon or shared names for different phenomena. Although a psychologist wrote one of the first practical guides to Bayesian statistical inference (Phillips, 1973), the normative theory is only indirectly available to most psychologists, through secondary and tertiary sources. In Fischhoff and Beyth-Marom (1983), we sought to make it more accessible, as well as providing an organizing framework for psychological phenomena. Edwards, Lindman, and Savage's (1963) more technical exposition still rewards readers.

Each of the chapters in this fascinating volume addresses the interests and standards of its authors' home discipline and theoretical perspective. As such, the chapters bring to behavioral decision research substantive content, without which its analytic perspectives are arid abstractions. They were not, by and large, concerned with creating the full normative–descriptive–prescriptive arc. However, readers are selfish in their own ways. Because these issues are often on my mind (e.g., Fischhoff, 1980, 1992, 1996, 1999, 2002), I read the volume in their light. What follow are some impressions of the state of the science, in these regards. The authors' and editors' admirable work has ensured the technical quality of the chapters. I focused on ways to extend the work in this direction.

NORMATIVE ANALYSIS

Decision theory adopts a normative standard that is foreign (even antithetical) to much of psychology. Shared with neoclassical economics, that standard evaluates choices in terms of their *rationality*, defined as whether they follow coherently from individuals' beliefs and values, in the sense of adhering to an axiomatically defined set of rules. From this perspective, good decision-making processes can be followed by unhappy outcomes—either because they get the best out of a bad situation or because they meet misfortune. Rational choices can also be ones that others deplore, but serve the decision maker's self-defined self-interest.

Given a decent explanation, any psychologist should accept the separation between choices and outcomes, thereby avoiding the confusion that Baron and Hershey (1988) called *outcome bias*. The *laissez faire* attitude toward the values motivating choices may be more problematic. Much psychological research focuses on changing behavior, in externally defined directions. Even if those changes are held to be in the manipulated individual's best interest (e.g., less drug use, more exercise), the attitude is not the accepting one that decision theory shares with neoclassical economics. Moreover, psychologists are not entirely immune to the natural temptation to tell other people how to run their lives, accepting whatever leverage their professional status affords.

A manipulative stance might be particularly tempting with adolescents, where the development of competence is a central research issue, and where funding often comes from agencies concerned with getting kids to do particular things. However, the chapters in this volume are distinguished by their respect for young people. The authors see young people as sentient beings, trying to live decent lives; in this spirit, the authors look hard at the decisions facing young people. These decisions often prove to be intellectually challenging, with complex, uncertain information, perhaps coming from questionable sources (such as adults who mix communication and manipulation).

This predisposition sometimes leads the authors to thought-provoking discussions of what we can learn from kids regarding the nature of optimal decision making, perhaps even challenging the standard notion of rationality (as codified by von Neumann & Morgenstern, 1994; Savage, 1954; and others). These thought-provoking proposals raise more interesting issues than can be addressed here, or even pursued fully in book chapters. Fuller pursuit would involve some of the following strategies, building on research prompted by other confrontations between descriptive and normative research:

1. Formally characterize the choices that individuals face and how their reformulations deviate from it. As anyone who has debated a neoclassical economist could testify, believers have enormous fluency in demonstrating the rationality of seemingly irrational choices. That fluency may be self-defeating, winning the battle but losing the war, by depriving rationality of meaning. Nonetheless, the translation process is an essential part of making fundamental claims regarding rationality.

2. Cast new claims in terms of other reformulations of rationality, expressed in alternative choice axioms. For example, Loomes and Sugden (1982) offered a "regret theory," which arose from some anomalous observations and has spurred much research. Gärdnefors and Sahlin (1990) collected (and proposed) alternative ways of dealing with uncertainty. Camerer (1999) and Camerer and Weber (1992) periodically summarized axiomatic attempts to take behavior seriously (see also Schoemaker, 1982).

3. Leave rationality to those committed to axiomatic treatments and focus on *optimality*, in the sense of effective decision making. As Simon (1957) argued, rationality is an impossible aspiration in many real-world situations. Rather, heuristic approaches are needed, either to simplify those situations or to sort through them, neglecting some details. Of course, not all heuristics are created equal nor equally effective in all settings. As a result, any endorsement

must be conditioned on specifying the range of application (or proposing that some applications are so important that getting them right justifies inefficiency elsewhere).

4. Reduce the emphasis on cognitive concerns of rationality. For example, demonstrate how suboptimal outcomes may be accepted in return for procedural benefits, such as feeling self-efficacy, achieving an emotional state, or participating in a social process. Convincing arguments for nonrational normative standards require showing that they have been accepted after thoughtful deliberation. They are more powerful, if shown to be widely applicable, rather than ad hoc excuses for individual deviations. That would mean endorsing a standard equivalent to the "stable preferences" assumption that is central to neoclassical economics (in principle, if not in practice; Becker, 1976). Sen's (1977) "Rational Fools" essay is a valuable touchstone for such arguments.

DESCRIPTIVE ANALYSIS

Thus, for behavioral decision researchers, a potentially important facet of the research reported here is its challenges to conventional notions of rationality. These challenges are particularly powerful, in coming from studies of adolescents, not normally seen as sources of normative insight. However, realizing that potential will require developmental researchers to engage the conventional normative discourse over rationality more fully. Given the excess baggage that "rationality" has accrued, partly reflecting the particular character of economics as an intellectual discipline, the independent course, of focusing on optimality, might be a better strategy.

Whatever strategy is taken, the developmental researchers represented in this volume can build on how well they have contextualized many of the behavioral regularities that they describe. That is, the researchers have often worked backward from specific tasks facing young people, toward alternative theoretical accounts. That strategy, arising from concern for young people, complements the usual behavioral decision research strategy of working forward from theoretical accounts, to plausible experimental concretizations. This deep familiarity with the worlds of young people affords ecological validity to the authors' descriptive accounts, however their normative claims are evaluated.

These accounts are further strengthened by the psychological theories in which they are embedded, both those of developmental psychology per se and those created by the researchers themselves. Thus, the accounts are informed by understanding what people of varying ages can and cannot do, cognitively. That knowledge is a critical antidote to claims to the effect that individuals have hyperrational ability to think their way through to optimal solutions for complex, novel problems. It has been pivotal in the debate between psychology and economics, so instrumental to the development of behavioral economics (McFadden, 1999). However, it can also discipline claims about heuristic or pattern-recognition alternatives to hyperrationality. The behaviors proposed here are ones that young people might actually execute.

The domain-specific research is distinguished by concern not only for the particulars of the choices, but also for the social, cultural, educational, and personal context within which they are made. That context determines the plausibility that a behavior will be in young people's repertoire of possibilities (e.g., through modeling or instruction) and that it will have been reinforced as a behavior, whatever the incentive properties of the outcomes that follow from it. The identity of choice options lies, of course, outside the purview of any abstract decision theory; so does the identity of the beliefs subjected to Bayesian (or other) evaluation. The studies here show how beliefs, too, can be socially constructed and promoted (e.g., base rates of risk behaviors).

Claims regarding the persistence and optimality of behavioral strategies are strengthened by accounts of the feedback properties of the environment: How well do young people who use a strategy fare? How well do they think they are faring? In an influential formal demonstration, von Winterfeldt and Edwards (1981) showed that, for many decisions with continuous choice options (e.g., invest $X, drive Y mph), the expected utility of the choice was relatively insensitive to the accuracy of individual input estimates (e.g., Federal Reserve rates, police surveillance intensity). This "flat maximum" theorem provided a valuable perspective for any demonstration of judgmental bias: Not every statistically significant deviation from normative perfection has practical significance.

The converse of this observation is that ineffective behavioral strategies may persist because individuals rarely receive sharp feedback regarding their limits. Thus, a generally forgiving environment can exact a price, when conditions change. For example, strategies honed with continuous options might face discrete choices (smoke/do not smoke). Strategies good enough for simple decisions may falter when complex decisions compound the errors of multiple imperfect inputs. Success with trial-and-error learning may be challenged by the need to get a decision right the first time. Reliable sources may lose their value when consulted in domains where they lack competence or have vested interests, distorting their advice.

The richness of the domain-specific accounts in many chapters might be tapped for accounts (or even formal models) of the feedback properties of pursuing the behavioral strategies that each has identified. Although circumstantial, the evidence from such analyses could clarify claims about the persistence and optimality of those strategies. Presumably, problems would differ in terms of how prompt and unambiguous feedback would likely be, allowing for a (somewhat predictably) variegated pattern of strengths and weaknesses.

Such formal analysis might facilitate integrating the heterogeneous accounts that are a strength of this volume. They discourage the sort of sweeping generalizations that have, to my mind, distorted much discussion of human judgment and decision making. They encourage showing how young people can be good at some things, but poor at others, reflecting the properties of choices as well as those of teens.

PRESCRIPTIVE ANALYSIS

Integrating normative and descriptive analyses sets the stage for conducting prescriptive research in a focused and behaviorally realistic way; that is, it allows addressing the most serious problems with strategies that young people could plausibly master. Before embarking on the design and testing interventions, though, one must ask whether young people are doing well enough without the proposed help. That means comparing typical choices with rational ones, then applying a standard for what constitutes "good enough." That standard represents a value judgment, regarding the tolerability of suboptimal decisions. It affects teens as a class, insofar as the status of young people in society depends on their decision-making competence. Two domains where teens' presumed competence plays a central role in policy debates are sex and violence, both thoughtfully represented in this volume. A sweeping assertion of competence would encourage granting teens reproductive rights, while exposing them to adjudication as adults. A sweeping assertion of incompetence would do the opposite.

With politicized issues, partisans will seize on whatever evidence serves their ends. Under those circumstances, researchers have a special obligation to do what they do best: delineating the features that different situations (e.g., sex, violence) do and do not share.[2] The set of potentially relevant features is familiar to psychologists: Decisions may pose different cognitive challenges. The young people in them may have different cognitive abilities (reflecting their education or maturational stage). They may have different degrees of familiarity with the consequences (hence, ability to weight them properly). They may face different emotional pressures (e.g., passion, anger, sadness), affecting their judgment and self-control. They may exert different degrees of situational control, determining their ability to act on their knowledge.

Research like that reported here can bound speculations about these factors, by showing how important they are, in general, and how they present themselves in specific decision-making situations. Young people deserve

---

[2]They also have a special obligation to word their results in ways that reduce the risks of being exploited for rhetorical purposes, although there may be no alternative to vigilantly monitoring citations and refuting inaccurate ones.

nothing less than an approach that can distinguish, say, between informed sexual choices and sexual coercion. Society (and psychology) does people (of any age) a disservice by giving them too much or too little credit for decision-making competence (Fischhoff, 1995).

One possible situation is finding that young people's chosen behavior is reasonably rational, but not optimal. A logical intervention is, then, providing better inputs to these, otherwise sound decision-making processes. This is the strategy of information-based programs, "If only teens knew X, then they would choose to Y." The missing pieces (X) could be facts about risks, social norms, or even emotional responses. If these pieces can be credibly and comprehensibly conveyed, then recipients might "do the right thing" of their own accord. Providing better information should be ethically neutral; providing "better" values cannot be. Certainly a common activity, value-change programs respect their targets' intellect, but not their moral judgment.

A second possible situation is finding that young people could make acceptable decisions in principle, but cannot do so in practice, because they lack the conditions for reasoned, rational decision making. Social skills training programs teach refusal skills in order to reduce the social coercion that can limit teens' ability to do what they believe is right. Emotion control and conflict resolution programs seek the same goal, by controlling other barriers to teens' realizing their cognitive potential. Young people's cognitive ability says little about the appropriate rights and protections, unless adequate cognitive and emotional control can be assured. Understanding their impacts and management is an important research topic.

A third possible situation arises when achieving the best outcome to a specific choice comes at the price of trial-and-error learning. With structured multiple-play tasks, one might model the costs and benefits of sampling experiences (Einhorn, 1986). It is much more difficult to characterize the appropriate balance between short-term optimality and long-term learning from an overall developmental perspective. Parents face this question when deciding how protective to be with their children. Research can inform this quest for properly graduated experimentation by clarifying the match between decision situations and young people's capabilities: What choices can they understand? What circumstances can they manage, socially and emotionally? What feedback can they utilize, by themselves, and with feasible help? What is the cost, and reversibility of error?

HALCYON DAYS REVISITED?

The research in this volume is noteworthy for what is has done—addressing all three elements of the normative–descriptive–prescriptive program, in ways that exploit the theories, results, and methods of developmental psychology. It is also noteworthy for some things that it has not done. One is not slavishly accepting results from behavioral decision research, and replicating them in new domains. That familiar strategy faces both a floor and a ceiling to the insight that research can provide. Well-honed tasks can create enough of their own reality to reproduce familiar results, or perhaps modest deviations from these results. The desire to show (or at least test the hypothesis) that young people or their circumstances are fundamentally different runs counter to the confirmation bias, implicit in the constructive replication strategy. It leaves the challenge of saying more than that young people behave differently in some specific situations.

A second well-avoided strategy is identifying decision-making research with linear models, combining beliefs and values. Assuming some insight into the concerns on decision makers' minds—and some orderliness to choices—such models should have some predictive validity. However, the statistical power of linear models means that their details cannot be taken too seriously. Simple models can mimic complex processes. Multiple models, representing very different theories, may predict the same phenomenon equally well. Although tempting to interpret, regression weights are often notably unstable. As a result, it is difficult to gain much psychological insight by comparing models. These fundamental results from relatively early behavioral decision research (Dawes, 1979; Dawes & Corrigan, 1974; Goldberg, 1968; Hoffman, 1960) diverted much of the field from its early focus on statistical modeling to experimental and observational approaches like those represented here. Investigators concerned with predictive ability per se, a completely legitimate activity for other purposes, have tended to drift out of the field.

In closing, let me mention two ways in which our own work has pursued these general goals. One is developing an individual differences measure of decision-making competence (DMC). Our strategy has been straightforward (although we hope that the execution is sophisticated). We have taken behavioral decision research tasks that are well-understood in laboratory settings and examined (a) the internal consistency of performance measures, building on research by Stanovich and West (1998, 2000) and others (e.g., Levin, Huneke, & Jasper, 2000); and (b) their predictive validity for real-world activities thought to be antecedents or consequences (or both) of poor decision making. Our initial results were taken from participants in the 8th to 10th year of a longitudinal study of environmental determinants of substance abuse (Parker & Fischhoff, 2004). We found that there was a common DMC factor, explaining a reasonable amount of the variance in performance in a set of tasks spanning the domain of behavioral decision research. Scores on that factor show substantial correlations with such real-world activities as delinquent activity, oppositional defiance disorder, and disrupted homes. These remained (and occasionally were strengthened) when measures of verbal and nonverbal (or fluid) intelligence were controlled for statistically. We currently are refining the set of measures so that they do a better job of representing the constituent cognitive skills.

A second research thrust has involved helping young people to understand the processes determining the risks that they face in their lives. Doing so has forced us to model those processes formally, using methods from decision and risk analyses, in order to identify the few facts most relevant to understanding complex processes (Fischhoff, 1999; Morgan, Fischhoff, Bostrom, & Atman, 2001). In cases where the processes are socially determined, doing so requires creating models that integrate diverse psychological theories (Fischhoff, Downs, & Bruine de Bruin, 1998), and hence may contribute to the development of predictive models of risk behavior. Once the modeling is complete, we conduct semistructured interviews, designed to elicit teens' *mental models* of the focal processes. These interviews accept participants' terminology and conceptualization directed at these topics. The prescriptive interventions seek to bridge the gap between the normative model and descriptive picture of current beliefs. A recently completed example is a DVD focused on facilitating young women's sex-related decision making. In a randomized control trial, it showed positive effects on knowledge, self-efficacy, reported condom use (and usability), and recurrence of sexually transmitted diseases (Downs et al., in press). We have been fortunate to have medical colleagues who have ensured the scientific accuracy and developmental focus of these projects.

REFERENCES

Baron, J., & Hershey, J. C. (1988). Outcome bias in decision evaluation. *Journal of Personality and Social Psychology, 64,* 347–355.

Becker, G. (1976). *The economic approach to human behavior.* Chicago: University of Chicago Press.

Camerer, C. (1999). Behavioral economics: Reunifying psychology and economics. *Proceedings of the National Academy of Sciences, 96,* 10575–10577.

Camerer, C., & Weber, M. (1992). Recent developments in modeling preferences: Uncertainty and ambiguity. *Journal of Risk and Uncertainty, 5,* 325–370.

Dawes, R. M. (1979). The robust beauty of improper linear models in decision making. *American Psychologist, 34,* 571–582.

Dawes, R. M., & Corrigan, B. (1974). Linear models in decision making. *Psychological Bulletin, 82,* 95–106.

Downs, J. S., Murray, P. J., Bruine de Bruin, W., White, J. P., Palmgren, C., & Fischhoff, B. (in press). An interactive video program to reduce female adolescents' STI risk: A randomized control trial. *Social Science & Medicine.*

Edwards, W. (1954). A theory of decision making. *Psychological Bulletin, 51,* 380–417.

Edwards, W. (1961). Behavioral decision theory. *Psychological Review, 12,* 473–498.

Edwards, W. (1968). Conservatism in human information process. In B. Kleinmuntz (Ed.), *Formal representation of human judgment* (pp. 17–52). New York: Wiley.

Edwards, W., Lindman, H., & Savage, L. J. (1963). Bayesian statistical inference for psychological research. *Psychological Review, 70,* 193–242.

Einhorn, H. J. (1986). Accepting error to make less error. *Journal of Personality Assessment, 50,* 387–395.

Fischhoff, B. (1980). Clinical decision analysis. *Operations Research 28,* 28–43.

Fischhoff, B. (1992). Giving advice: Decision theory perspectives on sexual assault. *American Psychologist, 47,* 577–588.

Fischhoff, B. (1995). Risk perception and communication unplugged: Twenty years of process. *Risk Analysis, 15,* 137–145.

Fischhoff, B. (1996). The real world: What good is it? *Organizational Behavior and Human Decision Processes, 65,* 232–248.

Fischhoff, B. (1999). Why (cancer) risk communication can be hard. *Journal of the National Cancer Institute Monographs, 25,* 7–13.

Fischhoff, B. (2002). Heuristics and biases in application. In T. Gilovich, D. Griffin, & D. Kahneman (Eds.), *The psychology of judgment: Heuristics and biases.* New York: Cambridge University Press.

Fischhoff, B., & Beyth-Marom, R. (1983). Hypothesis evaluation from a Bayesian perspective. *Psychological Review, 90,* 239–260.

Fischhoff, B., Downs, J., & Bruine de Bruin, W. (1998). Adolescent vulnerability: A framework for behavioral interventions. *Applied and Preventive Psychology, 7,* 77–94.

Gärdnefors, P., & Sahlin, N.-E. (Eds.). (1990). *Decision, probability and utility: Selected readings.* New York: Cambridge University Press.

Goldberg, L. R. (1968). Simple models or simple processes? Some research on clinical judgments. *American Psychologist, 23,* 483–496.

Hoffman, P. J. (1960). The paramorphic representation of human judgment. *Psychological Bulletin, 57,* 116–131.

Kelly, E. L., & Fiske, D. W. (1951). *The prediction of performance in clinical psychology.* Ann Arbor: University of Michigan Press.

Levin, I. P., Huneke, M. E., & Jasper, J. D. (2000). Information processing at successive stages of decision making: Need for cognition and inclusion-exclusion effects. *Organizational Behavior and Human Decision Processes, 82,* 171–193.

Loomes, G., & Sugden, R. (1982). Regret theory: An alternative theory of rational choice under uncertainty. *Economic Journal, 92,* 805–824.

McFadden, D. (1999). Rationality for economists. *Journal of Risk and Uncertainty, 19,* 73–106.

Meehl, P. E. (1954). *Clinical versus statistical prediction: A theoretical analysis and a review of the evidence.* Minneapolis: University of Minnesota Press.

Morgan, M. G., Fischhoff, B., Bostrom, A., & Atman, C. (2001). *Risk communication: The mental models approach.* New York: Cambridge University Press.

Parker, A., & Fischhoff, B. (2004). External validity of decision-making competence: An individual-differences approach. *Journal of Behavioral Decision Making, 17,* 1–27.

Phillips, L. D. (1973). *Bayesian statistics for social scientists.* London: Nelson.

Savage, L. J. (1954). *The foundations of statistics.* New York: Wiley.

Schoemaker, P. J. H. (1982). The expected utility model: Its variants, purposes, evidence, and limitations. *Journal of Economic Literature, 20,* 529–563.

Sen, A. (1977). Rational fools. *Philosophy and Public Affairs, 6,* 317–344.

Simon, H. A. (1957). *Models of mind: Social and rational.* New York: Wiley.

Slovic, P., & Lichtenstein, S. (1971). Comparison of Bayesian and regression approaches to the study of information processing in judgment. *Organizational Behavior and Human Performance, 6,* 649–744.

Stanovich, K. E., & West, R. F. (1998). Individual differences in rational thought. *Journal of Experimental Psychology: General, 127,* 161–188.

Stanovich, K. E., & West, R. F. (2000). Individual differences in reasoning: Implications for the rationality debate? *Behavioral and Brain Sciences, 23,* 645–726.

Strunk, W., Jr., & White, E. B. (1979). *The elements of style* (3rd ed.). New York: Macmillan.

von Neumann, J., & Morgenstern, O. (1947). *The theory of games and economic behavior.* Princeton, NJ: Princeton University Press.

von Winterfeldt, D., & Edwards, W. (1981). Costs and payoffs in perceptual research. *Psychological Bulletin, 91,* 609–622.

von Winterfeldt, D., & Edwards, W. (1986). *Decision analysis and behavioral research.* New York: Cambridge University Press.

Author Index

248, 249, 257, 273, 275, 285, 287,
288, 299, 300, 303, 323

C

Cacioppo, R., 42, 47, 73
Caffrey, C. M., 120, 125, 134, 154
Cairns, B. D., 162, 176
Cairns, R. B., 162, 176
Calderone, K., 216, 236, 308, 323
Calderone, K. S., 247, 248
Camerer, C., 338, 344
Camino, C., 183, 211
Campbell, S. B., 283, 301
Campione, J. C., 14, 36
Capaldi, D. M., 242, 248
Cappella, E., 214, 236, 243, 248
Carlsmith, J. M., 182, 210
Carmona, M., 214, 236
Carroll, A., 306, 324
Carver, C. S., 219, 236
Cashmore, J., 222, 237
Cauffman, E., 120, 156, 159, 173, 174, 176,
178, 256, 275, 278, 282, 288, 289,
292, 293, 294, 298, 299, 300, 301
Ceci, S. J., 60, 73
Chaiken, S., 41, 49, 73, 258, 259, 275
Champion, D. S., 160, 178
Chandler, M. J., 44, 45, 46, 73
Chao, R. K., 206, 210
Chartland, T. L. 7, 35, 48, 72
Chassin, L., 161, 178
Chen, E. C., 189, 210
Chen, H., 193, 210
Chen, S., 41, 49, 73, 258, 259, 275
Chen, X., 197, 210
Cheney, R., 44, 46, 75
Cheung, P. C., 196, 197, 211
Chow, C. W. K., 269, 272, 275
Christopherson, C. R., 263, 277
Chromiak, W., 157, 161, 177
Cialdini, R. B., 175, 177
Clasen, D. R., 261, 275, 293, 299
Clements, P., 261, 264, 276
Cocking, R. R., 216, 236
Code, L., 108, 112
Cole, M., 7, 36, 219, 236
Colecchi, C. A., 271, 278
Collins, J. L., 92, 93, 103
Collins, W. A., 260, 275

Combs, B., 160, 177
Compas, B. E., 247, 248
Conger, K. J., 162, 176
Connell, J. P., 219, 236
Connolly, J., 260, 275
Connor-Smith, J. K., 247, 248
Conrad, J. P., 281, 300
Cooper, D. K., 290, 299
Corrigan, B., 343, 344
Corty, E., 161, 178
Cotton, S., 222, 237
Cottrell, J., 40, 58, 63, 64, 71, 74, 140, 151,
154
Covey, S. R., 320, 322, 324
Covington, M. V., 306, 324
Cowan, P., 184, 195, 211
Cowden, V., 290, 299
Cozzarelli, C., 258, 270, 271, 277
Craig, W., 260, 275
Criss, M. M., 273, 276
Crosby, C., 259, 275
Crosby, M. C., 271, 275
Csikszentmihalyi, M., 159, 160, 162, 177,
262, 275
Curran, T., 77, 90, 106

D

Dalton, M., 273, 277
Darling, N., 242, 249, 263, 275
Das, J. P., 216, 219, 236, 238
Davidson, D., 53, 67, 73, 83, 86, 89, 99,
102, 158, 161, 176
Davies, M., 93, 105
Davis, W., 79, 104, 120, 155, 284, 300
Davison, M. L., 44, 46, 74
Dawes, R., 120, 154
Dawes, R. M. 157, 160, 176, 343, 344
Dempster, F., 90, 102
Denes-Raj, V., 58, 61, 62, 71, 73
Dent, C. W., 161, 171, 178
Devins, G. M., 165, 176
De Vries, N. K., 125, 126, 134, 148, 155,
156
Dewey, J., 329, 333
DiClemente, R. J., 32, 36
Dien, D. S., 189, 190, 210
DiIorio, C., 263, 275
Dinitz, S., 281, 300
Dishion, T. J., 258, 275

Laub, J. H., 172, *177*
Laupa, M., 184, 195, *211*
Lauritsen, J. L., 172, *177*
Laursen, B., 261, *278*
LaVeist, T. A., 96, *104*
Layman, M., 160, *177*
LeBoeuf, R. A., 111, *113*
Lee, J., 161, 162, 171, *178*
Lee, S., 221, *239*
Leevers, H. J., 50, *73*
Leggett, E. L., 307, 308, 320, *324*
Leibowitz, A., 269, 272, *275*
Leichtman, M. D., 90, *106*
Leiderman, H., 182, *210*
Leik, R. K., 92, *104*
Leith, K. P., 14, *36*
Leland, N., 93, 94, 95, 96, *103*
Lemon, S., 98, *102*
Lepper, M. R., 24, *37*
Levin, I. P., 89, *104*, 343, *345*
Lew, W. J. F., 196, *211*
Lewis, C., 120, *155*, 283, *300*
Lewis, C. C., 265, *277*, 294, *300*
Lewis, M., 259, 260, 262, *276*
Lexcen, F., 292, 298, *299*
Li, X., 93, *106*
Lichtenstein, S., 79, 88, *106*, 160, *177*, 336, *345*
Lidz, C. W., 283, *300*
Lie, E., 53, *75*
Lightfoot, C., 120, 148, *155*
Limber, S. P., 255, 260, 263, 266, 267, 268, 269, 271, *277*
Lindman, H., 337, *345*
Lindoerfer, J. S., 258, *275*
Lindsay, R., 244, *249*
Lipman, M., 329, *334*
Lipsey, M. W., 285, *300*
Little, B. R., 304, *325*
Lizotte, A. J., 242, *249*
Lloyd, F. J., 40, 49, 76, 77, 78, 80, 82, 86, 98, *105*
Locke, E. A., 307, 320, *325*
Loewenstein, G., 80, 82, 101, *104*
Logan, M. A., 148, *156*
Long, J. D., 306, *326*
Loomes, G., 338, *345*
Lowry, R., 92, *103*
Luiten, A., 158, *176*
Lyons, J. S., 271, *278*
Lysyuk, L. G., 307, *325*

M

Maccoby, E. E., 219, *238*
MacIver, D., 223, *236*
Mackerras, C., 190, *211*
Mackin, K. J., 268, *276*
Maggs, J. L., 97, *106*, 148, *155*
Mahapatra, M., 187, 191, 205, *211*
Main, D. S., 93, *104*
Major, B., 258, 265, 270, 271, *277*
Mann, L., 184, *211*, 259, *277*
Manstead, A. S. R., 124, *156*
Mao, S., 188, 203, *212*
Marche, T., 91, *105*
Marcia, J. E., 309, *325*
Mardh, P. A., 98, *102*
Markovits, H., 53, *75*
Marks, G., 160, 161, *178*
Markus, H. R., 187, *211*
Marlin, M. M., 265, *274*
Marshall, I. H., 173, *177*
Martinez, E. A., 227, *238*
Matusov, E., 308, *323*
May, R. M., 92, *104*
Mazzarella, S., 214, *239*
McAlister, A. L., 93, *102*
McCabe, J. B., 93, *103*
McClenny, B., 20, 21, 23, 24, 26, 36, 257, 275, 287, *299*
McCord, J., 258, *275*
McFadden, D., 340, *345*
McGloin, J., 93, *104*
McKee, G., 290, *299*
McMullen, M., 188, 203, *212*
McVaugh, B., 124, *153*
McVey, G., 256, 264, *278*
Medvec, V. H., 124, *154*
Meece, J. L., 306, *325*
Meegan, S. P., 216, *236*, 308, *323*
Meehan, A. M., 161, *178*
Meehl, P. E., 336, *345*
Meisel, A., 283, *300*
Mellers, B. A., 132, *155*
Melton, G. B., 256, *277*
Meltsas, M., 221, *239*
Merrill, A. R., 320, 322, *324*
Merrill, R. R., 320, 322, *324*
Mestel-Rauch, J. M., 161, 171, *178*
Meyer-Bahlburg, H. F. L., 272, *277*
Middlestadt, S. E., 92, *102*
Middleton, D., 218, *239*

Subject Index

A

Abortion, 255
Absolutist epistemology, 45, 65
Accuracy, 58
Accuracy motivation, 57, 72
Activity satisfaction, 224–225, 231–233
Adaptation, 5–6, 13
Adjudicative competence, 282, 291–292
Adult vs. peer interaction, 217–218
Affect, 125, 143–145
After-school activities, 219, 221–225,
    227–233
Analytic processing, 41, 48–53, 71
Anticipated outcomes, 145
Appeal to adult authority, 184–185, 199,
    201, 205
Authoritarian parenting, 196–197
Autonomy, 244–246

B

Base rates, 158, 160–163, 172–174
Behavioral decision theory, 286
Belief biases, 40, 43, 56–57, 72
Brain, 89, 91

C

Calibration, 15, 20–21
Category-cued goals, 311–312, 317, 319
Cognitive abilities, 119, 141
Cognitive competence, see Adjudicative
    competence
Cognitive development, 215, 218, 221–222,
    233–235
Collectivism, 186–187, 190, 193–196
Collectivistic societies, 187
Competence, 8–9, 12, 27, 31–32, 34,
    280
Confucianism, 189, 191–192, 196
Conjunction fallacy, 40, 53, 58
Conscious processing, 50
Consensus, 183, 185, 199–202, 204–205,
    207
Consultation, 255
Context, 7–8, 13, 16–17, 48–51, 65, 139,
    148
Counteracting strategies, 32
Counterfactual reasoning, 51, 61
Culpability, 280, 282, 292–295
Cultural practices, 233
Culture, 242–244

D

Decision-making autonomy, 181–186,
    206–207
Decision-making competence, 341–343
Decision theory, 337
Decline, 245
Decontextualization, 51, 60
Default processing, 49, 61, 71
Democratic centralism, 190, 204
Democratic decision making, 181
Descriptive analysis, 335, 339–341
Developmental fit, 223, 225, 231–232
Developmental goals, 309
Developmental mechanisms, 6, 17–18
Developmental variability, 52, 56
Domain specificity, 44
Dual processing, 89–91
Dual-process model of cognition, 247

E

Emotions, 15, 31–32, 89, 121, 123–124,
    132, 144–146
Episodic memory, 41
Epistemic development, 44
Estimation accuracy, 162
    gender, 162–163, 171–172
    prior experience, 162, 173
Estimation bias, 160–163
    depression, 171
    deviant behavior, 168
    gender, 168
    self-esteem, 171
    victimization, 171
Evidence-based reasoning, 47, 55–57
Executive function, 43, 51
Expected utility theory, 120–122, 126, 131,
    147
Expected value, 83–85, 99
Experience, 5, 18, 22–23, 27–28, 30, 34
Experiential processing, 40–41, 48–57, 71

F

False consensus effect, 160
Family, *see* Parents
Family democracy, 184, 189–190
Family socialization, 225

Feedback, 15, 22–26, 30
Flat maximum theorem, 340
Flexibility, 53, 65
Fundamental attribution error, 62
Fundamental computational biases, 110
Future-oriented behavior, 216
Fuzzy-trace theory, 77–81, 83, 88–90,
    97–101, 108–112

G

Gambler's fallacy, 58, 61, 71
Gender, 222, 227–228, 230–234
Gist, 77–79, 81
Goals, 215–219, 234–235
    complexity of, 306, 317
    controllability of, 317, 319
    definition of, 313
    difficulty of, 306, 319
    realism of, 317, 319
    setting of, 307, 310, 319, 327–329
    taxonomy of, 306
Growth, 245

H

Heuristic system, 110–112
Heuristics, 41–42, 45, 49–50, 53, 54, 56,
    58–60, 66–67, 69–72, 88, 97, 338
    make an exception heuristic, 69
    representativeness heuristic, 53
    "waste not" heuristic, 66–67, 69–70
Hierarchical systems, 193
Hierarchy, 81–82
    representations, 79–81, 89–90, 97
Hindsight bias, 58, 61

I

Identity, 332–333
Illusion of replacement, 109
Illusory correlations, 161
Image theory, 305
Immaturity, 280–281
Impulsivity, 13, 15, 32, 35
Independence, *see* Autonomy
Individual differences, 18, 23, 33, 35, 42,
    44, 46–47, 57, 138, 147, 149